Annotated Texts for Translation
English – French

TOPICS IN TRANSLATION

Series Editors: Susan Bassnett (*University of Warwick*)
André Lefevere (*University of Texas, Austin*)
Editor for Annotated Texts for Translation: Beverly Adab (*Aston University, Birmingham*)
Editor for Translation in the Commercial Environment: Geoffrey Samuelsson-Brown
(*Aardvark Translation Services Ltd*)

Other Books in the Series
Annotated Texts for Translation: French – English
BEVERLY ADAB
Linguistic Auditing
NIGEL REEVES and COLIN WRIGHT
Paragraphs on Translation
PETER NEWMARK
Practical Guide for Translators
GEOFFREY SAMUELSSON-BROWN
The Coming Industry of Teletranslation
MINAKO O'HAGAN
Translation, Power, Subversion
R. ALVAREZ and M. C-A VIDAL (eds)

Other Books of Interest
About Translation
PETER NEWMARK
Cultural Functions of Translation
C. SCHÄFFNER and H. KELLY-HOLMES (eds)

Please contact us for the latest book information:
Multilingual Matters Ltd,
Frankfurt Lodge, Clevedon Hall, Victoria Road,
Clevedon BS21 7SJ, England

TOPICS IN TRANSLATION 5
Series Editors: Susan Bassnett (*University of Warwick*)
André Lefevere (*University of Texas, Austin*)

Annotated Texts for Translation: English – French

B.J. Adab

MULTILINGUAL MATTERS LTD
Clevedon • Philadelphia • Adelaide

Library of Congress Cataloging in Publication Data

Adab, B.J. (Beverly Joan), 1953–
Annotated texts for translation: English–French/Beverly Adab.
Topics in translation: 5
1. English language – Translating into French. I. Title. II. Series.
PE1498.2.F74A26   1996
448'. 0221–dc20

British Library Cataloguing in Publication Data

A CIP catalogue record for this book is available from the British Library

ISBN 1-85359-320-6 (hbk)
ISBN 1-85359-319-2 (pbk)

Multilingual Matters Ltd

UK: Frankfurt Lodge, Clevedon Hall, Victoria Rd, Clevedon England BS21 7SJ.
USA: 1900 Frost Road, Suite 101, Bristol, PA 19007, USA.
Australia: P.O. Box 6025, 83 Gilles Street, Adelaide, SA 5000, Australia.

Copyright © 1996 Beverly Adab

Typeset by Archetype, Stow-on-the-Wold
Printed and bound in Great Britain by WBC Book Manufacturers Ltd

Contents

Acknowledgements

I would like to thank Professor Peter Newmark for his encouragement; Clothilde Jammes for her contribution in translating some of the source texts; also colleagues for their suggestions concerning the theoretical discussion (Christina Schäffner) and the production of target texts: Catherine Fieschi, Agnes Kukulska Hulme, Lorna Milne, Pam Moores, Catherine Pradeilles, Christophe Texier, Lynne Wilcox, Sue Wright. Thanks are also due to Linda Reeves for her assistance; and to Final Year Modern Languages students who have, over the years, helped me to try out my ideas and develop my approach to the discussion of problems.

A Conceptual Framework

This book is a follow-up to the first in the series of Annotated Texts, which considered both key concepts and issues of theory relating to the task of translation and gave practice in the specific language pair French–English (Adab, 1993). The raison d'être of the series is to offer a conceptual framework on which to base empirical analysis by means of the texts offered for analysis and translation. The reader is invited to reconsider concepts discussed in this first publication together with further relevant issues and new insights which would seem of equal importance.

For a more detailed and carefully structured coursebook for translation students, we would refer the reader to that comprehensive text by Newmark (*A Textbook of Translation*, 1990), also to texts by Hervey and Higgins (1992) and Delise (1994) which are intended to be just such a guide. All of these also have a similar objective in common with this series of Annotated Texts, namely that in which a knowledge of underlying theory informs the pragmatics of practice. As Newmark himself states in his introduction his aim is to offer, 'A course in translation principles and methodology for Final Year degree and post-graduate classes, autodidacts and home-learners'. The debt owed to Peter Newmark for the insights offered by his most perceptive and practically-oriented analysis of these problems is acknowledged by scholars of Translation Studies.

This publication is intended to offer a comprehensive collection of texts, which could be used in different ways in both the undergraduate and postgraduate fields of translation study and practice, as well as by the autodidact. It is therefore our intention to discuss, in this introduction, what seem to be the principal criteria which should inform and guide a intelligent and analytical approach to the task of translation. It is hoped that the method adopted, and the criteria used for guidance, will suffice to assist those who wish to use the book for teaching.

This method is intended to be eclectic, taking as its starting point an approach which could be described as combining aspects of text-linguistics and questions of cultural specificity in terms of the similarities and differences which will affect and determine the compatibility and accessibility of the Source Text's conceptual and factual content to the Target Culture. The text-linguistic parameters are intended to guide the selection of appropriate Target Language forms to express the Source Text substance. The method of translation-oriented text analysis of the Source Text, as first suggested by Christiane Nord, is intended to alert the translator not only to linguistic but also to cultural and stylistic factors of the Source Text. The purpose is to encourage an approach which identifies units of meaning, not units of linguistic form, so that what is sought in creating the Target Text (given functional constancy of both Source Text and Target Text as a presupposition) is similarity — aiming for identity or near-identity — of conceptual content in both Source Text and Target Text in order to ensure that all possible nuances and shades of meaning of the Source Text author's message are accessible to the Target Language reader.

Perhaps we should start by stating that we are interested, in this discussion, in translation as both *process* and *product* (see Bassnett-McGuire, 1980). Our interest in translation as product stems primarily from the fact that this collection is intended to assist those wishing to improve their understanding of and performance in this task, with a view to being able to undertake translation work in a professional capacity and at a professional level of competence. Naturally, in the teaching situation this process of development and improvement will be significantly enhanced by the contribution of the translation trainer, who will draw on his[1] own research and knowledge of translation theory for the benefit of his students.

The emphasis here is on the end-product of a series of choices and processes or strategies: we shall discuss these choices, and what motivates them, with the student or débutant translator as our intended target reader. This approach is what Gile describes as a training in *exploratory power*, where translators become able to understand *phenomena of production*, to identify *translation difficulties* and the reasons for these, and to understand *translation strategies*, including why these may or may not be acceptable within the parameters of a specific task, context and translation situation (Gile, 1995: 13). Holmes sums up this aim in his statement that (any theory of) translation should 'devote extensive attention to the way texts convey often very complex patterns of meaning, and to the manner in which they function communicatively in a given socio-cultural setting'.[2] The same is true for any approach to an understanding of translation difficulties and associated strategies.

Our interest in translation as a task is therefore a direct consequence of, and a pre-requisite to, this stated aim. It is through a better understanding of the processes involved that translation performance can be improved, and this understanding has to come, as in many subjects and skills, through exposure to examples of a problem-type; repeated attempts to solve these problems should allow progression from identification of the particular (relevant to the immediate text) to formulation of the general (but not in terms of an eternal truth, or fixed rule); in other words, to the ability to generalise the processes and patterns observed and look for them in other texts, contexts and situations. These processes are in fact translation strategies adopted during the task of transferring information from a Source Text (ST) in a Source Language (SL), to a Target Text (TT) in a Target Language (TL). Hewson and Martin describe these as 'an instrumental process or the cognitive operations involved in the production of a TT from an ST, involving cross-cultural issues, linguistic and *semiotic* (our italics) manipulations'. In their book *Discourse and the Translator*, Hatim and Mason (1990) expressed the need for just such a work, which would involve the comparison of ST and TT in order to discover techniques and effects. Newmark (1991) expresses the same need. Chuquet and Paillard (1989) similarly consider that translations from a given ST constitute a justifiable field of empirical research, in that they contain a number of regularities (i.e. recurrent translations between pairs of languages) which cannot be the result of (purely) arbitrary decisions. They define these strategies as constituting the observance of dominant grammatical patterns (1987: 135, quoted in Hewson and Martin, 1991), although we would prefer to exclude the term *grammatical* as being too restrictive in scope and concentrate on the term *patterns*, which better reflects the concept of generalisation of strategies by extension.

In agreement with Baker (1990) we hope to help the student to develop the critical ability to judge the appropriateness of choices made, by a study of actual practice and by the introduction of certain basic terms of metalanguage which can be used to explain and identify the nature of such choices. As Baker states, students need to develop a flexible approach, based on the context and the communicative intent of the particular text to be translated. To do this, they must be aware of the options available to them and of the consequences of choices made from amongst these options. A more systematic study of how signs, or units of meaning, acquire such meaning in context, or by virtue of association and consensus, can help students to improve their level of awareness. Their ability to access meaning in a given context, framed in a specific text in response to a given situation (text type and communicative function), can be further enhanced by the introduction of a basic theoretical framework establishing parameters for guidance in the selection of appropriate strategies and tactics, so that when new translation difficulties are encountered, strategies can be devised by reference to this framework:

a conceptual framework which explains phenomena, their cause and their possible consequences is easier to keep in mind than a

reference to the isolated rules of behaviour dictated by a
teacher. (Gile, 1995: 14)

The ability to access meaning is not, however, limited to competence
in terms of syntactic analysis of logical relations between units of meaning on the level of micro-units within a phrase, clause or sentence. There
is also the need to examine *how* these units function in the mind of the
text-interpreter, who for the purpose of this discussion is the translator.
He has to be able to identify and explain to himself how these units, or
signs, will be perceived by the target reader of the Source Text, and then
how these signs function in the domain of Jakobson's interlingual transfer,[3] i.e. in the mind of the translator as interlingual and intercultural
mediator, using his interpretation of sign function in the SL to guide his
choice of sign in the TL, complementing, supplementing or even replacing a purely comparative and contrastive approach at the level of syntax
and lexis.

Consideration of the metaphor developed by Holmes,[4] the *mind map*
of the ST meaning as developed by the translator in an intermediary
stage between decoding the ST message and encoding it into the TL, may
help to illustrate this approach. A map consists of symbols which represent concepts for the map reader, a pictorial or diagrammatic representation of information which is more economic and space saving than
the graphic representation of this information. Holmes extends this
comparison to encompass the notion of text function in relation to the
target reader, noting that:

> ... all translations are maps, the territories are the originals (i.e. the
> Source Texts). And just as no single map of a territory is suitable
> for every purpose, so is there no 'definitive' translation (of a
> poem)'.[5]

Although Holmes is making specific reference here to the translation
of poetry, the implication for non-literary texts is equally important.
Neubert also develops this concept of the mind map when he says,

> 'textual meaning is more than the accumulation or aggregation of
> smaller meaning units. Textual meanings are independent global
> units of cognition and communication...'[6]

When constructing his *mind map*, the translator also has recourse to
(mental) images to build up a picture, using what Peirce and others
describe as icons, indices and symbols. These different terms explain
how the information is perceived by the brain: either as index, where
there is some indirect physical or visual link between the sign and the

object referred to (e.g., the weather vane reminds us of the wind direction by its ability to rotate and by its form, or the roadsign P for parking); or as icon, by means of a direct and recognisable similarity of form between icon and object (as in road signs, where we have a picture of a child or elderly person, or on the computer screen when we see the picture of a disk, or of a piece of paper with a corner turned down to represent a file); or else as symbol, by virtue of association agreed by social consensus, as when the colour red is understood to mean danger, or when the rose symbolises love, emotion, devotion. Whilst semiotics originally arose from philosophical enquiry as to how the brain accesses signification in the intralingual situation, translation scholars have quickly seen the relevance of this approach to the interpretation of interlingual access to meaning. Thus we can find writings in which the fundamental principles of the two approaches, and indeed their respective metalanguages, are combined to give a new interdiscipline, the Semiotics of Translation.

The study of how signs function in this way is called *semiotics* or *sémiologie* and whilst the most obvious definition of a sign may be that of a visual image, the term can also be used to describe a single unit of meaning at the level of the word or combination of words. In the posthumous '*Cours de Linguistique Générale*' Saussure is credited with describing semiotics as 'une science qui étudie la vie des signes au sein de la vie sociale' (de Mauro, 1987: 33), or alternatively, 'dans les sociétés humaines', according to the new, third 'Cours' edited by Komatsu and Harris (1993: 71). For Saussure, 'l'association d'une idée avec un signe, c'est ce qui fait l'essence de la langue' (Komatsu, Harris, 1993: 71). So we find justification for the claim that words or units of meaning are in fact signs. It is to be noted that Saussure's main focus of interest is not so much what signs mean, but how they are linked or related to each other within a system or code, i.e. the horizontal associations between words, as opposed to what could be described as vertical hierarchies of meaning within a given unit or sign.

Cultural references or phenomena (such as the use of clothing or food as an expression of self image) also function as signs, according to Barthes (1967), who reinforces Peirce's view that 'knowledge is necessarily (stored) in signs and we think about signs in signs' (Gorlée, 1994: 42). Hence every unit of meaning of a text stands for something which could, as it were, be conceptualised mentally and separately from its immediate referent, in terms of another sign which stands in the relation of a synonym to that sign in the text. The term *sign* must be taken to refer to 'that which stands for something else (*aliquid stat pro aliquo*)'; the term *unit* here includes single or compound words, phrases, names, parts or the whole of a sentence or text.

In relation to the situation of interlingual translation, signs could be said to function as *indices* if there occurs in the mind of the translator an immediate connection between the SL sign and a given TL sign, rather like consulting a bilingual dictionary for a substitute term having the same or nearly the same meaning in both languages. Where there is no direct one-to-one substitution possible at this level of dictionary consultation, the translator may substitute word group for word group, as in the case of idiomatic expressions, where the individual components or units of the group may point to quite different meanings to that constituted by their occurrence in combination. This association between sign and concept or denotatum could be described as iconic, looking for a single image for a group of contributing elements of information.

Finally, where the association between sign and object of reference is arbitrary and based on social consensus, with no apparent direct or indirect linguistic clues as to this link, the sign function is symbolic and thus, for the translator, highly likely to be culture-specific. Further according to Peirce, a symbol:

> can only signify if it is interpreted according to some agreed-upon law-like rule or convention. Without such a common ground, which must be shared by sign producer and sign interpreter, successful interpretation of the symbol is hardly possible.[7]

It is our opinion that, in the context of the task of translation, this comment could be said to be true of all signs, not just symbolic ones. The process of interpreting one sign by reference to another (which represents the same or nearly the same concept as the first) is described by Peirce as *semiosis*, and the sign which recalls the meaning of the first sign is called its interpretant, this being the sign which comes into the mind of the sign interpreter (person, translator) on seeing the first sign.

Thus, for Gorlée, translation remains a 'dual incidence of semiosis', since the translator not only has to interpret for himself, in terms of different signs, the concepts embodied in the SL signs, but also to re-embody these concepts in TL signs in such a way as to make those concepts available to the TL reader through the process of semiosis (sign interpretation through other signs, an ongoing process):

> In order to function as a sign, a sign needs to lead to interpretations. And in order to be meaningful, a sign must invariably be embedded in a code or system … Meaning arises from exploratory interpretation of signs in their natural habitat: the world of context in which humans use verbal (and non-verbal) signs in order to

meaningfully (for themselves) organize the reality surrounding them ... this implies a partly experiential and partly cognitive frame of reference (1994: 67–69)

(see comments below relating to 'visions du monde').

In the context of Peircean semiotics these strategies of interpretation of the ST and selection of interpretant in the TL are the results of choices made by the translator. According to Gorlée, at the intuitive stage when a text is first read, 'a trained translator's mind ... will then, spontaneously and with practised ease, start generating a flow of ideas' (1994: 187). This flow can generate a process of growth of ideas, depending on the initial choices and subsequent refinements made by the translator in the process of developing an ever more accurate and TL appropriate version of the TT. Just as the process of *semiosis* points to a potentially and seemingly never-ending chain of further interpretants which should eventually run full circle to arrive back at the starting point of the first sign, so the process of translation involves a chain of interdependent choices which run throughout the text; these choices require constant revision, the cyclical nature of which is inherent in the creation of a coherent and accurate global message. The creation of this message is the final aim of the translator.

Petrilli further argues that, in interlingual translation, for the full and adequate reformulation of the SL message in the TL, it will be necessary to resort to Jakobson's *intralingual* translation. This is in essence a form of Hewson and Martin's paraphrase, but also and importantly, a form of *semiosis* (interpreting one sign by another, i.e. synonymy and paraphrase) in the search for equivalence of meaning and effect. Awareness of how a sign functions in the SL and how he has used this function to create his *mind map* should help the translator to evaluate the choices that he makes in his construction of the TT.

Perhaps it is pertinent to remind the reader at this point that, whilst we are aware that the information content and the intent of an utterance can be transferred from one language to another by both the written and the oral medium, when we speak of translation, we are in fact referring to that form of interlingual transfer which is represented through the medium of the written language. The oral form of this kind of transfer is interpreting, and this can take many forms, ranging from simultaneous or consecutive conference interpreting to liaison interpreting.

The central concept, or so it seems, in any act of translation (or interpreting) is that this is an *act of communication*, and that this act, in the form of a written text, is what Hatim and Mason (1990) call 'the result of motivated choices made by the text producer'. But these motivated choices made by the text-producer (here, the translator) are in turn guided by the choices made by the ST author, and by the translator's own understanding of the intentions of this author. As stated by Gorlée, the translator as communicator has thus a dual role. He or she:

> embodies both the addressee... of the original message, and the addresser of the translated message, both interpreter and utterer... thus he or she monopolises the whole sign-manipulative process in which translation consists (1994: 189).

It is intended to offer a discussion of the nature of the different potential choices available to the translator, which he will probably use in different combinations according to the context, text function and text type: to do this, an introduction and an overview should assist in the detailed consideration of such approaches.

Vinay and D'Arbelnet (1977) were perhaps the first to offer a means of describing generalised translation techniques, which they developed through an inductive rationalisation of actual practice, taken from real-life examples. They offered category-types within which to group together and define the different potential processes or strategies. Their observations also produced generalisations concerning the cultures of the respective societies in which the languages involved served as primary means of communication, although this was in the particular situation of a bilingual society. Thus an understanding of the cultural context and social parameters relating to the choice of use of language by an ST author were seen to be of equal importance in the task of translation as the actual language itself. This was also held to be essential to the accurate transfer of all possible intended meaning or meanings as created by the ST author through his use of particular aspects of lexis and syntax. Vinay and D'Arbelnet state:

> Une langue est à la fois le miroir d'une culture et son instrument d'analyse. Il ne faut pas s'étonner que les divergences entre deux langues soient particulièrement nombreuses sur le plan de la métalinguistique (1977: 260).

Furthermore, this understanding of social and cultural parameters was shown by these authors to be of equal importance in relation to the choices made by the translator when reproducing all this information in the TL, making of the translator what Hewson and Martin (1991) call 'an intercultural operator or mediator', through their discussion of this concept of conversion and transfer of information between cultures. The latter further describe the possible strategies for reconstruction alternatives as 'variations', recognising thereby the multiplicity of means (paraphrastic alternatives) available for the transfer of information, once one has accepted that this is the prime target of the translator, and not the literal transfer, unit for unit, of lexical and syntactical content.

In other words, given functional constancy between ST and TT, the translator has to be able to convey to his TT reader the same information, with the same nuances and resulting in the same effect on the reader, both of parts (or units) of the text as well as of the text as a whole. To do this, he has to understand not only the words and the syntax of the ST, but also to be able to decipher, or decode, any underlying meanings conveyed by effects such as a play on words, or direct or oblique cultural references. He has to know how the SL reader would have interpreted and reacted to these, in order to recreate these effects within the constraints of the TL norms and in terms of the experience offered to its members by the TL culture. Delisle supports this when he comments:

> Traduire consiste à accorder des concepts d'une langue avec ceux d'une autre langue dans une recherche d'adéquation la plus parfaite possible au sens global du message original. (1980: 43)

Delisle also notes:

> Traduire consiste à dissocier mentalement des notions de leurs formes graphiques afin de leur associer d'autres signes puisés dans un autre système linguistique. (1980: 40)

Here Delisle is using the definition of 'signe' offered by Saussure (de Mauro, 1987) to explain his interpretation of what translation is about. This definition states that the word 'signe' is used to denote the linguistic form used to describe an object or concept. This concept or object, in Saussure's terminology, becomes the 'signifié' (the thing designated by the 'signe') and the actual word or term used becomes a 'signifiant' (the thing doing the designating. In other words, all lexical units, whether one word or several words within a unit which refers to one concept, are 'signes', but each one is a different 'signifiant' for an individual and discrete 'signifié'.

It is also useful to note at this point another key concept taught by Saussure, that of the difference between 'langue' and 'parole', as this too is of supreme relevance to the translator. The word 'langue' is used to refer to the entire content of a language system, 'le produit social dont l'existence permet à l'individu l'exercice de la faculté du langage' (Komatsu and Harris, 1993: 66) rather like a totally comprehensive database of every single linguistic element that could possibly be used in combination with other elements to form an act of communication between members of the same language community. The term 'parole', on the other hand, refers to the use made by the individual of these elements of a language system; what could be described as the selection made from this vast range of potential elements, a selection based on the knowledge and personal preferences of the individual. This selection will be one which is highly unlikely to include every single potential element and whose size and extent will vary considerably. However, in most cases the context and ST structure will provide sufficient indications as to the appropriate interpretation of a unit, except in cases of ambiguity as a deliberate strategy or as a result of poor style on the part of the ST author.

The translator needs to be aware of as many as possible of these potential elements of the 'langue' of both language systems between which he is operating, since he cannot expect the 'parole' of the authors of all the texts he will have to translate to be composed of identical elements without any variations. His knowledge of the TL 'langue' (all potential units for combination) will have to be correspondingly wide, in order for his own 'parole' (individual selection from these) to be able to render the ST author's 'parole' as faithfully as possible, in terms of both content and intent (message). Hence the stipulation for the translator to possess native, or near-native competence in the foreign language (L2), as well as having an excellent understanding and command of his mother-tongue (L1).

Much has already been written on the subject of how a particular language system, by virtue of its structure in terms of syntax and lexis which is used to segment and present aspects of information, may be considered to shape the way in which we perceive the world, including this representative observation from Sapir and Whorf:

> Nous disséquons la nature suivant les lignes tracées d'avance par nos langues maternelles (Whorf, 1956)

Trier concurs with this view:

> Chaque langue structure la réalité à sa propre façon et par là même établit les éléments de la réalité qui sont particuliers à cette langue donnée (quoted in Mounin, 1976: 44);

and Mounin agrees with Whorf that:

> Chaque langue découpe dans le même réel des aspects différents (Language, 213, quoted in Mounin, 1976: 48),

whilst further concurring with Martinet's opinion that:

à chaque langue correspond une organisation particulière des données de l'expérience (Martinet, 1960: 16, quoted in Mounin, 1976: 58).

Mounin also presents Marcel Cohen's comment:

Chaque peuple a la logique que révèle la syntaxe de son langage (also quoted in Mounin, 1976: 48)

Some scholars have taken these comments to the extreme of suggesting that the structure of a language could be considered as indicative of the sophistication of the socio-cultural community by which it is used. Whilst this may be an extreme view, it would not appear unreasonable to concur that an individual can only interpret new phenomena in the light of what is known, and only describe these in terms which are already available to him within his own 'langue'; even when neologisms are created to denote new phenomena they have to be explained by existing terms.

All of these quotes serve to illustrate the point that each language uses a particular form of syntax to describe a certain kind of experience, and the building blocks for that description are the words, or lexical items, used to explain events or evoke feelings and reactions. Every language comprises this function of being able to relay to others who share mother-tongue knowledge of that language aspects of experience as lived, perceived and felt by the individual. This is made possible by the fact that all members of a linguistic community will have a fairly similarly generalised interpretation of what is meant by the use of a particular item of lexis or form of syntax, as well as being aware of less common but still potential meanings inherent in these. Where a less common meaning is to be inferred, rather than the most common one, there will be clues, in the form of contextual and situational input or information, which will aid the hearer or reader to select the most appropriate meaning for a particular unit within the specific utterance. Compare, for example, a simple comment such as 'I see', which could signify the simple fact of understanding; and the use of this same comment, within a context such as the repeated failure to complete a given task, where a person in a position of responsibility might reply, in a tone of sarcasm, 'I see', indicating vexation or disbelief. Consider also the frequently quoted example of what members of different linguistic communities understand by the word 'home' or 'privacy', according to their country of origin.

This line of reasoning has also been used to raise the question of *translatability* or of the impossibility of translation between two languages. Mounin asks this question, 'Is it therefore possible to represent for someone from a particular social group the perception of reality as seen by members of another social group?' (1976: 60). He reminds us that Nida talks of translation as being a search for equivalent concepts and terms, drawn from and relating to the environment and to aspects of material, social, religious and linguistic culture. To overcome this potential barrier Mounin describes how equivalences can be found: firstly, in terms of semantics, by referring to Saussure's description of the word as a written sign which represents a meaning or concept. The translator is thus looking to effect a transfer of concepts, not of actual words. Secondly, this realm of concepts may not coincide exactly but will have aspects or characteristics in common: it is thus a matter of finding the concept which encapsulates the greatest number of characteristics of the ST concept. Finally, the translator has to find the term, or lexical unit, in the TL which most closely and accurately conveys this concept, whilst accepting that a direct translational coincidence between two elements of lexis in two different languages will very rarely occur (Mounin, 1976: 78), but that interlingual communication will be possible on the basis of common elements of meaning. For further discussion of this concept of translatability the reader should consult: Catford (1974), Bassnett-McGuire (1980) and Neubert (1985). Where a breakdown in translatability does occur, it will be when there is what Pergnier (1980: 119) calls a 'non-coïncidence des découpages', but this should be less marked and less frequent, the more two languages are in contact.

Languages can be *in contact* in various ways, through travel, cultural or linguistic borrowing, new inventions which become internationally known, and in this century particularly, through mass media communications, including film, televised news, and the printed medium of the press including advertising. Another such instance of contact is the translation situation, when two or more languages are used by one person as interchangeable means of communication, so that the individual operates frequently and habitually in two or more languages.

Another approach considers the question of contact in terms of similarities and differences in world views. In other words, we can talk of languages being in contact to a greater or lesser degree, meaning that their perceptions of the world, their daily experience of life and their linguistic means for describing these perceptions and this experience can be either very different, or quite similar and close to each other, in the form which they adopt to present this information. This is certainly the case for two languages such as English and French, which are linked by geographical proximity as much as by shared historical and cultural tradition. Yet even these two socio-cultural communities may have quite different attitudes to some aspects of life, and may mean different things when using words which, on the surface, would seem to be more or less equivalent terms to describe a similar experience. Take, for example, the concept of the first meal of the day, known as 'breakfast' or 'le petit déjeuner' and the different types of food and drink implied by these two words. To continue this image, think of the different ways in which bread is made in the two countries, and therefore of the different words used to describe types of bread (shape, size, other characteristics). Or think of the structure of the education system, and what is meant by 'a school week' or 'access to university studies'. Mounin defines this difference: 'Les mots n'ont pas forcément la même surface conceptuelle dans les langues différentes' (1976: 23), and quotes Edmond Cary, 'la traduction est une opération sur les faits liés à tout un contexte culturel' (1976: 234) and Nida, 'Les mots ne peuvent pas être compris correctement séparés des phénomènes culturels localisés dont ils sont les symboles' (1976: 237).

Thus it is that the translator will need to be aware of these differences, whether minor or major, when seeking to understand the ST and the ST author's intention. Once he has done this, he then has to recreate the same intended meaning, with the self-same nuances and effects, through the medium of the TL, and within the constraints of the cultural experience of the TL reader. As seen above, the cultural experience of a member of the TL community has the potential to differ slightly, considerably, or somewhere in between, from that of the member of the SL community, and the translator has somehow to reconcile these differences through his search for the nearest possible equivalent term. Where this equivalent term fails to convey all the aspects of meaning of an SL term, the translator will have to make a decision as to how essential a complete understanding will be to the overall effect on and comprehension by the TL reader, and where appropriate, append a translator's note to explain more fully. To some extent this will also depend on the choice made by the translator, before commencing any decision-making, as to the 'initial norm' (Toury, 1980[8]) to be adopted, namely the choice between 'adequacy' to the ST meaning (an ST-oriented process) and 'acceptability' in the TL (a TL-oriented process). Both may be considered of equal importance. On the other hand, one or other may appear more essential, according to the context of the translation task and due account being taken of the communicative function of the source and target texts, which may or may not be identical.

In the above discussion some terms and concepts have been introduced which would appear to be of great importance for a translator. It would seem relevant, at this point, to discuss these terms in greater detail, and to refer the reader to useful sources for further explanation if required. These include textual considerations — text type and function; mechanisms of textual construction, coherence and cohesion; units of meaning; also sociocultural considerations relating to different world-views, symbolic associations and connotative values, cultural experience and culture-specific concepts.

Before any translator can begin to think about all the various aspects of his task or about all the relevant contributory factors in this process, he has to evaluate the text type, its target reader, and the ST author's aim in writing the text. In other words, is this text intended to create a particular reaction in the reader, to inform him, to stimulate discussion or to entertain through narrative? These considerations will influence the choice of approach to be adopted and serve as a guide to any decisions to be taken with regard to individual units of translation. This discussion will adopt the approach described by Pergnier (1980) among others, namely that a unit of translation consists of any word, or group of words, which has or have a single meaning, and which cannot be further broken down into individual components of meaning. Thus a unit will sometimes involve a single word, sometimes an idiom or fixed expression or phrase, and sometimes a clause or a complete sentence. The translator should always look for a unit which will be 'the smallest possible, but the largest necessary'. Once a preliminary draft has been produced, these units should always be reassessed within the context of their contribution to the immediate contextual message, as well as to the global, textual message.

This concept of the global message of the text is one which relates to a particular approach to be adopted, that which Newmark (1988, 1990) calls the 'Communicative Approach'. In his two major books on translation (1988, 1990, of which the second is an update and amended version of the first, with many additions but following the same basic principles), Newmark describes several possible approaches to the task of translation, before explaining his preferences. These approaches are widely accepted and quoted by other authors and so it would seem appropriate to recall them at this point.

The first such approach discussed is that of 'word for word', which is often written in interlinear form, with the ST sentence above and the translation immediately below. In this way words are translated one by one, according to their syntactical form or most common 'dictionary' meaning, without any consideration of the context in which they are used. As Newmark states, this process, if used, should be seen as a pretranslation process; in our opinion it may be helpful where the ST syntax is especially complex with deviations from the SL norms of style, but for would-be professional translators this process ought to operate on an automatic level, with no need for a written version, as a kind of initial conversion. It should certainly not be necessary to adopt this method for a whole text.

The second approach described is that of 'literal' translation, where the translator selects the nearest TL equivalent for the SL unit. This process does not relate each unit to its context, and should be seen as another pre-translation process. This method can, however, be useful in the preparation of a rough draft.

The 'faithful' approach is the third of Newmark's categories. This method aims to reproduce the exact meaning of the unit as dictated by its context, but within the limits imposed by the TL grammatical norms. Its advantage is that it does afford the opportunity to produce a complete version, and thus to review choices in the light of preceding and subsequent contexts.

Method number four is the 'semantic' method, which requires the translator to take more account of the aesthetic value of the individual unit than the third method, and thus permits greater flexibility and creativity, in that a choice which better conveys connotative or stylistic function within the TL may be preferred over one which is truly exact in its faithfulness to the ST. This is one of the two main methods advocated by Newmark; it still produces a version which is relatively faithful to the ST, and therefore somewhat literal, but does allow some freedom to the translator.

Another method is that of 'adaptation', which corresponds to Cicero's concept of 'ut orator' (giving precedence to oratorical skills rather than to exact fidelity to the text) and 'aemulatio' (taking the main themes and concepts but recreating them in the accepted style of the TL, i.e. without seeking to be faithful to the form of the ST). This method is used primarily for poetry and theatre, and so it is not proposed to discuss it further.

A 'free' method is one similar to the above, but in fact less free than the former, in that some form of paraphrase is still used to convey the meaning of the original. This usually leads to a somewhat longer TT than the ST. This method can be very useful for individual units, where there is no direct equivalent concept in the TL and therefore no direct semantically equivalent term. It should be used with caution, to avoid a kind of over-compensation in which the translator deliberately refrains from seeking or using a one-to-one equivalence, even where this exists and could be used quite legitimately within the TL.

An 'idiomatic' approach will reproduce the ST message but will sometimes distort nuances of meaning through a preference for a more colloquial style, thereby introducing a different register to that of the ST. This approach should only be used where the translator has a specific mandate to present his TT in such a register for a target reader, who will differ in characteristics of age, level of education and knowledge of the subject from the ST target reader.

Finally comes the approach most often advocated by Newmark, and one which it is aimed to follow wherever possible, within the constraints imposed by the genre, style, register and aims of each individual ST. This is the 'communicative approach', in which the translator attempts to render the exact contextual meaning of the ST, but does so through the medium of a TL which is acceptable to the TL reader and easily understood by him.

According to Newmark, only the semantic and communicative approaches fulfil the two main aims of translation, as he sees them. These are to render in the TL:

(i)   The expressive elements of the ST: if the text is informative, all this information must be clearly presented; if the text is intended to have an expressive function, this function and its intended impact on the target reader should also be respected and recreated.

(ii)   The cultural components of the ST: in informative texts these should be replaced with neutral terms (describing the general function) or TL cultural equivalents; in expressive texts these should be transferred intact.

He further states that a semantic approach will follow the thought processes of the ST author, while a communicative approach may involve the re-organisation of information and concepts into a different order of presentation, which will not alter the intended meaning or impact but will read more easily for the TL reader, and conform more closely to his thought-processes. Thus, although a semantic approach may aim to reproduce the ST impact and effect, the communicative approach will also do this, but in a more natural style, which will result from the translator's own ability to manipulate the TL. The semantic approach is also likely to lead to a longer translation, whilst the communicative approach allows a certain economy and concision of language. The former concentrates more on individual units, the latter on the overall effect and message (what Delisle, 1980, calls the sub-text, or the thoughts behind the ST units). At the basis of the latter is therefore the precept that it is the task of the translator to convey to his TL reader, in the most appropriate and natural style for that reader, the information which the ST author intended to impart to his target reader, the way in which the ST author wished his reader to understand and interpret that information, and the effect, in terms of thought and action, that this ST text was intended to have on the reader.

This principle of *equivalent effect* should therefore be the desired result for which the translator should aim. It is dependent on what Newmark describes in his definition of translation as the 'transfer of the meaning of a stretch or unit of language, the whole or part of a text, from one language to another'. For him, meaning is 'functionally relevant information' i.e. information which serves a purpose and therefore has a particular, intended effect on the reader. In order to transfer the overall meaning of a text the translator will have to reproduce all aspects of potential meaning: these include the explicit (obvious) meaning and the implicit (implied, underlying) meaning, which the translator will have to interpret, in order to recreate or reproduce this.

Nida and Taber call this the principle of *dynamic equivalence*, whose goal is that of creating or stimulating in the TL reader an equivalent response to that of the SL reader. They state that to preserve the content of the message, the form must be changed, and that the extent of this change will depend on the linguistic and cultural differences between the two languages. Their definition reads thus:

> Translating consists in reproducing in the receptor language the closest natural equivalent of the source-language message, first in terms of meaning, and second in terms of style (1974: 12)

and they thus advocate the aim of equivalence, rather than identity of form, so that dynamic equivalence takes priority over formal (syntactical and lexical) correspondence. They justify this aim by reference to the concept of Sapir and Whorf relating to how language shapes our perceptions of reality by the way this language segments and presents this reality to us and for us, so that each language can be said to possess its own system for symbolising meaning. Furthermore, the aim of dynamic equivalence also respects and takes into account the need of the TL reader, who may or may not have any linguistic competence in the SL, to have in front of him a text which is easily intelligible, so that he can read it with ease, perceive its relevance and respond to it in the manner intended by the ST author, on both its informative and its expressive level.

Catford (1974) also discusses this difference between textual equivalence in the TL of an SL form, where the information is conveyed in the appropriate TL form, and formal correspondence. This latter occurs when a TL category occupies as nearly as possible the same place in the TL as does a given SL category in the SL. This refers to a more or less direct equivalent in terms of word-class and structure, which can only ever be approximate, given the syntactical differences in the syntactical systems of L1 and L2. He further states that:

> Translation equivalence occurs when an SL and TL text or item are relatable to (at least some of) the same features of substance. (1974: 50).

Neubert limits the occurrence of equivalence in the following way:

> Equivalence only holds between SL and TL items within the framework of the individual texts (ST and TT). (1985: 142)

This is a valid restriction of the application of this term, and one which a translator should bear in mind when seeking to extrapolate generalised principles from his observations of translation practice. More recently, Gile has defined this effect in terms of 'successful communication' which he describes as taking place when 'Receivers of the Target language are successfully informed, understand the point and/or have been persuaded' (Gile, 1995: 27). Criteria pertaining to the success of this communicative process include 'ideational clarity, linguistic acceptability and terminological accuracy' (Gile, 1995: 34).

Thus it happens that there may be a loss of ST stylistic effect, in order to respect the TL reader's need for intelligibility whilst not allowing any loss of meaning or information. Sometimes, however, style and meaning are inextricably linked, with the former contributing to or even creating the latter, and this is where the translator's skill in interpretation of the ST and manipulation of the TL will be brought to bear.

To return to the term described at the beginning of this chapter, namely the *text-linguistic* approach, it may be useful to consider Neubert's comment that:

> The text is the central defining issue in translation. Texts and their situations define the translation process... the translation situation always determines the set of translation strategies to be used... differences in translation processes relate to variations in the translation situation.[9]

With this aim and these guiding principles in mind, the translator should then be able to adapt his approach according to the text. But in order to develop the ability to recognise which kind of approach is most relevant for a particular text, and then for each particular section of the text or for each unit of translation, we would suggest that the translator needs to undertake a process of reverse analysis of actual translation operations carried out within the context of authentic translation work. In other words, discourse analysis of both Source and Target Texts should provide, through comparison of the differences and similarities between form and style of the two texts, the opportunity for identification of the choices made and strategies adopted, and also the insight into the principles guiding those choices. Certain factors which could be expected to inform and motivate a translator's choices are listed by different authors. These factors, which find their echo in Newmark's, are discussed in the following points.

Beaugrande and Dressler (1981) introduced what they call 'seven standards of textuality', which are further developed in Neubert's work. The first two criteria are seen to be text-centred and these are: *cohesion*, which they see as related to and relying on the grammatical interdependence of different elements of the text; this cohesion gives stability to the text and allows for economy in the use of language; and *coherence*, which for them describes the 'configuration of concepts and relations which underlie the surface text' (i.e. the actual words used). In other words, there is a continuity of meaning and sense through the way in which these are arranged.

The others are seen as user-centred (in this case, the user being the translator in his role as mediator) and involve the consideration of *time*, in the sense of looking backwards to the intended direction of the text, and forwards to its anticipated result. Next comes *intentionality*, dealing with the attitude of the ST author; *acceptability*, which relates to the attitude and expectations of the TT reader; *informativity*, being the extent to which events of the text are expected or unknown (both within the reader's experience of the subject and as a result of previous indicators contained within the text); *situationality*, as those background, usually cultural, factors which make a text relevant to a situation or occurrence; and finally, *intertextuality*, meaning those factors which make production of one text dependent on a knowledge of one or more previously encountered texts of the same type.

The first set of guidelines towards discourse analysis are those offered by Grice and quoted in Neubert (1985), which are those of *quality, quantity, relevance* and *manner*. The maxim of *quality* imposes on the translator the obligation to find the best possible TL form in order to give as close a TL equivalent as can be achieved: in other words, to stick as closely as possible to the truth of the ST as the norms of TL syntax will allow him to do, without producing thereby an unnatural sounding TT. By *quantity* he means that the translator should only use those words, forms or units which are absolutely necessary to the accurate transfer of meaning; in other words, he should avoid excessive expansion and seek economy or compression of expression, so that the translation is just as informative as required, and not more. *Relevance* relates to the immediate situation within the sentence or paragraph, as well as to that of the whole text, and invites the translator to assist the TL reader by disregarding any syntactical relationships which are not directly pertinent to the message. His TT should also produce a network of sense relations which conform to the norms of TL syntax. Finally, the maxim of *manner* requires that the translator select the most appropriate TL form in terms of syntactical and stylistic norms, and that he should express these as clearly and as concisely as possible.

Neubert himself defines a wider set of criteria in terms of *intentionality, acceptability, situationality, informativity, coherence* and *intertextuality*, as he believes that Grice's maxims are not detailed enough and may lead to over-generalisation or a false identification of one system with another. Let us take each of these in turn and discuss their relevance to the task of translation.

The first factor is that of *intentionality*, which relates to the need for the translator to be sure that he has understood all aspects and nuances of the ST author's message, both implied and overt. If there are what Neubert calls 'breakdowns' in the process of communication in the ST, such potential ambiguities have to be assessed as to their nature, whether deliberate or as a result of poor style, and then dealt with appropriately, either by reproduction of that ambiguity in the TL or by its resolution through paraphrase, expansion or restructuring. This also presupposes, for Neubert, the existence of a principle of co-operation, in that the writer assumes the presence of a reader, and the reader assumes that the writer did in fact intend for his text to be a instrument of communication

The next criterion, that of *acceptability*, is seen by Neubert to be closely associated with intentionality, in that any linguistic communication has to be acceptable to the TL reader as a text in its own right, and for this to occur, the reader has to be able to identify with both form and content, although there may be some degree of tolerance with regard to the form. Different text types will therefore impose a greater or lesser number of constraints on the translator according to the norms of the particular genre.

For Neubert, *situationality* relates to the socio-cultural context of the text, in which a concrete situation can be seen to exemplify underlying truths or trends of the SL culture. Here again is the concept of the translator as mediator between two cultures, with the task of decoding information from the ST and encoding into the TL. Any obstacles to understanding of the ST meaning through lack of awareness of the SL culture on the part of the TT reader are to be removed through the mediation of the translator. This gives rise to the guiding principle of 'situational adequacy' and will involve an element of trade-off in terms of expansion or compression, and resultant gain or loss of information. It may involve a lot of deductive analysis, and even on occasion intelligent guesswork, on the part of the translator. Neubert even goes so far as to express the opinion that:

> If a situationality standard could be established for textual segments *qua* types, one would be able to account for textual shifts in the same way as one agrees to perform the necessary transpositions demanded by contrasting linguistic systems. (1985: 73)

This opens up quite another series of considerations which it is intended to address in a further study (forthcoming) on the role of cross-cultural differences and strategies for resolving these within the process of translation. The current collection does not allow enough scope for the exploration of this more specific possibility.

The criterion of *informativity* relates to the degree of certainty with which a TL reader can be expected to read of events, states and processes which were originally introduced within a situation or context which forms part of the cultural experience of an SL reader. There is thus a close affinity between situationality and informativity, and both will require a degree of pragmatic selection on the part of the translator when making choices as to expansion or compression of the SL term or reference, or gain or loss in terms of SL intended meaning. Obviously, any misunderstanding (what Neubert calls 'deviant knowledge') on the part of the translator, with regard to the SL culture and the situation of the text, may give rise to problems of understanding on the part of the TL reader.

The criterion of *coherence* is discussed by Neubert as relating to a 'continuity of sense', based on a clearly discernible coherence of structure in the ST. The translator needs to be able to perceive what mechanisms give this coherence to the ST, and then aim to create a similar structure of cohesive devices in his TT. The fact of aiming for coherence should preclude any tendency to over-reliance on literal translation, since the features which produce coherence in the TL text cannot be expected to replicate those of the SL text. Neubert's comment on this is as follows:

> Human communication relies in a critical way on the ability of the receiver to deduce a much more precise understanding of the intended meaning of an utterance than is conveyed by the words alone and the syntactic structure in which they are incorporated. (1985: 305)

The importance of textual coherence is also stressed by Beaugrande:

Coherence supplies a logical framework with which to achieve conceptual connectivity (1980: 19, quoted in Neubert, 1985)

A further feature of textuality is that of *cohesion*, which is concerned with the relationship between the underlying meaning of SL and TL utterances and the respective surface structures (linguistic forms) used to convey these meanings (e.g. surface structure: 'I am not averse to this amendment'; underlying meaning: 'I can accept or go along with this amendment'). These cohesive ties may differ from L1 to L2. They occur on several levels, including those of the word or lexical unit, of the sentence and of the text. They act as a signal or indicator to signpost relationships between previously introduced items and those about to be introduced. As Halliday and Hassan state, one element precedes another and relies on it for decoding (1976: 4, quoted in Neubert, 1985). Thus these cohesive devices provide clues for the translator, in terms of interpretation of meaning and linking relevant items of information with the language relating to each one.

For Neubert, lexical cohesion refers to the fact of lexis conforming to both immediate contextual meaning and to a theme, concept or semantic field running throughout the text. The ST author, and therefore the translator too, creates this is as a result of what Neubert calls 'textonymy' (1985: 22). This term refers to the associative network of word families which are linked in one of the following ways: synonymy, hyponymy, metonymy, metaphor, antonymy, complementarity, converseness, homonymy, gradation, thematic progression or lexical field. Syntactical cohesion also contributes to meaning by virtue of the form of syntax used (e.g. conditional or subjunctive forms for hypothesis or unfulfilled wish, Future Simple or Going To for intention) and thus contributes to the cohesive relationship between the different elements of the text. This is brought about through forms such as tenses, temporal relationships, dependency and subordination, use of adjectives to qualify nouns and adverbs to modify verbs, etc. Thus, for Beaugrande and Dressler (1981), cohesion is based partly on grammatical dependence.

The final point considered by Neubert is that of *intertextuality*, in which he seeks to remind the translator that any text is but one example of a text type, and that this text type will have its own particular characteristics of discourse which constitute the norm for that particular type. The translator needs to be aware of these norms and to avoid transferring the norms of the SL text type to those of the TT. The tolerance of any violation of these norms, on the part of the TL reader, will depend on the extent to which these norms are perceived as untouchable and essential to that text type. Thus an article in a medical journal could not contain any slang expressions, and would be highly unlikely to use the first person singular as a form of expression.

It is essential for the translator to have detailed knowledge both of his target text reader and the intended function of the TT, which may differ from that of the ST, according to the needs of both text giver and TT reader. Unless stated otherwise by a text provider, and definitely when using the texts in this collection, the translator could reasonably assume that he is to reproduce in the TL an equivalent text type to that of the ST, and he should inform his own knowledge of the norms for this text type in the TL by consultation of several examples of such a type, from authoritative sources such as books, journals or periodicals. Over a period of time, the translator should build up a library of notes on different text types, whether on card-index or database. The latter is preferable because of its flexibility but what is essential is to keep such records in some retrievable form. The number and range of text types observed will most probably be a direct result of texts tackled for translation, and so this will vary according to individual experience.

Delisle (1980) believes that translation is a process of operations effected on a segment of discourse, involving the skills of comprehension of the SL and reformulation in the TL, with the former being an interpretative process and the latter an expressive one. To explain this process more clearly, Delisle talks of 'les quatre paliers du maniement du langage' (the four landmarks or criteria for the use of language) with the same intention in mind, that of defining the major factors which govern our interpretation and understanding of a text, and which must therefore guide the translator in his construction of a Target Text. He describes these factors as being: the conventions of the written language, the need for lexical analysis, the interpretation of the stylistic effect and the overall textual coherence achieved.

By the conventions of the written language he refers to the norms, as established by usage, in terms of presentation, style and rules of syntax. Lexical analysis includes the decoding of the meaning of the various linguistic signs (cf. Saussure), and the selection of the actual meaning intended within the immediate context. For Delisle, style and form (syntax and lexis) are interlinked and both contribute to the overall meaning, or message, of the text, in terms of its denotative (what it refers to), connotative (what it suggests or recalls) and emotive (response) effect on the reader. The author, the subject, the medium of transmission and the target reader all influence the choice of style to be used. As for overall textual coherence, this refers to 'une logique interne qui rend le texte cohérent' and which therefore creates the 'dynamique générale du texte (overall text dynamics = effect). It involves consideration of the way in which utterances are linked, the relationships between various items of information, the rhythm and rate of presentation of ideas, and the way in which these are reinforced throughout the text. This requires from the translator the ability not only to undertake a detailed analysis of the different component units, but also to take an overview of the text as a whole in order to preserve the structure and relationships within the development of its line of argument. This may require him to re-organise the order of presentation of items of information; the compression of a number of ideas into a more concise form of expression; the elucidation (i.e. expansion in order to bring out the full meaning) or embedding (rendering implicit rather than explicit) of certain items of information; and the skilful use, or even introduction, of linking words in order to preserve this sense of textual organisation and structure.

This is then another element of the task of the translator; having already described him as a cultural mediator between two societies, reference can also be made to his role as linguistic mediator between the two language systems used by the members of these two social communities. The translator has at his disposal various techniques and mechanisms which will guide him in this task, relating to his re-formulation of the ST content in an acceptable TL form. These strategies are listed by various authors using different terms to describe their role and with differing interpretations of their scope, commencing, of course, with Vinay and D'Arbelnet. Discussion will be limited primarily to those terms and definitions of strategies as proposed by Newmark (1990, 1991), but with reference, where relevant, to other authors who have adopted a similar approach.

If cultural differences are to be perceived in terms of different ways of understanding and therefore of representing the world around us, and if the view is accepted that words are merely written signs which refer to and recall different aspects (concrete and conceptual) of the world as understood and described by a given linguistic community, then it would seem reasonable for the translator to ensure that he has a complete and accurate understanding of what is referred to, both denotatively (explicitly) and connotatively (implicitly, by association) by all the words, or lexical units, of the ST text, and by the way in which these words are linked to present concepts by means of the ST syntax and textual structure.

In order to reach an understanding of lexical items in cases of socio-cultural mismatch or contextual ambiguity, the translator has therefore to undertake a process of what used to be called *componential analysis* — namely the construction of a mental diagram of the network of inter-linked and/or clearly differentiated elements of meaning of a particular linguistic unit. This is discussed very clearly and at length by Nida (1979), who also describes this as the semantic structure of a sign, and taken up by Newmark (1990: 114); these two are the principal sources of reference for this process. Componential analysis of lexis involves the search for all nuances of meaning, both overt and implied (referential or pragmatic), which could be carried by a given lexical unit, firstly in its universal application, and secondly, by a process of elimination, in its immediate context. The ST term is then compared with possible TL equivalents in terms of its function within the text, its cultural content and connotations, its social usage (register) and its effect within the text.

However, componential analysis as a process has been somewhat displaced by newer theories of prototypes of denotation, as discussed by Taylor (1991), whose description of the categorisation of colour in different languages not only illustrates the comment that we segment reality into different 'bites' according to our sociocultural background, but also contributes to the concept of near-equivalence in translation by providing the term (also used in computer concordancing programmes) *fuzzy match*, where some, but not all, of the semantic characteristics of an L1 term will be present or contained in an L2 term. The appropriateness of the L2 term in context will depend on the extent to which this *fuzzy match* duplicates a sufficient number of features for the global message not to be deformed or misinterpreted.

Most comparisons by whatever method will reveal both similarities and differences between apparently equivalent terms in the SL and TL, and the translator's task is, as stated above, to select a term with maximum similarity to all aspects of the SL term (function and sense) whilst minimising the differences. This process assumes a native-speaker level of competence on the part of the translator, whilst also requiring him to reach beyond the limits of his own knowledge of the language in question through exhaustive use of all available sources, printed, electronic and human (the expert, or even another native speaker, since each native speaker will have his own range of lexis, 'parole', selected from the pool of lexis available to him in that language, 'langue'). Because of this, however, componential analysis cannot guarantee absolute comprehension and transfer of intended meaning. What it can do is to eliminate potential for ambiguity and misunderstanding.

To effect this process of analysis the translator will call on his knowledge of synonyms, of words that could be used, or are commonly used, with each term (collocations), of the semantic field (wider word-group) to which the lexical unit belongs and to any sub-divisions of that field within which the unit could be classed (e.g. agriculture — animal husbandry — cattle-farming — dairy farming). He also has to differentiate between potential ambiguities as a result of the use of homographs (words with a single form but different possible meanings, according to context, e.g. bear, as in animal, or, to put up with). Obviously, these perceived differences have to correspond to those which would be understood by a native speaker, and this is where the translator runs the risk of being the victim of an incomplete knowledge of either language, so that reference to a good thesaurus and a good monolingual dictionary should be a standard part of this process of analysis. For a discussion of the various aspects and definitions of meaning, refer also to Newmark (1991); his definition of this could be summed up by the statement that meaning is equal to the functionally relevant information contained in a unit, including intention, tone, impact, texture and function, with the word as minimal, and the text as maximal, potential unit. This meaning can further be cognitive (what is said), communicative (what is intended) and associative (the relationship between author and reader).

Thus the translator, in his role as linguistic mediator, operates on the level of the lexical content of the text and the meaning it conveys. As stated above, however, meaning is also conveyed by the form in which this meaning, or content, is presented, in other words, by the syntax used to link these units of meaning. It has also been stated that this syntax can either carry an element of meaning by itself (intention, doubt, manner of doing, indicating relationships between items of information: co-ordination of ideas, subordination, contrast); or it can contribute to a theme or intent, e.g. promises conveyed by naming an action to be undertaken and framing this action in a tense which implies intent: 'I will do that for you tomorrow'. All syntactical structures represent a particular way of using the building blocks of language to say something specific, but it does not mean that this is the only way in which this specific information could be conveyed. Consider, for example:

- John hit the ball. It rolled into the corner. The boy picked it up.
- The boy picked up the ball which John had hit into the corner.
- When John hit the ball, it rolled into the corner, where the boy picked it up.
- The ball rolled into the corner, hit there by John, and was picked up by the boy.

The sentences above all mean the same thing, but cast a slightly different emphasis, whether this is on the boy, the ball or the sequence of actions.

They are all *paraphrases* of each other, and this is an essential process in the task of translation. Just as the translator has to go through the process of componential analysis (CA) in order to discover the intended meaning of an item of lexis, so too, he needs to reformulate an SL sentence in his mind, in order to be sure of identifying where the emphasis lies, and what exactly is meant. Just as not every item of lexis will present a potential for misinterpretation, and therefore require CA, so that it will not be necessary to adopt the procedure of paraphrase for each and every sentence, or part of a sentence. Where any difficulty does arise in the initial decoding of the ST, however, this is a very useful process. The same process is also valid when reformulating the decoded ST meaning into the TL, in that the translator will find it useful to 'try out' several different ways of expressing the content and intent of a particular ST unit of translation (phrase, clause, sentence, even paragraph) in order to best conform to all the parameters he has set himself, in terms of ST style within TL norms.

A recent work by Hewson and Martin (1991) discusses this 'Variational Approach', again from the perspective of the translator as intercultural mediator, whose role is to effect an information transfer between cultures through the generation of what they call 'reconstruction alternatives'. They challenge Vinay and D'Arbelnet's approach as being one which aims to predict a series of translation techniques which could generally be reproduced, and claim that this is too restrictive. Their approach is intended to discover a variety of conversion strategies, which have then to be assessed in relation to the immediate requirements imposed by both Source and Target cultures, concurring with Beaugrande that translation is a comparative and adjustable process (1978: 14, quoted Hewson and Martin, 1991: 7). They call on Nida and Taber to support their belief that translation should be approached in the light of a range of potential translations, which will 'vary according to the relevant norms induced by the Language Cultures brought together in the act of translation' (1991: 8):

> The basic principle of translation means that no translation in a receptor language can be the equivalent of the model in the source language. (1969: 27)

> Translation will depend in a very large measure upon the purpose to be accomplished by the translation in question. (1969: 33)

Hewson and Martin explain their objection to a clearly-defined set of translation strategies being seen as universally applicable, on the grounds that possible translation alternatives do not necessarily qualify as regularities, and that just as conditions of translation production may vary, so will the potential alternatives, according to those conditions. Their conversion strategy places great emphasis on the need to consider how relationships, as perceived between different elements of the ST and dependent on the ST culture, can be accurately transferred into the TL. They are seeking to evaluate various degrees of equivalence, in order to 'bridge the communications gap' and so they give their own definition of translation as being:

> the individually- and interculturally-motivated choice, according to TL socio-cultural norms, by a mediator, from amongst sets of... related paraphrastic options (1991: 33)

and the term *variation* is explained thus:

> the set of all possible formulations that can be associated with any given identifiable situation. (1991: 40)

Thus they expect the translator to develop a range of possible reconstruction alternatives in the SL (paraphrastic options), in order to be able to do the same within the TL, until it becomes clear where the clearest match, or dynamic equivalence, will lie, between all these potential SL and TL paraphrases.

Fuchs sees this process of paraphrasing as being divided into three types of activity: firstly, there is a kind of subconscious process, which is followed whilst reading but without conscious effort. Then there is the deliberate effort to take into account all possible meanings. Finally, a process which lies between the two, in which the translator becomes aware of the subconscious process but has not deliberately set out to look at possible alternatives (1982: 169).

It seems to us that this method of approach is particularly advantageous to the translator. It encourages him not to reject different possible versions without first noting them down and proceeding to a systematic analysis. From this, and by a process of comparison between ST and TL paraphrastic options, he will be able to eliminate most possible choices, and this will allow for a logically founded and clearly motivated choice of his final TL version.

Hewson and Martin (1991) state that, 'Any specific translation is the product of the translator's predetermined, but in the final analysis, unpredictable choice'. It could be argued that these choices can in fact be predicted to a great extent, provided there are clear indications of the parameters (functional, textual and contextual) forming the basis for these choices. This is what the trainee translator has to accept as a guiding principle; namely, that there are degrees of suitability or appropriateness of choice, and that if selection is made according to context, text type and communicative function, then there will be valid arguments in favour of one choice as opposed to another. Just as for Saussure, 'in language there are only differences'[10] so for every translator, in the task of selection from alternatives, meaning is conveyed through a system of inclusion, exclusion and intersection, on the lines of Jakobson's *semantic* form of meaning.[11]

This is where pragmatics come into play, in that the translator's choice will involve giving precedence to one or more criteria, such as SL style and form, SL author's intention, TL style and syntax, and target reader's needs, to name but a few. Priorities will differ from one text and one situation to another, and so the translator will, if he adopts this approach, be assured of respecting all the parameters of a particular situation, provided of course that he has begun by a clear identification of these.

Although this approach may appear to conflict with the aims of this collection of texts, this is not necessarily the case. At the beginning of this chapter it was stated that the task of translation is concerned with a series of motivated choices, and so this 'variational' approach would seem to comply with this aim. The end result may not be a set of fixed categories of universally applicable translation strategies, but then neither was this the objective of this text. The stated aim was to enable the student translator to discover a series of potential strategies which could be applied in more than one situation, and which would therefore be worthy of consideration when tackling this task, but this does not mean that these could be fixed and eternalised. The intention is to enable the translator to become more sensitive to ST meaning, and more aware of potential TL strategies for expressing that meaning. The approach is thus non-prescriptive, non-normative and wholly empirical. It is process-oriented and context-bound, flexible and open-ended.

In summary, the starting point of this approach is the *translation oriented text analysis* of Christiane Nord,[12] which seeks to 'identify the functional concept of ST textual features and provide a reliable foundation for each and every decision of the translation process'; the intermediary stage is the creation of Holmes' *mind map*; the shape, composition and orientation of the TT will depend on the text type, its specific function in relation to the target reader and the medium of communication (cf. Vermeer's *skopos theory*[13]) and on the choice made by the translator as to the *initial norm* (Toury).

In the case of professional translation the translator may have many masters to serve: the ST author's intent, the client's aims and the target reader's needs, as well as his own interpretation. All of these have to be reconciled and ranked in order of priority. *Skopos theory* prioritises the function of the target text to be produced, but for this collection, functional constancy will be assumed as the norm and equal importance should be given to the integration of the ST parameters.

The aim of this collection is to encourage the translator to strive for accurate interpretation of the ST message, based on logical analysis of sign function and meaning, drawing on linguistic and sociocultural competence in the SL culture. This is then complemented by a pragmatic approach to the conceptual construction of the TT, accepting some loss as inevitable and introducing gain where this is desirable and where it reinforces the success of the global message. To close with the words of Delisle, the aim is to train the translator in an awareness of problems through 'le repérage des difficultés de traduction'. To do this, 'il faut s'habituer à lire l'original avec les "yeux d'un traducteur" afin de déterminer quel procédé de traduction il conviendra d'appliquer au moment du transfert de tel ou tel passage', one of the prerequisites for this being an awareness of 'les procédés de traduction' (1993: 94).

Notes

1. Whilst it is obvious that translators are not all male, for the purposes of economy and clarity, the third person pronoun 'he' will be used to refer to the translator.
2. Holmes, J. (1988), *Translated! Papers on Literary Translation and Translation Studies*. Amsterdam, Rodopi, p. 100.
3. Jakobson, R. (1959), 'On Linguistic Aspects of Translation'. In *On Translation*, ed. R. Brower, Cambridge (Mass), Harvard University Press, pp. 232–239. See also Bassnett-McGuire (1980) for discussion of this.
4. Hönig, H., 'Holmes's "Mapping Theory" and the Landscape of Mental Translation Processes'. In van Leuven Zwart and Naaijkens (eds) *Translation Studies: The State of the Art, Proceedings of the First James S. Homes Symposium on Translation Studies*. Amsterdam, Rodopi, pp. 77–89.
5. Holmes, H. (1988), p. 58.
6. Neubert and Shreve (1992), p. 136.
7. Gorlée (1994), p. 46.
8. Toury, G. (1980), *In Search of a Theory of Translation*. Tel Aviv, The Porter Institute.
9. Neubert and Shreve (1992).
10. De Saussure, F. (1987).
11. Jakobson, R., in Brower (1959).
12. Nord, C. (1991), *Text Analysis in Translation: Theory, Methodology and Didactic Application of a Model for Translation*. Amsterdam, Amsterdamer Publikationen zur Sprache und Literaturt.
13. Vermeer, H. J. (1978), 'Ein rahmen für eine allgemeine Translationstheorie'. In *Lebende Sprachen* 23 (3): 99–102, quoted in Schäffner, C. (1995), 'Skopos theory', forthcoming.

Preface to Texts

Any text to be translated requires a thorough decoding in order to acquire as clearly as possible an understanding of the intended meaning of each word, expression, clause, sentence and paragraph in the Source Text (ST). This will enable the translator to convey the most accurate interpretation in the Target Text (TT). To achieve this thorough decoding, the translator has to be aware of those linguistic and stylistic features which are most likely to carry both meaning and intended 'tone', and to pay particular attention to each of these during the process of translation.

The first points to note, when approaching a text with a view to translation, are the genre of this text, its source of publication and intended readership, as these will not only create certain expectations on the part of the translator (as for the SL target reader) in terms of style, syntax and lexis, but will also help to explain some of the choices made by the ST author and thus inform the TT author (i.e. the translator) in his own process of choice and decision-making. The alert student will recognise this as the first step in a textual commentary, and his ability to undertake a sensitive reading of the text with this kind of analysis in mind will greatly enhance his awareness of the factors contributing to the effect of the ST, thereby enabling him to create the best possible TT.

Another important element to note, before zooming in on a more detailed reading of individual units of the text, is the relationship between various parts of a sentence, in terms of the clauses and phrases thereof, and the degree of complexity conferred by these on the sentence itself. Further consideration has to be given to the potential for difficulty of interpretation of the message as a result of this complexity, and whether it is an intended factor of the ST author's style or the result of 'bad writing'. Then the translator will have to decide whether to reproduce this structure, or whether he will have to modify and re-order this in places, either to facilitate understanding or to conform to TL norms.

It is undeniable that whilst use of a particular form of syntax is sometimes dictated by linguistic norms, it is very often the result of a deliberate choice on the part of the author, and that whilst it may not be possible for the translator to use the same form of syntax in the TL, because of the norms of that language, he must however seek to reproduce the same effect as that of the SL syntax by his selection of the appropriate TL syntax. This may sometimes involve a direct equivalent, but will very often require a transformation in terms of verb forms (mood, aspect, person, tense) or of function as a part of speech (adjective to adverb and vice-versa, noun to gerund or verb, synthetic or single-word verb to phrasal verb, loss or insertion of definite article, etc).

Then, as discussed in the previous chapter, the production of a good translation requires the componential analysis (Newmark, 1991) of lexical items and the identification of appropriate semantic and terminological fields, as well as a clear understanding of the overall tone and intended message, in order to give the correct tone and interpretation of discrete units as well as of the text as a whole.

Almost any text will contain some stylistic features deliberately chosen by the ST author to create a particular effect, for the transmission of information or of his personal attitude, through a certain 'tone' or inflection of the message. These features could be termed 'stylistic devices' and they too have to be noted, in terms of specific examples of particular forms of style as well as in terms of the overall degree of, and impact occasioned by, the use of such features in the text as a whole. The translator will have to accept a certain degree of loss of these features, in that the very process of translation will incur such a loss by virtue of the inability within the TL to recreate the same lexical effect (e.g. alliteration, or a play on words) without subsequent loss of the message. It is generally true to say that it is the message which has to remain the prime consideration for transfer from ST to TT in a non-literary text, and that stylistic features have to take second place to this, whilst still seeking to retain these where possible. Within this category of non-literary texts, some genres will obviously contain a greater number of such rhetorical devices than others.

The elucidation, where necessary, of cultural references also constitutes an essential factor in the recreation of the global message of a text, and the translator will be failing in his duty if he does not bring out for the TL reader any nuances of meaning, whether overt or implied, denotative or connotative, which may be conveyed by these references and which may be considered to contribute to a better understanding of the ST author's message. Even the use of a particular form of punctuation will affect the structure of a sentence or paragraph and may hereby influence the meaning.

The aim of producing a text which reads as though it had been written in the Target Language (TL) therefore requires the translator to undertake an analysis and breakdown of:

(1) **Sentence Structure** to permit identification of main and subordinate clauses.

(2)   The use of **Syntax,** including the subject of each verb and the object of the action, the use of tense, number and parts of speech.

(3)   **Lexical Items** and units, including the implied slant and emphasis, either through denotative or connotative meaning.

(4)   **Stylistic Devices.**

(5)   **Cultural References.**

(6)   The use of **Punctuation.**

Peircean semiotics

The intricacies and complex subdivisions of Peirce's semiotics (see Conceptual Framework) are perhaps not of immediate help in this application of theory to analysis. However, his use of the three terms, *index, icon* and *symbol,* to describe the way in which meaning is accessed by the text interpreter, can be used to assist this process of interpretation through textual analysis, both by identifying how the translator has accessed particular units of meaning, and subsequently by training oneself to apply the same approach, where relevant, to ST units, in order to facilitate the selection of an appropriate TT unit.

For this reason, in the Annotations section there are also examples of how these three forms of sign interpretation seem to have been followed by the translator, whether consciously or not. These concepts are complementary to the categories described above and are intended to represent a further method of self-training in how to identify and access meaning, not to be applied dogmatically to every text or context, but as and when appropriate.

All of these procedures should help the translator bring out the nuances of the ST author's intended message through the information given and the language used. These will thus form the categories under which will be grouped discussion of particular points selected for discussion from each text, on the basis that such points will either pose a genuine problem for the translator or that they deserve his close attention in order to do full justice to the ST message as well as to the TL reader.

In this book the Annotations will not only indicate not only examples of linguistic categories of problem types but also select examples of how units of meaning can be interpreted by using terms from Peirce's semiotics as introduced in the previous chapter.

Suggested methodology

The process of translation requires the translator to demonstrate linguistic competence by the exercise of transfer of information from one language to the other.

In a professional context it is far more likely that this will involve translation into your mother-tongue (in this case, into English). It is well-known that the purpose of translation can serve several pedagogical objectives, but in our case, where the aim of the process is to produce target texts in French of a professional standard, this process will test the ability to understand relationships between parts of a sentence, a paragraph and a text, in order to convey, in a clear and accurate manner, both the overall message and the individual details of the Source Text. The task also tests control of expression in one's own language, and will very clearly highlight any misunderstandings of the ST. It further requires the demonstration of the ability to produce a coherent Target Text which conveys the content and which respects, as closely as possible within the TL norms, the stylistic characteristics of the Source Text. Note that it is very easy to produce a Target Text which is full of franglais and this is indicative of an excessive level of interference from the Source Text. In a professional context, evidence of lack of revision is not acceptable, and a final text has to read as though it had originally been written in the Target Language.

With experience, everyone develops a particular approach to the task of translation, but to begin with, it is advisable to stick to a single, disciplined and systematic method. Here are two possible initial approaches, both of which work equally well, and the translator should try both.

(1)   **Top to bottom**. In this approach the Source Text is read through carefully, to gain a clear idea of the overall message and subject-matter of the text. Then read each section again and within the section, each paragraph and then each sentence is read as a unit, so that by the time you begin the actual process of translation, you already have a clear picture of the relationship between the units of translation at each level.

(2)   **Bottom to top**. Here, you begin to translate straight away, after an initial reading but without undertaking a thorough study of the Source Text. After a brief reading, you start at the beginning and work through the text at the lowest level of translation unit (word, phrase, clause, sentence: each unit should be: 'the smallest possible, the largest necessary'), until you produce a rough draft. *A note of warning*: one possible drawback of this method is that misreadings of the Source Text are more likely, so it will be even more important, when adopting this approach, to check at the end that you have not jumped to the wrong conclusion or 'got hold of the wrong end of the stick'. This method requires that you constantly revise

or reassess your interpretation of preceding units, based on new denotative or connotative information in the unit you are in the process of translating. Although this is the method favoured by many professional translators, it will take some time to become adept at using this method and you must practise great self-discipline with regard to the need for constant revision. If in doubt, or not confident of your ability to maintain this approach, then I suggest you stick to the first method.

For both approaches, in the production of a first draft draft you need to note down (using brackets, dashes, etc.) whatever alternatives occur to you. Do not stop to agonise over the best choice at this point.

Having got this far, in both cases you will have some kind of draft, which will probably still read like a fairly literal translation, and which should have various possible versions for individual units of translation.

(3)   Now you need to return to the Source Text and make a note of:
   (i)   Any overall characteristics (register, sustained metaphor or imagery, tone, use of syntax, range of lexis) which you wish to preserve in your Target Text.
   (ii)   Any particular problems, in terms of syntax, lexis, cultural references or punctuation, and whether any cultural reference will require further explanation by means of information within brackets in the main body of the text, or else in a footnote. This will obviously depend on the TT reader's presumed knowledge.
   (iii) Any specific stylistic or syntactic features within a sentence or a paragraph which you wish to preserve.
   (iv)   Any ambiguities in the Source Text, and whether these are a stylistic feature to be preserved (i.e. deliberate) or a result of poor style on the part of the ST author. If the latter is the case, will it be necessary to reformulate the information in order to make it comprehensible for TT readers? If there is such ambiguity that the translator is obliged to made a choice based on his own interpretation, should the TT reader be informed of this by means of a translator's note, or is the informative content in this particular instance not so essential as to make a significant difference to the overall message?
   (v)   The lexical field or fields to which choice of vocabulary should aim to conform.
When making these decisions, you should assume that your Target Reader will have the same social characteristics and level of education as the reader of the Source Text, unless informed otherwise.

(4)   Having identified both problems and characteristics, you can then
        return to your draft and work from the Source Text, taking each
        unit of translation in turn and selecting from any alternatives
        according to your criteria of register, style, syntax and lexis. At the
        end of each sentence you should reread the sentence to make sure
        it 'fits in' with the preceding sentence, and in order to be aware of
        the contextual and syntactical framework for the following sen-
        tence. At the end of each paragraph, you should reread the whole
        paragraph and assess it in the same way. At each of these stages
        you should check that not only is your draft linguistically accurate,
        but that it also accurately conveys the information inherent in each
        unit of translation, both denotative (what does it say) and conno-
        tative (what does it imply, what associations does it evoke).
        Attention should also be paid to the linking mechanisms between
        each section (sentence, paragraph, section of text).

(5)   Once you have a complete, revised version of your text, you can
        then systematically work through both Source and Target texts, to
        assess your TT in terms of:
        (i)   Its internal coherence (syntax, lexis, style, balance).
        (ii)   How far it respects the criteria identified: style, tone, syntax,
                lexis.
        (iii)   The overall accuracy of the transfer of the 'message' of the
                Source Text, and of the individual details of that message.

(6)   Finally, and very importantly, you have to set aside the Source Text
        and read your Target Text, assessing its naturalness and readability
        as a text in its own right, as if there had been no Source Text from
        which to work. It is a good idea, at this stage, to ask a native speaker
        of the TL to also read the text, since another person, who has not
        seen the ST, may bring to bear a greater degree of objectivity, free
        from any SL/ST interference or expectations.

As you will see from the above this exercise involves, as previously
stated, the skill of commentary, in that you need firstly to be able to identify
the message and how it is conveyed in terms of the linguistic, stylistic and
thematic characteristics of the Source Text, and also to be able to reproduce a similar message in a similar textual form in the Target Language.

It also requires a high degree of accuracy and fluency of expression in
both languages in relation to one another, together with the ability to
manipulate language to create effect and convey information. It is the
ultimate test of your command of both languages, in that you are
required to switch from one to the other, rather than perform within the
parameters of one language, as is the case in other linguistic activities.

Like all other language skills, competence in this exercise improves with frequent practice. By keeping up with reading and listening related to contemporary affairs, from both French and English sources, a translator should build up a range of vocabulary and expression, as well as a certain level of awareness, which will be of relevance in this exercise. Do not expect to reach your peak without plenty of practice, and do not be satisfied with a version which is merely, or at best, adequate. There is a great difference between being able to convey the gist of the ST meaning and producing a carefully crafted Target Text. It is within your power to surprise yourself; the more you practise, the better you will perform, and the more you will enjoy the whole exercise as a creative process, as well as producing an even more professional standard of work.

Finally, all these revisions must be undertaken within the framework of the final objective, which is to produce a naturally flowing TT with appropriate register, word order and stylistic devices. An over-reliance on a literal translation in the final version will indicate a lack of understanding of the SL and a lack of 'polishing-up' within the global context of the intended impact of the ST in terms of the TT.

How to use these texts and annotations

Although there can be no one, fixed way in which to use the opportunity for self-testing and improvement offered by this collection of annotated Source Texts and suggested Target Texts, we would like, nonetheless, to offer some ideas on how they could be used.

For all texts, the student is to assume that the target reader is an educated but non-specialist reader, who could be expected to share the intellectual and social characteristics of the target reader of the ST. By the same token, it will be assumed that the source of publication or dissemination of the TT will be similar to the medium of publication of the ST. Suggested TT versions and discussion of problems for the translator will be based on these assumptions, since the aim of this book is to practise and develop the basic skills of translation, and does not include the further skill of transposition from one register or text genre to another. We expect the student to develop his or her critical faculties with regard to the effectiveness and appropriateness of the suggested target texts, through reading the guided discussion of the solutions suggested for each perceived problem of translation within a given text.

Discussion of problems for translation is intended to be of practical relevance and is directed towards the student translator who may be working alone. Points discussed sometimes take the form of notes rather than adopting a more abstract or theoretical approach.

All references to line numbers in brackets refer to the text in the language of the preceding quote (i.e., if in French — to Source Text, if in English — to Target Text)

In many cases the translation shifts or strategies adopted by the translator would be equally valid for use when translating from French into English, in which case they should obviously be applied in reverse.

Although all of the texts except one follow a clearly defined structure and approach, the first text is somewhat of an exception. This text is divided, for the purpose of analysis, into segments or units of meaning, pairing parallel segments and commenting on all aspects worthy of note from the point of view of translation. The pairing of segments follows the linear sequence of the text.

This way of tackling initial identification of problems mirrors the sequence adopted when reading a text for the first time, where the translator makes a mental comment or note as he reads, rather than grouping problems under particular categories. This should be the approach adopted by the trainee translator. In effect, the grouping of types of problem is intended to show how patterns can be identified, whereas the intensive reading model as exemplified by the *Ouistreham* text illustrates the actual process of identification in operation, rather like the think-aloud protocols of Lörscher[1] *et al.* It is suggested that, for each text, trainee translators adopt the model of the *Ouistreham* text for the initial reading of a Source Text, but that they then group their findings into particular categories as is done in the Annotations section. This way the trainee benefits from both aspects of translation-oriented text analysis and gains an overview of patterns as well as an in-depth familiarity with each text.

On a more practical note, most of the chosen texts are of a non-literary, sometimes semi-specialised nature and their lexical content should be readily available in bilingual, non-specialist dictionaries, although in a few cases access to a specialised dictionary may be necessary. They will be informative, of descriptive or discursive style, with no real narrative or dialogue.

Do not forget, however, that dictionaries, whether printed or electronic, are not the only source of information. Other sources include publications in the field of the topic, other papers written on a similar subject, and of course the human source, the expert working in a particular field. This latter is of especial value in a field such as computer technology, where the lexical content is constantly being revised and updated to take account of new developments; or in medicine, where new discoveries in diagnosis and treatment are being reported and old beliefs questioned and revised.

The texts are grouped in separate sections (Source Texts, Target Texts,

Annotations) to give the opportunity for self-testing. It is to be remembered that there is no such thing as a perfect, definitive version of a translation, given the importance of the translator's own interpretation and idiolect, and so the fact of having adopted a different strategy or chosen a different form of lexis or syntax does not necessarily imply error of interpretation or judgement. What is important is to try to analyse and explain the reason for any differences between your TT and the suggested version.

It would therefore be beneficial to approach the ST from the point of view of analysis of potential problems first. Your assessment of such problems and ideas for solutions could then be compared with those suggested, either before tackling the text or after having produced an initial draft.

We would suggest that the former be the method adopted to begin with, in order to become familiar with the approach adopted and with the range of problems that can reasonably be expected to be present in a text for translation. As you gain in confidence this comparison can serve as feedback, following and supplementing your own analysis.

A final step would be to compare your own, finalised and revised version of a Target Text with that suggested, again noting and analysing the reason for differences of interpretation and choice of lexis, syntax and style.

The number of texts and the opportunity to tackle both shorter and longer texts should enable the student-translator to build up his speed and improve his performance through a steady programme of timed effort and production, once a certain level of familiarity with the approach and sensitivity to the types of problem has been developed.

In the same way that one learns the basics before progressing to a more instinctive and non-analytical use of language, so too can the internalisation of such strategies only be achieved through repeated practice and analysis, until the translator is able to tackle a text and consider all such criteria on an almost subconscious level.

Thus the gradual discovery of a generalised tendency towards the use of a specific strategy for dealing with a particular problem in translation from French to English should be borne in mind when reading all annotations of the Source Texts. These strategies will not always be universally applicable but should provide both insight into potential solutions and a clearer overall understanding of some of the ways in which aspects of the process of translation can be approached. The availability of a series of texts of differing length should, as stated above, also enable the student-translator to build up his competence and speed.

It is the purpose of this book to contribute to such a process of internalisation and self-improvement through repeated practice.

Note

1. Lörscher, W. (1987) *Übersetzungsperforanz, Übersetzungsprozess und Übersetzungsstrategien.* Habiliationsschrift, Universität Essen.

Bibliography

Baker, M. (1990) *Linguistics and the Training of Translators and Interpreters*. In 'Translation and Meaning' Part I, M. Thelen, B. Lewandowska-Tomaszczyk (eds), *Proceedings of the 1990 Maastricht-Lódz Duo Conference held in Maastricht, 4–6 January 1990*. Euroterm, pp. 167–175.

Baker, M. (1992) *In Other Words*. London: Routledge.

Ballard, M. (1984) *La Traduction: De la Théorie à la Didactique*. Presses Universitaires de Lille.

Ballard, M. (1987) *La Traduction de l'Anglais au Français*. Paris: Nathan University.

Barthes, R. (1967) *Le Système de la Mode*. Paris: Seuil.

Bassnett-McGuire, S. (1980) *Translation Studies*. London: Methuen.

Beaugrande, R.A. and Dressler, U.D. (1981) *Introduction to Text Linguistics*. London: Longman.

Catford, J.C. (1974) *A Linguistic Theory of Translation*. London: Oxford University Press.

Chuquet, H. and Paillard, M. (1989) *Approche Linguistique des Problèmes de la Traduction*. Paris: Ophrys.

Delisle, J. (1980) *Analyse du Discours comme Méthode de Traduction*. Ottawa: Ottawa University Press.

Delisle, J. (1993) *La Traduction Raisonnée: Manuel d'initiation à la Traduction professionnelle de l'anglais vers le français*. Ottawa: Presses Universitaires d'Ottawa.

De Mauro, Tullio (ed.) (1987) *F. de Saussure: Cours de Linguistic Générale, 1910–1911*. Paris: Payot.

Dressler, U. (1978) *Current Trends in Text Linguistics*. New York: de Gruyter.

Duff, A. (1981) *The Third Language: Recurrent Problems of Translation*. Oxford: Pergamon.

Fuchs, C. (1982) *La Paraphrase*. Paris: Presses Universitaires de France.

Gentzler, E. (1993) *Contemporary Translation Theories*. London: Routledge.

Gile, D. (1995) *Basic Concepts and Models for Interpreter and Translator Training*. Amsterdam: John Benjamins.

Gorlee, D.L. (1994) *Semiotics and the Problem of Translation*. Amsterdam: Rodopi.

Guillemin-Flescher, J. (1981) *Syntaxe Comparée du Français et de l'Anglais*. Paris: Ophrys.

Hatim, B. and Mason I. (1990) *Discourse and the Translator*. New York: Longman.

Hervey, S. (1982) *Semiotic Perspectives*. London: George Allen & Unwin.

Hervey, S. and Higgins, I. (1992), *Thinking Translation: A Course in Translation Method: French to English*. London: Routledge.

Hewson, L. and Martin, J. (1991) *Redefining Translation: The Variational Approach*. London: Routledge.

Komatsu, E. and Harris, R. (eds) (1993) *Saussure's Third Course of Lectures on General Linguistics (1910–1911)*. Oxford: Pergamon.

Ladmiral, J.R. (1979) *Traduire: Théorèmes pour la Traduction*. Paris: Payot.

Larose, R. (1989) *Théories Contemporaines de la Traduction*. Presses Universitaires de Québec.

Maingeneau, D. (1976) *Initiation aux Méthodes de l'Analyse du Discours*. Paris: Hachette.

Mounin, G. (1976) *Les Problèmes Théoriques de la Traduction*. Paris: Gallimard.

Neubert, A. (1985) *Text and Translation*. Leipzig: VEB Verlag Enzyklopädie.

Neubert, A. and Shreve, G.M. (1992) *Translation as Text*. London: Kent State University Press.

Newmark, P. (1988) *Approaches to Translation*. Oxford: Pergamon.

— (1990) *A Textbook of Translation*. New York: Prentice Hall.

— (1991) *About Translation*. Clevedon: Multilingual Matters.

Nida, E.A. (1969) *Towards a Science of Translating*. Leiden: Brill.

— (1979) *Componential Analysis of Meaning*. The Hague: Mouton.

Nida, E.A. and Taber, C.R. (1974) *The Theory and Practice of Translation*. Leiden: Brill.

Pergnier, M. (1980) *Les Fondements Sociolinguistiques de la Traduction*. Paris: Champion.

Savory, T. (1957) *The Art of Translation*. Cape: London.

Sperber, D. and Wilson, D. (1986) *Relevance: Communication and Cognition*. London: Blackwell.

Steiner, G. (1975) *After Babel*. London: Oxford University Press.

Taylor, J. (1991) *Linguistic Categorisation*. Oxford: Clarendon.

Toury, G. (1980) *In Search of a Theory of Translation*. Tel Aviv: The Porter Institute for Poetics and Semiotics.

Vinay, J.-P. and D'Arbelnet, J. (1977) *Stylistique Comparée de l'Anglais et du Français*. Paris: Didier.

Whorf, B. (1956) *Language, Thought and Reality*. Cambridge, MA: MIT Press.

Williams, G. (1992) *Sociolinguistics: A Sociological Critique*. London: Routledge.

Part 1:
Source Texts

Welcome to Ouistreham

This is the procedure for vehicle embarkation at OUISTREHAM

1. Embarkation of vehicles will commence approximately 45 minutes before time of departure.
2. If you are transporting animals please ensure you have all the relevant documentation and declare them to our Freight Office here in the Terminal Building.
3. At car control you will have been given boarding cards. Any special attention you may need (with disabilities, illness, vehicles, etc.) should have been requested at the car control desk. Please advise us now if you have not already done so.
4. You will then be directed into the correct lane depending on vehicle categories. Loading will be prioritised where possible.
5. You will be advised by public address announcement to return to your vehicle immediately prior to vehicle embarkation.
6. Please have your boarding cards and passports ready for inspection prior to embarkation.
7. A large number of vehicles of differing sizes need to be loaded safely. This takes time so please wait patiently until you are called to board, even when you appear to be moving slowly.
8. Finally, remember your passport must be checked at the UK Immigration Control on board so take your passport and anything else you require during the crossing with you when you leave the car deck.

May we wish you a pleasant crossing and thank you for your co-operation

NOTE: this envelope contains documents you will need for your crossing

Brittany Ferries Travel Document

The Pedigree of Plain English

1 The history of plain English is measured not in years or even decades
2 but in centuries. The term itself is on record since 1500, but the compiler
3 of the first ever dictionary of English in 1604 appears to have been the
4 first to use it in a technical sense. He was the schoolmaster Robert
5 Cawdrey, whose *Table alphabeticall* was intended to explain 'hard usual
6 words' (borrowing from such other languages as Latin, Greek and
7 Hebrew) by means of 'plain English words'.
8   In the long subtitle to this work Cawdrey showed that he wanted to
9 make hard words accessible to 'Ladies, Gentlewomen, or any other
10 unskilfull persons'. Such a statement sounds highly sexist and patronis-
11 ing in the late 20th century, but was intended quite differently in those
12 days, about a year after the death of Elizabeth the First.
13   Cawdrey was aware of the extent to which most (though not all)
14 women of his class were cut off from the commanding heights of
15 language. They lost out because they either had not had private family
16 tutors or could not attend the Church-based or Church-linked (and
17 therefore all-male) 'grammar schools' in which Latin was taught and
18 English heavily Latinized. As a result, such women had no easy way of
19 appreciating the layer of Latinity that had formed, as it were, along the
20 top of traditional English.
21   Most upper- and middle-class women (and all lower-class women,
22 along with the vast majority of their men) did not know high, golden
23 English. Some women, however, were on the borderline; 'unskilful' not
24 by being illiterate as such but because of limited literacy that did not
25 include classical borrowings — the 'hard usual words' of English. Things
26 have improved greatly since Cawdrey's time, but the classical legacy is
27 still strong, and despite its many positive aspects it often continues to
28 leave people out in the linguistic cold.
29   Towards the end of the 14th Century, the poet Geoffrey Chaucer was
30 writing the Canterbury Tales. Chaucer's English had become a hybrid
31 language that had only recently regained its status as the national
32 language of England, after some 200 years of second-class status. Before
33 there was official English there was official French, the language of
34 government and law — and above them both was official Latin, used
35 internationally by the Roman Catholic Church. To be fully literate in
36 those days to any significant extent generally meant being male, part of
37 the religious establishment and knowledgeable in both French and Latin.

38 However, the idea of plainness in language goes back much further
39 than Chaucer. The adjective *plain* itself derives from Latin *planus* which
40 can be translated as 'flat, even, level, low, clear, intelligible, evident' and
41 the like. It was used in a three-part gradation of style employed and
42 taught by orators in ancient Rome under the influence of rhetoricians
43 from Greece: first and most prestigious was the *grand* or *high style*, then
44 came the *middle style* and finally the *plain* or *low style*, and each was said
45 to have its virtues and its vices.
46 The middle style is by and large the one I am using to give this address.
47 I'm not using plain English — my style may be plainish quite often, but
48 is not uniformly plain or low, because there are things that I want to say
49 and effects that I want to produce that cannot be achieved in a really
50 plain style. In fact, people can and do play the three great rhetorical styles
51 like a piano, and traditionally 'good' orators and writers have been
52 expected to be able to do such things. There is no one style of English in
53 which everything can be done, on all occasions, for all purposes, in front
54 of all people. To hope for such a state of affairs — whatever the style
55 concerned — is to put the language in a straitjacket.
56 In the 1970s people on both sides of the Atlantic began to be interested
57 in plain English not in terms of such ancient matters as rhetorical style
58 or separating the Germanic side of English from its Latin heritage, but
59 in terms of such practical matters of communication as functional liter-
60 acy and how business organisations could communicate clearly and
61 simply with their publics, especially avoiding unnecessary jargon, tech-
62 nical language and convoluted syntax when talking to or writing for
63 non-technical audiences and readerships.
64 By and large there appear to be two approaches to the propagation of
65 plain usage in public life. One can be called the *top-down* approach, in
66 which existing institutions — governments, professional bodies, or com-
67 mercial organisations — take the initiative. For example, the NCTE (the
68 National Council of Teachers of English in the US), presented its first
69 annual Doublespeak Awards in 1974. Since then the Awards have be-
70 come a national event.
71 In the UK, however, the tendency is generally a *bottom-up* approach,
72 the grassroots putting pressure on governments and organisations to
73 make changes. In 1979 the PEC was founded; as a result of media
74 attention it grew larger, and in due course brought out its Plain English
75 Awards, which have also become annual national events.
76 Both approaches are useful, but still more effective is long-term
77 two-way co-operation among all concerned. There are, I think, signs of
78 an increase in such co-operation, between the consumers, customers,
79 victims or whatever you like to call them, on the one hand, and the

80 institutions, organisations, corporate bodies and so forth on the other,
81 providing each other with appropriate feedback, so that the right style
82 is chosen for an audience or readership on as many occasions as possible.

Tom McArthur, *The Linguist*, Vol. 32, no.6, 1993, pp. 182–185

The above text is a composite of extracts from the revised version of the
opening address to the first National Plain English Conference held in
Cambridge, UK.

Bless Thee Burgess, Thou Art Translated[1]

1   Good evening, ladies and gentlemen. The term 'translation' has taken on
2   a new connotation for me since I have recently been undergoing clinical
3   tests which point to a very dark end, so please forgive me if by 'transla-
4   tion' I am beginning to think of a possible transmigration or elevation,
5   or certainly the beginning of a new life — a meaning not normally there
6   in the word. In fact there is no spiritual dimension for the word 'trans-
7   lation' except when we talk about bishops being translated from one
8   diocese to another.
9   Shakespeare, as usual, got the meaning right when he has Snug say
10 to Bottom, who has just emerged from a brake with an ass's head, 'Bless
11 thee Bottom, thou art translated', because there is something essentially
12 asinine about translation. I prefer in some ways the German word
13 *übersetzung* which implies 'setting a thing over there', crossing a kind of
14 Red Sea, moving from one world into another.
15   Let me first say something about translation from a superficial angle.
16 When I see on the cover of a book by Agatha Christie, Jack Higgins or
17 Freddie Forsyth, 'translated in 76 languages, including Upper Stobovian
18 and Middle Ruritanian' and so forth, I am expected to feel immense
19 envy, because though I am translated I am not quite so multitudinously
20 translated. In fact to be translated is horrific and the more ignorant the
21 author is of foreign languages the better off he is. If an author can be
22 translated into innumerable languages he is not strictly speaking a
23 practitioner of literature at all, because literature cannot be translated,
24 only the appearance of literature, the arrangement on a page of words
25 which do a minimal job, that of describing action, feelings and dialogue
26 of a fairly easily translatable kind.
27   Indeed if a book is translatable one may say it is yearning for the
28 ultimate translation, which is to be turned into a film, and when this
29 happens a book is no longer a verbal construct. It becomes a play of
30 characters. The cinema is the final goal of all popular fiction, and some-
31 times one feels that when people praise a translatable book they are
32 discounting the literary angle altogether. Lord Archer was recently said
33 by one of his colleagues to be a good writer in that he forgets about words
34 and gets on with the job, and the job is a cinematic one.
35   Of course you could say: 'Look, the great writers have produced great
36 characters, great figures, easily separable from the words in which they
37 were first presented — Don Quixote and Sancho Panza, for instance'.

38   People used to believe that they knew Dickens because they had the
39   complete collection of cigarette cards, showing the various characters
40   portrayed. Or people listen to, say, Rimsky-Korsakov's *Sheherazade* and
41   think they have read the Arabian Nights.
42   The point is that we do tend to feel we know foreign literature, because
43   so much of it has been translated. It is assumed that it is enough with a
44   novel to know the work in translation Poetry, of course, is different,
45   because poetry is nothing unless made out of words. But here is a
46   curious — personal — example of the manner in which our conception
47   of what we think we know about world literature can go wrong.
48   Some years ago I lived in a part of Rome called Trastavere, and at the
49   opening to this district, just by the Ponte Garibaldi, there is a statue of a
50   man wearing 19th century dress and a top hat. He is a poet named
51   Giuseppe Gioacchino Belli, widely known to the denizens of Trastavere
52   and to other Romans. But nobody else knows him. Why? Belli has never
53   been translated into English, for the simple reason that he wrote not in
54   Italian but in a dialect that nobody not Roman can possibly know,
55   namely the Roman dialect, Romanesco. This is the dialect of the street,
56   the gutters; it is foul, obscene, blasphemous, but it's what the Romans
57   speak, and Belli took it upon himself to produce three volumes of
58   sonnets, written in an aggressive classical Petrarchan form but loaded
59   with these Roman qualities of blasphemy and obscenity, in which he
60   recorded for all time the spirit of Rome.
61   There are some rare occasions when a translation becomes greater
62   than the original — this has happened with Sir Thomas Urquhart's
63   Rabelais. It is as though the French language in Rabelais' time was not
64   capable of carrying the huge burden of obscenity and scatology that a
65   drunken Scotsman was able to give it. There are originals too, which
66   quail before the advent of the translation. This happened, as far as the
67   Germans are concerned, with their own translation of Shakespeare. They
68   consider that Schlegel's version of Shakespeare is better than the original,
69   and is some ways it is.
70   Well, translation can revivify a language and revivify a culture, and
71   there is no doubt that Schlegel's Shakespeare revivified not only German
72   literature but also German music. So it is possible to regard translation
73   as a means of inaugurating an new era in a native literature.
74   I want to deal finally with an aspect of translation which is not literary
75   at all: dubbing. The commonest way of hearing a foreign film at least on
76   the continent of Europe, is to suffer the illusion that the actors on screen
77   are actually speaking the language of the audience. The other way, still
78   the better of the two, is to hear the original dialogue, with a translation
79   on the screen in sub-titles. In multi-lingual communities, such as Malay-

80 sia, the second method is the only practical one. From an aesthetic angle
81 it is hard to defend dubbing since the way an actor uses his voice is an
82 important part of his artistic equipment.
83   The confusion of tongues means the confusion of all civilised endeav-
84 our. This confusion is genuine, and it lies wholly in the slippery, devilish,
85 disobedient organ known as the tongue. I don't think that Babel will ever
86 be unbuilt, and so people like me will continue to give the most confused
87 dissertations on this whole problem of translation. And no bishop,
88 however often translated, can do anything to exorcise the curse.

Extracts from a lecture given by Anthony Burgess at the Cheltenham
Festival of Literature, 1993 (© CFL Ltd).

1. (Note at head of article: 'Anthony Burgess died this week. In a recent lecture
    he reflected on the uneasy world of the translator').

Preaching Community

1 Suddenly, 'community' is every political thinker's Big Idea. Tony Blair,
2 Labour's leader-in-waiting, puts it at the centre of his manifesto, pub-
3 lished on June 23rd. A new pamphlet by John Gray, a conservative
4 philosopher, laments that market forces 'unsettle communities and legiti-
5 mate traditional institutions'. David Willetts, a formerly Thatcherite
6 philosopher, announces 'the collapse of neo-liberalism as a significant
7 intellectual force' in a new pamphlet entitled 'Civic Conservatism' pub-
8 lished by the Social Market Foundation. Mr Willetts, like Mr Gray, frets
9 about the health of civic institutions. 'The challenge facing both our main
10 political parties now is to formulate a coherent set of policies which
11 shows that... there must be a role for collective action but that collective
12 action does not necessarily mean state action. The race is on', he writes.
13   Not that there is anything new about the concept of community in
14 politics. On the Tory side, it owes it origins to Edmund Burke and the
15 'little platoons' that he thought were the secret of a well-functioning
16 society. On the Labour side it can be traced to Christian socialism —
17 about which Mr Blair is evangelical — and the co-operative movement.
18 Even the Liberals gave it an outing in the 1970s with 'community
19 politics', though in practice this meant little more than agitating for clean
20 drains.
21   Nor should anyone be surprised at the current revival of interest in
22 community. The British are not, right now, a happy people. One reason
23 is a growing feeling of insecurity brought on by rapid, boneshaking
24 change, its victims now the middle classes who fear for their jobs as much
25 as any factory worker. Another reason for unhappiness is a widespread
26 cynicism, not just about John Major's government but about the power
27 of any government to mitigate this insecurity. Amid this swirl of cyni-
28 cism and worry, the warm, vague word 'community' shines like a
29 beacon.
30   For Labour politicians, it summons visions of terraced streets in the
31 late 1940s: the people poor but honest, mums borrowing cups of sugar
32 from each other, bobbies on bikes clipping delinquents' ears, all wrapped
33 in the comfort of the new-born welfare state. (They conveniently forget
34 that the generation which grew up in those stultifying communities took
35 the first opportunity to flee.) Conservatives think of 1950s villages where
36 benevolent squire and kindly vicar presided over people who knew their
37 place, and there were crumpets still for tea. (People fled them too for

38 cities and suburbs, for sex, drugs and rock 'n roll.) Each vision responds
39 to present pains by conjuring past Edens, ignoring the fact that such
40 paradises passed away for good reasons.
41   There are differences between the two sides as to the cause of present
42 discontent. For Labour (and for Mr Gray too), they stem from a one-sided
43 concentration on the free market. This produced, at the very least, a
44 culpable blindness to the duties individuals owed to one another and to
45 the broader society; beyond that, to a selfish dog-eat-dog, me-here-now
46 philosophy, whose symptoms include crime, marital break-up and wel-
47 fare fraud.
48   Mr Willetts denies that the free market is to blame. He prefers to finger
49 a still-overmighty and centralising state whose over-arching power
50 drains the life-blood out of other community institutions. This was so,
51 he says, even in the nominally anti-state 1980s. Even then, the state
52 imposed new regulation: on charity trustees, for example, which put
53 people off serving; and with new food-hygiene rules that limited the
54 variety of meals-on-wheels for the elderly. His is a cry to supplement the
55 free market with localism, volunteerism and deregulation: Thatcherism
56 plus.
57   When historians turn to our times, they may see both views as correct.
58 The great American sociologist, Daniel Bell, in 'The Cultural Contradic-
59 tions of Capitalism' argued as long ago as 1976 that: 'The economic
60 dilemmas confronting western societies derive from the fact that we
61 have sought to combine bourgeois appetites which resist curbs on
62 acquisitiveness, either morally or by taxation; a democratic polity which,
63 increasingly and understandably, demands more and more social serv-
64 ices and entitlements; and an individualist ethos which at best defends
65 the idea of personal liberty, and at worst evades the necessary social
66 responsibilities and social sacrifices which a communal society
67 demands.'
68   Mr Blair, out of this list, may dislike selfish individualism. Mr Willetts
69 may complain about the demands of the polity on the public purse. But
70 the essence is not that one or the other threatens economic and social
71 success. It is the combination of all three factors that seems to cause
72 discontent.
73   Mr Blair enjoys the luxury of opposition. He can argue for a market
74 economy together with a redefined socialism. And, delivered with his
75 smiling fluency, the contradictions between the two may go unnoticed.
76   There are contradictions, nonetheless. Consider the requirements of
77 a vibrant market economy: a mobile workforce; ambitious entrepreneurs
78 willing to work all hours for more money; competition, redundancies
79 and work incentives. And consider the requirements for stable com-

80   munities: people who stay in one place, able volunteers with time and
81   energy to devote outside work to the common weal, co-operation, job
82   security and generous welfare safety nets. Governments around the
83   world are wrestling with those contradictions. Most of them are far from
84   convinced you can enjoy both. Mr Blair's appeal to the British people is
85   that you can. They will be tempted to believe him; as a vote-winner,
86   community may indeed be Labour's long-sought Big Idea. But when it
87   comes to the hard, practical task of formulating policies while in office,
88   community may prove to be just another disappointing tub-thumper's
89   premise.

Bagehot, *The Economist*, June 25th 1994, p. 33.

Defining a European Immigration Policy

1   By any measure, the search for 'European Immigration Policy' is frus-
2   tratingly elusive. It would be impossibly so without first attempting to
3   define all three words in the title in such a way as to make possible some
4   kind of description of an otherwise indescribable concept.
5   • What is 'European'? For the purpose of this article it makes sense to
6   use it in the limited sense of the 12 Member States of the European
7   Community since no other major grouping has really made a collec-
8   tive attempt jointly to define something which might deserve the
9   name of an 'immigration policy' as such. But 'European' can also
10   be used in the wider sense of 'the Atlantic to the Urals', in which
11   case the whole examination of migration issues would look very
12   different.
13 • What is 'immigration'? By limiting the definition of 'European' to
14   mean western European, it is possible also to limit the definition of
15   'immigration' to the phenomenon of people wishing or attempting
16   to move into the area being considered. But if the geographical scope
17   is widened to include the whole European continent, the definition
18   would need to be extended to include the separate phenomenon of
19   people seeking to move out of the area in question. That wider
20   subject is perhaps better described as migration — but it almost by
21   definition escapes the scope of the third word in the title, 'policy'.
22 • What is 'policy'? Here some generosity is needed. A rigorous defi-
23   nition would almost immediately lead to the conclusion that the
24   title itself is far too ambitious. The number of countries that can be
25   said to have a genuine 'immigration policy' in the sense of an active
26   search for people to populate and become nationals of the country
27   concerned is very limited — and probably excludes any European
28   country. By such a definition, probably only the huge geographical
29   spaces of the New World (the Americas and Australasia) and the
30   special case of Israel could lay claim to such a portentous aspira-
31   tion as an 'immigration policy'. To justify the use of the word
32   'policy' in the European context it is necessary to broaden it to
33   include the dispersed and often improvised reactions to shifting
34   pressures (ranging from the active search for immigrant labour of
35   the 1950s and 1960s to the more closed door policies of today) and
36   the attempt to pull these together into something deserving of the
37   name 'policy'.

38   In order therefore to make some sense of the concept of *European*
39   *Immigration Policy*, this article will use the phrase to mean the moves by
40   EC Member States to develop a co-ordinated approach to the question
41   of third country nationals either already present in or seeking to move
42   to an EC country.
43
44   **The need for a collective answer**
45   What has led the countries of the European Community to grope now
46   and collectively for an immigration policy when for so many years,
47   indeed centuries, immigration was more inclined simply to happen
48   without anybody feeling any great need of organising it into a policy
49   doctrine? A combination of factors might explain it.
50   • By the second half of the 20th century a certain stability of national
51   boundaries had established itself — at least until the recent upheav-
52   als and the emergence of the new republics in ex-Yugoslavia, the
53   break-up of the old Soviet Union into new states and the splitting of
54   Czechoslovakia into its components (*sic*) parts. Most of the world,
55   especially the industrialised world, is now organised in such a way
56   that governments are attached to having a real say and control over
57   who should be allowed to take up residence, work and ultimately
58   hold nationality in their territory. The need for something approach-
59   ing a national 'policy' on immigration is widely felt, especially in
60   Europe.
61   • This has, however, been overlain by some important distorting
62   factors, namely wars and their consequences, but also, in peace time,
63   economic pressures which in post-war western Europe initially led
64   to a relatively *laissez-faire* approach that appeared to suit everyone
65   well in a period of sustained economic growth, but became increas-
66   ingly unacceptable to public and political opinion as unemployment
67   figures began to rise, leading in turn to calls for 'policies' to control
68   immigration.
69   • The imperceptible (and unplanned) shift from 'temporary' immigra-
70   tion (in the sense of earning money in one country with a view to
71   returning home to spend it later) to 'permanent' immigration with
72   its potential for ghettoisation and communal disharmony.
73   • The slowing down of European immigration to the New World and
74   the gradual transformation on different time scales of all western
75   European countries, except Ireland, into countries of net immigra-
76   tion
77   • The collapse of the Iron Curtain which confronted the free world,
78   especially western Europe, with the consequences of its own rheto-
79   ric. Having for years berated the Communist powers for blocking

80   their citizens' wishes to move to the West, the West was suddenly
81   confronted with the Eastern exit doors being unlocked without the
82   Western entry doors being ready.
83 • The European Community's own declared and widely supported
84   aspiration of removing its own internal frontier controls, i.e. a major
85   instrument which in the minds of both governments and public
86   opinion was available to exercise some kind of control over immi-
87   gration flows.
88
89 **No welcome mats**
90   This link with the aspiration of a frontier-free Community has had
91 one unfortunate but perhaps inevitable consequence. It has meant that
92 nearly all the Community's early efforts to forge the beginnings of an
93 immigration policy appeared to be directed towards keeping people
94 out — partly because, for other, primarily economic reasons, this was
95 increasingly the trend in national policies anyway, and partly because
96 Member States were searching for ways to ensure that the controls at
97 their shared external frontier would be as reliable as the ones they would
98 be losing at the frontiers between them.

Adrian Fortescue, Director with responsibility for Co-operation in the
fields of Justice and Home Affairs in the Secretariat General of the
European Commission.

Published in a discussion paper published by the Philip Morris Institute,
entitled *Towards a European Immigration Policy*, October 1993, pp. 33–39.

Jobs and Competitiveness: The UK Approach

1 In March 1994, the Group of Seven major industrial countries held a
2 conference in Detroit — a conference about jobs. For 30 years many
3 industrial countries have seen national income rising hand in hand with
4 unemployment. The old notion that growth alone can eradicate unem-
5 ployment and human misery has been exploded by experience. Where
6 before one person in every 40 was unemployed, it is now three people
7 in every 40.
8 　　The human costs of such high unemployment, the wasted potential,
9 are both incalculable and unacceptable, and no industrialised country is
10 immune. Everyone knows we all have to search for ways to do better.
11 But everyone also knows the painful truth that there are no easy answers
12 and no magic single solutions.
13 　　The G-7 jobs conference therefore represented an opportunity to pool
14 our countries' knowledge and experience on effective ways of tackling
15 unemployment and achieving sustainable increases in jobs. The confer-
16 ence proved its worth in helping to think further and more deeply about
17 these policies and they will be further developed at the G-7 summit in
18 Naples this July when heads of government again consider policies to
19 tackle unemployment.
20
21 **Common ground**
22 　　There is, of course, a great deal of common ground between the major
23 industrialised countries. We have to create the conditions for growth, in
24 which businesses can flourish and new jobs can be created. That means
25 we have to achieve both low inflation on a permanent basis and sound
26 public finances.
27 　　At the same time, each country must promote free trade and ensure
28 that markets are really open to competition. Trade works to everyone's
29 benefit — increasing prosperity and jobs — which is why the GATT
30 agreement needs to be implemented quickly and why it is so important
31 that we remove the remaining barriers to the Single Market in Europe.
32
33 **The European perspective**
34 　　All that is valuable. But we in Europe face the most acute problems.
35 Most OECD countries have high unemployment, but Europe faces noth-
36 ing short of a jobs crisis. Twenty million people unemployed and almost
37 half of them unemployed for over a year.

38   In large measure, we know what we have to do about this crisis. The
39 European Council in Brussels last December endorsed three key objec-
40 tives based on employment. The EU heads of government agreed that to
41 combat unemployment we must ensure a stable economic framework,
42 we must ensure that the Community is internationally competitive and
43 open to international trade, and we must pursue labour market reforms.
44   Knowing what we have to do is one thing, doing it is another. Time
45 and again the OECD and others have told us that overly rigid labour
46 markets and excessive non-wage costs attached to employing people lie
47 at the heart of Europe's poor performance on jobs and unemployment.
48 Inflexible wages, high non-wage labour costs and needless regulation
49 have made too many jobs uneconomic and have erected too many
50 barriers to new job creation. Too much of our emphasis in Europe has
51 been on the short-term interests of employed people, far too little on the
52 needs of those who are unemployed.
53
54 **The UK approach**
55   In Britain we are committed to reducing unemployment on a sustain-
56 able basis. Low inflation, sound public finances, free trade and
57 competition are fundamental to our approach. Over the last 13 years we
58 have also been working to encourage enterprise and to make markets of
59 all kinds work better. And nowhere have our reforms been more funda-
60 mental than in the labour market.
61   The labour market is very special — a market made up of people, one
62 which concerns their living standards, their skills, and their ambitions,
63 and one which brings job-seekers and potential employers together. A
64 lot of hopes rest on the labour market. Inefficient labour markets carry
65 a high price in unemployment, and inefficient labour markets have
66 plagued Western Europe as our economies have struggled to compete.
67   Britain in 1979 was little different. We had too many obstacles in the
68 way of jobs and too little incentive for employers to create new employ-
69 ment opportunities.
70
71 **Making the labour market more efficient**
72   Step by step over the last 15 years we have worked to change that.
73 Our labour market reforms have focused on three aspects of perform-
74 ance in particular: increasing labour market efficiency; enhancing the
75 ability of unemployed people to compete effectively for jobs; and en-
76 couraging investment in skills by both individuals and their employers.
77   Our reform of industrial relations means that we in the United King-
78 dom now lose fewer days through strikes than at any time in over a
79 century. We have left employers and employees free to negotiate pay

80 and conditions for themselves and encouraged new, decentralised and
81 more flexible pay arrangements.
82   We have removed those unnecessary regulations which impeded
83 much needed job creation. And we have ensured that regulation does
84 not discriminate against the sort of flexible opportunities, like part-time
85 jobs, which employers want to create and which, above all, millions of
86 people clearly want to take up.
87   A more effective jobs market must be underpinned by a strong
88 welfare state — one which targets help on those who need it most, and
89 preserves incentives to work for individuals. That is why our system
90 now includes benefit help for workers who are on low incomes and who
91 have families. Nearly everyone can now be better off in work than by
92 remaining unemployed.
93   At the same time we have maintained essential employment protec-
94 tion legislation. There is a balance to be struck between the pressures of
95 the market and regulated standards in employment. Some regulation is
96 essential. Britain's system of protection of health and safety at work, for
97 example, is among the best in the world and we fully intend to keep it
98 that way. We also have wide-ranging legal rights for people at work. But
99 the hard lesson that has to be learned is that unnecessary regulation can
100 damage the interests of the very people it is intended to protect by
101 reducing the employment opportunities available to them.

David Hunt,[1] extract from a paper published in a collection entitled 'Jobs
and Competitiveness', by the Philip Morris Institute, Brussels, June 1994.

1. David Hunt was the UK's Secretary of State for Employment at the time of
    writing.

Law & Disorder

1 *Computers have given rise to a sinister new crime wave, but what is being done*
2 *to prevent it. Gus Chandler investigates...*
3   Anonymous white collar, not really doing any individual harm —
4 that's often the public misconception of computer. The truth is very
5 different, though. Imagine a large American city left without its phone
6 system for hours or days — a recipe for anarchy? Well, on 4th July 1989
7 it almost happened to the cities of Atlanta, Georgia; Denver, Colorado;
8 and Newark, New Jersey. A hacker broke into a series of switches
9 (telephone routing exchanges) and planted 'logic bombs' that were set
10 to 'explode' on American Independence Day. Fortunately, disaster
11 didn't happen on that occasion: the telephone company spotted the
12 attack in time and after massive resources were deployed checking
13 exchange software across the USA, the problem was defused. An
14 extreme example? Perhaps, but it illustrates well the potential disaster
15 that can be caused by a hacker attack.
16
17 **Hacking**
18   Hacking has its roots in the American West Coast culture of the late
19 60s and early 70s. At that time a number of individuals — known as
20 'phreakers' — perfected ways of using the American telephone system
21 for free. In fact, the methods they employed to obtain free calls were
22 ridiculously simple. The American phone system then operated by using
23 a tone at a frequency of 2,600 hertz to switch the billing equipment on
24 and off. By sending that tone at the time the connection was made you
25 could call anywhere in the world for free. To start with, these phreakers
26 used a purpose-built tone generator — called a 'blue box' or 'MF'er'
27 within the fraternity — to generate the signal. In 1970, though, a large
28 breakfast cereal manufacturer happened to give away a children's toy
29 whistle that generated a 2,600 hertz tone. From that point phreakers no
30 longer needed the blue boxes to generate the tones — they could simply
31 whistle up a free phone call. For the most part there was nothing
32 particularly malicious about their actions; they were doing it for no other
33 reason than because they could.
34   With the advent of personal computers and modems, people who had
35 been happy to use the phone system for free set about cracking access to
36 corporate and governmental computers. Again the motivation that
37 drove them — and still drives the modern-day hacker — is the challenge

38 of being able to beat the system. Very few people try to break into
39 computer systems with the object of taking something — like money or
40 data — or to cause wilful damage, but they do tend to leave clues for
41 operators that they have been there. In a way it's akin to the graffiti artist
42 'tagging' property.
43
44 **Access all areas**
45   Hacking into computer systems often isn't all that difficult. While
46 almost any commercial system has some safeguards to try and prevent
47 unauthorised access, these controls can often be circumvented by the
48 determined and informed hacker.
49   The usual approach to security is to issue legitimate users with an
50 identity code and password. Both have to be correctly entered to gain
51 entry to the system. However, passwords only offer a limited level of
52 protection, and in the case of Digital's VAX computers, for several years
53 during the 80s they offered no security at all. The VAX mainframe has
54 long been popular with the US government and military. While the
55 VAX/VMS operating system was designed to perform a security check
56 each time a user logged on to the system, the software had a fatal flaw.
57 If an incorrect identity code or password was entered the user would be
58 denied entry to the system — all well and good. However, if no identity
59 code and password were supplied — the user simply pressed Return at
60 each prompt — the system would allow immediate access. As a result
61 of this major oversight, VAXs became a popular target for hackers for
62 some years. The problem was finally resolved in 1986 with a new issue
63 of the system software.
64   While any password is better than none, people often choose ones that
65 can be guessed quickly — and hackers are well versed in the psychology
66 of discovering passwords. Until recently it was extremely difficult to
67 prosecute an individual for gaining unauthorised access to a computer
68 system — the prosecuting authorities had to come up with imaginative
69 charges such as 'theft of electricity'. While the US Congress passed the
70 Computer Fraud and Abuse Act in 1986 to protect US computer instal-
71 lations from hackers, in the UK we had to wait until the 1990 Computer
72 Misuse Act was taken through Parliament as a private member's bill for
73 legislative protection.
74   The first widely reported case on hacking in this country — and the
75 one that persuaded legislators to take action — was that of Steve Gold
76 and Robert Schifreen. The pair had hacked into British Telecom's Prestel
77 service and managed to access a mail box that belonged to Prince Philip.
78 They weren't out to do damage, they simply wanted to explore the
79 system. The most malicious action they took was to change the £/$ rate

80 in the Prestel financial area. For a little while the pound was worth $50.
81 Both Gold and Schifreen were eventually traced after a complicated
82 police hunt and were prosecuted on a fraud charge. Two years later after
83 the case had gone all the way to the House of Lords they were acquitted,
84 their Lordships finding that the law as it then stood didn't cover the
85 pair's actions. Schifreen is now a poacher turned gamekeeper, running
86 a business as a computer security consultant.
87   Most hackers do it for fun — the intellectual excitement of beating the
88 system — rather than profit. Attacks against businesses in an attempt to
89 gain money are rare. Shadowy hacker organisations do exist through
90 which the digital burglars exchange details of their activities. In recent
91 years the most prominent of these have been The Legion of Doom in the
92 US and the Chaos Computer Club in Germany. Much of the information
93 is exchanged via pirate bulletin boards, but for some years the Chaos
94 club has organised annual meetings which are attended by hackers from
95 around the world.

Extract from an article by Gus Chandler, *Computer Shopper Magazine*,
June 1994, pp. 456–458.

Doctor on Screen

Videos can help patients assess risks and benefits of treatment

1 When Gordon Rock started having prostate problems, he realised that
2 he knew as much about his prostate gland as he did about his hypothala-
3 mus. And when his doctor suggested that he might need an operation,
4 he felt about as ready for it as a footballer for a hip replacement.
5   But Mr Rock was fortunate. He was given access to the most up-to-
6 date research evidence on the pros and cons of surgery. Every year in
7 Britain, 30,000 men have an operation to reduce the size of their prostate,
8 which often gets larger in later life, making urination difficult, but not
9 all of them get the risks of and alternatives to surgery fully explained.
10   It has been quite common for surgeons just to tell patients that they
11 need an operation and that they will be sent a date for admission as soon
12 as possible. A junior doctor then explains the risks the night before the
13 operation and usually writes in the medical notes 'UWG' or Usual
14 Warning Given.
15   Now an American organisation, the Foundation for Informed Medical
16 Decision-Making, has produced an inter-active video which outlines the
17 relative risks and benefits of immediate surgery versus 'watchful wait-
18 ing' (waiting with regular medical check-ups) so that they can make an
19 informed decision. The theory behind it is that surgeons do not give an
20 unbiased picture of the relative risks and benefits. To them, prostrate
21 operations are routine, but to patients they are not.
22   Researchers from the London School of Hygiene and Tropical Medi-
23 cine are using the video at Ashford Hospital Trust, Middlesex, to
24 discover how it influences patient choice. The project, initially backed by
25 the King's Fund Centre, is now financed by the North Thames Health
26 Authority. 'I found it extremely useful' said Mr Rock, 56, an assistant
27 caretaker from Feltham, west London. 'It put my mind at rest and helped
28 me to decide what to do.'
29   When it starts, the programme looks like a standard video on an
30 ordinary television. But it is controlled by a 12-inch laser disc player and
31 can be programmed with the patient's details (age and severity of
32 symptoms) so that the information shown is relevant to that particular
33 patient. It has a touch-sensitive screen, which the patient can press to
34 indicate what he wants to find out. If, for example, he or she wants to
35 know more about drug treatments, they can press the 'Learn More'
36 section on the screen. At the end, they receive a print-out of all the
37 information.

38   Perhaps the most telling evidence is the personal testimony from two
39 patients, one of whom had surgery and one of whom decided to wait for
40 a while. The former spoke of his joy after the operation at being able to
41 urinate properly again.
42   His testimony did not convince Mr Rock, however, who decided that
43 he did not want an operation for the time being. 'My symptoms are at
44 an early stage. I do not have to get out of bed several times at night, like
45 some people do, so I've decided to wait. The video did not frighten me.
46 In fact, the risks from the operation for a man of my age seem quite small.
47 But I discovered that the effects of the operation are not permanent. It
48 has often been repeated three years later. That made me think I would
49 sooner wait.'
50   'I also found it interesting to learn about the various drug treatments,
51 but I got the impression that these have not been used long enough for
52 us to know all the side-effects. So I decided against them. It took about
53 an hour to watch. You cannot imagine a doctor speaking to you for a
54 whole hour, can you? It means I am better-informed when I see the
55 consultant.'
56   Mr Rock was unusual in seeing his doctor relatively early on in the
57 course of his trouble, benign prostatic hyperplasia (BPH) which affects
58 more than two million men in Britain (one in three between 50 and 79).
59 But his response to the video was typical in one respect — it made him
60 more sceptical about the advantages of surgery.
61   That has been common. In the US, where it has been shown to more
62 than 1000 patients, the response has been to turn away from surgery and
63 towards 'watchful waiting'. Robert Maxwell, secretary of the King's
64 Fund, says 'Patients turn out to be more risk-adverse to surgery than
65 their surgeons.'
66   Such a discovery has important implications for the health service. If
67 surgeons are painting too rosy a picture of surgery — emphasising the
68 benefits and minimising the risks — they may be performing more
69 operations than they need. If patients were given a more balanced
70 picture, the number could fall. Certainly in the US, health-maintenance
71 organisations are using these inter-active videos partly to reduce the
72 amount surgery carried out.
73   It is too early to say what exactly the project will show in Britain, but
74 the first findings are following the American pattern. Mrs Jeremy Stone,
75 the research nurse who sets the machine for patients, said that most
76 comments are positive. 'A small proportion of patients, about four per
77 cent, have difficulties in understanding it. We think it is valuable because
78 the pressures on us are such that we have not got the time to sit down
79 with patients and explain everything to them. We have had patients

80   come back who say that they were never warned that the operation did
81   not always work'.
82   The video makes it clear even after surgery, six per cent of patients
83   still have severe symptoms and another 18 per cent moderate symptoms.
84   Mrs Hilary Gilbert, project manager for 'Promoting Patient Choice' at
85   the King's Fund Centre, said: 'Our aim is to increase the amount of
86   unbiased, research-based and user-friendly information for patients,
87   because our research shows that there is a dearth of it.'

Article by Annabel Ferriman, *The Guardian*, 4th January 1995.

The Inhumanity of Medicine

Time to stop and think

1 In the past few months... I have been made aware of a large number of
2 cases of disturbingly callous and rude behaviour by consultants and
3 general practitioners towards patients... might I suggest that courses to
4 remind (or perhaps teach) doctors how to behave to their patients be put
5 high on the agenda.
6   This extract from a letter received recently by the editor of the *BMJ*
7 and the articles in a similar vein (p. 1696, p. 1699, p. 1700), raise some
8 disturbing questions for us to ponder on over the Christmas season. The
9 excuse that only bad news is newsworthy will not wash; such stories are
10 becoming commonplace and encompass so much of current clinical
11 practice that we seem to be becoming a profession of uncaring techno-
12 crats.
13   In seeking solutions to these problems it is important to see them in
14 their historical perspective. Are they new? I know of no evidence that
15 doctors of the past were so much better at handling their patients. I still
16 vividly remember one of my first teaching rounds as a medical student,
17 over 30 years ago. We had arrived at the end of the bed of a patient who
18 had been found to have an inoperable lung cancer. The senior and much
19 respected physician who was conducting the round suddenly veered
20 away from the bed and collected together the throng of staff and students
21 in the middle of the ward into what resembled a huddle of American
22 football players planning their next play. The diagnosis and prognosis
23 were discussed in hushed whispers, after which we returned to the
24 bedside, a few banalities were exchanged, and we moved on to the next
25 patient. Such behaviour was common during my student days. And, as
26 so well portrayed on page 1714, for centuries journalists, cartoonists,
27 novelists, and playwrights have castigated us for our pomposity, inhu-
28 manity, and cruelty. Such attacks continue, as exemplified by Alan
29 Bennett's recent play *The Madness of George III*.
30
31 **Patients are taken to the limit**
32   But although doctors may always have had a limited facility to treat
33 their patients as humans, there is no doubt that the current medical scene
34 is highlighting our deficiencies. Oncology, the basis of two articles in
35 today's journal, is a good example. Patients are often subjected to the
36 most intensive protocols of chemotherapy, some of which require them
37 to be taken to death's door in an attempt to eradicate their tumours. One

38 hundred years hence we may look back on all this in the same light as
39 we do on bleeding and cupping today. But this is what is currently
40 believed to be the most effective way to manage these diseases; in almost
41 every field of modern high technology patch-up practice, patients are
42 pushed to the extremes of their endurance, and not always for reasons
43 that include a careful appraisal of what is meant by the quality of life.
44   Our patients' problems are compounded by our current systems of
45 medical care because they are not geared to support very sick people.
46 Above all else, those with distressing chronic or terminal illnesses need
47 continuity of care — that is, the attention and friendship of one doctor
48 whom they can come to trust and with whom they can share their hopes
49 and fears. Yet this kind of relationship is all too rarely available to them.
50 Too few consultants exist to look after the increasing numbers of patients
51 undergoing periods of intensive treatment or in their final illness.
52
53 **No continuity**
54   Because young doctors are constantly rotating through different train-
55 ing programmes, and as a consequence of the new regulations to limit
56 their working hours, there is lack of day to day continuing of care at all
57 junior grades. Patients are looked after by continuously changing teams
58 of doctors and nurses, a pattern of care that also spills over into general
59 practice, where the chances of them always seeing their own family
60 doctor are equally limited.
61   And in the frenetic reorganised NHS, doctors and nurses are spending
62 more and more time on committees, organising their business plans and
63 contracts, and less with their patients; managerial efficiency and an
64 increasingly rapid turnover of patients, while they may make for impres-
65 sive statistics, do not necessarily reflect a caring attitude on the part of
66 doctors. At the same time patients and relatives are much more demand-
67 ing than they used to be and, not unreasonably, expect more time and
68 explanation of their doctors. Thus it is most surprising that the deficien-
69 cies that have dogged us for the past 2000 years are being accentuated.
70   To what extent are our shortcomings a reflection of the pattern of
71 medical education? Many of the criticisms levelled at doctors are not
72 about their clinical competence; rather, they seem to reflect a deficiency
73 of the basic skills of handling sick people as humans, poor communica-
74 tion, lack of kindness, thoughtlessness, and, in short, all the facets of good
75 interpersonal relationships that society has a right to demand of its
76 doctors. Can such attitudes be taught? And even if they can, given our
77 poor track record who is to teach them?
78   Concerns along these lines have led to radical revisions of medical
79 education in several countries. For example, the General Medical Coun-

80 cil suggests that there should be less emphasis on the basic sciences and
81 more on ethics, communication skills, and the social sciences, with
82 earlier exposure to patients and their families. Few people would dis-
83 agree that two years spent in the company of a corpse is not the most
84 imaginative introduction to a profession that, more than any other, needs
85 to develop the skills of talking to distressed people.

This is the first half of an article by D. J. Weatherall, Regius Professor of
Medicine, University of Oxford, John Radcliffe Hospital. In *The British
Medical Journal*, Vol. 309, pp. 1671–72, December 1994.

Black Death

1   *Journalist and broadcaster John Hosken recalls the Great Plague and is amazed*
2   *to discover that bubonic plague is still very much alive.*
3   Three sailing ships limped into Genoa harbour in 1348, drifting with
4   little or no seamanship, sails flapping. They brought cargoes from the
5   Far East. They brought something else as well. The Black Death. The
6   people of Genoa, anxious for trade, made the plague ships secure at their
7   docks. The strangely-dead sailors and the moribund were brought
8   ashore. But these mariners were not the culprits who caused bubonic
9   plague to sweep Europe, killing half the population of a continent in half
10 a century, changing the tide of history. The real culprits were black rats,
11 themselves infected with plague and which ran down the ropes the
12 Genoans had so conveniently provided.
13   Once ashore, the rats scurried to find food. The food was always close
14 to humans; and people began to die. And to die by the thousands most
15 horribly. They had caught a disease nature had intended for rats. But
16 nobody, God help the millions who have died of plague, knew what
17 caused the dreadful visitations. Many died bellowing and without useful
18 aid. No-one could stop the plague. No-one could cure the plague.
19 No-one knew *why*. Yet there was an answer at once so simple but so
20 convoluted, that it look until the 1890s to unravel it.
21   Plague was now endemic in Europe. It flared up here and there. It
22 scythed through the people of western Europe in 1664, crossing the
23 Channel to London in 1665. Up to 100,000 people died in London that
24 year and part of the following year. Still no-one knew *why*.
25   And what a London it became! So many were dying by the late
26 summer of 1665 that normal funerals were no longer possible. Between
27 dusk and dawn dead carts roamed the streets, preceded by a man with
28 a bell who shouted. 'Bring out your dead... bring out your dead.'
29 Corpses were tossed onto the carts like the household junk we place on
30 the carts of modern-day bellmen, to be taken to huge burial pits (one of
31 the biggest lies under Liverpool Street Station) and covered over before
32 dawn. Such was the desperation of the afflicted and the endangered that
33 ghastly events happened. Daniel Defoe in his *A Journal of the Plague Year*
34 recorded, 'For people that were infected and near their end, and delirious
35 also, would run to those pits, wrapt in blankets or rugs, and throw
36 themselves in. And when they came to bury others and found them
37 there, they were quite dead, though not cold.'

38 Searchers, mostly old women with long noses for other people's
39 business, were recruited by the magistracy to walk through infected
40 areas to find out any signs of plague in the houses. If such a house were
41 discovered then it must be shut up, the well people incarcerated with the
42 sick. A sign was daubed on the door in red — a cross with the words
43 'Lord have mercy upon us'.
44   Outside these houses, which grew in number by the week, stood a
45 watchman to prevent people getting out. But these men were frequently
46 tricked or bribed so that people often escaped from their quarantined
47 homes into the streets and the nearby countryside remembering, no
48 doubt, that many of the rich and most of the doctors of London had fled
49 in their coaches at the first signs of plague, leaving their sick and their
50 servants to take the blow.
51   The plague abated in London after a dreadful autumn, only to re-
52 emerge in the spring. But it was weaker then and dying out. Indeed,
53 contrary to some lingering popular belief, the Great Fire of London
54 which broke out as late as 1st September 1666 (a Saturday) had nothing
55 to do with the curtailment of the Great Plague of London.
56   Broadly speaking, the fire consumed the City; the poorer parishes
57 where plague had been most virulent were largely excused the flames.
58 The Great Plague, its awsome work complete, was limping into the pages
59 of history already.
60   By now, the bubonic plague was entrenched in our heritage. Children
61 sang about it. 'Ring-a-ring-o'-roses. A pocketful of poses. Atichoo!
62 Atichoo! We all fall down.' Sneezing was one the first signs of bubonic
63 plague, which is why we still say 'bless you' today when someone
64 sneezes.
65   Then there was the pocketful of poses. These 'poses' were the black
66 buboes which erupted under the armpits and in the groin and were
67 excruciating. They still are. Physicians, believing these buboes should
68 burst to save the patient, would slice through them or, even worse, put
69 living fire and red hot metal against them so that plague victims died
70 screaming and of the pain alone.
71   The doctors still didn't know *why*. The medical profession, such as it
72 was, had two schools of thought. One was the miasmatists, the other the
73 contagionists. The miasmatists believed that plague was caused by fogs
74 arising from the ground, whilst the contagionists believed the disease
75 was transmitted from person to person or by articles, such as clothing,
76 which others handled. And much derided were the fools who suggested
77 there were monsters in the air, too small to be seen, in the shapes of
78 dragons, snakes, serpents and devils, which caused bubonic plague to
79 spread.

80   This fanciful theory proved to be nearest the truth, but still far short
81 of it. Plague, for all its blatant attacks against the human race, was too
82 subtle for any of that. It took a French physician born in Switzerland,
83 Alexandre Yersin, to isolate a germ whose peregrinations were so con-
84 voluted that its ability to kill man was almost an impossibility, yet if it
85 could strike it was deadly. The germ is *Yersenia Pestis*. Now they knew
86 *why*.

From an article by John Hosken, journalist and broadcaster, in *Mensa Magazine*, October 1994, pp. 11–12.

Our Children's Education —
The Updated Parent's Charter

1 Schools have changed a lot in recent years. Standards have improved,
2 and there is wider choice.
3   Teachers, governors and parents have all played their part to bring
4 this about. So have the Citizen's Charter and the Parent's Charter. They
5 have brought:
6 *On standards*
7 • new rights to information on how schools are performing;
8 • better arrangements for inspecting them;
9 • clear National Targets for Education and Training — for schools and
10   colleges, employers and the Government.
11 *On choice*:
12 • new targets of school;
13 • more rights for parents; and improvements for parents of children
14   with special needs.
15 This updated Parent's Charter tells you all about these improvements.
16 It is of particular importance to the parents of 5–16 year olds. But
17 everyone, not just parents, should benefit from improved standards and
18 choice. The Charter reforms are always the key to making the country
19 more competitive. That is why we have sent this charter to every home
20 in the country.
21
22 **The right to know**
23 *The five key documents:*
24 1. A report about your child.
25 2. Regular reports from independent inspectors.
26 3. Performance tables for all your local schools.
27 4. A prospectus or brochure about individual schoools.
28 5. An annual report from your school's governors.
29   Under the Government's reforms you should get all the information
30 you need to keep track of your child's progress, to find out how the
31 school is being run, and to compare all local schools. The five main
32 documents are explained below.
33   Better information about schools is also important for raising stand-
34 ards. For example, publishing tables which compare the performance of
35 schools has encouraged many schools to take a hard look at the exami-
36 nation results the pupils achieve and how the schools can help the pupils
37 to do better.

38 **1. A report about your child**
39 You will receive a written report on your child's progress at least once
40 a year. It will tell you about:
41 • How your child is getting on in all the subjects taught under the
42   National Curriculum, including your child's results in the national
43   tests at the ages of 7, 11 and 14.
44 • The results your child gained during the year in public examinations
45   such as GCSEs, GCE A-levels and job-related qualifications like
46   GNVQs.
47 • What your child has achieved in other subjects and activities.
48 • How your child's results in national tests at 7, 11 and 14 compare
49   with the results of other children of the same age.
50 • Your child's general progress and attendance record. This informa-
51   tion will be provided by the headteacher or class teacher; and
52 • Who to contact about your child's report and how to arrange an
53   appointment.
54 At other times during the year you will be able to see the work of the
55 school and talk to the staff. This will help you to find out how your child
56 is being taught and what you can do to help.
57 The school will keep records about your child's attendance, behaviour
58 and achievements. You have a right to see those records. If you ask the
59 school, they will let you look at the information about your child.
60 When your child leaves school to go on to further education, training
61 or work, he or she will receive a report. This will usually be in the form
62 of a National Record of Achievement, which gives a summary of his or
63 her achievements in school and elsewhere. This helps young people plan
64 further and higher education in employment.
65
66
67 **2. Regular reports from independent inspectors**
68 A new, independent organisation now monitors standards in our
69 schools. The Office for Standards in Education (OFSTED) is led by Her
70 Majesty's Chief Inspector of Schools. OFSTED is in charge of the new
71 inspection arrangements. These started in September 1993 for secondary
72 schools in England and will start for all other schools in September 1994.
73 The new arrangements mean that:
74 • All state schools, including special schools, are inspected at least
75   every four years. The people who lead inspection teams have to be
76   approved by OFSTED. OFSTED regularly checks that they are doing
77   a thorough job.
78 • Reports on all schools cover the same main points, so you can
79   compare how all the schools in your area are performing.

80 • All inspection teams include at least one person who has not worked
81   in education. This means the inspection team has an 'outside' view.
82   Before the team inspects the school, they must hold a meeting to talk
83   about the school.
84 • After an inspection, the inspectors must publish a report. The school
85   must act on the report. The school will send you a summary of the
86   report, prepared by the inspector, which sets out the school's
87   strengths and weaknesses. You will also receive the governing
88   body's plans to develop the school and solve any problems which
89   the inspection brought to light.
90 • You, and parents who are thinking of sending their children to the
91   school, can ask the school for a full copy of the report. The school
92   may charge for this. The report will also be available in local libraries.
93 • A summary of the latest report and an update on action the school
94   has taken will go in the governing body's annual report which is sent
95   to parents.
96 • At the annual parents' meeting the governing body must explain
97   what they have done to carry out their plans; and
98 • If an inspection report states that a school is failing to give an
99   acceptable standard of education, special measures will apply.
100   These are designed to tackle the school's problems and make sure
101   that the standard of education at the school is improved as quickly
102   as possible. If necessary, the school will be managed by an Education
103   Association brought in by the Secretary of State; he may close the
104   school if it does not improve.

Extract from 'Our Children's Education, The Updated Parent's Charter'
issued by the Department for Education (1994). Reproduced with the
permission of HMSO.

Charter 88

1   We have been brought up in Britain to believe that we are free: that
2   our Parliament is the mother of democracy; that our liberty is the envy
3   of the world; that our system of justice is always fair; that the guardi-
4   ans of our safety, the police and security services, are subject to
5   democratic, legal control; that our civil service is impartial; that our
6   cities and communities maintain a proud identity; that our press is
7   brave and honest.
8   Today such beliefs are increasingly implausible. The gap between
9   reality and the received ideas of Britain's 'unwritten constitution' has
10   widened to a degree that many find hard to endure. Yet this year we
11   are invited to celebrate the third centenary of the 'Glorious Revo-
12   lution' of 1688, which established what was to become the United
13   Kingdom's sovereign formula. In the name of freedom, our politi-
14   cal, human and social rights are being curtailed while the powers
15   of the executive have increased, are increasing and ought to be
16   diminished.
17   A process is underway which endangers many of the freedoms we
18   have had. Only in part deliberate, it began before 1979 and is now
19   gathering momentum. Scotland is governed like a province from White-
20   hall. More generally, the government has eroded a number of important
21   civil freedoms: for example, the universal rights to habeas corpus, to
22   peaceful assembly, to freedom of information, to freedom of expression,
23   to membership of a trade union, to local government, to freedom of
24   movement, even to the birth-right itself. By taking these rights from
25   some, the government puts them at risk for all.
26   A traditional British belief in the benign nature of the country's
27   institutions encourages an unsystematic perception of these grave
28   matters: each becomes an 'issue' considered in isolation from the rest.
29   Being unwritten the constitution also encourages a piecemeal approach
30   to politics, an approach that gives little protection against a deter-
31   mined, authoritarian state. For the events of 1688 only shifted the
32   absolute power of the monarch into the hands of the parliamentary
33   oligarchy.
34   We have had less freedom than we believe. That which we have
35   enjoyed has been too dependent on the benevolence of our rulers. Our
36   freedoms have remained their possession, rationed out to use as subjects
37   rather than being our own inalienable possession as citizens. To make

38 real the freedoms we once took for granted means for the first time to
39 take them for ourselves.

The Observer Magazine, Colour Supplement, 29 July 1990.

The NHS Reforms and You

1 The National Health Service and Community Care Act 1990 will bring
2 about important changes in the way our caring services are run. There
3 have also been changes in the way the family doctor service operates.
4 Others are planned for dental care. These changes, and those arising
5 from the Act, are designed to give you a more efficient and an even
6 better run service — above all, a service that puts you, the patient,
7 first.
8   They are designed to reinforce the main aim of the National Health
9 Service — to help people live longer and enjoy a better quality of life. As
10 a matter of fact, today's NHS, employing record numbers of doctors and
11 nurses, is treating more people than ever before.
12   As now, the NHS will continue to be open to all, regardless of income,
13 and paid for mainly out of general taxation. NHS services will continue
14 to be largely free at the point of use.
15
16 **A word of reassurance**
17   Changes in the health services affect everyone. Some people are
18 worried about what services will be available. Some of the questions
19 being asked are:
20   – Will my doctor be able to spend as much time with me? **Yes.**
21   – Will I continue to get my prescriptions, even if the medicines are
22   expensive? **Yes.**
23   – If my family doctor has a practice fund, will I still get the treatment
24   I need? **Yes.**
25   – Can I still have treatment at a local hospital? **Yes.**
26   – Will I still have a choice about where I have my baby? **Yes.**
27   – Will hospitals which become self-governing NHS Trusts stay com-
28   pletely within the NHS? **Yes.**
29 So, quite simply, the answer to all these questions is 'Yes'.
30   This booklet explains the changes and how they will affect you.
31
32 **You and your family doctor**
33   Family doctors — also known as General Practitioners (GPs) — will
34 be able to offer you and your family a wider range of services. There will
35 be more emphasis on the promotion of good health and the active
36 prevention of disease. This section looks at the range of services and how
37 the family doctor service will be run to meet your needs.

38 **Services for the family**
39   Good health care is not just about treating you when you are ill, but
40 also giving help and advice so that you stay fit and well.
41   The Government's Chief Medical Officer says:
42 *'Prevention is better than cure. A better quality of life comes from better*
43 *health. The range of services available from your GP will help you to*
44 *maintain or improve your health and reduce the risk of illness. Of course*
45 *these services are optional — it is up to you whether you decide to make use*
46 *of them. For the sake of your own good health I would strongly urge you to*
47 *do so.'*
48 What services should you now look out for?
49
50 **For all adults**
51   • Regular 'life-style' check-ups will be available. These will be
52   offered to you when you first register with a doctor or if you have
53   not seen your doctor for some time. The purpose of these check-ups
54   is to:
55   – give you the chance to discuss anything worrying you;
56   – provide an opportunity to carry out a few simple tests (such as
57   checking your blood pressure);
58   – offer professional advice if needed on such matters as diet, exer-
59   cise, smoking and alcohol consumption.
60 In other words, your GP can advise you on how to look after yourself.
61 This may include recommending that you attend one of the practice's
62 health promotion clinics. The 'Health Check' in the centre pages of this
63 booklet gives further advice on healthy living.
64   • GPs will be encouraged to provide more health promotion clinics.
65   These may include clinics giving detailed advice on diet, blood
66   pressure, giving up smoking, diabetes, heart disease, alcohol
67   control and stress management. There could also be well-person
68   clinics.
69
70 **Family planning services**
71   • Family planning services are available from most GPs and from
72   health authority family clinics, which also make services avail-
73   able to men. You can choose where to go for family planning
74   advice.
75 If you prefer to get advice from a GP about contraception, you may
76 choose to see a GP other than your own family doctor, if that GP is willing
77 to accept you. Information about whether particular GPs provide con-
78 traceptive services is now more readily available (see 'More information
79 for patients' on p. 11).

80   Family planning services are provided free of charge to encourage all
81   those who wish to use the services to do so.

Extract from a brochure entitled *The Health Service, The NHS Reforms and You*, pp. 2–8, published by the Department of Health in July 1990. Reproduced with the permission of HMSO.

The Wrong Way to Defend a Culture

1 'You cannot defend values militarily' the maverick British politician,
2 Enoch Powell, once observed. Sadly, the European Union has yet to
3 grasp a similar truth: you cannot defend a culture by legislative fiat.
4   Just over three years ago, a directive designed to keep non-European
5 programmes off European television screens came into force throughout
6 the European Union. In recent months the directive has become a bone
7 of contention at the GATT talks on global trade liberalisation.
8   The misleadingly named 'television without frontiers' directive in fact
9 aimed to erect formidable frontiers around the EU. Few more blatant
10 examples of the Fortress Europe mentality can be conceived. Articles 4
11 and 5 of the directive stipulate that, with certain exceptions, 'Member
12 States shall ensure... that broadcasters reserve for European works... a
13 majority proportion of their transmission time'. The main exceptions are
14 news and sports programmes.
15   The European Union's fear of foreign TV programmes has its roots in
16 economics. The European market for film and television is highly frag-
17 mented: 80% of films made in Europe do not cross the borders of their
18 country of origin. They are rarely able to recoup their production costs
19 from foreign sales. State-owned TV channels seeking to reduce over-
20 heads have every incentive to buy in cheap US programmes that have
21 already paid their way in their vast home market.
22   But it is worth asking whether the imposition of import quotas will
23 really help redress the balance. Two related questions arise: are Europe's
24 attempts to protect its film-makers feasible, and, if feasible, are they
25 desirable?
26   Feasibility first. Doubts are not hard to find. They nestle in the
27 directive itself. EU member states are given a wide margin of discretion
28 over how to implement the directive. They must ensure that European
29 works account for over half of programmes broadcast, 'where practica-
30 ble'. They must work to coax broadcasters in this direction 'progres-
31 sively' — but the deadlines are relaxed. New channels have two years in
32 which to get into their stride before the European content rule begins to
33 affect them. The biggest problem lies in trying to regulate an industry that
34 is evolving far faster than the regulators. Terrestrial TV channels, broad-
35 casting from within the frontiers of EU member states, can be brought
36 into line easily enough. But far greater difficulties are posed by satellite
37 channels beaming programmes from outside the European Union.

38   The Commission expects that, by 1995, over 16 million European
39 homes will be receiving satellite television. An official at DGX, the
40 European Commission's division for audio-visual policy, admits that
41 controlling satellite channels based outside the EU may prove 'very
42 difficult'. The Commission is hoping that satellite broadcasters will have
43 at least some physical representation within the European Union
44 through which pressure can be brought to bear.
45   If this hope proves groundless, the television without frontiers direc-
46 tive will come under serious strain. Satellite operators within the EU will
47 want to know why they are being penalised financially by being forced
48 to buy high-cost European programmes, while their counterparts else-
49 where can transmit whatever they wish.

William Pitt, *EuroBusiness*, December 1993/January 1994, p. 65.

We Are...

1 What is the European Bureau for Lesser Used Languages? How did it
2 begin? What does it hope to achieve?
3   The Bureau is in a sense a product of the 'roots phenomenon' — this
4 undefined movement of peoples seeking their identity and the human
5 rights ensuing from their ethnicity. It came into being at a colloquium
6 held in Brussels in May 1982 to consider the implications of the Arfe
7 Report which the European Parliament had adopted the previous Octo-
8 ber. The representatives of the various 'small peoples' who attended this
9 colloquium expressed their support for the establishment of a body
10 which would act on their behalf at Community level with the various
11 institutions of the EEC, the Council of Europe, etc. Its constitution
12 defines this general aim — 'to preserve and promote the lesser used
13 autochthonous languages of the member states of the European Com-
14 munities, together with their associated cultures'.
15   The European Community is, essentially, a community of nation-
16 states, i.e. independent states considered by their governments to be
17 nations, in the 19th century meaning of that term. State and nation are
18 not, however, synonymous and in every member state of the European
19 Community there exists at least one nation or community which differs
20 from the majority in that state insofar as they possess their own language
21 and their own particular identity. In fact, there are only two countries in
22 western Europe that do not have such internally different communi-
23 ties — Iceland and Portugal — and neither of these are members of the
24 European Community.
25   The European Community recognises seven official working lan-
26 guages — French, English, German, Italian, Dutch, Danish and Greek.
27 Irish is a 'treaty language'. That is to say that the text in Irish of the
28 treaties carries equal authority with the same text in the seven working
29 languages. Irish is also 'an official working language of the European
30 Community'.
31   There are over 30 million citizens in the European Community whose
32 mother tongue is a language other than the seven official working
33 languages. In reality this means that there exists a large number of people
34 within the Community who do not enjoy the same linguistic status as do
35 the majority language speakers.
36   The communities who use these less widely spoken languages are
37 various:

38 (i)   Small nations without their own state e.g. the Welsh, the Bretons
39   and the Frisians.
40 (ii)   Small independent nation states whose language is not now widely
41   spoken e.g. the Irish.
42 (iii) Communities who speak a minority language but do not consider
43   themselves a nation (in the accepted use of that term) e.g. the
44   Ladins of the Alpine regions.
45 One may add to these three groups:
46 (iv) Extra-territorial minorities e.g. communities within one country
47   who speak the majority language of another e.g. the Danish speak-
48   ers of Schleswig-Holstein, the French speakers of Val d'Aosta.
49 It cannot be denied that these communities of lesser-spoken languages
50 are not without their problems. Indeed, one might well ask whether they
51 can possibly have a future in the modern world. There is, however,
52 strong evidence to suggest that they do indeed have a future and a most
53 viable one, once some basic facts are acknowledged.
54   These languages are an integral part of the cultural heritage of Europe.
55 They include some of the oldest languages of Europe with a rich litera-
56 ture and folk tradition. If they have been ignored in the past by the
57 institutions of the European Community, this is no longer the case. In
58 1979, for example, John Hume (Member of the European Parliament for
59 Northern Ireland) put forward in the Parliament a motion demanding
60 certain basic rights for speakers of such languages, as well as supportive
61 measures from Community institutions. In the following year, four other
62 separate motions were tabled, all centring on the same areas of concern.
63 These motions were discussed in detail at Parliamentary Committee
64 level and, as a result, Gaetano Arfe (an Italian member of the Committee)
65 was requested to draw up a document encompassing the points made
66 in the various motions tabled. Signor Arfe performed this function so
67 efficiently that the outcome was the adoption by the European Parlia-
68 ment of the document now known as the Arfe Report on the 16th October
69 1981.
70   This Report comprises basically a charter of rights with some indica-
71 tors as to possible action. It is, in every sense, a basic foundation upon
72 which to build.
73   The building has begun.

This is an incomplete extract of an article by Dónall Ó Riagáin, 'We are…', *Contact Bulletin*, published by the European Bureau for Lesser Used Languages, no. 1, November 1983.

Unhappy Families

Obsessively, government ministers are arguing about what to do about the British family. In a speech on June 20th, Peter Lilley, the social-security secretary, described the growth of family breakdown as 'deeply disturbing' and 'manifestly' the cause of serious social problems. This seemed to contradict a speech last month by Virginia Bottomley, the health secretary (and the cabinet's official spokesperson on the family), which argued that there never was a 'golden age' of the family, and that the size or shape of a family mattered less than its commitment to raising children.

In fact, Mr Lilley agreed his speech with Mrs Bottomley — and they may both be correct. Mrs Bottomley is right that there was no golden age. At the end of the 19th century, about 5% of all children lived with a father or mother who was not their natural parent. Today, according to an article by John Haskey in this summer's *Population Trends*, 6% of children are in that step-child situation.

Mrs Bottomley may even be right that commitment to raising children, rather than the shape of the family, matters most. Unfortunately, recent research suggests that the shape of the family affects that commitment. So Mr Lilley may also be right to worry about the trend of family breakdown.

The British family is more diverse than it has ever been. Only 73% of children under the age of 16 live with both their natural, married parents. While death disrupted the Victorian household, today's families are shaped by a different attitude to marriage. Most of the children who now live with just one natural parent have, unlike their Victorian counterparts, another natural parent still alive.

Such 'reordering' of their domestic life is bad for children, according to a study by Monica Cockett and John Tripp of the Department of Child Health in Exeter. They interviewed 152 children, half of whom had always lived with their natural parents and half of whom had seen their natural parents' marriage collapse. Preliminary results, published by the Joseph Rowntree Foundation, suggest that children in the 'reordered' families were more likely to suffer from problems with school work and behaviour, low self-esteem and bad health than children whose parents stayed married. When parents stayed together but had frequent rows, their children were more likely to suffer such problems than the children of happy marriages; but much less likely than children whose parents split up.

38   Moreover, the more changes in their domestic arrangements children
39 experienced, the more miserable they were. This may be because chil-
40 dren who went through several family breakdowns were more likely to
41 lose contact with their absent parent and less likely to enjoy the support
42 of other members of the family, such as grandparents.
43   One reason why some children in 'reordered' families may be un-
44 happy is apparent from a study of the relationship between battered
45 children and broken homes published earlier this year by Robert Whelan
46 of the Institute for Economic Affairs, a right-wing think-tank. Mainly
47 using figures collected by the National Society for the Prevention of
48 Cruelty to Children between 1973 and 1990, Mr Whelan argues that
49 children who live only with their natural mother are roughly four times
50 as likely to be physically abused as children who live with both natural
51 parents; and between six and ten times as likely if they live with their
52 natural mother and a stepfather.
53   Mr Lilley, who links family breakdown with the fall in the relative
54 pay of the unskilled, sees the cure in terms of better training and a reform
55 of social benefits. 'It will take a generation', he believes. By that time, lots
56 more youngsters will have grown up as unhappy as Cinderella, before
57 her fairy god-mother appeared.

The Economist, 25th June 1994, pp. 29–32 (author unknown).

Age of Stress Dawns for the Middle Class

Psychologist warns job insecurity will take its toll

1 The middle classes are entering a highly stressful 'age of uncertainty' in
2 which many of them will only work on a freelance basis, according to a
3 leading psychologist.
4   While the new work environment will affect everyone, the change will
5 be at its most fundamental for professional and white-collar workers,
6 Professor Gary Cooper told the British Psychological Society's occupa-
7 tional psychology conference at Warwick University. 'A good education
8 used to be a ticket to success and a permanent job. That's no longer the
9 case.'
10   Professor Cooper, of the University of Manchester Institute of Science
11 and Technology, said the present 'feel bad' factor was not simply caused
12 by job insecurity, but a deep concern that permanent posts will be simply
13 unavailable in future.
14   Already companies routinely contracted out personnel department
15 and information technology functions and were increasingly employing
16 general managers on a project by project basis only, he said in his keynote
17 address.
18   He predicted that by the end of the millennium many organisations
19 would rely on contractors for all but the production process, so blue-
20 collar workers would feel more secure than their white-collar colleagues.
21   'We are not so much entering the age of the entrepreneur as the age
22 of uncertainty where a great deal of work will be on a freelance basis. I
23 am deeply worried that people will not be able to cope with such a
24 fundamental shift in the world of work', said Professor Cooper.
25   The new working patterns were likely to increase stress at the work-
26 place, which was already at historically high levels in Britain, Professor
27 Cooper said. Absence through sickness was already costing British
28 industry £11 billion a year, much of it stress-related. Sickness rates in
29 Britain stood at around 3.5 per cent compared with between one and two
30 per cent among our competitors.
31   The cost to employers was likely to soar in the wake of the successful
32 case brought by John Walker, a social-work manager who suffered two
33 nervous breakdowns and who is now claiming £200,000 in compensa-
34 tion from Northumberland County Council. The High Court judgement
35 meant that employers now had a 'duty of care' for their employees, but
36 it also meant some companies might be tempted to get rid of workers at
37 the very first sign of strain.

38   Stress among contract workers was invariably high, Professor Cooper
39 said. They often went without holidays and took on jobs for which they
40 were not qualified just in case the work dried up. Working as a freelance
41 required a whole range of skills which the average manager or profes-
42 sional did not possess such as accounting, contract law, information
43 technology and marketing expertise. People would have to learn to work
44 from home.
45   Society as a whole was ill-equipped for the new era, he said. More
46 than 65 per cent of women between 16 and 59 were now working so that
47 increasingly parents found it difficult to combine employment with
48 family. Irregular contract employment would make the situation more
49 difficult.

Barrie Clement, Labour Editor, in *The Independent*, 4th January 1995.

Deliver Us from Motor Hell, Dr Mawhinney

1 The minister must be brave. Only radical change can save Britain from
2 the car, says Christian Wolmar.
3   Today the Institute of British Geographers will receive a paper from
4 a team at the London School of Economics and King's College saying
5 that only a massive investment in public transport can save the roads
6 from an explosive increase in traffic and all the environmental damage
7 associated with that. The researchers found that energy use for travel to
8 work in Manchester and the West Midlands had increased dramatically
9 per job, while in London, where good public transport systems have
10 survived, there was little increase.
11   This is only the latest evidence of the misguided thinking that has
12 steered roads policy for countless governments. Its central tenet — that
13 we must increase road capacity in order to build ourselves out of
14 congestion — is revealed as fatally flawed.
15   Last year several events, from the Royal Commission on Environ-
16 mental Pollution's report to new Department of Environment planning
17 advice on out-of-town shopping centres, made the previous policy
18 appear totally impractical. The most recent was the publication of a
19 report by an advisory committee of the Department of Transport which
20 found that new roads generate extra traffic — axiomatic to most of us.
21   But how should we go about replacing a road-building policy with a
22 transport policy? Brian Mawhinney, Transport Secretary since July, is
23 giving it a go: already there have been concrete signs of a shift in policy.
24 Road schemes have been scrapped, more is being spent on bus lanes and,
25 amazingly, £3m is being spent to start work on a 1220 mile cycle network
26 in London.
27   In a speech last month to a conference on air quality, Dr Mawhinney
28 said he wanted to break through the entrenched positions which the two
29 sides in the transport debate — broadly, the environmentalists and the
30 pro-roaders — had reached.
31   But there are no easy answers and no easy votes to be won — indeed,
32 Dr Mawhinney is hamstrung by his own party's ideological obsession
33 with the car. In fact, the solutions are so difficult that it must be tempting
34 for transport ministers to throw up their hands in the air and do nothing.
35 As David Mackenzie, regional director of Transmark, which has studied
36 transport problems around the world, put it: 'It is extremely difficult to
37 get a sensible transport policy based on what the community at large is

38   prepared to accept. Most solutions put forward by governments are
39   nibbling at the edges of the problem.'
40   As Dr Mawhinney pointed out in his speech, the anti-roads lobby can
41   be just as facile and wrong-headed as its opponents. The constant cries
42   for 'more and better public transport' or for 'putting more freight on rail'
43   are often as irrelevant as slogans such as 'we need roads to keep industry
44   moving'.
45   The awful truth is that a coherent transport policy, with set objectives,
46   requires an answer to the question: 'What sort of society do we want to
47   live in?' Take leisure. Cars have made it much easier for people to visit
48   national parks and areas of outstanding natural beauty. But their pres-
49   ence reduces the aesthetic appeal of such areas. Introducing high charges
50   to drive on local roads has obvious appeal, but that will only deter those
51   new to car ownership. The rest will stump up with bad grace. What looks
52   like a transport issue is actually a much more profound political and
53   social question.

Extract from an article by Christian Wolmar in *The Independent*, 4th
January 1995.

Deaths Linked to London Smog

1 When a latter-day smog enveloped London in 1991 the number of deaths
2 shot up by 10 per cent, according to an unpublished report for the
3 Department of Health. The figures suggest that the smog killed about
4 160 people. The episode presents the first direct evidence of deaths from
5 air pollution in Britain for more than 30 years and has forced the
6 government to order a review of its air quality guidelines.
7   The smog, which built up from traffic fumes during four windless
8 days in December 1991, was the worst in Britain in recent years. Many
9 of those who died had probable been suffering from heart disease and
10 respiratory problems.
11   Evidence of the deaths has been compiled by Ross Anderson, an
12 epidemiologist at St George's Hospital in South London. He will present
13 a summary of his results to a meeting of the British Thoracic Society next
14 week.
15   But Anderson's results have already convinced the Department of
16 Health to act. Under air quality guidelines which it set last year, no public
17 warning would be given if the 1991 smog was repeated today, because
18 the level of pollutants would not be high enough.
19   The smog blanketed London from the morning of Thursday 13 De-
20 cember until winds cleared the air the following Sunday evening. Two
21 pollutants reached exceptionally high concentrations: nitrogen dioxide
22 levels peaked at 423 parts per billion, the highest level ever recorded in
23 Britain, and particulates, measured as the amount of black smoke in the
24 air, reached 228 micrograms per cubic metre.
25   By looking at the number of people in London who died the week
26 before the smog, and the number who died in the same week in previous
27 years, Anderson calculated the expected number of deaths for the seven
28 days starting on 12 December. He then compared this figure with the
29 number of people who actually died.
30   Anderson found that 10 per cent more people than expected died
31 during the smog. He declined to say how many deaths make up the 10
32 per cent or to comment on his findings until next week's meeting.
33   But government figures show that about 1700 people were registered
34 dead during the fateful week, suggesting that about 160 extra people
35 died during the smog.
36   Anderson found the number of people who died from respiratory
37 diseases, including asthma and severe lung disease, was 22 per cent

38 higher than expected during the week of the smog. The number of people
39 who died from cardiovascular disease was 14 per cent higher.
40   An epidemiological study such as Anderson's cannot prove that air
41 pollution caused the extra deaths. But the abstract of Anderson's paper
42 concludes: 'The results suggest an increased mortality occurred during
43 the episode week. This is consistent with an effect of air pollution.'
44   According to John Bower of the National Environmental Technology
45 Centre near Culham, Oxfordshire, episodes as bad as the 1991 smog are
46 rare, but they remain possible, despite new regulations intended to
47 reduce vehicle emissions. 'If the same weather happens again, it would
48 happen again', he says.

From an article by William Bown, *The New Scientist*, 25th June 1994, p. 4.

One-Stop Quality

1 *A team from the UK's Leicester Royal Infirmary beat finalists from across*
2 *Europe to pick up this year's European Golden Helix Care award for an initiative*
3 *aimed at providing a quality service for outpatients.*

4 The UK entry to the European Golden Helix Care Award, Leicester
5 Royal Infirmary NHS Trust, has won the 1994 competition outright.
6 Held in Geneva in June, the Award finals featured teams from Germany,
7 Austria, Denmark, France, Italy, the Netherlands and Spain, as well as
8 the UK. Each team had already won its own national Golden Helix
9 Award.

10 Set up in 1991 and sponsored and co-ordinated at UK and European
11 levels by Hewlett-Packard, the Award exists to promote greater aware-
12 ness of quality and its benefits throughout healthcare. Each team must
13 demonstrate how its quality improvement project has measurably raised
14 standards within a healthcare institution. The President of the European
15 Golden Helix Board is Simone Veil, Minister of State for Social Affairs in
16 the French Government.

17 The other teams to reach the finals were the Vienna City Hospital
18 Association, Austria; the Bispebjerg Hospital, Copenhagen, Denmark;
19 the Centre Hospitalier Regional Universitaire. Rennes, France; the Ev.
20 Waldkrankenhaus Spandau, Germany; UCL 9, Reggio Emilia, Italy; the
21 Academisch Ziekenhuis, Rotterdam, Netherlands; and the Severo Ochoa
22 Hospital, Madrid, Spain.

23 The Leicester Royal Infirmary NHS Trust's single visit neurology
24 outpatient process has established an outpatient process which is sub-
25 stantially more convenient and less stressful for patients. This is achieved
26 through completing the entire process in one day, including the patient's
27 initial consultation with a specialist, a full series of complex investiga-
28 tions, a follow-up session with the consultant to discuss results and
29 treatment, and decisions about treatment options.

30 Previously, this process would have taken several weeks and have
31 involved multiple trips to the hospital. In addition, the Leicester Royal
32 Infirmary Team set themselves a set of strict quality targets, which
33 included:

34 • 100 per cent of appropriate patients to have finished their consult-
35 ations with all diagnostic investigations completed and reported
36 within one visit.

37 • 100 per cent availability of notes and results at consultation.

38   • All patients to be seen within 30 minutes of appointment time.
39   • All expected patients to attend the clinic.
40   • 100 per cent of GPs to receive a full report within 24 hours; GPs felt
41   this last target was unnecessary, and it was subsequently changed
42   to 48 hours.
43   These targets contrast with the initial project baseline. Before the
44   quality project was implemented at the hospital, no patients requiring
45   complex investigations completed their consultation within one visit;
46   three visits were the average. Only 50 per cent of patients were seen
47   within 30 minutes of their appointment time, and only 93 per cent of
48   notes and results were available at consultation time. In addition only
49   90 per cent of patients with appointments actually attended the clinic,
50   and no GPs received a report of the consultation by the next day.
51   The team achieved all quality targets. Not only can patient need for
52   medical or other treatment now be promptly and accurately determined,
53   but the time spent at, and travelling to, the hospital is greatly reduced.

From: Euroquan newsletter,* 5th October 1994, Vol. 9, no. 2, p. 13.

* Produced by the Royal College of Nursing Dynamic Quality Improvement
  Programme and the Foundation of Nursing Studies, in association with the
  Nursing Standard.

Chaos Theory — Achieving a Balance

1   *'The philosophers have only interpreted the world in various ways; the point is*
2   *to change it'. Marx's words are being taken to heart in the science of chaos.*
3   Chaos theory, as the science of non-linear dynamics was sexily rechris-
4   tened in the 1970s, has been a mixed blessing. Its central insight, that
5   processes described by simple physical laws could, under the right
6   conditions, be entirely unpredictable — is hugely illuminating. All sorts
7   of bizarrely fluctuating things, such as populations of animals, bubbling
8   pots on a stove or measles epidemics, can now be understood in princi-
9   ple. For people studying such phenomena this has been a great step
10 forward. But for those who hoped to make predictions through the
11 careful application of hard-won physical laws the news has been bad.
12 No longer can they hope that the mysteries of the weather, or the
13 sudden flurries of instability that rock fast aeroplanes, will one day yield
14 to better application of the rules. The instabilities are inherent in the
15 system.
16   Yet this despair is not wholly justified. Chaos theory says that, left to
17 themselves, seemingly simple systems end up behaving unpredictably.
18 But why leave things to themselves? Chaos theory may lack predictive
19 power, but if you are willing to get involved rather than just observe, it
20 can provide deft ways to control the world.
21
22 **It's just a phase it's going through**
23   Engineers are now trying to tame chaos in all sorts of places: the
24 muscles of the heart; the rhythms of the brain; the flames of industrial
25 furnaces. Wherever they find the chaos, though, all the researchers go to
26 the same place to control it — phase space.
27   Mathematicians invented the notion of phase space in the 19th cen-
28 tury. It is a place where every direction has its own meaning. Consider
29 a simple pendulum. Its movement can be described by a two-dimen-
30 sional phase space with two axes. One provides a measure of the
31 pendulum's velocity, the other records its position. Each point in this
32 phase space represents a particular state of the system in which the
33 pendulum has a given velocity and position. As the state of the system
34 changes, so does the point that represents it. Back-and-forth motion by
35 an ideal pendulum is a perfect circle in phase space.
36   All sorts of systems can be described by the shapes they produce in a
37 phase space — often one with more than two dimensions. Much of chaos

95

38 theory stems from the fact that seemingly random processes in the real
39 world look more regular in phase space. The patterns they make are not
40 the closed loops produced by a pendulum, a system which keeps coming
41 back to exactly the same state. Chaos patterns look more like tangled
42 skeins of wool, looping endlessly around without ever touching the
43 same spot twice.

Extract from an article in *The Economist*, 25th June 1994, pp. 105–106 (no author's name given).

Great Expectations for Optical Card Trial

1   The rising tide of malpractice suits in Britain could finally provide the
2   financial incentive for the wider use of patient records held on memory
3   cards and owned by the patient.
4   In an 18-month clinical trial beginning this autumn, pregnant women
5   receiving antenatal care at the new Chelsea and Westminster Hospital
6   will be given optical memory cards which can store X-rays, ultrasound
7   scans and medical records. Altogether, each 'Clinicard' can hold the
8   equivalent of 1000 pages of information, safe from accidental erasure or
9   alteration, on a space the size of a credit card.
10   The trial is part of a project that has been under way for almost eight
11 years. British Telecom originally licensed the technology in 1986, but
12 only began its first trial — involving 200 volunteers at a London hospi-
13 tal — in 1989 (*Technology*, 10 December, 1988) because of delays caused
14 by difficulties in finding and paying for equipment capable of reading
15 the cards. BT Tallis, an offshoot of BT, is managing the trial and provid-
16 ing optical scanners.
17   The principal benefit of the card in this trial should be that the women
18 will receive all the tests appropriate to their condition. 'Studies a few
19 years ago in the National Health Service found that of the standard
20 courses of action — such as specific tests for conditions — which should
21 have been done during pregnancy — only 25 per cent were...', says Tony
22 Brown, principal consultant at BT Tallis. 'That has implications if there
23 is a malpractice case, which is very common in the US and becoming less
24 rare here. What these cards provide is a clear audit trail, so that if, for
25 example, a woman says that her baby has Down's syndrome but that she
26 was never given a test for it, we can check that against the record.'
27   Each card can hold 2–4 megabytes of formatted data, which is written
28 onto it by burning microscopic pits, like those on a compact disc, with a
29 laser. A less powerful laser can then read the data. Each card presently
30 costs about £4, but that should halve with mass production.
31   The trial will try to develop software, supplied by Nippon Conlux of
32 Japan, to automatically suggest the correct tests to administer at each
33 stage of pregnancy, based on changes in factors such as the mother's
34 weight and blood pressure. 'In traditional paper systems it's just written
35 down, and it relies on the midwife or doctor to put the information
36 together and suggest the appropriate checks', says Brown.
37   Although such cards can bring clear health benefits — by alerting

38   doctors to allergies, for example, if the patient is brought in for an
39   emergency operation — health economists have previously rejected
40   wider use, because the financial benefits have been unclear. But Brown
41   says that the growing number of malpractice suits in Britain could
42   provide the financial impetus. 'By having a clear audit trail of what
43   advice was given when, and by whom, you have a far better case if it
44   comes to court and you're arguing over whether a test was carried out
45   and what the results were', says Brown.
46   The cards will be able to hold digital scans of X-rays, which when
47   compressed can be squeezed into less than 15 kilobytes. Ultrasound
48   scans lasting 10 seconds could also be stored, since the TV picture is
49   already in digital form, though the compression technique for this has
50   not been picked.

Charles Arthur, *The New Scientist*, 25th June 1994, p. 20.

Britain Under Siege

1   While the British and Irish governments continue to search for peace in
2   Northern Ireland, a surge in violence makes that goal seem more remote
3   than ever. In the first part of a two-week series describing the complex
4   attitudes underlying 25 years of the 'troubles' we examine the Protes-
5   tants.
6   On June 18th, pubs across the British Isles were full of drinkers
7   cheering on Ireland's underdog team as it played Italy in the World Cup.
8   For those in the Republic of Ireland, their team's victory over the Italians
9   was a cause for national celebration. For English fans, the Irish team —
10   coached by a famous English footballer and containing players who
11   normally play for English or Scottish teams — was a good proxy for their
12   own, which had failed to qualify for the contest. For the 24 fans gathered
13   in Height Bars in the quiet village of Loughinisland in County Down,
14   the cheering was followed by carnage.
15   Two men walked into the pub and sprayed the room with bullets,
16   killing six and wounding five, and then fled laughing. The Ulster Vol-
17   unteer Force, a Protestant terrorist group, later claimed it had carried out
18   the attack. It chose the pub only because it knew that those gathered to
19   support Ireland's team would be Catholic.
20   Yet again, after 25 years of strife, Northern Ireland was faced with
21   violence whose ferocity seems incomprehensible to outsiders. Only a
22   tiny minority of Protestants, or of Catholics, have any hand in the
23   shootings and bombings done in their name. But many people on each
24   side of the province's sectarian divide are fearful and suspicious of those
25   on the other — and such feelings have helped fuel a violent conflict
26   which shows no sign of abating despite scores of peace 'initiatives' from
27   both governments and citizen groups.
28   Northern Ireland's Protestants are perhaps in the more anomalous
29   position. They call themselves British but know that the people of
30   mainland Britain do not always see them as such. They describe their
31   political allegiance as Unionist but recognise that the British Parliament
32   and people do not feel as strongly as they do about the Union of Great
33   Britain and Northern Ireland.
34   Some 900,000 Protestant Unionists share the north-eastern corner of
35   the island of Ireland with 6,000,000 Catholics, whose Irish identity is now
36   recognised, at least verbally, by British ministers as enjoying equal
37   validity with the claimed Britishness of many Protestants. In Unionist

38 eyes, even this verbal concession seems to imply that the union with
39 Britain which they cherish is slipping away. Unionist politicians refuse
40 to take part in negotiating any framework for future government which
41 would recognise the Irishness of their Catholic neighbours by estab-
42 lishing cross-border institutions with southern Ireland (as suggested on
43 June 20th by Albert Reynolds, Ireland's Prime Minister, to Unionist
44 indignation). 'Loyalist' paramilitaries attempt to subvert any such goal
45 by brutal, random killings of Catholics, as at Loughinisland.
46   Since the latest round of secret contacts, proposals and discussions
47 began last year — which Catholics term the 'peace process' — many
48 Protestants have become more worried than ever that Britain may be
49 tempted to do a deal with the IRA. They believe that covert steps towards
50 shared sovereignty with the government of the Irish Republic are meant
51 to soften them up for eventual absorption into a predominantly Catholic
52 united Ireland.

Extracts from an article in *The Economist*, 25th June 1994, pp. 25–26 (no
author's name given).

The Policy Paper that caused the Storm

1 **The problem**
2 The problem of European unification has reached a critical juncture
3 in its development. If, in the next two to four years, no solution to the
4 causes of this critical situation is found, the Union, contrary to the goal
5 of an ever-closer association invoked in the Maastricht Treaty, will, in
6 essence, become a loosely knit grouping of states restricted to certain
7 economic aspects and composed of various sub-groupings of states. The
8 main causes include:
9 • Over-extension of the institutions, which, originally set up for six
10 member countries, must now cater for a membership of 12, soon to
11 rise to 16.
12 • An increase in 'regressive nationalism' in (almost) all member coun-
13 tries. Fear and anxiety tempt people to seek if not a solution, then at
14 least refuge in a return to the nation-state and all things national.
15
16 **Institutional overhaul**
17 All existing institutions — the Council, the Commission, the presi-
18 dency and the European Parliament — must be reformed. The changes
19 must be geared to concepts for a new institutional balance, according to
20 which the Parliament will increasingly become a genuine law-making
21 body with the same rights as the Council; the Council, in addition to
22 performing tasks in the intergovernmental field, will assume the func-
23 tions of a second chamber; and the Commission will take on features of
24 a European government.
25 With regard to the Council, democratisation means striking a better
26 balance between the equality of all member states, on the one hand, and
27 the ratio of population size to number of votes in the Council, on the
28 other.
29
30 **Multi-speed Europe**
31 To achieve this, the 'variable geometry' or 'multi-speed' approach
32 should be sanctioned and institutionalised in the Union treaty or the new
33 quasi-conditional document. Otherwise, this approach might well en-
34 courage a trend towards a 'Europe à la carte'. It must therefore be
35 decided whether, in the case of amendments to the Maastricht Treaty,
36 the principle of unanimity laid down in Article N should be replaced by
37 a quorum yet to be more specified. It is essential that no country should

38 be allowed to use its right of veto to block the efforts of other countries
39 more able and willing to intensify their co-operation and deepen inte-
40 gration.
41   The task of the hard core is, by giving the Union a strong Centre, to
42 counteract the centrifugal forces generated by constant enlargement.
43   To this end, the countries of the hard core should be recognisably
44 more community-spirited in their joint action than others.
45   In the monetary field, too, there are strong signs that a hard core of
46 five countries is emerging. They (together with Denmark and Ireland)
47 are the ones which come closest to meeting the convergence criteria
48 stipulated in the Maastricht Treaty. This is especially important since
49 monetary union is the cornerstone of political union (and not, as believed
50 in Germany, an additional element of integration alongside political
51 union).

The European, 9–15th September 1994. Extracts from the CDU/CSU
document (Germany's ruling parliamentary group at the time).

EU Fugaces Labuntur Communitates

1   Just as most people had stopped talking about the 'Common Market'
2   and become used to calling it the European Community, the Maastricht
3   treaty comes along and confuses everyone by creating something called
4   the European Union. What is it, and why has *The Economist* reluctantly
5   decided to abandon the now familiar EC for the something-between-a-
6   sigh-and-an-expletive EU?
7   The viscosity of the answer reflects that of the Maastricht treaty, which
8   came into force on November 1st, bringing the Union with it. It is yet
9   another masterpiece of Euro-fudge. The new Union is the old Commu-
10   nity with two additions. One is a common foreign and security policy;
11   the other is co-operation between the 12 governments in justice and
12   police matters. The rest of what Maastricht is supposed to do — open
13   the road to economic union and a single currency, strengthen the Euro-
14   pean Parliament, give Brussels new powers over industrial policy,
15   consumer affairs, health and education — stays four-square within the
16   EC.
17   The whole construction — EC plus foreign and security policy plus
18   justice and police co-operation — adds up to the European Union. On
19   the other hand, it does not add up to one single decision-taking process
20   but to three separate ones. Moreover, the European Union has no legal
21   persona. Only the EC, and/or the member-states, can conclude inter-
22   national agreements, for instance.
23   In other words, confusion reigns. It certainly does among the Union's
24   architects. At a press conference after the recent Brussels summit, John
25   Major fluffed his first attempt to explain what the European Union is and
26   why he would be using the name sparingly. He eventually spoke of a
27   'three-pillared union' within which EC work would continue as before,
28   while anything to do with foreign and security matters or justice and
29   police would be strictly Union business. The main reason for this sepa-
30   ration is the desire of several countries, led by Britain and France, to keep
31   the Maastricht additions as much as possible out of the hands of the
32   Brussels commission and the European Parliament. British officials in
33   Brussels say they will try to maintain the distinction in day-to-day
34   European affairs.
35   *The Economist* reckons that effort will be forlorn. Some people will go
36   on talking about the Community regardless of legal accuracy, others will
37   increasingly refer to the Union in all contexts except historical ones. We

38 have decided to opt for the Union, believing (perhaps wrongly) that in
39 time this term will prevail.
40   We have not had much help from the authorities in reaching our
41 decision. On November 8th the Council of Ministers, the Community's
42 main decision-taking body, became the 'Council of Ministers of the
43 European Union'. But on November 17th the commission in Brussels
44 evaded the question by rebaptising itself the 'European Commission',
45 which nearly everybody thought was its name anyway. The judges of
46 the European court in Luxembourg, conservatives to a man, have de-
47 cided to remain the 'Court of Justice of the European Communities', a
48 reminder that the European Coal and Steel Community and the Atomic
49 Energy Community still exist.

From the (unnamed) Brussels correspondent of *The Economist*, 20th
November 1993.

Q. Europe by Eurotunnel?
A. The Easy Way To Go!

1 The traveller's guide to Eurotunnel

2

3 **1. The smart route to Europe**
4 *When will Eurotunnel open?*
5 Euroshuttles are scheduled to carry cars and freight vehicles from 15
6 June 1993, and coaches and caravans from Autumn 1993. (British Rail
7 and SNCF's through-train services are also scheduled to run from 15
8 June 1993.)

9

10 *How do I travel through the tunnel?*
11 The Channel Tunnel is actually two single-track railway tunnels and
12 a smaller service tunnel which link Britain and continental Europe. Road
13 vehicles will be carried through the tunnel in Eurotunnel shuttles, and
14 through-trains (operated by national railways) will carry passengers and
15 freight.

16

17 *Where is it?*
18 The Eurotunnel shuttle service will run between two terminals, one
19 near Folkestone in Kent, with direct access from the M20, and one just
20 outside Calais with links to the continental motorway system.

21

22 *Who can use it?*
23 In addition to through-railway services, the tunnel will be open to
24 most road vehicles. Depending on their height, coaches, cars (with
25 caravans or trailers) and motor-bikes will be directed to single-deck or
26 double-deck shuttles, and most passengers will travel with their vehi-
27 cles. Heavy goods vehicles will be carried in special shuttles with a
28 separate passenger coach for their drivers. Terminals and shuttles will
29 be well-equipped for disabled passengers.

30

31

32 **2. Quickly and easily across the Channel**
33 *Do I drive my car through the tunnel?*
34 No, you drive your car onto one of the shuttles which will carry you
35 and your vehicle in safety. As all the railway and shuttle locomotives
36 using the tunnel will be electric, the air will not be polluted with exhaust
37 fumes.

38 *How long will the journey take?*
39   About thirty-five minutes from platform to platform, with twenty-
40 five minutes in the tunnel itself.
41
42 *How will I know if there is a queue?*
43   With passenger shuttles leaving every 15 minutes at peak time,
44 queues will be rare. By telephoning the Eurotunnel Information Line, or
45 listening to Eurotunnel Radio as you approach the terminal, you will be
46 able to find out when the next shuttle leaves, how busy we are, plus the
47 latest news, weather and traffic information.
48
49 *How do the shuttles travel through the tunnel?*
50   There will be an electric locomotive at each end of the shuttle, each of
51 which is capable of powering the shuttle at speeds of up to 80mph.
52
53 **3. No stress**
54 *Will the tunnels leak?*
55   The tunnels are between 80–150 feet below the sea-bed in a layer
56 of water-impermeable chalk marl. The concrete tunnel lining forms a
57 waterproof seal, so the risk of leakage is almost non-existent.
58
59 *What happens if there is a fire?*
60   In the rare event of a fire breaking out, passengers will be evacuated
61 by staff into an adjoining shuttle wagon. Staff, sophisticated fire detec-
62 tion and suppression systems will identify and extinguish any fire,
63 which would be contained by sealed and fire-resistant doors. In most
64 cases the shuttle would continue its journey to the terminal where further
65 action would be taken if necessary.
66
67 *Do I need a passport?*
68   Yes, passengers will pass through the same frontier controls as those
69 at ferry and hovercraft terminals. However, the coming of the single
70 European market will mean the end of passport controls within Europe.
71
72 *What frontier controls will there be?*
73   Although the actual frontier is in the middle of the Channel, you will
74 pass through British and French customs and immigration controls
75 before you board the shuttle. There will be no further controls on
76 arrival.
77
78 *Can I take my pet?*
79   Only if you comply with the existing regulations governing export/

80 import and quarantine. Because of British laws to prevent accidental
81 import of rabies, strict security procedures will be used to enforce these
82 regulations.
83
84 *What about rabies?*
85   Several types of barriers are being installed above and below ground
86 to prevent animals straying into the tunnel. Surveillance at the terminals
87 will mean that the risk of animals being smuggled through is certainly
88 no greater than on other cross-Channel routes.
89
90
91 **4. No booking, no deadlines**
92   **Just turn up and go**
93 *Do I need to book my journey?*
94   No, you do not need to book but you can purchases tickets in advance.
95 You can arrive at the terminal whenever it suits you. At peak periods
96 there will be up to four shuttles an hour, so queues will be rare.
97
98 *How long in advance do I need to come to the terminal?*
99   You will not have to arrive at any specific time. Once you are at the
100 terminal, you will be put onto the next available shuttle, so there is no
101 'slot' to miss if you are unexpectedly delayed.
102
103 *How much will it cost?*
104   Prices are expected to be similar to those charged by the ferries, with
105 a simple fare structure.
106
107 *What about facilities for disabled passengers?*
108   Special measures have been taken to make the journey as easy as
109 possible for disabled passengers, and there will always be members of
110 staff to assist when required.
111
112
113 **5. Round the clock reliability 365 days a year.**
114 *Will it be open at night?*
115   Yes, the shuttles will operate twenty-four hours a day, 365 days a year,
116 with at least one service an hour during the night.
117
118 *How do I find the terminals?*
119   The terminals will be well signposted from motorways and other
120 approach roads on both sides of the Channel. As you drive into the
121 terminals you will see clear signs in both English and French.

122 *What facilities will the terminals have?*
123   Both terminals will have extensive passenger facilities — cafes, res-
124 taurants, toilets, shops and bureaux de change. You can either stop there
125 or go straight to the shuttle.
126
127 *How do I pay?*
128   You pay your fare to a member of staff at a tollbooth at the terminal
129 entrance. You can pay in cash (sterling or French francs), by cheque or
130 major credit, debit and charge cards.
131
132 **6. Drive in, switch off**
133 *How do I get my car into the shuttle?*
134   A well-signposted route from the tollbooths leads you to your allo-
135 cated departure platform, where the staff will be guiding vehicles into
136 the shuttle through a wide loading door. Inside the shuttle there is a
137 continuous 'roadway' and you will have to drive forward along this until
138 directed to stop, put the hand-brake on and switch off the engine.
139
140 *How long will it take to load the shuttle?*
141   About eight minutes, if it is completely full.
142
143 *What happens if my car breaks down?*
144   There will be an emergency repair service at both terminals.
145
146 **7. The comfort factor**
147 *How comfortable will it be?*
148   The rail track has been specially designed so that the ride will be
149 smoother than on a normal train journey — and you certainly won't feel
150 seasick! The noise level will be similar to that on a modern express train.
151
152 *Do I have to stay in my car?*
153   No, you will be able to walk around in the shuttle, chat to staff and
154 other passengers, and use the toilet facilities. You may choose to rest,
155 plan your journey, listen to Eurotunnel Radio, or watch the indicator
156 boards which show how the journey is progressing.
157
158 *Will I feel claustrophobic?*
159   The shuttles are air-conditioned and very well lit, with room to walk
160 around and stretch your legs during the short journey. The shuttle has
161 small windows, but once in the tunnel there will be nothing to see!

From *The Traveller's Guide to Eurotunnel*, pp. 1–3.

Lucrative Fishing in Foreign Labour Pools

1 A ruling by the European Court allows employers to transfer immigrant
2 workers to anywhere in the Union. Electoral accountability will be the
3 first casualty, writes Alastair McAlpine.

4 One of the great bonuses of the European Union — possibly its
5 greatest — is that its citizens can seek employment anywhere within its
6 boundaries. People from the rest of the world must apply for work
7 permits from the member state where they wish to be employed. This,
8 at least, was how the matter used to stand. But a ruling by the European
9 Court has since changed all this.

10 A group of Moroccans employed by a Belgian demolition contractor
11 wished to work on a contract that he had won in France. The French
12 immigration officials, as had always been their practice, insisted that
13 these Moroccan building workers needed French work permits. The
14 court ruled otherwise. It seems that an employer can now transfer
15 immigrant labour in his employ anywhere within the European Union
16 regardless of national boundaries.

17 The construction industry is a large employer of unskilled labour. The
18 first requirement for obtaining work as a labourer on a building site is
19 strength and the next, stamina. Builders have traditionally sought un-
20 skilled labour from overseas. The governments of the countries where
21 these contractors operate have regulated the flow of this labour. The
22 construction industry is a highly competitive world where builders
23 compete ferociously. This new ruling from the European Court changes
24 the whole ball game.

25 The most competitive builder will no longer be the best organised or
26 the most experienced, but the builder who has access to the largest pool
27 of the cheapest foreign labour. For example, an Italian builder will
28 negotiate with the Italian government to be given permits for, say, North
29 African workers who will work for him on contracts that he may have
30 won in the City of London. The Italian officials and, for that matter, their
31 master, Italian politicians, will have little interest in refusing these per-
32 mits, since the employment taken by these migrant workers from North
33 Africa will be the jobs of British construction workers who do not vote
34 in Italian elections.

35 In any case, the wealth created by the cheap and successful Italian
36 contractor will find its way back to Italy, while the social costs of his
37 workforce will be a charge on the British taxpayer. The conse-

38 quences of a decision by an Italian official will be totally detached
39 from Italy.
40   In time the need to compete will ensure that all construction workers
41 are immigrants. The social strains in the countries where they work will
42 be intolerable.
43   The governments who suffer at second hand from the decisions of
44 officials in other countries of the European Union can huff and puff as
45 much as they like, for the law now clearly says that migrant workers have
46 the right to work in any country of the European Union where their
47 employer chooses to conduct his business.
48   I have taken the example of the construction industry, for it is a very
49 obvious one. The principle, however, can be applied to manufacturing,
50 tourism or any other sector. Nothing but chaos and strife will come from
51 this court's decision.

Extract from an article by Alistair McAlpine, *The European*, 9–15th September 1994.

Euro-Court Extends UK Workers' Rights

1   A far-reaching European Court decision affecting the rights of millions
2   of British workers threw the Government on the defensive last night over
3   its failure to give employees a voice in their futures.
4   In a ruling variously interpreted as a devastating blow to the Govern-
5   ment and a matter of little practical consequence, the European Court of
6   Justice said that workers' representatives had a right to be informed and
7   consulted about large-scale redundancies or when a business was trans-
8   ferred from one owner to another, including when it was privatised.
9   The European Commission said that Britain would have to change its
10 legislation on workers' rights. Padraig Flynn, the social affairs commis-
11 sioner, said: 'There is no question that changes will have to be put in
12 place to satisfy the court ruling.'
13   Mr Flynn would not say whether he thought the ruling would open
14 the way to compensation claims by workers whose jobs were switched
15 from the public to the private sector in the 1980s.
16   However, last night, Jack Dromey, the Transport and General Work-
17 ers' Union official in charge of public services, called on the Government
18 to negotiate compensation for all those who had suffered as a result of
19 compulsory competitive tendering — or fight the unions through the
20 courts.
21   He said the TGWU would take legal action against any local authority
22 which tried to derecognise unions. 'We believe this decision will put an
23 end to derecognition in public services.'
24   The Employment Minister, Michael Forsyth, said that the Govern-
25 ment would have to consider the judgement, but its effects were
26 extremely limited. Employers would not have to recognise unions as a
27 result of redundancy and transfers, but workers would have to be
28 consulted.
29   John Hendy, QC, chairman of the Institute of Employment Rights,
30 said: 'The significance of the decision is not the question of possible
31 compensation but a step towards democracy at the workplace.'
32   The ruling led to a clash between John Major and Labour's environ-
33 ment spokesman, Jack Straw, during the European election press
34 conferences yesterday. Mr Major said it was based on a European
35 directive approved by the Labour government in 1975.
36   But Mr Straw insisted that the ruling was based on a law signed by
37 the Government 13 years ago. 'It is now going to be enforced to give

38 British workers the same rights as those enjoyed by workers across
39 Europe.'
40   John Monks, the TUC general secretary, described the decision as a
41 'devastating blow' for the Government. 'Once again British workers
42 have been shown to be denied rights that are accepted in law in all other
43 European Union countries.'
44   The rulings came in two cases brought by the European Commission
45 against the Government for incorrectly implementing EU legislation.
46 The first concerning the acquired rights directive — known as Tupe in
47 Britain — which protects workers' wages and conditions in a sale or
48 transfer of their enterprise. The second involved legislation protecting
49 their rights in collective redundancies. British unions have used Tupe to
50 challenge the practice of worsening pay and conditions when public
51 services are transferred to the private sector.

Extract from an article by Keith Harper, Julie Wolf and Seumas Milne,
The Guardian, 9th June 1994, p. 2.

Choosy Employers Search for Skilful Team Players

1 *New business survey paints a rosy picture of life in the service sector, reports*
2 *Clive Woodcock.*
3 Employers are still having problems finding the right kinds of staff in
4 spite of the recession and high jobless levels, according to a new report
5 on employment in small service firms. This is partly because they are
6 very careful about whom they take on; it is not just a matter of having
7 the right skills, the new employee also has to be somebody who will 'fit
8 in', say the authors of the study from Kingston University's Small
9 Business Research Centre.
10 A small firm has to have team players; where employees have contacts
11 with customers, common in services, they also need the right social and
12 personal skills. Relations between employers and staff were mainly
13 found to be conflict-free. Employees felt that their bosses were generally
14 fair, and supervision was rarely interpreted as close or overbearing.
15 Relations between employees themselves were also good — essential to
16 the successful running of a small business, the researchers point out.
17 Most employees as well as their employers found it difficult to recall
18 a dispute of any real seriousness in the businesses. Little evidence of
19 the sweatshop small firm was found, or even of the poor employer–
20 employee relations often reported previously in industries such as
21 catering.
22 More than 270 employers and employees were interviewed; some of
23 the firms were in traditional services such as small garages and catering
24 businesses, while others were in modern areas such as computer services
25 and recently expanding fields such as business services. A high propor-
26 tion of jobs were part-time or temporary rather than the permanent
27 full-time jobs typical of the past. A substantial number were held by
28 women, another marked feature of jobs in the service sector. Many of the
29 jobs were filled by people who wanted part-time or temporary jobs to fit
30 in with domestic commitments and education. Former full-time employ-
31 ees doing part-time work were uncommon.
32 The researchers say that the increasing importance of services and
33 small firms in the UK economy means that if trades unions are to reverse
34 their decline they need to recruit heavily from these kinds of firms. The
35 interviews with employees, however, suggested that unions were going
36 to find it difficult to make an impact. The great majority of employees
37 felt unions had no role to play in a small firm. While many employers

38   were against unions representing their employees, a surprisingly high
39   proportion said they would accept union representation if their employ-
40   ees wanted it.
41   Pay and fringe benefits in small firms are generally seen as poorer
42   than in larger firms and the findings of the study confirmed the general
43   picture, though showing big variations between firms in different sec-
44   tors. Employers were keen to tailor pay and benefits to the individual
45   employee.
46   Employers showed little enthusiasm for more training or for Training
47   and Enterprise Councils as a source of training. They reported that a
48   great deal of training was being carried out in their firms, much of it
49   informal but geared closely to the needs of the business. Employees
50   themselves also lacked enthusiasm for big increases in training.

*Employment and Employment Relations in the Services Sector Small Enter-
prise, £40, from Small Business Research Centre, Kingston University,
Kingston Hill, Surrey KT2 7LB.*

Clive Woodcock, *The Guardian*, 4th May 1993.

Marks and Spencer

1   **1. Principal Activities**
2   Marks and Spencer is a major international retailer selling clothing,
3   household goods and foods under the 'St Michael' trade mark in the
4   United Kingdom and the Republic of Ireland, France, Belgium, Spain,
5   Holland and Hong Kong.
6   In North America, a range of St Michael merchandise and other
7   consumer goods is sold through stores in Canada. Quality clothing is
8   sold through Brooks Brothers in the United States and Japan, and foods
9   through Kings Super Markets in the United States.
10 Marks and Spencer is committed to providing its customers, through-
11 out the world, with quality, value and service.
12

13 **2. Company Facts (1991/92)**
14 • Turnover exceeded £5.7 billion
15 • Pre-tax profits over £615 million
16 • Over 690 stores world-wide
17 • 74,000 employees
18 • 15 million customers each week
19 • AAA credit rating
20 • Over £5 million invested in a wide range of community activi-
21 ties.
22

23 **3. Europe**
24 *United Kingdom*
25 Over the last two years, the Company has added approximately
26 1 million square feet and now operates on approximately 10 million
27 square feet. The Company's high street, edge of town, and neighbour-
28 hood food stores will continue to be expanded during 1992/93.
29

30 *Continental Europe*
31 The Company's 17 stores on the Continent performed outstandingly
32 during 1991/92, with operating profits increasing 38% on the year
33 before. Stores were opened in Spain and Holland for the first time. The
34 Company aims to quadruple selling space on the Continent during the
35 next four years.
36 Development throughout Europe means there will be a number of
37 opportunities for graduates of the highest calibre.

38 **4. Graduate Opportunities**
39   Opportunities exist for graduates of any discipline in one of the three
40 areas of Store Management.
41
42 *Commercial Management*
43   Responsible for maximising sales and making the most of business
44 opportunities. Commercial Managers are concerned with providing
45 high standards of customer service, ensuring the optimum use of selling
46 space, controlling costs and developing operational efficiency.
47
48 *Personnel Management*
49   Responsible for the cost-effective use of a store's most valuable
50 resource, its people. Personnel Managers implement the Company's
51 personnel policy, carrying out recruitment, training and development
52 programmes as well as caring for individual needs and solving personal
53 and professional problems.
54
55 *Administration Managers*
56   Responsible for controlling and developing the financial, information
57 and systems areas which are vital to the profitable running of the store.
58 Administration Managers implement and manage computer systems,
59 oversee budgets and ensure costs are controlled.
60   All successful applicants are offered a structured training programme
61 with career development based solely on individual performance.
62   Starting salaries are competitive and come with a comprehensive
63 benefits package.
64
65 **5. Graduate Requirements**
66   Personal skills are as important as academic qualifications for all
67 positions.
68   Whilst graduates should have completed a first degree, in any subject,
69 successful applicants will be able to show outstanding personal skills. In
70 particular, they should be able to demonstrate strong leadership skills,
71 along with a clear commitment to, and interest in, retailing.
72   All candidates must be able to communicate must be able to commu-
73 nicate fluently in English and, for positions on the Continent, at least one
74 of the following languages: Dutch, Flemish, French, Spanish.
75   If you are interested in a career with Marks and Spencer and would
76 like further information, please write to one of the addresses below,
77 stating whether you are interested in working on the Continent or in the
78 UK initially.
        From *European Graduates' Career Guide, 1993, EC, Brussels.*

Part 2:
Target Texts

Bienvenue a Ouistreham

Ceci est la procédure relative à l'embarquement des véhicules à OUISTREHAM

1. L'embarquement des véhicules commencera environ 45 minutes avant l'heure de départ.
2. Si vous transportez des animaux, assurez-vous que vous possédez tous les documents nécessaires et venez les déclarer à notre bureau frêt en Gare Maritime.
3. Lors du contrôle de votre billet, il vous a été remis des cartes d'embarquement. Tous cas particuliers (incapacité, maladie, problème de voiture...) doivent être signalés au contrôle. Merci de nous en informer dans le cas où vous ne l'auriez pas fait.
4. Nous vous indiquerons ensuite dans quelle file garer votre véhicule, ceci en fonction des catégories de voitures.
5. Une annonce sera faite pour vous prévenir de regagner immédiatement votre voiture avant l'embarquement des véhicules.
6. Préparez vos cartes d'embarquement et vos passeports pour le contrôle précédant l'embarquement.
7. Un grand nombre de véhicules de différentes tailles doit être embarqué sans risques. Cela prend du temps; merci d'attendre patiemment jusqu'à ce que vous soyez appelés pour embarquer, même si vous avez l'impression d'avancer lentement.
8. Enfin nous vous rappelons que votre passeport doit être contrôlé à bord, au bureau de l'immigration britannique. Aussi avant de quitter votre véhicule, assurez-vous que vous avez sur vous votre passeport et tout ce dont vous pourriez avoir besoin durant la traversée.

Nous vous souhaitons une agréable traversée et vous remercions de votre collaboration.

NOTA: Cette enveloppe contient tous les documents dont vous aurez besoin durant votre voyage.

Brittany Ferries: documents pour le passager.

La généalogie de l'anglais dit 'simple et clair'

1   L'histoire de l'*anglais simple* ne se calcule pas au nombre des ans ni même
2   des décennies, mais des siècles. Le terme même, l'*anglais simple*, fait sujet
3   de record depuis l'an 1500, mais celui qui rédigea le tout premier
4   dictionnaire de l'anglais en 1604 semble avoir été le premier à l'employer
5   dans un sens technique. Il s'agit du maître d'école, Robert Cawdrey, dont
6   la '*Table alphabétique*' visait l'explication des 'mots habituels difficiles' (les
7   emprunts des langues telles le latin, le grec et l'hébreu) par moyen des
8   'mots simples anglais'.
9   Dans un long sous-titre à cette oeuvre, Cawdrey a fait preuve de sa
10 volonté de rendre plus accessible à 'Mesdames, Gentilles femmes ou
11 d'autres personnes non-qualifiées' les mots plus difficiles. Une telle
12 forme d'adresse paraît ouvertement préjugée contre les femmes, avec
13 même un air de condescendance, pour nous les citoyens de la dernière
14 partie du 20e siècle, mais à l'époque, à environ un an après le décès de
15 la reine Elisabeth I, l'intention était tout autre.
16   Cawdrey était pleinement conscient du point auquel la plupart des
17 femmes de sa classe sociale, bien que pas toutes, furent privées des
18 avantages qu'apporte la compétence linguistique. Elles étaient perdan-
19 tes à cause du manque d'enseignement en famille, ou bien de l'accès aux
20 écoles de 'grammaire', où l'on enseignait le latin et un anglais fort
21 latinisé, puisque l'accès à ces écoles, basées dans où liées à l'Eglise, était
22 strictement limité au sexe masculin. Par conséquent, de telles femmes ne
23 bénéficiaient pas de moyen d'apprécier la couche de 'latinité' qui s'était
24 pour ainsi dire formée en dessus de l'anglais traditionnel.
25   La plupart des femmes des classes supérieures et moyennes (ainsi que
26 toutes les femmes de classe ouvrière et la plupart des hommes de cette
27 classe) ne connaissaient point la forme la plus haute de l'anglais de l'âge
28 d'or. Quelques unes d'entre elles, pourtant, en franchissaient presque les
29 limites; certes elles étaient 'non-qualifiées', mais non pas illettrées, à
30 cause d'une instruction limitée qui ne comprenait pas les emprunts des
31 langues classiques — ces 'mots habituels difficiles' de l'anglais. La situ-
32 ation s'est beaucoup améliorée depuis l'époque de Cawdrey, mais le
33 patrimoine des classiques se fait toujours fort valoir, et malgré de nom-
34 breux aspects positifs de celui-ci, il continue à laisser beaucoup de gens
35 dans une sorte de désert linguistique.
36   Vers la fin du 14e siècle, le poète anglais Geoffrey Chaucer écrivait les
37 Contes de Cantorbéry. L'anglais du temps de Chaucer était devenu une

38 langue hybride, qui venait tout récemment de regagner son statut
39 comme langue nationale de l'Angleterre, après quelques 200 ans de
40 statut de 2e classe. Avant qu'il n'y eût l'anglais officiel il y avait eu le
41 français officiel, la langue du gouvernement et du droit — et plus impor-
42 tant que ces deux-ci, il y avait eu le latin officiel, langue d'usage
43 internationale de l'église catholique romaine. A cette époque, pour se
44 considérer comme doté d'un niveau important d'éducation, il fallait
45 généralement être du sexe masculin, faire partie de l'établissement re-
46 ligieux et avoir de bonnes connaissances du français et du latin.
47   Pourtant, l'idée de la clarté et de la simplicité linguistique remonte à
48 beaucoup plus loin que l'époque chaucerienne. L'adjectif *clair* peut se
49 traduire par *plain* en anglais, et ce mot anglais vient du mot latin, *'planus'*,
50 ce qui peut se traduire comme, entre autres, 'plat, bas, simple, applani,
51 clair, compréhensible, évident'. Ce mot servait à définir un genre à trois
52 degrés, un style employé et enseigné par les orateurs de la Rome antique
53 sous l'influence des rhétoriciens grecs: de ces trois degrés, le plus impor-
54 tant et le plus prestigieux, c'était le *grand ou le haut style*; venait ensuite
55 le *style moyen*, et enfin le style *bas* ou *'planus'*. Chacun de ces styles avait
56 ses propres vertus et ses propres vices.
57   Le style dont je me sers, pour la plupart, pour vous parler aujourd'hui,
58 c'est le style dit *moyen*. Je ne me sers pas de l'anglais *simple*, bien que
59 l'anglais que j'utilise puisse paraître parfois simple, sans être pourtant
60 entièrement dans ce style, puisque il y a des choses que je veux dire et
61 des effets que je souhaite créer qui ne sauraient se faire dans un vrai style
62 simple. A vrai dire, on peut faire jouer les trois grand styles rhétoriques
63 comme l'on joue au piano, ce qui arrive souvent, et on s'est toujours
64 attendu à ce que les 'bons' orateurs et les 'bons' écrivains du genre
65 traditionnel sachent le faire. Il n'existe pas de style unique de l'anglais
66 dans lequel on saurait tout faire, à toute occasion, à tout objectif, devant
67 tout le monde. Quel que soit le style choisi, ce ne serait que de limiter la
68 portée d'une langue que d'espérer qu'elle puisse ainsi fonctionner.
69   Aux années 70, certains locuteurs des deux côtés de l'Atlantique ont
70 commencé à s'intéresser à une forme simple de l'anglais, pas en ce qui
71 concerne les matières anciennes comme le style rhétorique ou la sépara-
72 tion du vocabulaire anglais d'origine germanique du patrimoine
73 d'origine latine. Il s'agissait plutôt des moyens pratiques de communi-
74 cation tel l'instruction fondamentale et comment les organisations
75 commerciales pourraient communiquer entre elles ou avec leur clients
76 de façon claire et simple, surtout afin d'éviter là où il le serait possible le
77 jargon, le langage technique et la syntaxe complexe au moment de
78 s'adresser à une audience ou un lectorat non-techniques.
79   En gros il semble y avoir deux façons d'aborder la question de la

80   propagation de l'usage simple dans la vie publique. L'une, que l'on
81   pourrait qualifier comme 'du haut en bas', implique une prise d'initia-
82   tive par les institutions actuelles, comme les gouvernements, les organes
83   professionnels, les organisations commerciales. Par exemple, le
84   NCTE[1] (Conseil National des Professeurs d'anglais aux Etats Unis), a
85   décerné en 1974 les premiers prix annuels de 'Doublespeak' (parler
86   ambigu). Depuis lors, la présentation de ces prix est devenu un événe-
87   ment d'intérêt national.

88   Pourtant, au Royaume Uni la tendance serait plutôt celle du 'bas vers
89   le haut', à savoir des initiatives de la part des groupes de citoyens qui
90   cherchent à exercer de la pression sur les gouvernements et les organi-
91   sations afin d'effectuer des changements. L'année 1979 a vu la création
92   de la PEC[2] (Commission pour l'anglais simple); celle-ci a grandi grâce à
93   l'intérêt médiatique, avec pour conséquence l'introduction de ses pro-
94   pres prix pour l'anglais clair, qui sont devenus à leur tour un événement
95   d'importance nationale.

96   Les deux approches sont également utiles, mais ce qui serait d'autant
97   plus efficace, ce serait une co-opération bilatérale parmi tous les in-
98   téressés. A mon avis il y a en effet des indices d'un accroissement d'une
99   telle co-opération entre d'un côté les consommateurs, les clients, les
100   victimes (on peut les appeler ainsi), et d'autre côté les institutions, les
101   organisations, les sociétés et ainsi de suite. Chacun d'entre eux fournit
102   aux autres un retour d'information appropriée pour que l'on puisse
103   choisir le style qui convient à une audience ou à un lectorat dans le plus
104   grand nombre de cas possible.

Tom McArthur, *The Linguist*, Vol. 32, no. 6, 1993, pp. 182–185.

Extraits d'une version abrégée d'un discours présenté au premier Congrès national de l'anglais simple à Cambridge, au RU.

1.   The National Council of Teachers of English.
2.   Plain English Commission.

Que Dieu vous bénisse, M Burgess, on vous a traduit[1]

1 Mesdames et Messieurs, bonsoir. Le mot 'traduction' a assumé pour moi
2 une connotation toute nouvelle puisque je viens de subir récemment des
3 tests cliniques qui me promettent une fin peu joyeuse; il faut donc me
4 pardonner si, en parlant du mot 'traduction' je commence à y voir la
5 possibilité d'une transmigration ou d'une élévation, le début au moins
6 d'une vie nouvelle, même si l'on n'associe pas d'habitude ce dernier
7 sens-là à ce mot. A vrai dire, ce mot 'traduction' ne possède pas de
8 dimension spirituelle sauf quand on parle, en anglais, du transfert d'un
9 évêque d'un diocèse à un autre.[2]
10 C'est Shakespeare qui a choisi, comme toujours, le mot juste quand il
11 fait dire par Lecoin à Bottom,[3] qui vient de sortir d'une buisson avec une
12 tête d'âne, 'Dieu te bénisse, Bottom, Dieu te bénisse, tu es métamor-
13 phosé'[4] (dans le sens de la métamorphose), parce que la traduction a en
14 effet quelque chose d'asinien. Je préfère, à certains égards, le mot alle-
15 mand *übersetzung* puisque celui-ci implique le transfert d'une chose vers
16 un autre endroit, là-bas, la traversée d'une sorte de Mer rouge, le mou-
17 vement d'un monde vers un autre.
18 Permettez-moi de vous parler tout d'abord de la traduction sous un
19 angle assez superficiel. Quand je vois, sur la couverture d'un livre par
20 Agatha Christie, Jack Higgins ou Freddie Forsyth,[5] la phrase 'traduit en
21 76 langues, y compris le haut-Stobovien et le moyen Ruritanien,[6] je
22 devrais ressentir une forte jalousie, puisque bien que mes oeuvres soient
23 traduites dans d'autres langues, ces deux-là ne figurent pas au compte.
24 A vrai dire, la traduction des oeuvres est à redouter, et le moins que
25 connaît l'écrivain des langues étrangères, le mieux il s'en tire. Si l'on peut
26 traduire les oeuvres d'un écrivain en de nombreuses langues il s'ensuit
27 que celui-ci ne pratique pas *stricto sensu* la littérature, car la littérature ne
28 se traduit pas, seulement son apparence, la mise en page des mots qui
29 remplissent une fonction minime, celle de la description des actions, des
30 sentiments et du dialogue du genre relativement facile à traduire.
31 On peut même dire que si un livre s'avère traduisible, c'est qu'il
32 soupire après l'ultime traduction, à savoir, se faire convertir en un film;
33 quand ceci lui arrive, le livre n'est plus une construction verbale, il
34 devient un jeu de personnages. Le cinéma est le but final de toute fiction
35 populaire, et l'on a parfois l'impression que quand on chante les
36 louanges d'un livre dit 'traduisible' on fait par là l'abstraction de l'aspect
37 littéraire. Un des collègues du Lord Archer a expliqué récemment que

38 celui-ci méritait la description de 'bon écrivain' en ce qu'il sait oublier
39 les mots pour se concentrer sur la tâche principale, celle cinéma-
40 tographique.
41   On pourrait bien sûr affirmer que 'Les plus grands écrivains ont créé
42 de grands personnages, de grandes personnalités, facilement différenti-
43 ables des mots à travers lesquels ils ont été présentés initialement — Don
44 Quichotte et Sancho Panchez, à titre d'exemple. On croyait naguère
45 connaître Dickens par le simple fait de posséder la collection complète
46 des cartes de cigarette afffichant le portrait des personnages divers. Ou
47 bien, on écoute La Shéhérazade de Rimski Korsakov et l'on croit avoir
48 lu les Mille et une Nuits.
49   L'important, c'est que nous avons tendance à croire connaître de la
50 littérature étrangère simplement parce qu'un si grand nombre d'oeuvres
51 ont été traduites. On prétend qu'il suffit de lire la traduction d'un roman
52 pour connaître l'oeuvre. La poésie est tout naturellement différente,
53 puisque la poésie ne consiste en rien que des mots. Voici un exemple
54 personnel de la manière dont notre conception de nos connaissances de
55 la littérature du monde peut se révéler fausse.
56   Il y a quelques ans, je vivais dans un quartier de Rome qui s'appelle
57 Trastavere. A l'entrée de ce quartier juste à côté du pont Garibaldi, il se
58 trouve une statue d'un homme au costume du 19e siècle avec un chapeau
59 haut de forme. Il s'agit d'un poète, un certain Giuseppe Gioacchino Belli,
60 très connu aux habitants de Trastavere et aux autres Romains, mais
61 personne d'autre ne le connaît. Pourquoi? L'on n'a jamais traduit les
62 oeuvres de Belli en anglais pour la simple raison qu'il n'écrivait pas en
63 italien mais dans un dialecte connu par les seuls Romains, à savoir, le
64 dialecte romain, le romanesco. Celui-ci est le dialecte des rues, des
65 gouttières; il est grossier, obscène, blasphématoire, mais c'est ce que
66 parlent les Romains, et Belli a entrepris de produire trois tômes de
67 sonnets, dans un style pètrarquiste classique et agressif, qui était pour-
68 tant chargé des qualités romaines du blasphème et de l'obscénité, à
69 travers lequel il a noté pour l'histoire l'esprit de Rome.
70   Il y a de rares occasions où une traduction devient plus grande que
71 l'original, ce qui est arrivé au Rabelais de Sir Thomas Urquhart. C'est
72 comme si le français du temps de Rabelais n'était pas capable de sup-
73 porter le fardeau onéreux de l'obscénité et de la scatologie que saurait
74 lui donner un Ecossais en état d'ivresse. Il y a aussi des originaux qui
75 tremblent devant la traduction. Voici ce qui est arrivé, selon les Alle-
76 mands, avec leur propre traduction de Shakespeare. Ils sont d'avis que
77 la traduction de Shakespeare par Schlegel est supérieure à l'original, ce
78 qui est vrai dans une certaine mesure.
79   Eh bien, une traduction peut raviver une langue et une culture, et il

n'est guère contestable que le Shakespeare de Schlegel ait ravivé non
seulement la littérature allemande mais aussi la musique allemande.
Ainsi, il est possible de considérer la traduction comme moyen d'in-
augurer une nouvelle ère dans une littérature indigène.
    Je veux conclure par traiter d'un aspect de la traduction non-littéraire,
celui du doublage des films. La façon la plus habituelle d'écouter un film
étranger, du moins en Europe, c'est de souffrir l'illusion que les acteurs
sur l'écran sont en train de parler la langue de l'audience. L'autre façon,
toujours la meilleure, c'est d'écouter le dialogue original avec une traduction sur l'écran en forme de sous-titres. Dans des communautés
multi-lingues, telles la Malaisie, la seconde méthode est la seule pratica-
ble. Du point de vue esthétique, le doublage est difficile à défendre,
puisque la modulation de la voix fait partie importante des outils artis-
tiques de l'acteur.
    La confusion des langues mène à la confusion de tout effort de
civilisation. Cette confusion est authentique, et elle se trouve entièrement
enracinée dans cet organe d'une désobéissance rusée et diabolique qu'est
la langue. Je ne crois pas que Babel puisse jamais se déconstruire et c'est
pour cela que des gens comme moi-même continueront de donner des
dissertations très confuses au sujet du problème de la traduction. Aucun
évêque, aussi souvent qu'il soit traduit (= transféré) ne saurait conjurer
cette malédiction.

Anthony Burgess: Extraits du reportage, en forme abrégée, d'un
discours inaugural présenté lors du festival de la littérature de
Cheltenham, 1993.

1. (Note paru en tête de l'article: 'M Burgess est décédé cette semaine. Il a fait
   part recemment, dans une addresse publique, de ses réflexions concernant
   le rôle perturbant du traducteur').
2. L'anglais emploie ici le mot 'translation' (traduction) là où le français exige
   le mot 'transfert'.
3. Deux des personnages du 'Songe d'une nuit d'été' de Shakespeare. D'après
   le texte source de Burgess c'est le personnage de Snug (Etriqué) qui s'adresse
   à Bottom, tandis que d'après la traduction c'est Lecoin (anglais — Peter
   Quince). En effet, d'après *The Complete Works of William Shakespeare* (oeuvres
   complètes), Spring Books, London 1970, c'est le traducteur français qui a
   raison et non pas M. Burgess.
4. Traduction de F.V. Hugo, revue par Yves Florentine et Elisabeth Duret, avec
   annotations par Yves Florentine, Livre de Poche.
5. Écrivains contemporains.

6. Noms de pays fictifs, tirés peut-être d'un film avec l'acteur anglais Peter Sellers, intitulé *The Mouse that Roared* ('La souris qui rugit' — traduction littérale: il se peut qu'il y ait un titre officiel en français que je n'ai pas pu découvrir).

Prêcher la doctrine de la communauté

1   Le concept de la 'communauté' fait soudain figure de Grande Idée pour
2   tout homme politique. M Tony Blair, leader présomptif du parti Travail-
3   liste, a placé ce concept au coeur de son manifeste, paru le 23 juin. Dans
4   un nouveau tract John Gray, philosophe conservateur, regrette que les
5   forces du marché puissent 'troubler les communautés et les institutions
6   traditionnelles légitimes'. Dans un autre nouveau tract intitulé 'le Con-
7   servatisme civique' et publié par la Fondation du Marché Social, M
8   David Willetts, ancien philosophe et partisan loyal de Mme Thatcher,
9   annonce 'l'effondrement du néolibéralisme comme force intellectuelle
10 importante'. L'état de santé des institutions civiques trouble M Willetts
11 tout comme M Gray. 'Le défi que doivent confronter nos deux princi-
12 paux partis politiques est de formuler une série cohérente de politiques
13 qui démontrera que... l'action collective doit y jouer un rôle, mais que
14 cette action collective ne doit pas forcément être une action étatique.
15 Voilà que la course est partie', écrit-il.
16   Non pas que le concept de la communauté soit quelque chose d'inno-
17 vateur dans la vie politique. Du côté des Conservateurs, ce concept
18 retrouve ses origines dans l'oeuvre d'Edmund Burke[1] avec les 'petits
19 platons' qu'il croyait être à la base d'une société ayant un bon fonction-
20 nement. Du côté des Travaillistes, il remonte au socialisme chrétien —
21 au sujet duquel le discours de M Blair devient évangélique — et au
22 mouvement des associations co-opératives. Même le parti Libéral a
23 ressorti ce concept aux années 70 avec l'idée de la 'politique communau-
24 taire', bien que celle-ci ne s'exprimât de manière pratique qu'au moyen
25 des revendications des égouts plus propres.
26   Personne ne devrait non plus se laisser surprendre par le renouveau
27 d'intérêt actuel envers l'idée de la communauté. De nos jours le peuple
28 britannique est peu content. Une des causes de ce mécontentement, c'est
29 le sentiment toujours croissant d'insécurité soulevé par des changements
30 rapides et fondamentaux, dont les victimes sont les classes moyennes
31 qui craignent la perte de leurs emplois autant que le fait l'ouvrier d'usine.
32 Un autre facteur est un cynisme largement répandu, non seulement
33 concernant le gouvernement de John Major mais aussi à l'égard de la
34 capacité potentielle de n'importe lequel gouvernement à mitiger cette
35 insécurité. Dans toute cette confusion de cynisme et de soucis, le mot
36 bien chaleureux et vague de 'communauté' brille comme un phare.
37   Pour les hommes politiques du parti Travailliste, ce mot évoque des

38 visions des années 40, des rues longées de maisons rangées en ligne et
39 accrochées les unes aux autres: des visions aussi d'un peuple pauvre
40 mais honnête, des mères de famille qui vont emprunter du sucre l'une à
41 l'autre,[2] des 'bobbies'[3] à bicyclette qui poursuivent les petits délinquents
42 pour leur filer deux claques, le tout enveloppé dans le confort que leur
43 apporte l'état providence nouveau-né. (Ils oublient volontiers que ceux
44 de la génération qui avait grandi dans de telles communautés accablan-
45 tes ont saisi la première occasion pour s'enfuir.) Les Conservateurs par
46 contre pensent aux villages des années 50 où le seigneur de village
47 bienveillant et le vicaire de paroisse règnaient sur des habitants bien
48 conscients de leur statut social, à une époque où il y avait encore des
49 'crumpets'[4] à l'heure du thé anglais. (Les gens se sont échappés de ces
50 villages pour aller dans les grandes villes et les banlieues, à la recherche
51 d'un comportement sexuel libre, de la consommation des drogues et de
52 la musique 'rock and roll'.) Chaque vision répond aux angoisses actuels
53 en évoquant des paradis d'antan, tout en faisant peu de cas de la
54 disparition de ces paradis sont disparus pour des raisons entièrement
55 valables.

56   Les deux côtés proposent des explications différents de la cause des
57 sentiments de mécontentement actuels. Pour le parti Travailliste (et pour
58 M Gray aussi), ces sentiments sont dûs à une concentration unilatérale
59 sur le marché libre, avec pour résultat une cécité répréhensible en ce qui
60 concerne les devoirs réciproques de l'individu envers son prochain ainsi
61 qu'envers la société au plan plus large; avec, en plus, une philosophie de
62 chacun pour soi, moi, maintenant, parmi les symptômes de laquelle
63 figurent le crime, la dissolution du mariage et l'abus fraudulent de la
64 securité sociale.

65   M Willett refuse de condamner le marché libre. Il préfère rejeter la
66 blâme sur un état toujours archicentralisé et trop puissant dont le pou-
67 voir excessif fait saigner la force vitale des autres institutions
68 communautaires. Il en était ainsi, prétend-il, même pendant la décennie
69 nominalement anti-état des années 80. Même à cette époque, l'état avait
70 imposé de nouveaux règlements: par exemple, sur les administrateurs
71 des associations à but non lucratif, ce qui avait découragé la participation
72 des volontaires; de surcroît, de nouveaux règlements gouvernant l'hy-
73 giène alimentaire, limitaient la gamme des repas pour livraison à
74 domicile pour les retraités.[5] M Willetts plaidoye pour que le localisme,
75 le volontarisme et la dérégulation viennent suppléer au marché libre; un
76 genre de Thatcherisme avec une plus-valeur.

77   Quand les historiens se référeront à notre époque, il est bien possible
78 qu'ils attribuent aux deux points de vue une valeur égale. Le grand
79 sociologue américain, Daniel Bell prétendait déjà en 1976, dans 'Les

80 contradictions culturelles du capitalisme', que 'les dilemmes économ-
81 iques auxquels doivent faire face les sociétés occidentales sont
82 attribuables au fait que nous avons cherché à allier des appétits bour-
83 geois lesquels résistent à toute tentative de limiter l'acquisivité, soit
84 moralement soit par imposition fiscale; une politique démocratique qui,
85 de plus en plus souvent et de façon compréhensible, exige un niveau de
86 service social et des droits sociaux toujours accroissant; et un éthos
87 individualiste qui tout au mieux défend l'idée de la liberté individuelle,
88 et qui, au pis aller, s'esquive des responsabilités et des sacrifices sociaux
89 qu'exige une société communautaire.
90   Dans toute cette liste, il est probable que M Blair ne favorise pas
91 l'individualisme égoïste. M Willetts se permet certes de se plaindre des
92 exigences du corps politique auprès des fonds publics. Mais l'essentiel,
93 ce n'est pas que l'un ou l'autre menace le succès économique ou social.
94 C'est la combinaison des trois facteurs qui semble donner lieu au mécon-
95 tentement.
96   M Blair jouit du luxe de faire partie de l'opposition. Il peut se permet-
97 tre de plaider le cas d'une économie du marché allant de pair avec un
98 socialisme redéfini. Qui plus est, les contradictions entre ces deux con-
99 cepts pourraient bien passer inaperçues, grâce à sa façon souriante et
00 éloquente de les présenter.
01   Il existe néanmoins bien des contradictions. Considérons les exi-
02 gences d'une économie du marché palpitante d'activité: une main-
03 d'oeuvre mobile; des entrepreneurs ambitieux prêts à travailler 24
04 heures sur 24 afin de gagner plus d'argent; de la concurrence, des
05 licenciements et des primes de rendement. Considérons également les
06 exigences des communautés stables: des gens qui restent sur place, des
07 volontaires habiles ayant du temps et de l'énergie pour se dévouer à un
08 effort pour le bien commun, de la co-opération, de la sécurité de l'emploi
09 et des mesures généreuses de protection sociale supplémentaire. Dans
10 tous les pays du monde les gouvernements luttent avec ces contradic-
11 tions, la plupart d'entre eux étant loin d'être convaincus de la possibilité
12 de jouir des deux en même temps. Le charme de M Blair pour le peuple
13 britannique réside dans l'avis positif qu'il avance quant à cette possi-
14 bilité. On sera tenté de le croire; le concept de la communauté peut bien
15 être la Grande Idée tant recherchée par le parti Travailliste pour attirer
16 les voix électorales. Cependant, une fois au pouvoir et le moment venu
17 pour remplir la tâche dure de formuler des politiques pratiques, le
18 concept de la communauté pourrait bien s'avérer n'être qu'encore un
19 devis décevant du démagogue.

Un article de Bagehot, publié dans *The Economist*, le 25 juin 1994, p. 33.

1. Philosophe britannique du 18e siècle qui fut écrivain politologue.
2. Metaphore, dans la langue source, pour l'aide réciproque que se donnent les voisins dans les communautés défavorisées.
3. Surnom affectueux que l'on donne au gendarme local qui font la patrouille à pied à travers les rues.
4. Sorte de crêpe rotie ou grillée.
5. Service offert aux retraités de faible revenu, assuré par des volontaires.

Définir une politique commune
de l'immigration

1   L'approche d'un concept aussi insaisissable que la 'politique européenne
2   de l'immigration' s'avère constituer un exercice pénible. Il serait com-
3   plètement impossible de se lancer dans une telle opération sans tenter
4   au préalable de définir les trois termes du titre, de façon à rendre possible
5   quelque description d'un concept autrement indescriptible.

6   – que signifie 'européenne'? Dans le cadre de cet article, il est logique
7   d'entendre par l'adjectif 'européenne' les 12 Etats membres de la
8   Communauté européenne, étant donné, notamment, que jusqu'à
9   présent aucune autre entité majeure n'a réellement tenté collective-
10   ment de mettre en place quelque chose qui puisse mériter le nom
11   de 'politique d'immigration'. Cependant, 'européenne' peut aussi
12   être utilisé dans le contexte plus large 'de l'Atlantique à l'Oural',
13   auquel cas l'examen des questions liées aux migrations prendrait
14   une toute autre dimension.

15   – qu'est-ce-que l'"immigration'? Si l'on limite la définition d'"europ-
16   éenne' à l'Europe occidentale, il est également possible de limiter
17   la définition de l'"immigration' au phénomène de personnes
18   désirant ou tentant d'entrer dans le territoire considéré. Mais si le
19   champ géographique est élargi au point d'inclure tout le continent
20   européen, la définition doit être étendu afin de prendre en compte
21   le phénomène séparé de personnes désirant se déplacer hors de la
22   région considérée. Ce sujet plus large est peut-être mieux défini par
23   le terme de migration, qui échappe, presque par définition, à
24   l'application du mot 'politique'.

25   – qu'est-ce-qu'une 'politique'? Ce terme doit, dans le cadre de notre
26   discussion, être interprété au sens large. Une définition rigoureuse
27   risquerait de déboucher sur la conclusion que le titre lui-même est
28   beaucoup trop ambitieux. Le nombre de pays qui peuvent être
29   considérés comme ayant une véritable 'politique d'immigration'
30   (comprise dans le sens d'une recherche active de personnes dis-
31   posées à peupler et à devenir citoyens de l'un de ces pays), est très
32   limité et ne comprend certainement aucun pays européen. Dans le
33   sens d'une telle définition, probablement seuls les vastes espaces
34   géographiques du Nouveau Monde (les Amériques et l'Australie)
35   et le cas particulier d'Israël pourraient revendiquer une ambition
36   aussi extraordinaire qu'une 'politique d'immigration'. Afin de
37   justifier l'utilisation du terme 'politique' dans le contexte européen,

38   sa définition doit être élargie pour comprendre les réactions dis-
39   persées et souvent improvisées face aux pressions changeantes
40   (allant de l'incitation active à l'afflux de main d'oeuvre immigrée
41   dans les années 50 et 60 aux politiques actuelles plus orientées sur
42   la fermeture des frontières) ainsi que la tentative de les réunir sous
43   la forme de ce qui l'on pourrait apeller une 'politique'.
44   Ainsi, afin de donner un certain contenu au concept de politique
45   européenne d'immigration, dans cet article, l'expression sera utilisée
46   pour couvrir les actions que les Etats membres de la CE ont entrepris (*sic*)
47   en vue de développer une approche coordonnée de la question relative
48   aux ressortissants des pays tiers présents dans l'un des Etats membres
49   ou désireux de s'y établir.
50
51   **La nécessité d'une réponse commune**
52   Qu'est-ce-qui a poussé les pays de la Communauté européenne à
53   chercher aujourd'hui à tâtons une politique de l'immigration de manière
54   collective, alors que pendant de nombreuses années, des siècles en fait,
55   l'immigration ne faisait que 'se produire', sans que quiconque ne res-
56   sente vraiment le besoin de l'organiser dans une doctrine politique. Une
57   combinaison de facteurs pourrait l'expliquer:
58   – Au cours de la deuxième moitié du 20ème siècle une certaine
59   stabilité des frontières nationales s'était établie d'elle-même — du
60   moins jusqu'aux bouleversements récents et à l'émergence de nou-
61   velles républiques dans l'ex-Yougoslavie, à la dissolution de
62   l'Union soviétique en de nouveaux Etats et à la division de la
63   Tchécoslovaquie. La majeure partie du monde, et notamment du
64   monde industrialisé, est actuellement organisée de façon telle que
65   les gouvernements tiennent à disposer d'un droit d'intervention et
66   de contrôle sur la question de savoir qui aura le droit de résider,
67   de travailler et en fin de compte d'acquérir la nationalité sur leur
68   territoire. Le besoin de mettre en place une sorte de politique
69   nationale de l'immigration se fait ressentir partout, et particulière-
70   ment en Europe.
71   – Cependant ceci a été ajourné en raison d'un certain nombre de facteurs
72   de distorsion importants: les guerres et leurs conséquences; mais aussi
73   en temps de paix, des pressions économiques dans l'Europe occiden-
74   tale de l'après-guerre ont initialement conduit à une approche de
75   laissez-faire relatif en matière d'immigration, qui semblait convenir à
76   tout le monde dans une période de développement économique
77   soutenu, mais qui est devenue de plus en plus inacceptable aux
78   yeux de l'opinion publique et politique lorsque les taux de
79   chômage ont commencé à grimper, ce qui a entraîné des demandes

80   pressantes pour des 'politiques' de contrôle de l'immigration.
81   – La mutation imperceptible et non planifiée de l'immigration
82   temporaire (au sens de gagner de l'argent dans un pays puis de
83   retourner à la maison plus tard pour le dépenser) en une immigra-
84   tion 'permanente', avec tous les risques de constitution de ghettos
85   et de désordres locaux que cela comporte.
86   – Le ralentissement de l'émigration européenne en direction du
87   Nouveau-Monde et la transformation progressive de tous les pays
88   d'Europe occidentale, à l'exception de l'Irlande, en pays de nette
89   immigration.
90   – La chute du rideau de fer qui a mis le monde libre, plus particu-
91   lièrement l'Europe occidentale, face aux conséquences de sa propre
92   rhétorique. Après avoir longtemps houspillé les régimes commu-
93   nistes parce qu'ils contrariaient la volonté de leurs citoyens de se
94   rendre à l'Ouest, l'Ouest a été soudainement confronté à l'ouver-
95   ture des portes de sortie à l'Est, alors que les portes d'entrée à
96   l'Ouest n'étaient pas prêtes.
97   – La volonté déclarée et largement soutenue de la Communauté
98   européenne pour éliminer ses contrôles aux frontières internes,
99   c'est-à-dire de se priver d'un instrument essentiel capable aux yeux
100   des gouvernements comme de l'opinion publique d'exercer une
101   sorte de contrôle sur les flux d'immigration.
102
103   **Accès interdit aux étrangers**
104   Ce même lien avec la volonté d'une Communauté sans frontières
105   internes a eu une conséquence regrettable mais peut-être inévitable. Il a
106   entraîné que presque tous les premiers efforts de la Communauté pour
107   initier une politique d'immigration ont paru avoir comme objectif de
108   maintenir les étrangers à l'extérieur, en partie parce que de toute façon
109   pour d'autres raisons, essentiellement économiques, cette tendance était
110   de plus en plus présente dans les politiques nationales; et en partie parce
111   que les Etats membres étaient à la recherche de moyens pour garantir
112   que les contrôles à leur frontière extérieur commune seraient aussi
113   efficaces que ceux auxquels ils renonçaient entre eux.

Adrian Fortescue, Directeur en charge de la Coopération dans les domaines de la Justice et des Affaires Intérieures, au Secrétariat général de
la Commission des Communautés européennes.

Extrait d'un article paru dans: 'Vers une Politique Européenne de l'Immigration', publication de l'Institut Philip Morris (PMI), Bruxelles,
octobre 1993.

Emplois et compétitivité: l'approche britannique

1 En mars 1994, le Groupe des Sept principaux pays industrialisés a tenu
2 une conférence à Detroit sur le thème de l'emploi. Depuis 30 ans,
3 plusieurs pays industriels connaisssent une croissance simultanée de
4 leur revenu national et de leur taux de chômage. La réalité est venue
5 invalider le vieux concept selon lequel la croissance peut à elle seule
6 porter remède au chômage et à la pauvreté. Il y a actuellement trois
7 personnes sur 40 qui sont sans travail, là où il n'y en avait qu'une
8 auparavant.
9   Les coûts sociaux d'un chômage aussi important et le potentiel inu-
10 tilisé sont à la fois inestimables et inacceptables. Aucun pays industrial-
11 isé n'est à l'abri de ce problème. Chacun sait que nous devons tous
12 rechercher des moyens de mieux faire. Mais chacun connaît aussi la triste
13 réalité: il n'existe ni réponse facile, ni recette miracle.
14   Par conséquent, la conférence de G7 sur l'emploi constituait une
15 occasion de mettre en commun le savoir-faire et l'expérience de nos pays
16 sur les moyens efficaces de lutte contre le chômage et de création durable
17 d'emplois. La conférence a permis d'élargir et d'approfondir la réflexion
18 sur ces politiques. Ces sujets seront repris et développés au cours du
19 prochain sommet du G7 à Naples en juillet 1994, lorsque les chefs de
20 gouvernement discuteront à nouveau des politiques de lutte contre le
21 chômage.
22
23 **Des bases communes**
24   Selon toute évidence, les principaux pays industrialisés ont beaucoup
25 en commun. Il nous incombe de créer les conditions de la croissance qui
26 favorisent le développement des entreprises et la création des emplois.
27 Cela signifie qu'il faut à la fois endiguer l'inflation de façon durable et
28 veiller à la saine gestion des finances publiques.
29   En même temps, chaque pays doit favoriser le libre-échange et garan-
30 tir que les marchés soient véritablement ouverts à la concurrence. En
31 accroissant la richesse et les emplois, le commerce oeuvre à l'intérêt
32 général, c'est pourquoi l'Accord du GATT doit être appliqué rapidement
33 et la raison pour laquelle il est tellement important d'éliminer les
34 derniers obstacles au Marché unique eeuropén.
35
36 **La perspective européenne**
37   Tout cela est important, mais c'est nous, en Europe, qui sommes

38 confrontés aux problèmes les plus graves. La plupart des pays de
39 l'OCDE ont un taux de chômage élevé mais ce que subit l'Europe n'est
40 rien de moins qu'une véritable crise de l'emploi: 20 millions de
41 chômeurs, dont environ la moitié au chômage depuis plus d'un an.
42   Nous savons en grande partie comment remédier à cette crise. Réuni
43 à Bruxelles en décembre dernier, le Conseil européen a approuvé trois
44 objectifs majeurs fondés sur l'emploi. Les chefs de gouvernement de l'UE
45 se sont accordés à dire que, pour combattre le chômage, il convient de
46 préserver un environnement économique stable, d'assurer la compéti-
47 tivité internationale de la Communauté et son ouverture au commerce
48 international et de réformer les marchés de l'emploi.
49   Savoir ce qu'il convient de faire est une chose, l'appliquer en est une
50 autre. Notre expérience, ainsi que celle de l'OCDE et d'autres pays, nous
51 ont montré que la mauvaise performance de l'Europe en matière d'em-
52 ploi et de chômage est imputable à la trop grande rigidité des marchés
53 de l'emploi et aux coûts non-salariaux excessifs liés à l'embauche. Des
54 salaires rigides, des coûts non-salariaux de l'emploi élevés et des régle-
55 mentations inutiles ont rendu de nombreux emplois anti-économiques
56 et ont érigé trop d'obstacles à la création de nouveaux postes de travail.
57 En Europe, nous avons trop privilégié les intérêts à court terme des
58 travailleurs et beaucoup trop négligé les besoins de ceux qui sont au
59 chômage.
60   Aussi, en Europe devons-nous passer des paroles aux actes pour
61 réformer le marché de l'emploi. C'est ce que nous tentons de faire depuis
62 1979 au RU.
63
64 **L'approche britannique**
65   En Grande-Bretagne nous nous sommes engagés à réduire le chômage
66 de façon durable. Notre approche repose sur une inflation limitée, des
67 finances publiques saines, le libre-échange et la concurrence. Au cours
68 des 13 dernières années nous nous sommes également efforcés d'encour-
69 ager l'entreprise et d'améliorer le fonctionnement de tous les types de
70 marchés. Et le marché de l'emploi, plus que tout autre, s'est révélé un
71 terrain fondamental de nos réformes.
72   Le marché de l'emploi est très particulier: c'est un marché fait de
73 personnes, un marché qui conditionne leur niveau de vie, qui implique
74 leurs compétences et leurs ambitions ainsi qu'un marché où se rencon-
75 trent les demandeurs d'emploi et les employeurs potentiels. Nombre
76 d'espoirs reposent sur le marché de l'emploi. Les marchés de l'emploi
77 inefficaces coûtent cher en termes de chômage et ce sont eux qui portent
78 la responsabilité de la crise en Europe occidentale, dans la mesure où nos
79 économies ont dû se battre pour rester concurrentielles.

80   En 1979, la situation en Grande Bretagne était peu différente. Il y avait
81   trop d'obstacles à l'emploi et trop peu de motivations pour que les
82   employeurs créent de nouvelles opportunités d'emploi.
83
84   **Rendre le marché du travail plus efficace.**
85   Au cours des 15 dernières années, nous nous sommes employés peu
86   à peu à inverser cette situation. Pour y parvenir, nos réformes ont plus
87   particulièrement mis l'accent sur trois éléments: améliorer la capacité des
88   chômeurs à prétendre effectivement à des emplois et encourager les
89   investissements en formation, tant de la part des individus que celle des
90   employeurs.
91   Un marché du travail véritablement efficace récompense, développe
92   et encourage les compétences. Il soutient la croissance économique, ce
93   qui conduit à une production plus importante, à la création d'emplois et
94   à la baisse du chômage. La création d'emplois est plus importante
95   lorsque les salaires et les aménagements du travail s'adaptent rapide-
96   ment aux pressions du marché et aux performances des entreprises et
97   des personnes. Les employeurs sont plus enclins à recruter davantage
98   de personnel s'ils peuvent le faire sans engager de frais excessifs, qui sont
99   irréductibles en cas de modification de la demande des consommateurs
100   ou de difficultés liées à une crise industrielle accidentelle.
101   Notre réforme des relations industrielles a abouti à ce qu'aujourd'hui,
102   au Royaume Uni, nous sommes arrivés au minimum de pertes de
103   journées de travail pour cause de grève jamais enregistré au cours du
104   siècle. Nous avons laissé la liberté aux employeurs et aux employés de
105   négocier entre eux leurs salaires et leurs propres conditions de travail et
106   nous avons encouragé de nouvelles formules de rémunération plus
107   décentralisées et plus flexibles.
108   Nous nous sommes débarrassés de ces réglementations inutiles qui
109   entravaient la création d'emplois tant désirée. Et nous avons fait en sorte
110   que la réglementation n'écarte pas les diverses possibilités d'emploi
111   flexible tels les emplois à temps partiel, que les employeurs veulent créer,
112   et surtout que des millions de personnes sont clairement prêtes à accep-
113   ter.
114   Améliorer l'efficacité du marché de l'emploi nécessite un système de
115   protection sociale solide, un système dont l'objectif soit s'aider ceux qui
116   en ont le plus besoin et qui entretienne des motivations individuelles au
117   travail. C'est la raison pour laquelle notre système comprend maintenant
118   des allocations pour les travailleurs à faible revenu qui ont une famille.
119   Actuellement, presque tout le monde a davantage intérêt à travailler
120   qu'à rester au chômage.
121   En même temps, nous avons préservé les lois essentielles de protec-

22 tion de l'emploi. Il faut trouver un équilibre entre les pressions du
23 marché et les normes réglementaires. Il est nécesaire de maintenir un
24 certain niveau de réglementation. A titre d'example, le système britan-
25 nique de santé et de sécurité sur le lieu de travail est parmi les meilleurs
26 au monde et nous sommes fermement décidés à ce qu'il le reste. Nous
27 disposons également de toute une gamme de normes juridiques pour les
28 travailleurs. Néanmoins, l'enseignement à retenir est qu'une réglemen-
29 tation superflue peut aller à l'encontre des intérêts des personnes qu'elle
30 est censée protéger en réduisant les possibilités d'emploi qui leur sont
31 offertes.

Extrait d'un article de David Hunt, Secrétaire d'Etat à l'Emploi du
Royaume Uni lors de la publication de cet article dans 'L'emploi et la
compétitivité: L'Europe face au dilemme', L'Institut Philip Morris (PMI),
Bruxelles, juin 1994.

Désordre Public

L'informatique a créé une sinistre vague de crimes d'un nouveau type, mais que fait-on pour les prévenir? Gus Chandler mène l'enquête...

Des employés de bureau anonymes qui ne font pas vraiment de mal à qui que ce soit — c'est souvent la fausse image qu'a le public des criminels de l'informatique. La vérité est cependant bien différente. Imaginez une grande ville américaine sans système téléphonique pendant des heures, ou des jours: le secret de l'anarchie? Eh bien, c'est ce qui a failli se passer dans les villes d'Atlanta en Géorgie, de Denver dans Colorado et de Newark dans le New Jersey, le 4 juillet 1989. Un pirate informatique est entré par effraction dans un système de commutateurs (central de routage téléphonique) et y a installé des 'bombes logicielles' qui étaient programmées pour 'exploser' le jour de la célébration de l'indépendance américaine. Heureusement, le désastre ne s'est pas produit cette fois-là: la compagnie téléphonique avait repéré l'attaque juste à temps et, après qu'elle ait déployé des ressources importantes à travers les Etats-Unis pour vérifier tous les programmes d'échanges téléphoniques, l'incident était clos. Un exemple extrême? Peut-être, mais il illustre bien le désastre potentiel qui pourrait être causé par l'attaque d'un pirate informatique.

Piratage informatique

Le piratage informatique est né de la culture de la côte ouest des Etats-Unis à la fin des années 60–début des années 70. A cette époque, un certain nombre d'individus — connus sous le nom de 'Phreakers' — mettaient au point des moyens pour utiliser le système téléphonique américain gratuitement. En fait, les méthodes qu'ils utilisaient pour obtenir des appels gratuits étaient un jeu d'enfant. Le système téléphonique américain opérait, à l'époque, grâce à une tonalité d'une fréquence de 2600 hertz qui allumait et éteignait l'équipement de facturation. En envoyant un signal de cette fréquence au moment de la connection téléphonique, vous pouviez appeler n'importe quel numéro dans le monde, gratuitement. Au début, les Phreakers utilisaient un générateur de tonalité construit spécialement, appelé 'boîte bleue', ou 'boîte FM' entre confrères, pour créer le signal. Cependant, en 1970, il s'est trouvé qu'un fabriquant de céréales pour le petit-déjeuner offrait des sifflets pour enfants qui produisaient un signal de 2600 hertz. A partir de ce moment, les Phreakers n'ont plus eu besoin

38 des boîtes bleues pour créer le signal: ils n'avaient qu'à donner un coup
39 de sifflet pour obtenir un appel gratuit. Pour beaucoup, il n'y avait rien
40 de bien méchant à agir de sorte, ils le faisaient parce qu'ils pouvaient le
41 faire.
42   Avec la venue des ordinateurs personnels et des modems, les gens qui
43 utilisaient volontiers le téléphone gratuitement, se sont mis à forcer
44 l'accès aux ordinateurs appartenant à des corporations, ou au gouverne-
45 ment. Cette fois encore, leur motivation était (est elle est restée la même
46 pour les pirates modernes) le défi de pouvoir contourner le système. Très
47 peu de gens tentent de forcer l'accès à des réseaux informatiques dans
48 le but d'en retirer quelque chose — argent ou information —, ou de
49 causer des dommages prémédités, mais ils ont tendance à laisser des
50 indices pour que les utilisateurs sachent qu'ils sont passés par là. C'est
51 en quelque sorte leur façon de marquer une propriété, comme les artistes
52 qui dessinent des graffitis le feraient.
53
54 **Acceder à tous les domaines**
55   Pirater un système informatique n'est, bien souvent, pas si difficile.
56 Bien que presque tous les systèmes commercialisés ont une sécurité pour
57 tenter de prévenir leur accès sans autorisation, ces contrôles peuvent
58 souvent être contournés par le pirate déterminé et informé.
59   La façon habituelle d'aborder le problème de sécurité est de délivrer
60 un code d'identité et un mot de passe aux utilisateurs autorisés. Les deux
61 codes doivent être entrés correctement pour obtenir l'accès au système.
62 Cependant, les mots de passe n'offrent qu'une protection limitée et, dans
63 le cas des ordinateurs digitaux VAX pendant plusieurs années dans les
64 années 80, ils n'offraient aucune sécurité. Le système central VAX a
65 longtemps été populaire auprès des gouvernements politique et mili-
66 taire américains. Bien que le système opérationnel VAX/VMS ait été créé
67 pour exécuter un contrôle de sécurité à chaque fois qu'un utilisateur
68 entrait dans le système, le programme avait un inconvénient qui lui était
69 fatal. Si un code d'identité incorrect ou un mot de passe était entré
70 incorrectement, l'utilisateur se voyait refuser l'accès au système, pas
71 d'inconvénient jusqu'ici. Cependant, si aucun code d'identité ou mot de
72 passe n'était donné, l'utilisateur n'avait qu'à appuyer sur la touche-
73 Retour à chaque demande de code et le système autorisait l'accès
74 immédiatement. C'est à cause de cet oubli important que VAX devint
75 une cible populaire auprès des pirates informatiques pendant plusieurs
76 années. Le problème fût finalement résolu en 1986 grâce à une nouvelle
77 version du programme informatique.
78   Bien qu'un mot de passe quelconque soit toujours mieux que pas de
79 mot de passe du tout, les gens choisissent souvent des mots de passe qui

80 peuvent être devinés rapidement, et les pirates sont des maîtres dans la
81 psychologie de la découverte de mots de passe.
82   Il y a encore peu de temps, il était très difficile de poursuivre en justice
83 un individu qui avait obtenu accès à un programme informatique sans
84 autorisation. Les autorités plaignantes devaient trouver des accusations
85 imaginaires telles que 'vol d'électricité'. Bien que le Congrès américain
86 ait voté la loi 'Fraude et Abus Informatiques' en 1986 pour protéger les
87 installations informatiques américaines contre les pirates, il nous a fallu
88 attendre jusqu'en 1994 en Grande Bretagne: la loi 'Usage Abusif de
89 l'Informatique' a été passée au Parlement comme projet de loi d'un
90 parlementaire privé, pour la protection legislative.
91   Le premier cas de piratage qui ait fait du bruit en Grande Bretagne (et
92 également celui qui a persuadé les législateurs à agir) était celui de Steve
93 Gold et Robert Schiffren. Ensemble, ils ont piraté le service Prestel de
94 British Telecom et ont réussi à accéder à la messagerie de Prince Philip.
95 Ils ne l'ont pas fait avec de mauvaises intentions en tête, ils voulaient
96 simplement explorer le système. L'action la plus criminelle qu'ils aient
97 commise était de changer le taux de change de la Livre Sterling et du
98 Dollar dans le secteur financier de Prestel. Pendant un moment, la Livre
99 Sterling valait $50. Gold et Schiffren ont finalement tous deux été retrou-
100 vés après une enquête de police compliquée et ont été poursuivis en
101 justice, accusés de fraude. Deux ans après que le dossier soit allé jusqu'à
102 la Chambre des Communes, ils ont été acquittés: le juge a trouvé que la
103 loi telle qu'elle était alors, ne couvrait pas les actions des compères.
104 Schiffren est maintenant un braconnier devenu garde-chasse, dirigeant
105 une société de consultants en sécurité informatique.
106   La plupart des pirates le sont pour le jeu, pour l'exaltation de con-
107 tourner le système, plutôt que pour l'argent. Les attaques contre les
108 sociétés dans le but de faire de l'argent sont rares. Des organisations-
109 fantômes de pirates existent, à travers lesquelles les cambrioleurs
110 digitaux échangent les détails de leurs activités. Durant ces dernières
111 années, la plus connues de ces organisations était La Légion du Destin
112 aux Etats-Unis et Le Club Informatique Chaos en Allemagne. La plupart
113 des informations sont échangées à travers des tableaux d'affichage mais,
114 depuis quelques années, le Club Chaos a également organisé des assem-
115 blées annuelles auxquelles participent des pirates du monde entier.

Extrait d'un article de Gus Chandler, *Computer Shopper Magazine*, juin
1994, pp. 456–458.

Un docteur à l'écran

Des vidéos peuvent aider les patients à estimer les risques et les avantages d'un traitement

1 Lorsque Gordon Rock a commencé à avoir des problèmes de prostate, il
2 a réalisé qu'il en savait autant sur la glande prostate que sur l'hypotala-
3 mus. Et lorsque son docteur lui a suggéré qu'il pourrait avoir besoin
4 d'une opération, il s'est senti aussi prêt pour cette opération qu'un joueur
5 de football pour un remplacement de la hanche.

6 Mais Monsieur Rock a eu de la chance: il a eu accès aux résultats des
7 recherches les plus récentes sur les avantages et les inconvénients de
8 l'opération. Chaque année en Grande Bretagne, 30.000 hommes subis-
9 sent une opération pour réduire la taille de leur prostate qui grossit
10 souvent à un âge avancé, rendant l'action d'uriner difficile; mais pas tous
11 ne sont pas bien informés des risques encourus et des solutions autres
12 que la chirurgie. Il est devenu commun pour les chirurgiens de dire à
13 leurs patients qu'ils ont besoin d'une opération et qu'on leur commu-
14 niquera une date pour admission à l'hôpital aussitôt que possible. Un
15 jeune docteur explique les risques encourus la nuit précédant l'opéra-
16 tion, et écrit normalement dans le dossier médical 'DAH' pour 'Donné
17 Avertissement Habituel'.

18 Une organisation américaine, la Fondation pour l'Information dans
19 les Décisions Médicales, a maintenant produit une vidéo 'inter-active'
20 qui souligne les risques liés à l'opération immédiate et ses avantages, et
21 fait la comparaison avec 'l'attente surveillée' (attendre avec un suivi
22 médical régulier), de sorte que les patients peuvent prendre leur décision
23 basée sur l'information reçue. La théorie sous-jacente est que les chirur-
24 giens ne donnent pas une image préconçue des risques possibles et des
25 avantages de l'opération. Pour eux, les opérations de la prostate sont
26 courantes, mais elles ne le sont pas pour les patients.

27 Les chercheurs de l'Ecole d'Hygiène et de Médecine Tropicale de
28 Londres utilisent la vidéo à l'hôpital de Ashford dans le Middlesex, pour
29 découvrir comment elle influence le choix des patients. Le projet, initiale-
30 ment supporté par le King's Fund Centre, est maintenant financé par le
31 Ministère de la Santé de North Thames. 'Je l'ai trouvée très utile', dit
32 Monsieur Rock, un assistant-concierge de 56 ans qui vit à Feltham, à
33 l'ouest de Londres. 'Elle m'a rassuré et m'a aidé à prendre ma décision'.

34 Au début, le programme ressemble à une vidéo normale sur un écran
35 de télévision ordinaire. Mais il est contrôlé par une platine laser 25
36 centimètres et peut être programmé avec les détails du patient (âge et

37 grâvité des symptômes) de sorte que l'information donnée ait rapport
38 avec le patient en question. Il a un écran tactile sur lequel le patient peut
39 indiquer ce qu'il désire savoir. Si par exemple il/elle veut en savoir plus
40 sur les traitements médicaux, il/elle peut appuyer sur la section 'Pour
41 en savoir plus' de l'écran. A la fin, il/elle reçoit un rapport imprimé
42 résumant toute cette information.

43   La preuve la plus parlante est sans doute le témoignage de deux
44 patients, l'un ayant été opéré, l'autre ayant choisi d'attendre un peu. Le
45 premier a expliqué qu'il était heureux de pouvoir de nouveau uriner
46 proprement après l'opération.

47   Son témoignage, cependant, n'a pas convaincu Monsieur Rock qui a
48 décidé qu'il préfèrait ne pas être opéré pour le moment. 'Les symptômes
49 ne viennent que de commencer pour moi. Je n'ai pas besoin de me lever
50 plusieurs fois dans la nuit, comme le font certains, alors j'ai décidé
51 d'attendre. La vidéo ne m'a pas fait peur. En fait, les risques encourus
52 par un homme de mon âge pour cette opération semblent minimaux.
53 Mais j'ai découvert que les effets de l'opération n'étaient pas perma-
54 nents. L'opération doit souvent être répétée après trois ans. Ceci m'a fait
55 penser que je ferais mieux d'attendre.'

56   'J'ai également trouvé l'information sur les différents traitements
57 médicaux intéressante, mais j'ai aussi l'impression qu'on ne les a pas
58 utilisés depuis suffisamment longtemps pour connaître tous leurs effets
59 secondaires. Alors j'ai décidé de ne pas les prendre. J'ai passé à peu près
60 une heure à regarder la vidéo. Vous avez du mal à imaginer qu'un
61 docteur puisse passer une heure entière avec vous, non? Ceci prouve que
62 je suis mieux informé quand je vois un médecin-consultant.'

63   Monsieur Rock n'est pas un exemple type: il a consulté son docteur
64 plutôt au début de ses problèmes dûs à une hyperplasia bénine de la
65 prostate (HBP), problèmes qui touchent plus de deux millions
66 d'hommes en Grande Bretagne (un homme sur trois entre 50 et 79 ans).
67 Mais ses réactions sur la vidéo sont, en quelque sorte, typiques: elle lui
68 a donné un doute sur les avantages de la chirurgie.

69   Ceci est courant. Aux Etats-Unis, où la vidéo a été passée à plus de
70 mille patients, la réaction a été d'attendre sous surveillance plutôt que
71 de choisir l'opération. Robert Maxwell, secrétaire du King's Fund, ex-
72 plique: 'Il s'avère que les patients sont plus hostiles au risque que le sont
73 leurs chirurgiens.'

74   Une telle découverte a des répercussions importantes sur le service
75 de la Santé: si les chirurgiens dépeignent la chirurgie trop rose, insistant
76 sur les avantages mais diminuant l'importance des risques, ils pour-
77 raient bien opérer plus souvent qu'il n'en est besoin. Si l'image donnée
78 aux patients était plus proche de la réalité, leurs nombre pourrait di-

minuer. Il n'y a aucun doute sur le fait que les organisations médico-sociales aux Etats-Unis utilisent ces vidéos inter-actives pour réduire le nombre des opérations effectuées.

Il est trop tôt pour dire exactement ce que le projet indiquera en Grande Bretagne, mais les premiers résultats suivent le modèle américain. Madame Jenny Stone, l'infirmière qui installe la machine pour les patients, dit que les commentaires sont positifs. Une proportion peu importante de patients — environ 4 pour cent — ont des difficultés à la comprendre. Nous pensons que c'est important, parce les contraintes qui nous sont imposées sont telles que nous n'avons pas le temps de nous asseoir près des patients et de tout leur expliquer. Nous avons vu des patients revenir pour nous dire qu'ils n'avaient jamais été prévenus que l'opération ne marchait pas à chaque fois.'

La vidéo insiste bien sur le fait que, même après l'opération, six pour cent des patients ont toujours des symptômes grâves et 18 pour cent des symptômes moins importants.

Madame Hilary Gilbert, responsable du projet 'Promouvoir le Choix du Patient' au King's Fund Centre, explique: 'Notre but est d'augmenter le volume d'informations objectives, basées sur des recherches, et de lecture simple pour les patients, parce que nos recherches montrent qu'il y a une pénurie à ce niveau.'

Un article de Annabel Ferriman paru dans *The Guardian*, le 4 janvier 1995.

Medecine inhumaine

Prendre le temps de s'arreter et de reflechir

1 'Ces derniers mois, j'ai été informé d'un grand nombre de cas de com-
2 portements déconcertants car insensibles et impolis, de la part de
3 médecins spécialistes et de praticiens généralistes vis-à-vis de leurs
4 malades. Puis-je suggérer de prévoir, en bonne place dans l'ordre du jour
5 des médecins, des cours pour leur rappeler (ou peut-être leur enseigner)
6 le comportement à adopter vis-à-vis de leurs malades.'
7   Cet extrait d'une lettre reçue récemment par le rédacteur en chef du
8 BMJ,[1] et les articles d'un esprit similaire (pages 1696, 1699, 1700), font
9 surgir des questions dérangeantes sur lesquelles nous pourrons réfléchir
10 pendant la période de Noël. L'excuse selon laquelle seules les mauvaises
11 nouvelles valent la peine d'être publiées ne prendra pas; de telles his-
12 toires deviennent trop ordinaires et contiennent tant de pratiques
13 cliniques actuelles qu'il semble que nous devenions une profession de
14 technocrates qui ne se soucient pas des autres.
15   En recherchant des solutions à ces problèmes, il est important de les
16 placer dans leur contexte historique. Sont-ils nouveaux? Rien ne m'a
17 jamais prouvé que les médecins du passé prenaient leur malades en main
18 beaucoup mieux que maintenant. Je me souviens encore, comme si j'y
19 étais, d'une de mes premières visites d'enseignement en tant qu'étudiant
20 en médecine, il y a plus de trente ans. Nous étions arrivés au pied du lit
21 d'un malade à qui on avait diagnostiqué un cancer du poumon non
22 opérable. Le chef de clinique très respecté qui dirigeait la visite s'éloigna
23 soudainement du lit et réunit la foule de membres du personnel et
24 d'étudiants au milieu de la salle dans ce qui donna l'allure d'une mêlée
25 de joueurs de football américain qui préparent leur prochain jeu. Les
26 diagnostic et pronostic fûrent discutés dans des chuchotements étouffés,
27 après quoi nous retournâmes près du lit, quelques banalités fûrent
28 échangées et nous continuâmes avec le malade suivant. Un tel comporte-
29 ment était courant à l'époque où j'étais étudiant. Et, comme cela a bien
30 été dépeint en page 1714, pendant des siècles les journalistes, caricatur-
31 istes, romanciers et auteurs dramatiques nous ont critiqués sévèrement
32 pour nos manières pompeuses, notre manque d'humanité et notre cruauté.
33 De telles critiques continuent, comme l'exemple nous en est donné dans
34 la récente pièce de théatre de Alan Bennett, *La Folie de Georges III*.[2]
35
36 **Les malades sont poussés aux limites**
37   Mais bien que les médecins aient toujours eu des moyens limités pour

traiter leurs malades humainement, il n'y a aucun doute sur le fait que
la scène médicale actuelle mette nos imperfections en lumière. L'oncolo-
gie, le sujet de deux des articles de la revue d'aujourd'hui, est un bon
exemple. Les malades sont souvent soumis aux protocoles de
chimiothérapie les plus intensifs, certains d'entre eux nécessitant que les
malades se retrouvent aux portes de la mort dans la tentative de supprimer leurs tumeurs. D'ici une centaine d'années, nous porterons
peut-être le même regard sur tout cela que celui que nous portons
aujourd'hui sur les saignées et les ventouses. Mais c'est ce que l'on pense
être le moyen le plus efficace actuellement pour traiter ces maladies; la
technique de 'raccommodage' dans presque tous les domaines de haute
technologie moderne pousse les malades à l'extrême de leur résistance,
et pas toujours pour des raisons qui répondent à une appréciation
conforme à ce que signifie la qualité de la vie.

Les problèmes de nos malades sont aggravés par nos systèmes
médico-sociaux actuels, lesquels ne sont pas adaptés au soutien de gens
très malades. Ceux qui souffrent de maladies chroniques pénibles ou de
maladies dans leur phase terminale ont besoin, par dessus tout, de
continuité dans les soins qu'ils reçoivent, c'est à dire de l'attention et de
l'amitié d'un médecin en qui ils peuvent apprendre à avoir confiance et
avec qui ils peuvent partager leurs espoirs et leurs craintes. Cependant
ce type de relation est bien trop peu souvent à leur disposition. Il existe
trop peu de médecins-consultants pour s'occuper du nombre croissant
de malades qui suivent des périodes de soins intensifs ou qui sont dans
la phase finale de leur maladie.

Pas de continuité

Parce que les jeunes médecins tournent constamment dans des programmes de formation différents, et parce que de nouvelles réglementations visent à limiter leurs heures de travail, il y a un manque de
continuité journalière dans les soins, à tous les niveaux subalternes. Des
équipes de médecins et d'infirmières qui changent continuellement
s'occupent des malades; un mode de soin qui s'étend aux consultations
de généralistes qui font que les chances des malades de toujours consulter leur propre médecin de famille sont tout aussi limitées.

Et les médecins et infirmières du frénétique Service National de la
Santé réorganisé passent de plus en plus de temps en réunion, à organiser leurs projets d'affaires et leurs contrats, et moins de temps avec leurs
patients; l'éfficacité directoriale et un défilé incroyablement rapide de
malades, bien qu'ils donnent des statistiques impressionnantes, ne sont
pas nécessairement le reflet de médecins qui prennent soin de leurs
patients. Dans le même temps, les malades et leur famille sont beaucoup

80 plus exigeants qu'ils ne l'étaient, et, non sans raison, comptent sur leurs
81 médecins pour leur offrir davantage de temps et d'explications. Il n'est
82 donc pas étonnant que l'accent soit mis sur les imperfections qui ne nous
83 lâchent pas depuis 2000 ans.
84   Dans quelle mesure nos défauts sont-ils le reflet du modèle de l'édu-
85 cation médicale? La plupart des critiques formulées à l'encontre des
86 médecins ne portent pas sur leur compétence clinique, mais elles sem-
87 blent plutôt refléter un manque de compétences élémentaires à
88 considérer les malades comme des humains, une pauvreté en commu-
89 nication, un manque d'amabilité, une insouciance, et, en bref, tous les
90 aspects de bons rapports entre individus que la société est en droit
91 d'exiger de ses médecins. Peut-on enseigner un tel état d'esprit? Et même
92 si on le pouvait, étant donné nos maigres résultats, qui les enseignera?
93   Les inquiétudes de ce type ont mené à des modifications radicales
94 dans l'éducation médicale de plusieurs pays. Par exemple, le Conseil
95 Général de Médecine suggère qu'on mette moins l'accent sur les sciences
96 de base, et davantage sur la morale, l'aptitude à communiquer et les
97 sciences sociales, avec un contact plus précoce avec les malades et leurs
98 familles. Beaucoup de gens conviendront que passer deux ans en com-
99 pagnie d'un cadavre n'est pas l'initiation la plus originale à une
100 profession qui nécessite, plus que toute autre, le développement d'apti-
101 tudes à parler aux gens qui souffrent.

Ceci représente la première partie d'un article de D.J. Weatherall, Regius
Professor of Medicine, University of Oxford, John Radcliffe Hospital,
paru dans *The British Medical Journal*, Vol. 309, pp. 1671–72, le 24–31
décembre 1994.

1. *British Medical Journal* — le journal britannique de la médecine (hebdo-
   madaire).
2. Pièce de théâtre qui, ayant connu un grand succès au théâtre londonien, s'est
   vu tourner en film en 1994.

La Mort Noire

John Hosken, journaliste et personnalité des média audiovisuelles, rappelle la Grande Peste. Il s'étonne de découvrir son existence persistente.

Trois voiliers regagnèrent le port de Gênes tant bien que mal en 1348, laissés à la dérive avec peu ou pas du tout de matelotage, les voiles battantes. Ils rapportaient des cargaisons du Moyen-Orient. Ils rapportaient aussi autre chose: la Mort Noire. Les habitants de Gênes, inquiets pour leur commerce, amarèrent les voiliers de la peste. Les marins décédés d'une mort étrange et les moribonds furent portés à terre. Mais ces marins n'étaient pas les coupables qui amenèrent la peste bubonique à balayer l'Europe, tuant la moitié de la population du continent en un demi siècle et changeant le cours de l'Histoire. Les vrais coupables étaient les rats noirs, eux-mêmes contaminés par la peste et courant le long des cordes que les Gênois avaient fournies si à-propos.

Une fois à terre, les rats partaient à la débandade pour trouver à manger. La nourriture était toujours proche des humains, et les gens commencèrent à mourir. Ils moururent par milliers, d'une manière horrible. Ils avaient attrappé une maladie que la nature avait destinée aux rats. Mais personne (que Dieu veille sur ceux qui sont morts de la peste) ne savait quelle était la cause de ces effroyables épreuves. Beaucoup moururent en beuglant et sans aide réelle. Personne ne pouvait arrêter la peste. Personne ne pouvait soigner la peste. Personne ne savait *pourquoi*. Cependant il y avait une solution à la fois si simple et si tordue qu'il fallut attendre les années 1890 pour la trouver.

La peste était alors endémique en Europe. Elle éclatait ici et là. Elle faucha les habitants d'Europe de l'ouest en 1664, traversant la Manche pour atteindre Londres en 1665. Jusqu'à 100.000 personnes moururent à Londres cette même année et durant une partie de l'année suivante. Et on ne savait toujours pas *pourquoi*.

Et qu'advint-il de Londres? Tant de gens mourraient à la fin de l'été 1665 qu'il devenait impossible de procéder aux funérailles habituelles. Entre le coucher du soleil et l'aube les charettes des morts parcouraient les rues, précédées d'un homme qui sonnait une cloche et criait 'Sortez vos morts... sortez vos morts!' Les corps étaient jetés sur les charettes comme on jette le bric-à-brac ménager sur les charettes des ferailleurs des temps modernes, pour être emmenés dans les fosses publiques géantes (l'une des plus importantes gît sous la gare de Liverpool Street) et enterrés avant l'aube. Le désespoir de ceux en détresse et en danger

38 était tel que des choses horribles se passèrent. Daniel Defoe nota dans
39 son *Journal de l'Année de la Peste*: 'Les gens qui étaient contaminés et
40 proches de la fin, et délirant également, couraient vers ces fosses, en-
41 veloppés dans des couvertures et des plaids, et s'y jetaient. Et quand ils
42 venaient enterrer d'autres personnes et qu'ils les trouvaient là, ils étaient
43 bien morts alors qu'ils n'étaient pas déjà froids.'
44   Des chercheurs, principalement des vieilles femmes qui aimaient
45 mettre leur nez dans les affaires des autres, furent recrutés par la magis-
46 trature pour traverser les endroits contaminés à pied et découvrir des
47 signes de la peste dans les maisons. Si une telle maison était découverte,
48 elle devait être fermée, les gens en bonne santé étaient incarcérés avec
49 les malades. Un signe était barbouillé en rouge sur la porte: une croix
50 accompagnée des mots 'Que Dieu ait pitié de nous'.
51   Devant ces maisons, dont le nombre augmentait chaque semaine, se
52 tenait un garde qui empêchait les gens de sortir. Mais ces hommes étaient
53 fréquemment dupés ou corrompus de sorte que les gens s'échappaient
54 souvent de leurs maisons en quarantaine et allaient dans les rues et la
55 campagne proche, pensant, sans aucun doute, aux nombreux riches et à
56 la plupart des médecins de Londres qui avaient fui dans leurs voitures
57 aux premiers signes de la peste, laissant leurs malades et leurs domes-
58 tiques à la merci de la maladie.
59   La peste prit moins d'importance à Londres après un automne terri-
60 ble, mais refit surface au printemps. Elle était plus faible cependant et
61 disparaissait. En fait, contrairement aux croyances populaires persistan-
62 tes, le Grand Incendie de Londres qui éclata le premier septembre 1666
63 (un samedi) n'avait rien à voir avec l'extinction de la Grande Peste de
64 Londres.
65   En bref, l'incendie consuma la Cité. Les paroisses les plus pauvres, où
66 la peste avait été la plus virulente, avaient en grande partie évité les
67 flammes. La Grande Peste, une fois sa tâche terrifiante achevée, dis-
68 paraissait déjà tranquillement dans les pages de l'Histoire. La peste
69 bubonique était alors ancrée dans notre patrimoine. Les enfants la chan-
70 taient 'Autour des roses faisons la ronde, de pustules nos poches sont
71 fécondes. Atchoum! Atchoum! Nous voilà tous à terre'. Eternuer était
72 l'un des premiers symptômes de la peste bubonique et c'est la raison
73 pour laquelle nous disons encore 'A vos souhaits' aujourd'hui lorsque
74 quelqu'un éternue.
75   Venait ensuite les pustules. Ces pustules étaient des poches de pus
76 noires qui faisaient éruption sous les aisselles ou dans l'aine et qui
77 faisaient atrocement mal. Elles font toujours aussi mal. Les médecins,
78 croyant que ces poches devaient être percées pour sauver le malade, les
79 taillaient ou, encore pire, les brûlaient ou y posaient un fer rouge, de sorte

que les victimes de la peste mouraient en hurlant de la seule douleur. Les médecins ne savaient toujours pas *pourquoi*.

La profession médicale telle qu'elle existait, avait deux écoles: celle des tenants du Miasme et celle des tenants de la Contagion. Les tenants du Miasme croyaient que la peste était due aux brouillards qui émanaient du sol, alors que les tenants de la Contagion croyaient que la maladie était transmise d'une personne à l'autre, ou par l'intermédiaire des choses telles que les vêtements, que d'autres personnes touchaient.

Et les imbéciles qui suggéraient qu'il y avait dans l'air des monstres à la forme de dragons, de serpents et de diables, trop petits pour être vus, qui causaient la propagation de la peste bubonique, étaient compléte-ment tournés en ridicule. Cette théorie fantaisiste était finalement la plus proche de la réalité, mais toujours loin d'être vraie. La peste, bien qu'attaquant la race humaine injustement, était trop subtile pour tout ceci. Il a fallu un médecin français né en Suisse, Alexandre Yersin, pour isoler un germe dont les pérégrinations étaient si circonvolues qu'il lui était quasi-impossible de tuer un homme, mais qui, s'il pouvait frapper, était mortel. Le germe est le *Yersenia Pestis*. Ils savaient alors *pourquoi*.

Extrait d'un article de John Hosken, Journaliste et speaker dans les média audio-visuelles paru dans *Mensa Magazine*, October 1994, pp. 11–12.

L'education de nos enfants —
la nouvelle Charte des Parents

1 Les écoles ont beaucoup changé ces dernières années. Leur niveau s'est
2 amélioré, et leur choix est plus large. Professeurs, directeurs d'écoles et
3 parents ont tous joué un rôle dans ces changements. Tout comme la
4 Charte des Citoyens et la Charte Parentale. Ces chartes ont apporté:
5   – pour l'amélioration de la qualité des écoles;
6   – de nouveaux droits à l'information sur la performance;
7   – de nouvelles directives pour les inspecter;
8   – de clairs Objectifs Nationaux pour l'Education et la Formation,
9   pour les écoles, les collèges, les employeurs et le gouvernement;
10   – pour un choix d'écoles plus important;
11   – de nouveaux types d'écoles;
12   – davantage de droits pour les parents; et
13   – des améliorations pour les parents d'enfants qui ont des besoins
14   particuliers.
15   Cette Charte Parentale a été mise à jour, et vous donne toutes les
16 informations concernant ces améliorations. Elle est particulièrement
17 importante pour les parents d'enfants de cinq à seize ans, mais tout le
18 monde, pas uniquement les parents, devrait tirer avantage d'une amélio-
19 ration dans la qualité et le choix des écoles. Les réformes de la Charte
20 sont également le facteur-clé qui rendra le pays plus compétitif. C'est
21 pour cette raison que nous avons envoyé une copie de la Charte à chaque
22 foyer du pays.
23
24 **Le droit à l'information**
25 *Les Cinq Documents-Clés*:
26 1. Un Rapport sur votre Enfant.
27 2. Des Rapports Réguliers par des Inspecteurs Indépendants.
28 3. Des Classements de Performance pour toutes vos Ecoles Locales.
29 4. Un Prospectus ou une Brochure sur les Ecoles Individuelles.
30 5. Un Rapport Annuel des Membres Dirigeants de votre Ecole.
31   Selon les réformes gouvernementales, vous devriez obtenir toutes les
32 informations dont vous avez besoin pour suivre les progrès de votre
33 enfant, pour savoir comment l'école est dirigée, et pour comparer cette
34 école avec toutes les écoles locales. Les cinq documents principaux sont
35 expliqués ci-dessous.
36   Une meilleure information sur les écoles est également importante
37 pour l'amélioration du niveau des écoles. La publication de tableaux de

48 classements qui comparent les performances des écoles, par exemple, a
49 encouragé beaucoup d'écoles à sérieusement étudier les résultats des
40 examens de leurs élèves et à se demander comment l'école peut aider les
41 élèves à faire mieux.
42
43 **1. Un rapport sur votre enfant**
44   Vous recevrez un rapport écrit sur les progrès de votre enfant au
45 moins une fois par an. Ce rapport vous informera sur:
46   – Les progrès de votre enfant dans les matières du Programme
47   d'Enseignement National, y compris les résultats aux tests na-
48   tionaux qu'il ou elle passera à l'âge de 7, 11 et 14 ans.
49   – Les résultats que votre enfant a obtenus aux examens publiques
50   tels que les 'GCSE' (Brevet des Collèges), les 'GCE A-Levels'
51   (Baccalauréat) et les qualifications professionnelles telles que les
52   GNVQ (CAP et BEP).
53   – Les résultats obtenus par votre enfant dans d'autres matières et
54   activités.
55   – Une comparaison des résultats de votre enfant aux tests nationaux
56   passés à 7, 11 et 14 ans, avec les résultats d'autres enfants du même âge.
57   – Les progrès d'ensemble de votre enfant et son taux d'absentéisme.
58   Cette information sera donnée par le directeur d'école ou le maître
59   d'école.
60   – Qui contacter pour parler du rapport sur votre enfant et comment
61   organiser un rendez-vous.
62   Vous aurez la possibilité de voir le travail de l'école et de parler à son
63 personnel à d'autres moments de l'année. Ceci vous aidera à découvrir
64 le type d'enseignement suivi par votre enfant et ce que vous pouvez faire
65 pour l'aider.
66   L'école prendra note des absences de votre enfant, de son comporte-
67 ment et de ses résultats. Vous avez le droit de consulter ces notes. Si vous
68 en faites la demande à l'école, elle vous laissera regarder les informations
69 sur votre enfant.
70   Lorsque votre enfant quittera l'école pour suivre des études
71 supérieures, faire un stage ou travailler, il recevra un rapport. Celui-ci
72 sera présenté sous forme d'un Relevé National de Résultats qui donne
73 un résumé des résultats scolaires et extra-scolaires de l'enfant. Ceci aide
74 les jeunes gens à penser à des études supérieures ou à des stages de
75 formation. Ils devraient également mettre leur dossier à jour au fil de
76 leurs études supérieures et de leurs emplois.
77
78 **2. Des rapports réguliers préparés par des inspecteurs indépendants**
79   Une nouvelle organisation indépendante contrôle désormais les per-

80   formances de nos écoles. Le Bureau pour la Qualité de L'Education
81   (Office for Standards in Education, ou OFSTED) est dirigé par l'Inspec-
82   teur Principal des écoles, sous les ordres de Sa Majesté la Reine.
83   L'OFSTED est responsable de l'organisation des nouvelles inspections.
84   Ces dernières ont débuté en septembre 1993 pour les écoles secondaires
85   en Angleterre et débuteront en septembre 1994 pour toutes les autres
86   écoles. La nouvelle organisation se traduit par:
87   – L'inspection, au moins une fois tous les quatre ans, de toutes les
88   écoles publiques, y compris les écoles spécialisées. Les personnes
89   qui dirigent les équipes d'inspection devront être approuvées par
90   l'OFSTED. L'OFSTED vérifie régulièrement que ces équipes font
91   un travail en profondeur.
92   – La couverture des mêmes points principaux dans les rapports de
93   toutes les écoles afin que vous puissiez comparer les performances
94   de toutes les écoles de votre région.
95   – Au moins une personne qui n'a pas travaillé dans l'éducation fera
96   partie des équipes d'inspection. Ceci permet à l'équipe d'inspec-
97   tion d'avoir l'avis d'une personne non-concernée. Avant une
98   inspection, l'équipe doit tenir une assemblée de parents pour
99   parler de l'école.
100 – Les inspecteurs doivent publier un rapport après une inspection.
101   L'école doit se conformer au rapport. L'école vous fera parvenir un
102   résumé du rapport, préparé par l'inspecteur, qui établira les points
103   forts et les points faibles de l'école. Vous recevrez également du
104   corps dirigeant les plans de développement de l'école, ainsi que les
105   solutions proposées pour répondre aux problèmes éclairés par
106   l'inspection.
107 – Vous pouvez, ainsi que tous les parents qui pensent envoyer leur
108   enfant dans la même école, demander à l'école qu'elle vous fasse
109   parvenir une copie du rapport complet. Il se peut que l'école vous
110   fasse payer pour ce rapport. Le rapport sera également disponible
111   dans les bibliothèques municipales.
112 – Un résumé du dernier rapport en date et une mise à jour sur les
113   actions prises par l'école seront inclus dans le rapport annuel du
114   corps dirigeant qui sera envoyé aux parents.
115 – Lors de l'assemblée générale annuelle des parents, le corps
116   dirigeant de l'école doit expliquer comment leurs plans ont été
117   suivis; et
118 – Si un rapport d'inspection établit que l'école n'offre pas un niveau
119   d'éducation acceptable, des mesures spéciales seront applicables.
120   Celles-ci ont pour but d'attaquer les problèmes de l'école et de
121   s'assurer que le niveau d'éducation de l'école est amélioré aussi

22   rapidement que possible. L'école sera dirigée par une Association
23   Educative choisie par le Secrétaire d'Etat si nécessaire. Ce dernier
24   peut fermer l'école si son niveau ne s'améliore pas.

Extrait d'un papier blanc, 'Our Children's Education, The Updated
Parent's Charter' (l'Education de nos enfants, la nouvelle charte des
parents) émis par le Département pour l'Education (1994).

La Charte 88

1 Ici en Grande Bretagne nous avons grandi dans la conviction de notre
2 liberté: avec la ferme conviction aussi que notre parlement symbolise la
3 démocratie même; que le monde entier convoîte notre liberté; que notre
4 système judiciaire est toujours équitable; que les gardiens de notre
5 securité, à savoir, la police et les services de sureté, sont soumis à un
6 contrôle judiciaire et démocratique; que nos fonctionnaires sont impar-
7 tiaux; que nos villes et nos communes maintiennent un sentiment de
8 fierté en leur identité; et enfin, que notre presse fait preuve de courage
9 et d'honnêteté.
10 De nos jours, des convictions pareilles deviennent de plus en plus
11 invraisemblables. L'écart entre la réalité et les idées reçues au sujet de la
12 'constitution non-écrite' de la Grande Bretagne s'est creusé au point où
13 beaucoup le trouvent difficile à supporter. Et pourtant, cette année on
14 nous invite à commémorer le 3e centenaire de la 'Révolution Glorieuse'
15 de 1688,[1] qui a vu naître ce qui allait devenir la formule souveraine du
16 Royaume Uni. Au nom de la liberté, nos droits politiques, civils et
17 sociaux se voient imposer des limites, tandis que les pouvoirs de l'ad-
18 ministration ont augmenté, vont en s'augmentant, qui devraient par
19 contre se faire restreindre.
20 Il existe actuellement un processus par lequel sont mises en danger
21 beaucoup des libertés dont nous avons joui jusqu'à présent. Erosion en
22 partie involontaire qui a commencé avant 1979, et qui ne fait que de
23 gagner de la vitesse. L'Ecosse se fait gouverner à partir de Whitehall,[2]
24 tout comme une province.[3] De façon plus générale, le gouvernement a
25 erodé bon nombre des libertés civiles fondamentales: par exemple, les
26 droits universels à l'habeas corpus, le droit à l'association paisible, au
27 libre accès à l'information, à la liberté d'expression, à l'adhésion à un
28 syndicat, au gouvernement local, à la libre circulation, même le droit de
29 naissance. A force de soustraire ces droits à certains, le gouvernement
30 les met en danger pour tous.
31 Une foi britannique traditionnelle en le caractère bénin des institu-
32 tions du pays encourage une perception non-systématique de ces
33 questions graves; chacune d'entre elles devient un problème à considérer
34 isolément des autres. Comme elle n'est pas écrite, cette constitution
35 encourage elle-aussi une approche peu-systématique d'aborder la poli-
36 tique; cette approche ne protège guère contre un état autoritaire et
37 volontariste qui ne fait point de concessions. En tout état de compte les

événements de 1688 n'ont fait que de déplacer le pouvoir absolu d'un
monarque pour le mettre entre les mains d'une oligarchie parlementaire.
On nous a accordé moins de libertés que nous ne le croyions. Celles
qui nous ont été permises ont trop dépendu de la bonté de nos souverains. En tant que citoyens, nos libertés nous ont été rationnées par nos
souverains, entre les mains de qui elles sont restées, au lieu de nous être
données comme droit inaliénable. Afin de rendre réelles les libertés que
nous considérions une fois comme admises, il faudra pour la première
fois les saisir pour nous-mêmes.

The Observer Magazine, Colour Supplement, le 29 juillet, 1990.

1. Date où le pouvoir de la monarchie a été confié à la fille du roi catholique
   Jaques II, qui était, avec son mari Guillaume, de religion protestante. C'est
   alors que les pouvoirs du souverain ont été limités tandis que ceux du
   parlement se sont vu accroître, afin de protéger le peuple contre les abus de
   pouvoir connus sous les souverains précédents, Jaques I, Charles I et II,
   Jaques II. Révolution dite Glorieuse car il n'y a pas eu de sang versé lors du
   transfert du pouvoir et de l'arrivée des nouveaux monarques.
2. Whitehall est le lieu, la grande avenue à Londres où se trouve de nombreux
   ministères.
3. Il importe de savoir qu'une partie de l'Ecosse souhaiterait une certaine
   indépendence avec son propre parlement.

Les réformes du Service National de la Santé et vous

1 Le Service National de la Santé et la loi de 1990 sur les services médico-
2 sociaux vont introduire des changements importants dans la gestion des
3 services médico-sociaux. Des changements ont également été effectués
4 dans la façon de gérer les services du médecin de famille. D'autres sont
5 prévus dans le secteur dentaire. Ces changements, ainsi que ceux qui
6 émanent de la sus-dite loi, sont destinés à vous offrir un service plus
7 efficace et de meilleure qualité; un service qui avant tout vous place,
8 vous, le patient, en première position.
9 Ils visent à renforcer le but principal du Service National de la Santé:
10 aider les gens à vivre plus longtemps et à profiter d'une vie de meilleure
11 qualité. En effet, le Service national de santé, qui emploie aujourd'hui un
12 nombre record de médecins et d'infirmières, traite plus de patients que
13 jamais.
14 Pour le moment les services de la Service national de santé resteront
15 ouverts à tous, quel que soit le revenu des patients, et seront couverts
16 par les împôts généraux. Les secours du Service national de santé
17 resteront, pour la plupart, gratuits et ce dès le début des soins.
18
19 **Pour vous rassurer**
20 Les changements dans les services médicaux touchent tout le monde.
21 Certains s'imquiètent et se demandent quels services seront disponibles.
22 Voici certaines des questions posées:
23 – Est-ce que mon médecin pourra passer autant de temps en consult-
24 ation avec moi? OUI.
25 – Est-ce que j'obtiendrai toujours mes médicaments, même si ceux-ci
26 coûtent cher? OUI.
27 – Est-ce que je pourrai toujours recevoir le traitement qu'il me faut
28 si le cabinet de mon médecin de famille reçoit des fonds extérieurs?
29 OUI.
30 – Est-ce que je peux toujours être soigné(e) par un hôpital local?
31 OUI.
32 – Est-ce que je pourrai toujours choisir où accoucher? OUI.
33 – Est-ce que les hôpitaux qui deviennent des unités financières
34 autonomes du Service national de santé vont rester partie in-
35 tégrante du Service national de santé? OUI.
36 Alors finalement la réponse à toutes ces questions est 'OUI'.
37 Ce livret explique les changements et en quoi ils vous touchent.

Vous et votre médecin de famille

Les médecins de famille — aussi connus sous le nom de médecins généralistes — seront capables de vous offrir, à vous et à votre famille, une sélection de services plus étendue. L'accent sera davantage mis sur la campagne pour la Bonne Santé et la médecine préventive. Cette section est consacrée à la sélection des services offerts par votre médecin, et à la façon dont son cabinet sera géré pour répondre à vos besoins.

Des services pour la famille

Le but d'un service médico-social de qualité n'est pas seulement de vous soigner lorsque vous êtes malade, mais également de vous offrir aide et conseils afin que vous restiez en forme et en bonne santé.

Le Directeur général de la Santé Publique au gouvernement déclare: *'Mieux vaut prévenir que guérir. On profite d'une meilleure qualité de la vie lorsqu'on est en meilleure santé. La sélection des services offerts par votre médecin-généraliste va vous aider à rester en bonne santé ou à améliorer votre santé, et à réduire le risque de maladie. Ces services ne sont pas obligatoires bien sûr, c'est à vous de décider si vous voulez en profiter. Mais je vous les recommande vivement, par égard pour votre santé.'*

Quels services devriez vous guetter?

Pour les adultes:
- Des bilans de santé 'Style de Vie' réguliers seront disponibles. Ils vous seront offerts lorsque vous irez chez un médecin pour la première fois, ou lorsque vous retournez chez votre médecin que vous n'avez pas vu depuis longtemps. Ces bilans de santé ont pour but:
  - de vous donner la possibilité de parler de tout ce qui vous inquiète;
  - de vous donner l'occasion de passer des examens médicaux simples tels que prendre votre tension;
  - de vous offrir les conseils professionnels sur des sujets qui vous touchent tels que faire un régime, l'exercice physique, la consommation de tabac et d'alcool.

Pour résumer, votre médecin généraliste peut vous donner des conseils sur la façon de prendre soin de vous-même. Il peut, dans ce but, vous recommander de participer au programme de l'une des cliniques de son cabinet qui suit une campagne médicale pour l'amélioration de la santé. La partie 'Bilan de Santé' au centre de ce livret vous donne des conseils complémentaires sur la façon de mener un style de vie sain.
- Les médecins-généralistes seront incités à ouvrir davantage de cliniques dans leur cabinet, dans le but de poursuivre des campagnes médicales, qu'il s'agisse de cliniques qui donnent des conseils

80   sur les régimes à suivre, sur la tension, comment arrêter de fumer,
81   le diabète, les maladies du coeur, avoir le contrôle sur l'alcool ou
82   gérer son niveau de stress. Il pourrait aussi y avoir des cliniques
83   pour le Bien-Etre.
84
85   **Les services du Planning Familial**
86   – Les services du Planning Familial sont disponibles chez la plupart
87   des médecins-généralistes et dans les cliniques du Planning Famil-
88   ial du Service national de santé, qui sont également ouvertes aux
89   hommes. Vous pouvez choisir où aller pour recevoir des conseils
90   sur le planning familial.
91   Si vous préférez recevoir les conseils d'un médecin-généraliste sur la
92   contraception, vous pouvez choisir de voir un autre médecin-généraliste
93   que votre médecin de famille, toutefois si ce médecin-généraliste est prêt
94   à vous recevoir. Il est maintenant plus facile de savoir si certains
95   médecins-généralistes offrent des conseils sur la contraception (référez-
96   vous à la partie 'Informations complémentaires pour les patients', page
97   11).
98   Les services du Planning Familial sont offerts gratuitement afin d'en-
99   courager leur utilisation par tous ceux qui le souhaitent.

Extraits d'une brochure publiée par le Service National de la Santé en Grande Bretagne, traitant des réformes du service et intitulée: *The Health Service, The NHS Reforms and You*, pp. 2–8.

Une façon erronée d'assurer la défense d'une culture

1 Selon M Enoch Powell, dissident politique britannique, 'l'option mili-
2 taire ne peut point constituer la meilleure défense des valeurs'.
3 Malheureusement, l'Union européenne tarde toujours à comprendre
4 une pareille vérité: on ne saurait défendre une culture par moyen de
5 décret législatif.

6 Il y a un peu plus de 3 ans, une directive a été introduite partout dans
7 la UE, visant la protection de l'accès aux petits écrans contre des émis-
8 sions d'origine non-européenne. Plus récemment, cette directive est
9 devenue la pomme de discorde des négotiations du GATT (AGETAC)
10 en ce qui concerne la libéralisation du commerce global.

11 Cette directive, au nom quelque peu trompeur de 'télévision sans
12 frontières' visait en effet l'érection des frontières encore plus redoutables
13 autour de la UE. On ne peut guère concevoir d'exemple plus éhonté de
14 la mentalité 'forteresse Europe'. Les articles 4 et 5 de la directive stipulent
15 que, certaines exceptions faites, 'les états membres doivent veiller à ce
16 que les chaînes de télévision réservent aux émissions européennes une
17 proportion majoritaire du temps de transmission', les principales excep-
18 tions étant les actualités et les émissions sportives.

19 La crainte ressentie par la UE envers les émissions d'origine
20 étrangères a pour base des soucis d'ordre économique. Le marché
21 européen du film et de la télévision est en état de fragmentation grave;
22 80% des films tournés en Europe ne franchissent pas les frontières du
23 pays d'origine. Ils n'arrivent que rarement à se rattraper des frais de
24 production par des ventes à l'étranger. Les chaînes de télévision pub-
25 liques qui cherchent à réduire leurs frais généraux ont déjà une grande
26 motivation vers l'achat des émissions américaines lesquelles, ayant déjà
27 assuré le recouvrement des frais de production sur le vaste marché
28 intérieur, se vendent à un prix très raisonnable.

29 Il vaut tout de même la peine de se demander si l'imposition des
30 quotas d'importation aidera réellement à redresser l'équilibre. Deux
31 questions pertinentes se posent: est-ce que les tentatives de protection
32 de l'industrie cinématographique par l'Europe sont faisables et si oui,
33 sont-elles souhaitables?

34 Considérons d'abord la question de la faisabilité. Les doutes se lais-
35 sent facilement identifier. Il sont au coeur de la directive même. Les
36 états-membres de la UE ont une marge de discretion assez large quant à
37 l'implémentation de la directive. Ils doivent assurer, dans les contextes

38 où il serait 'faisable' de le faire, que plus que la moité des émissions
39 transmises soient d'origine européenne. Ils doivent aussi oeuvrer pour
40 persuader les émetteurs de s'orienter progressivement vers une telle
41 politique, mais les dates limites ne font pas l'objet d'un horaire stricte.
42 Les nouvelles chaînes auront deux ans pour établir un certain élan avant
43 d'être soumises à la règle de la proportion du contenu européen.
44   La tentative de réglementation d'une industrie qui évolue beaucoup
45 plus rapidement que ne le font les régulateurs européens pose la plus
46 grande difficulté. Les chaînes de télévision terrestres, émettant de l'in-
47 térieur des frontières des états membres de la UE se laissent assez
48 facilement mettre au pas. Mais pour ce qui est des chaînes satellites
49 émettant d'en dehors de la UE, le problème est d'autant plus difficile à
50 cerner.
51   La Commission s'attend à ce que plus de 16 millions de domiciles
52 seront capables, d'ici 1995, de capter les émissions satellites. Un officiel
53 de la DGX, la division de la Commission qui est responsable de la
54 politique audio-visuelle, admet que le contrôle des chaînes satellites
55 ayant leur base de transmission en dehors de la UE pourrait s'avérer 'très
56 difficile'. La Commission espère que les émissions satellites auront au
57 moins une quelconque représentation physique à l'intérieur de la UE par
58 intermédiaire de laquelle on pourra leur faire pression.
59   Si cet espoir devait s'avérer inutile, la directive de la télévision sans
60 frontières subirait des tensions graves. Les opérateurs satellites à l'in-
61 térieur de la UE voudront savoir pourquoi ils doivent subir des peines
62 financières en étant obligés d'acheter des émissions coûteuses européen-
63 nes tandis que leurs homologues ailleurs peuvent transmettre tout ce qui
64 bon leur semble.

Extrait d'un article par William Pitt, *Eurobusiness*, décembre 1993/
janvier 1994, p. 65.

Ce que nous sommes ...

1 Qu'est le Bureau européen pour les langues moins répandues? Com-
2 ment commença-t-il? Qu'espère-t-il accomplir?
3   D'une certaine manière le Bureau est le produit du 'phénomène des
4 racines', ce mouvement en évolution de peuples cherchant leur identité
5 et les droits de l'homme découlant de leur ethnicité.
6   Il se créa lors d'un colloque à Bruxelles en mai 1982 qui examinait les
7 implications du rapport Arfe adopté par le parlement européen en
8 octobre 1981. Les représentants des différents 'petits peuples' qui
9 prenaient part à ce colloque exprimaient leur solution pour la mise en
10 place d'un organisme qui agirait dans leur intérêt au niveau de la
11 Communauté avec les diverses institutions de la CEE, le Conseil de
12 l'Europe, etc. Sa constitution en définit le but principal: 'préserver et
13 promouvoir les langues autochtones les moins répandues des états
14 membres de la Communauté ainsi que les cultures qui y sont associées'.
15   La Communauté européenne est essentiellement une communauté
16 d'états nations, c'est à dire des états indépendants considérés comme
17 étant des nations par leur gouvernement au sens du XIXe siècle du terme
18 'nation'. Cependant, états et nations ne sont pas synonymes et il existe
19 dans chaque état membre de la communauté européenne au moins une
20 nation ou une communauté qui se distingue de la majorité de cet état par
21 leur propre langue et leur identité propre particulière. En fait il n'y a que
22 deux pays en Europe de l'ouest qui n'ont pas de communauté interne
23 différente, l'Islande et le Portugal, et aucun des deux n'est membre de la
24 Communauté européenne.
25   La Communauté européenne reconnaît sept langues officielles de
26 travail; le français, l'anglais, l'allemand, l'italien, le néerlandais, le danois
27 et le grec. L'irlandais est 'langue de traité'. Ceci signifie que le texte en
28 irlandais des traités a même autorité que le même texte dans les sept
29 langues de travail. L'irlandais est aussi 'une langue officielle de travail
30 de la Cour européenne'.
31   Il y a plus de 30 millions de citoyens dans le (*sic*) Communauté
32 européenne dont la langue maternelle est une langue autre que l'une des
33 sept langues de travail. En réalité ceci veut dire qu'il y a un nombre
34 important de personnes qui ne jouissent pas du même status linguistique
35 que ceux parlant une langue majoritaire.
36   Les communautés qui utilisent ces langues moins parlées sont di-
37 verses:

38 (i)   des petites nations sans leur propre état, par exemple les Gallois,
39   les Bretons et les Frisons;
40 (ii)   des petites nations-états indépendantes dont la langue n'est pas
41   maintenant largement parlée;
42 (iii) des communautés qui parlent une langue minoritaire mais qui ne
43   se considèrent pas comme étant une nation (dans l'usage accepté
44   de ce terme), par exemple les Ladins de la région des Alpes.
45 On pourrait ajouter à ces trois groupes:
46 (iv)   des minorités extraterritoriales, c'est à dire des communautés à
47   l'intérieur d'un pays parlant la langue majoritaire d'un autre, par
48   exemple les habitants de langue danoise de Schleswig-Holstein, les
49   francophones du Val d'Aoste.
50   Il est indéniable que ces communautés de langues moins répandues
51 ne sont pas sans problèmes. En fait, on peut se demander si elles peuvent
52 avoir un futur dans le monde moderne.
53   Cependant tout semble indiquer qu'elles ont un futur des plus viables
54 une fois que certains faits fondamentaux sont reconnus.
55   Les langues font partie intégrale de l'héritage culturel de l'Europe.
56 Parmi elles il y a quelques unes des plus vieilles langues d'Europe avec
57 une littérature et un folklore traditionnel riches. Si elles n'ont pas été pris
58 (*sic*) en considération dans le passé par les institutions de la Commu-
59 nauté européenne, cela n'en est plus le cas. En 1979, par exemple, John
60 Hume (Membre du Parlement européen pour l'Irlande du nord) proposa
61 au parlement une motion exigeant certains droits fondamentaux pour
62 ceux parlant des langues ainsi que des mesures en leur faveur des
63 institutions de la Communauté. L'année suivante, quatre autres motions
64 séparées furent mises à l'ordre du jour, toutes portant sur le même
65 domaine de préoccupations. Ces motions furent discutées en détail au
66 niveau du comité parlementaire et, en conséquence, Gaetano Arfe, (un
67 membre italien du comité) fut prié de rédiger un document comprenant
68 les propos des diverses motions à l'ordre du jour. Signore Arfe s'acquita
69 (*sic*) de cette tâche d'une manière si efficace que le résultat en fut
70 l'adoption par le Parlement européen du document connu maintenant
71 sous le Rapport Arfe le 16 octobre 1981.
72   Fondamentalement ce rapport comprend une charte des droits ainsi
73 que des indications pour d'éventuelles actions. C'est une base fonda-
74 mentale sur laquelle on peut bâtir.
75   Et nous avons commencé à bâtir.

Extrait d'un article de Dónall Ó Riagáin, *Contact Bulletin*, journal d'information du Bureau européen pour les langues moins répandues, No.1,
novembre 1983.

Des familles malheureuses

1 Les ministres au gouvernement sont en désaccord obsessif sur ce qui
2 devrait être fait pour la famille britannique. Dans un discours du 20 juin,
3 Peter Lilley, secrétaire d'état à la Sécurité Sociale, décrit l'effondrement
4 croissant de la Famille comme la cause manifeste et profondément
5 troublante de sérieux problèmes sociaux. Ceci semblait aller à l'encontre
6 d'un discours prononcé le mois dernier par Virginia Bottomley, ministre
7 de la Santé (et porte-parole officiel du Cabinet pour les Affaires Sociales),
8 qui soutenait qu'il n'y avait jamais eu un âge d'or de la Famille et que la
9 taille ou la forme de la Famille importait moins que la responsabilité qui
10 lui encourait d'élever les enfants.
11   En fait Mr Lilley accorda son discours avec celui de Mme Bottomley,
12 et tous deux pourrait bien avoir raison. Mme Bottomley a raison
13 lorsqu'elle dit qu'il n'y avait pas d'âge d'or de la Famille. A la fin du 19ème
14 siècle, environ 5% des enfants vivaient sans doute avec un père ou une
15 mère qui n'était pas leur parent naturel. Aujourd'hui, selon un article de
16 John Haskey paru dans *Les Tendances Populaires*, 6% des enfants sont
17 dans cette situation de beau-fils ou de belle-fille.
18   Mme Bottomley pourrait même bien avoir raison lorsqu'elle explique
19 que la responsabilité d'élever les enfants est plus importante que la
20 forme de la Famille. Malheureusement des recherches récentes sug-
21 gèrent que la forme de la Famille affecte cette responsabilité. Mr Lilley
22 pourrait donc bien avoir raison de s'inquiéter de la tendance à l'effon-
23 drement de la Famille.
24   La famille britannique est plus variée qu'elle ne l'a jamais été. Seule-
25 ment 73% des enfants de moins de 16 ans vivent avec leurs parents
26 naturels mariés. Alors que la mort perturbait les ménages de l'ère
27 Victorienne, les familles d'aujourd'hui doivent leur forme à un état
28 d'esprit différent face au mariage. La plupart des enfants qui ne
29 vivent maintenant qu'avec un seul de leurs parents ont, au contraire
30 de leurs homologues de l'ère Victorienne, un autre parent naturel
31 vivant.
32   Selon une étude de Monica Cockett et John Tripp du Département de
33 la Santé des Enfants situé à Exeter, une telle réorganisation de leur vie
34 familiale n'est pas saine pour les enfants. Ils ont fait une enquête sur 152
35 enfants dont la moitié avaient toujours vécu avec leurs parents naturels
36 et l'autre moitié avaient vu le mariage de leurs parents s'effondrer. Les
37 premiers résultats, publiés par la Fondation Joseph Rowntree, suggèrent

38 que les enfants des familles 'réorganisées' avaient plus de chances de
39 souffrir de difficultés dans leur travail scolaire et de problèmes de
40 comportement, de manque d'amour propre et d'une mauvaise santé,
41 que les enfants dont les parents étaient toujours mariés. Lorsque les
42 parents n'étaient pas séparés mais se disputaient fréquemment, les
43 enfants avaient de plus grandes chances de souffrir de tels problèmes,
44 que les enfants de mariages heureux, mais beaucoup moins de chances
45 que les enfants de parents séparés.
46   De plus, plus les changements dans leur vie familiale étaient nom-
47 breux, plus les enfants étaient malheureux. Ceci pourrait s'expliquer par
48 le fait que les enfants qui avaient traversé plusieurs périodes difficiles au
49 sein de leur famille, avaient plus de chances de perdre contact avec celui
50 de leurs parents qui était absent, et moins de chances d'apprécier le
51 soutien d'autres membres de leur famille tels que leurs grands-parents.
52   Une étude sur la relation entre les enfants battus et les foyers brisés,
53 publiée au début de cette année par Robert Whelan de l'Institut des
54 Affaires Economiques, un 'puits de pensées' de la Droite, fait ressortir
55 l'une des raisons pour lesquelles certains des enfants qui appartiennent
56 à des familles 'réorganisées' sont malheureux. Utilisant en grande partie
57 des chiffres rassemblés entre 1973 et 1990 par la Société Nationale pour
58 la Prévention de la Cruauté envers les Enfants, Mr Whelan soutient que
59 les enfants qui ne vivent qu'avec leur mère naturelle ont à peu près
60 quatre fois plus de chances d'être physiquement maltraités que les
61 enfants qui vivent avec leurs deux parents naturels; et que ceux qui
62 vivent avec leur mère naturelle et un beau-père voient leurs chances
63 multipliées par six ou dix.
64   Mr Lilley, qui établit un lien entre l'effondrement de la Famille et la
65 baisse des salaires relatifs aux gens non-qualifiés, pense que la solution
66 se trouve dans une formation de meilleure qualité et une réforme des
67 prestations sociales. Il pense qu'il faudra une génération pour que ceci
68 soit mis en place. 'D'ici là bien d'autres jeunes auront grandi pour
69 devenir des adultes, tout aussi malheureux que Cendrillon avant que
70 n'apparaîsse sa marraine la fée'.

Un article d'auteur anonyme publié dans *The Economist*, le 25 juin 1994,
pp. 29–32.

Naissance de l'ère du stress dans la classe moyenne

Un psychologue nous met en garde contre le prix que l'insécurité au travail nous fera payer

1 Selon un psychologue de premier ordre, les classes moyennes entrent
2 dans une ère d'incertitude très difficile durant laquelle beaucoup ne
3 travailleront qu'en tant que collaborateurs indépendants.
4   Le Professeur Gary Cooper a annoncé à l'Association des Psy-
5 chologues Britanniques, lors de leur conférence professionnelle tenue à
6 l'université de Warwick que, bien que le nouvel environnement au
7 travail touchera tout le monde, le changement sera encore plus fonda-
8 mental pour les professionnels et les employés de bureaux. 'Une bonne
9 éducation garantissait succès et emploi permanent. Ce n'est plus le cas.'
10   Le Professeur Cooper, de l'Institut des Sciences et de la Technologie
11 de l'université de Manchester a expliqué que le 'sentiment de malaise'
12 actuel n'était pas uniquement dû au manque de sécurité de l'emploi,
13 mais à une profonde inquiétude que les postes permanents ne soient plus
14 disponibles à l'avenir.
15   Il a annoncé, dans la note dominante de son discours, qu'il était déjà
16 courant pour les sociétés de sous-traiter leur service du personnel et leur
17 service informatique, et d'employer des responsables sur la base de leurs
18 projets seulement.
19   Il a prédit que d'ici à la fin du millenaire, de nombreuses sociétés
20 compteraient sur des entrepreneurs pour assurer toutes les tâches de la
21 société sauf la production, de sorte que les ouvriers se sentiraient plus
22 en sécurité au travail que leurs collègues employés de bureaux.
23   'Ce n'est pas tant l'ère de l'entrepreneur dans laquelle nous entrons,
24 que l'ère de l'incertitude où une partie importante du travail sera offerte
25 à des collaborateurs indépendants. J'ai bien peur que les gens ne parvi-
26 endront pas à faire face à un changement de cette importance dans le
27 monde du travail', dit le Professeur Cooper.
28   Le Professeur Cooper a expliqué que ce nouveau type d'emploi était
29 susceptible d'augmenter le taux de stress au travail dont le niveau était
30 déjà au plus haut historiquement en Grande Bretagne. Les congés-
31 maladie coûtent déjà 11 milliards de Livres Sterling par an à l'industrie
32 britannique, la plupart d'entre eux sont dûs au stress. Le taux de congés-
33 maladie en Grande Bretagne est d'environ 3,5 pour cent, contre un à deux
34 pour cent parmi nos concurrents.
35   Le coût subi par les employeurs risque de monter en flèche à la suite
36 du procès que John Walker, responsable d'un service social qui a eu deux

37 dépressions nerveuses, a intenté contre les Services Municipaux de
38 Northumberland, et à la suite duquel sa demande de dommages et
39 intérêts de 200.000 Livres a été reçue. La décision de la Cour Suprême
40 signifie qu'il est maintenant du devoir des employeurs de prendre soin
41 de leurs employés, mais elle signifie également que certaines sociétés
42 pourraient être tentées de se débarrasser des employés qui montreront
43 le moindre signe de fatigue.

44   Le Professeur Cooper a indiqué que le niveau de stress chez les
45 employés sous contrat à durée déterminée était invariablement élevé. Ils
46 se passent souvent de vacances et acceptent des emplois pour lesquels
47 ils ne sont pas qualifiés, pour le cas où il viendrait à manquer de travail.
48 Travailler comme collaborateur indépendant nécessite toute une gamme
49 de connaissances que le responsable de service moyen ou le profession-
50 nel ne possèdent pas, telles que la comptabilité, la loi du travail,
51 l'informatique et l'expertise en marketing. Les gens vont devoir appren-
52 dre à travailler à la maison.

53   Il a ajouté que la Société toute entière n'était pas prête pour cette
54 nouvelle ère. Plus de 65% des femmes entre 16 et 59 ans travaillent, de
55 sorte que les parents trouvent qu'il est de plus en plus difficile de
56 combiner travail et famille. Des contrats de travail irréguliers rendraient
57 la situation encore plus difficile.

Extrait d'un article de Barrie Clement, redacteur en chef pour les questions sur l' Emploi, *The Independent*, le 4 janvier 1995.

L'enfer motorisé

1 Le Ministre doit se montrer courageux. Seuls des changements fonda-
2 mentaux nous sauveront de la voiture, constate Christian Wolmar.
3   L'Institut des Géographes Britanniques recevra aujourd'hui une
4 étude d'une équipe de l'Ecole de Commerce de Londres et du King's
5 College, qui annonce que seul un investissement très important dans les
6 transports en commun peut sauver les routes d'une explosion de la
7 circulation routière et des problèmes écologiques qui y sont associés. Les
8 chercheurs ont découvert que la consommation d'énergie liée aux trajets
9 pour se rendre au travail dans la région de Manchester et celle des West
10 Midlands avait considérablement augmenté proportionnellement au
11 nombre d'emplois, alors qu'à Londres, où de bons réseaux de transports
12 en commun ont subsisté, l'augmentation était très faible.
13   Ceci n'est que le dernier témoignage en date de l'idée malencontreuse
14 qui a guidé la politique d'aménagement des routes sous tant de gou-
15 vernements. Son principe de base — qu'il nous faut accroître la capacité
16 routière pour nous sortir de l'encombrement des routes — s'est révélé
17 tout aussi fatalement imparfait.
18   Cette politique est apparue bien peu réaliste à la suite d'événements
19 de l'an dernier, tels que le rapport de la Commission Royale sur la
20 Pollution de l'Environnement, ou les nouveaux conseils de planification
21 donnés par le Ministère de l'Environnement concernant des centres
22 commerciaux situés en-dehors des villes. L'événement le plus récent
23 était la publication d'un rapport par un comité consultatif du Ministère
24 des Transports, qui annonçait que de nouvelles routes créaient davan-
25 tage de circulation (ce qui semble évident pour la plupart d'entre nous).
26   Mais que devrions-nous faire pour remplacer une politique
27 d'aménagement des routes par une politique des transports? Brian
28 Mawhinney, Ministre des Transports depuis le mois de juillet, s'y essaie:
29 on a déjà noté les signes concrets d'un changement de politique. Des
30 projets d'aménagement routiers ont été abandonnés, des sommes plus
31 importantes sont utilisées pour créer des voies réservées aux bus et,
32 chose étonnante, trois millions de Livres Sterling financent le début des
33 travaux de création d'un réseau de pistes cyclables de 1800 kilomètres à
34 Londres.
35   Dr Mawhinney a annoncé, dans un discours prononcé le mois dernier
36 lors d'une conférence sur la qualité de l'air, qu'il voulait comprendre les
37 positions très arrêtées qu'avaient atteint les deux partis — grossière-

38 ment, les écologistes et les partisans de la construction routière — dans
39 le débat sur les Transports.
40   Mais il n'existe pas de réponse simple ou de votes remportés facile-
41 ment. En effet, Dr Mawhinney se retrouve pieds et poings liés parce que
42 son propre parti est idéologiquement obsédé par la Voiture. En fait, les
43 solutions sont si difficiles, qu'il doit être tentant pour les ministres des
44 transports de baisser les bras et de ne rien faire. Comme l'expliqua David
45 Mackenzie, directeur régional de Transmark qui a étudié les problèmes
46 de tranports dans le monde entier: 'Il est extrêmement difficile de trouver
47 une politique des Transports qui soit simple mais qui soit basée sur ce
48 que l'ensemble de la Communauté est prêt à accepter. La plupart des
49 solutions proposées par les gouvernements ne font que frôler le
50 problème'.
51   Comme le souligna Dr Mawhinney dans son discours, le lobby anti-
52 routes peut être tout aussi facile et entêté que son opposant. Pleurer en
53 permanence pour avoir 'davantage de transports en commun de
54 meilleure qualité' ou 'davantage de marchandises sur les voies ferrées'
55 est tout aussi peu à-propos que des slogans tels que 'il nous faut des
56 routes pour faire avancer l'Industrie'.
57   La triste vérité est qu'une politique des Transports cohérente, qui
58 établit des objectifs, se doit de répondre à la question 'dans quel type de
59 Société voulons-nous vivre?'. Prenez les loisirs. Les voitures ont facilité
60 les visites de parcs nationaux et de régions d'une beauté hors du com-
61 mun. Leur présence, cependant, a rendu ces régions moins attrayantes
62 esthétiquement. L'introduction de taxes élevées ouvrant l'accès aux
63 véhicules sur les routes locales est évidemment une mesure attrayante,
64 mais elle ne dissuadera que les gens qui ont une voiture pour la première
65 fois. Le reste des conducteurs casqueront de mauvaise grâce. Ce qui
66 ressemble à un problème lié aux transports est en fait une question
67 politico-sociale bien plus approfondie.

Extrait d'un article de Christian Wolmar dans *The Independent*, le 4 janvier
1995.

Décès à la suite d'un brouillard londonien

1 Selon un rapport rédigé pour le Département de la Santé mais
2 jusqu'alors non-publié, lorsque un brouillard contemporain, le smog,[1] a
3 voilé la ville de Londres en 1991, le nombre de décès enrégistrés a connu
4 une augmentation en flèche d'environ dix pour cent. Cet épisode révèle
5 la première preuve depuis 30 ans des décès directement attribuables à
6 la pollution de l'air en Grande Bretagne, et il a poussé le gouvernement
7 à commander une révision de la politique de contrôle de la qualité de
8 l'air.

9 Le smog avait résulté d'une accumulation des gaz d'échappment qui
10 a eu lieu pendant quatre jours sans vent au mois de décembre 1991: il
11 s'est avéré être le pire qu'eût connue la Grande Bretagne pendant les
12 dernières années. Il est probable que nombreux des décédés souffraient
13 déjà des maladies cardiaques ou des problèmes respiratoires.

14 Ross Anderson, épidémiologue à l'hôpital sud-londonien de St Geor-
15 ges, a su réunir des preuves de la cause de ces décès. Il doit présenter un
16 rapport sommaire des résultats obtenus, lors d'une réunion de la Société
17 britannique de la thoracique[2] la semaine prochaine. Mais les résultats
18 obtenus par M Anderson ont déjà su convaincre le Département de la
19 Santé de la nécessité d'agir. Selon les directives réglant la qualité de l'air,
20 imposées l'année dernière par ce département, si le smog devait se
21 reproduire actuellement, il n'y aurait aucun avertissement public, puis-
22 que le niveau de polluants n'atteindrait pas la limite fixée.

23 Le smog a enveloppé la ville de Londres du matin du jeudi 13 décem-
24 bre jusqu'à ce qu'il fût dissipé par le vent le dimanche suivant, au soir.
25 Deux des polluants ont atteint des niveaux de concentration très impor-
26 tants: le dioxyde d'azote a atteint le plus haut niveau jamais enrégistré
27 en Grande Bretagne, à 423 parties pour un milliard: calculés en tant que
28 la quantité de fumée noire dans l'air, les particulaires ont atteint 228
29 microgrammes par mètre cube.

30 En faisant l'analyse du nombre d'habitants de Londres décédés pen-
31 dant la semaine qui a précédé le smog, et par comparaison avec le nombre
32 de décès pendant la même semaine aux années précédantes, Anderson
33 a su calculer le nombre de décès que l'on aurait pu prevoir pour les huit
34 jours à partir du 12 décembre. Ensuite il a comparé ce chiffre avec le
35 nombre de décès effectivement survenus.

36 Anderson a trouvé une hausse de 10 pour cent, pendant le smog, sur
37 le nombre de décès prévus pour cette période. Il refuse de faire le calcul

38   du nombre de décès dont seraient composés ces dix pour cent; il ne veut
39   pas non plus faire de commentaire au sujet de ses découvertes avant la
40   réunion prévue pour la semaine prochaine.
41   Mais les chiffres gouvernementaux montrent qu'environ 1700 décès
42   ont été déclarés pendant la semaine fatidique, ce qui pourrait suggérer
43   qu'il y ait eu environ 160 décès supplémentaires pendant le *smog*.
44   Anderson a trouvé que le nombre de décès dûs aux maladies respira-
45   toires, y compris l'asthme et la maladie sérieuse des poumons, était de
46   l'ordre de 22 pour cent plus élevé que prévu pour la semaine du *smog*.
47   Le nombre de décès dûs à la maladie cardiovasculaire était de quatorze
48   pour cent plus élevé que prévu.
49   Une étude épidémiologique telle que celle menée par M Anderson ne
50   saurait apporter la preuve définitive de ce que la pollution de l'air soit
51   la cause des décès supplémentaires. Mais comme le conclut le résumé
52   du papier de M Anderson: ' Les résultats suggèrent qu'une hausse de la
53   mortalité se soit produite pendant la semaine de cet épisode, ce qui serait
54   conforme aux effets à prévoir à la suite d'une pollution de l'air'.
55   Selon M John Bower, du Centre national de la Technologie de l'Envi-
56   ronnement,[3] près de Culham dans l'Oxfordshire, rares sont les épisodes
57   aussi sévères que celui du brouillard de 1991. Mais ils restent toujours
58   possibles, malgré de nouvelles dispositions visant la réduction des taux
59   de gaz d'échappement. 'Dans de pareilles conditions météorologiques,
60   l'épisode se renouvelerait', constate-t-il.

Extrait d'un article de William Bown, paru dans *The New Scientist*, le 25
juin 1994, p. 4.

1.   Le *smog* — le dense brouillard contemporain causé par et cemprenant un haut
     niveau de pollution/fumées — dictionnaire Collins Robert.
2.   British Thoracic Society.
3.   National Environmental Technology Centre.

La qualité du service — tout en une seule visite

1 *Une équipe de l'hôpital de Leicester (Royal Leicester Infirmary) au Royaume*
2 *Uni a battu les finalistes de toute l'Europe et remporté le Prix Hospitalier*
3 *Européen 'Golden Helix' de cette année grâce à une initiative visant à fournir*
4 *un service de qualité aux malades non-hospitalisés.*

5   Les participants au Prix Hospitalier Européen 'Golden Helix', équipe
6 de l'hôpital de Leicester appartenant au Service de la Santé National (le
7 Leicester Royal Infirmary NHS Trust), a remporté la compétition de 1994
8 haut la main. Tenues en juin à Genève, les finales du Prix ont mis en
9 vedette les équipes d'Allemagne, d'Autriche, du Danemark, de France,
10 d'Italie, des Pays-Bas et d'Espagne ainsi que du Royaume Uni. Chaque
11 équipe avait déjà remporté son propre prix 'Golden Helix' national.

12   Etabli en 1991 et soutenu et coordonné aux niveaux du Royaume Uni
13 et de l'Europe par Hewlett-Packard, la raison d'être du prix est de
14 promouvoir une plus grande reconnaissance de la qualité et de ses
15 avantages dans le domaine de la Santé. Chaque équipe doit démontrer
16 comment son projet de l'amélioration de la qualité a relevé les normes
17 d'une manière quantitative au sein de l'institution de la Santé. Le Prési-
18 dent de la Commission Européenne Golden Helix est Simone Veil,
19 ministre d'Etat chargé des Affaires Sociales et de la Santé dans le gou-
20 vernement français.

21   Les autres équipes admises en finale étaient l'Association Hospitalière
22 de Vienne, Autriche; l'hôpital Bispebjerg de Copenhague, Danemark; le
23 Centre Hospitalier Régional Universitaire de Rennes, France; le Ev.
24 Waldkrankenhaus Spandau, Allemagne; le UCL 9, Reggio Emilia, Italie;
25 l'Academisch Ziekenhuis de Rotterdam, Pays bas; et l'hôpital Severo
26 Ochoa de Madrid, Espagne.

27   Le service spécialisé en neurologie de l'hôpital de Leicester du Service
28 national de la Santé (le Leicester Royal Infirmary NHS Trust) auquel
29 s'adressent les malades non-hospitalisés pour une visite unique, a établi
30 une méthode de prise en charge de ces malades nettement plus com-
31 mode et moins contraignante pour les malades non-hospitalisés. Celle-ci
32 consiste en un déroulement complet, en une seule journée, de la première
33 consultation du malade par un médecin-spécialiste, toute une série
34 d'examens médicaux complexes, une séance de suivi avec le médecin-
35 consultant pour parler des résultats et du traitement et décider du choix
36 du traitement.

37   Précédemment, ce processus aurait pris plusieurs semaines et im-

38 pliqué de multiples va-et-vient à l'hôpital. De plus, l'équipe du Leicester
39 Royal Infirmary s'est fixé un ensemble d'objectifs de qualité stricts qui
40 comprenait:
41   – Un diagnostic complet et documenté à la suite de la consultation
42   et lors de la même visite pour 100% des malades affectés.
43   – Des notes et des résultats disponibles au moment de la consultation
44   médicale dans 100% des cas.
45   – Tous les malades vus dans les trente minutes de l'heure du rendez-
46   vous.
47   – Tous les malades sur rendez-vous vus à la clinique.
48   – Réception dans les 24 heures d'un rapport complet par 100% des
49   médecins-généralistes; les médecins-généralistes ont estimés que
50   ce dernier objectif n'était pas indispensable et il fût transformé en
51   conséquence en 48 heures.
52   Ces objectifs contrastent avec la ligne de point de départ du projet.
53 Avant que le projet de qualité ne soit mis en place à l'hôpital, aucun
54 malade nécessitant des examens compliqués ne complétait sa consult-
55 ation en une seule visite; la moyenne était de 3 visites. Seulement 50%
56 des malades voyaient le médecin dans les trente minutes suivant l'heure
57 de leur rendez-vous, et seulement 93% des notes et des résultats étaient
58 disponibles au moment de la consultation médicale. De plus, seulement
59 90% des malades qui avaient un rendez-vous voyaient effectivement
60 quelqu'un à la clinique, et aucun médecin-généraliste ne recevait un
61 rapport sur la consultation le jour suivant.
62   L'équipe a atteint tous les objectifs de qualité. Non seulement le
63 traitement, médical ou autre, dont le malade a besoin peut être défini
64 rapidement et précisément, mais le temps passé à l'hôpital et celui du
65 voyage pour s'y rendre, sont grandement réduits.

Extrait d'un article publié dans, *Euroquan newsletter*, un magazine pour infirmières et autres employés au secteur des soins médicaux — le 5 octobre 1994, Vol. 9, no. 2: 13. (Publication de: The Royal College of Nursing Dynamic Quality Improvement Programme and the Foundation of Nursing Studies, in association with the *Nursing Standard*.)

La théorie du chaos

1 *'Les philosophes n'ont fait qu'interpréter le monde de façons diverses: le*
2 *problème, c'est de le changer'.* Les paroles de Marx sont prises très au sérieux
3 dans la science du chaos.
4 La théorie du chaos, comme a été rebaptisé pendant la décennie 1970
5 d'un nom plus sexy la science de la dynamique non-linéaire, a fait double
6 tranchant. Son aperçu principal — que les processus décrits par des lois
7 physiques simples pourraient, sous des conditions favorables, devenir
8 tout à fait imprévisibles — nous donne une vision extrêmement éclai-
9 rante. Toutes sortes de choses, sujettes à des variations bizarres, comme
10 la démographie des espèces animales, les casseroles qui mijotent sur la
11 cuisinière, ou des épidémies de rougeole, peuvent dorénavant se com-
12 prendre en principe. Pour ceux qui étudient de tels phénomènes, ceci
13 représente un grand pas en avant. Mais pour ceux qui espéraient pouvoir
14 faire des prévisions en appliquant méticuleusement des lois physiques
15 découvertes après tant d'efforts, c'était une mauvaise nouvelle. Ils ne
16 peuvent plus espérer que les mystères concernant le climat, les gru-
17 meaux qui obstruent les processus chimiques, ou les rafales d'instabilité
18 qui secouent les avions rapides, cèdent tous un jour devant une com-
19 préhension plus précise des règles. Les instabilités font partie intégrale
20 du système.
21 Pourtant, ce désespoir n'est pas totalement justifié. La théorie du
22 chaos dit que, livrés à eux-mêmes, les systèmes simples en apparence
23 finissent par se comporter de façon imprévisible. Mais pourquoi laisser
24 les choses à elles-mêmes? La théorie du chaos peut bien manquer de
25 pouvoir de prédiction, mais si l'on veut bien se laisser impliquer dans le
26 calcul au lieu de se limiter à une simple observation, ceci peut mener à
27 des façons très habiles de contrôler le monde.
28
29 **Ce n'est qu'une étape du développement**
30 Les ingénieurs cherchent actuellement à dompter le chaos dans des
31 endroits très divers: les muscles du coeur; les rythmes du cerveau; les
32 flammes des fourneaux industriels. Et pourtant, là où se trouve le chaos,
33 toutes les recherches ont recours à la même méthode pour le contrôler —
34 l'espace de phase.
35 Les mathématiciens ont inventé le concept de l'espace de phase au 19e
36 siècle. C'est un espace où chaque direction a sa propre signification.
37 Prenons, par exemple, un simple pendule: son mouvement peut se

38 décrire comme un mouvement de phase à deux dimensions avec deux
39 axes. L'un permet de mesurer la vitesse du pendule, l'autre enregistre la
40 position de celui-ci. Chaque point dans cet espace de phase représente
41 un état spécifique du système dans lequel le pendule possède une vitesse
42 et occupe une position données. Le point qui le représente change au fur
43 et à mesure que change l'état du système. Le mouvement d'un pendule
44 idéal dessine un cercle parfait dans l'espace de phase.
45   Toutes sortes de systèmes peuvent se décrire d'après les formes qu'ils
46 dessinent dans un espace de phase, qui aura souvent plus de deux
47 dimensions. Une grande partie de la théorie du chaos a pour point de
48 départ le fait que les processus apparemment aléatoires dans le monde
49 réel prennent en effet une forme plus régulière dans l'espace de phase.
50 Les figures qu'ils dessinent ne sont pas celles produites par le pendule,
51 qui agit selon un système qui le pousse à se retrouver toujours au même
52 état. Les dessins du chaos ressemblent plutôt aux écheveaux de laine
53 embrouillés, qui forment des spirals sans fin sans jamais revenir deux
54 fois au même endroit.

The Economist, le 25 juin 1994, pp. 105–106 (auteur anonyme).

De grands espoirs pour la carte à lecture optique — mise à l'essai

1 Le nombre toujours accroîssant du flot de procès pour cause de négli-
2 gence pourrait enfin fournir l'impulsion financière à l'usage plus étendu
3 d'un fichier du malade enrégistré sur une carte à mémoire qui resterait
4 entre les mains du malade lui-même.
5   Au cours d'un essai clinique de 18 mois qui doit commencer cet
6 automne, les femmes enceintes recevant les soins prénatals au nouvel
7 hôpital londonien de Chelsea et Westminster, recevront aussi une carte
8 à mémoire optique capable de stocker des radiographies, des échog-
9 raphies et des fichiers médicaux. En tout, chaque 'Clinicarte' pourra
10 stocker l'équivalent de 1000 pages d'informations, protégées contre
11 toute modification ou effacement, dans un espace pas plus grand que
12 celui d'une carte de crédit.
13   Cet essai fait partie d'un projet qui dure depuis presque huit ans. La
14 British Telecom (PTT britannique) avait accordé la première autorisation
15 de cette technologie en 1986, mais les premiers essais n'ont commencé
16 qu'en 1989, avec 200 volontaires dans un hôpital londonien, (voir *Tech-*
17 *nology*, 10.12.1988) à cause du retard dû aux difficultés dans la recherche
18 et le financement du matériel capable de lire les cartes. BT Tallis, filiale
19 de la BT, gère l'essai et fournit les scanners optiques.
20   Le principal avantage de la carte dans cet essai devrait résider dans
21 ce que les femmes recevront toutes les analyses appropriées à la mater-
22 nité. 'Des études menées il y a quelques années au coeur du NHS (Service
23 de Santé publique) ont trouvé que seulement 25 pour cent des analyses
24 habituelles qui devraient se faire pendant la grossesse, telles des tests
25 spécifiques pour certaines conditions, ont été faites', dit Tony Brown,
26 principal expert-conseil chez BT Tallis. 'Ceci revête des implications
27 importantes au cas d'un procès pour cause de négligence, ce qui arrive
28 très fréquemment aux Etats Unis et qui devient de moins en moins
29 rare en Grande Bretagne. Ces cartes permettront un contrôle détaillé,
30 ainsi, par example, dans le cas où une mère dont le bébe souffre du
31 syndrome de la trisomie, devait affirmer qu'elle n'a jamais été testée
32 pour ce syndrome, nous pourrions constater la vérité d'après les
33 fiches.'
34   Chaque carte pourra enrégistrer 2–4 megaoctets de données élec-
35 troniques, imprimées par laser sur la carte sous forme des alvéoles
36 microscopiques, comme ceux d'un disque compact. Un laser moins
37 puissant pourra alors entreprendre la lecture des données. Chaque carte

38   coûte actuellement environ quatre livres sterling (circa 32 fr) mais ce prix
39   devrait se réduire de moitié à la suite de la fabrication en série.
40   Cet essai tentera de développer le logiciel fourni par la société Nippon
41   Conlux du Japon, afin de permettre le rappel automatique des tests
42   appropriés à faire à chaque étape de la grossesse, basés sur des change-
43   ments dans des facteurs tels que le poids et la pression du sang maternel.
44   'Dans les systèmes basés sur des fiches en papier traditionnels, ce sera
45   noté quelque part, et tout dépendra de la sage-femme ou du médecin
46   pour le rassemblement des informations et le rappel des contrôles ap-
47   propriés' constate M Brown.
48   Bien que de telles cartes puissent apporter de nets avantages en ce qui
49   concerne les soins médicaux — en alertant, par example, les médecins à
50   la possibilité des réactions allergiques si le malade doit subir une opéra-
51   tion d'urgence — les économistes de la santé ont jusqu'alors rejeté l'idée
52   d'un usage plus étendu, parce que les avantages financiers n'ont pas
53   paru très clairs. Mais selon M Brown, le nombre accroissant des procès
54   pour cause de négligence en Grande Bretagne pourrait fournir l'impul-
55   sion financière nécessaire. 'Le fait d'avoir un moyen organisé de contrôle
56   des conseils donnés, quand et par qui, permettra une meilleure défense
57   en cas de procès, quand il pourrait y avoir dispute au sujet des tests faits
58   et des résultats obtenus.'
59   Les cartes seront aussi capables de stocker des images numériques des
60   radiographies, qui, une fois compactées, pourraient se faire enrégistrer
61   en moins de 15 kilo-octets. Les échographies de moins de dix secondes
62   pourraient aussi se stocker, puisque l'image télévisée sera déjà sous
63   forme numérique, bien que la technique pour le compactage de tels
64   renseignements n'ait pas encore été choisie.

Charles Arthur, *The New Scientist*, le 25 juin 1994, p. 20.

Etat de siège

1 Tandis que les gouvernements britannique et irlandais poursuivent la
2 recherche de la paix en Irlande du Nord, un resurgence de la violence
3 repousse à nouveau la réalisation de cet objectif. Dans la première partie
4 d'une série d'articles présentés au cours de deux semaines, traitant des
5 attitudes complexes qui sous-entendent 25 ans des 'perturbations', nous
6 faisons l'examen du cas de l'église protestante en Irelande du Nord.

7 Le 18 juin, partout dans les 'pubs'[1] aux îles britanniques, on buvait au
8 succès éventuel de l'équipe irlandaise, qui avait peu de chances de
9 gagner, lors du match de football entre celle-ci et l'équipe italienne dans
10 le cadre du Coupe mondial. Pour les habitants de la République d'Ir-
11 lande, la victoire contre les Italiens par leur équipe nationale donnait lieu
12 à des manifestations de réjouissement. Pour les supporters anglais,
13 l'équipe irlandaise — entraînée par un ancien joueur célèbre anglais et
14 composée des joueurs faisant normalement partie des équipes anglaises
15 ou écossaises, était un substitut acceptable pour la leur, qui n'avait pas
16 su se qualifier pour la compétition. Pour les 24 passionnés du football,
17 réunis au 'Heights Bar' dans le village tranquille de Loughinisland dans
18 le County Down, la fête fut suivie d'un massacre.

19 Deux hommes entrèrent dans le 'pub'; ils arrosèrent la salle de balles,
20 tuant six hommes et faisant cinq blessés. Puis ils s'enfuirent en riant. Un
21 peu plus tard, la Force volontaire d'Ulster,[2] groupe terroriste protestant,
22 a revendiqué l'attaque. Le 'pub' avait été choisi en sachant que ceux qui
23 s'y seraient rassemblés seraient des supporters catholiques de l'équipe
24 irlandaise.

25 Une fois de plus, après 25 ans de lutte, l'Irlande du Nord se trouvait
26 confrontée à la violence dont la férocité semble incompréhensible pour
27 les étrangers. Seule une petite minorité de Protestants, ou de
28 Catholiques, participent aux coups de feu et aux bombardements que
29 l'on commet à leur nom. Mais ils sont nombreux, des deux côtés du fossé
30 sectaire de la province, à ressentir des craintes et des soupçons à l'égard
31 de ceux de l'autre camp; de tels sentiments ont contribué à l'escalade
32 d'un violent conflit qui ne donne guère de signe d'affaiblissement,
33 malgré de nombreuses 'initiatives' de paix émanant des groupes gou-
34 vernementaux ainsi que des citoyens.

35 Les Protestants de l'Irlande du Nord se trouvent peut-être dans une
36 position plus ambigüe. Ils se disent britanniques, tout en sachant que les
37 habitants du continent britannique ne les considèrent pas toujours ainsi.

38 Ils affirment une allégeance politique unioniste[3] tout en admettant que
39 le parlement et le peuple britanniques ne partagent pas leurs sentiments
40 au sujet de l'Union de la Grande Bretagne et l'Irlande du Nord.
41   Quelque 900 000 Unionistes protestants co-habitent la partie nord-est
42 de l'île d'Irelande avec 600 000 Catholiques, dont l'identité irlandaise a
43 été reconnue, du moins verbalement, par les ministres britanniques
44 comme l'égale à l'identité britannique qu'affirment beaucoup de Protes-
45 tants. Aux yeux des Unionistes, même cette concession verbale semble
46 impliquer que l'union tant prisée avec la Grande Bretagne est en train
47 de leur échapper. Les hommes politiques unionistes refusent de par-
48 ticiper aux negociations concernant le cadre d'un gouvernement futur
49 qui reconnaîtrait l'identité irlandaise de leurs voisins catholiques à trav-
50 ers l'établissement des institutions communes pour les deux parties de
51 l'île, le nord et le sud (comme l'avait suggéré Albert Reynolds, Premier
52 ministre de la République d'Irelande, ce qui avait provoqué la plus
53 grande indignation auprès des Unionistes). Les paramilitaires 'loyal-
54 istes'[4] cherchent à détourner de tels objectifs par des massacres brutaux
55 de Catholiques, faits au hasard, comme celui de Loughinisland.
56   Depuis le début, l'année dernière, de la série la plus récente des
57 contacts, des propos et des discussions secrets — appelée par les
58 Catholiques le 'processus de la paix' — beaucoup de Protestants
59 craignent plus que jamais que les Britanniques ne se laissent tenter par
60 la perspective de conclure un accord avec la IRA.[5] Ils sont d'avis que des
61 pourparlers secrets avec le gouvernement de la République d'Irlande,
62 visant une souveraineté partagée, sont destinés à amadouer l'opposition
63 à une intégration finale en une Irlande unie de tendance majoritaire
64 catholique.

Extrait d'un article publié dans *The Economist*, le 25.6.94, pp. 25–26
(auteur anonyme).

1. Bistrots britanniques.
2. Ulster Volunteer Force.
3. L'Union (The Act of Union) entre la Grande Bretagne et l'Irlande, conclue le
    1 janvier 1801, entre les Britanniques protestants et les Irlandais et modifiée
    en 1922 quand vingt six des provinces de l'Irlande du sud ont obtenu leur
    indépendance pour devenir le pays nommé Eire.
4. Dans ce contexte, loyaliste veut dire loyal à l'Union, donc protestant.
5. L'Armée républicaine irlandaise, groupe terroriste catholique (Irish Repub-
    lican Army).

Le livre blanc qui a déchaîné la tempête

Le problème

Le problème de l'union européenne a atteint une étape décisive de son développement. Si d'ici deux à quatre ans l'on n'arrivait pas à trouver une solution aux causes de cette situation critique, il en résultera que l'Union deviendra pour ainsi dire un rassemblement décousu d'états entre lesquels les seuls liens seront d'ordre économique, divisé d'ailleurs en de petits groupuscules d'états, et ceci contrairement au but d'une association de plus en plus étroite telle que prévue dans le traité de Maastricht. Parmi les principales causes figurent les suivantes:

– La surextension des institutions, qui, prévues d'origine pour six pays membres, doivent dorénavant pourvoir aux exigences de 12 pays, qui seront bientôt 16.

– Une augmentation du niveau de 'nationalisme regressif' dans (presque) tous les pays membres. La peur et l'inquiétude poussent à chercher, sinon une solution alors au moins un refuge dans le retour au concept de l'état-nation et tout ce qui a rapport aux interêts nationaux.

Révision des institutions

Toutes les institutions actuelles — le Conseil, la Commission, la présidence et le parlement européen — doivent être réformées. Les changements doivent viser des concepts prévoyant un nouvel équilibre institutionnel, selon lequel le parlement européen aura de plus en plus de pouvoirs comme vrai organe de législation possédant les mêmes droits que le Conseil. En plus de s'acquitter des tâches dans le domaine intergouvernemental, celui-ci assumera les fonctions d'une seconde assemblée, et la Commission de sa part se verra doter des fonctions d'un gouvernement européen.

Pour ce qui est du Conseil, la démocratisation exigera un meilleur état d'équilibre entre d'une part l'egalité parmi tous les états membres et le rapport, d'autre part, entre la population et le nombre de votes au Conseil.

Une Europe multivitesse

Afin de réaliser tout ceci, la 'géométrie variable', ou bien l'approche 'multivitesse', devrait être approuvée et institutionalisée dans le traité d'union ou dans le nouveau document quasi-conditionnel. Sinon, cette

38 approche risquerait de favoriser une tendance vers une 'Europe à la
39 carte'. Il faut ainsi décider si, dans le cas des amendements au traité de
40 Maastricht, le principe de l'unanimité comme prévu dans l'Article N
41 devrait être remplacé par celui d'un quorum qu'il resterait à préciser. Il
42 est essentiel qu'aucun pays ne puisse se servir du droit de véto pour
43 bloquer les efforts d'autres pays plus capables et plus désireux d'inten-
44 sifier le niveau de co-opération et d'approfondir celui de l'intégration.
45   La tâche du noyau dur sera de donner à l'Union un centre solide afin
46 de faire contre-équilibre aux forces centrifuges générées par un élargis-
47 sement perpetuel.
48   A cette fin, les pays du noyau dur devraient faire preuve d'un degré
49 d'esprit communautaire dans leurs actions collaboratives qui sera plus
50 élevé et beaucoup plus évident que celui des autres pays.
51   Dans le domaine monétaire aussi, il y a de fortes indications qu'un
52 noyau dur de cinq pays soit en voie d'émergence. Ceux-ci, avec la
53 Danemark et l'Irelande, seront ceux qui rempliront de plus près les
54 critères de convergence prévus dans le traité de Maastricht. Ceci est
55 particulièrement important puisque l'union monétaire constitue en effet
56 l'élément clé de l'union politique (et non pas, comme on le croit en
57 Allemagne, un élément supplémentaire de l'intégration qui va de pair
58 avec l'union politique).

Extraits d'un document CDU/CSU publié par le groupe majoritaire au
parlement allemand à cette époque: ces extraits ont paru dans *The
European*, 9–15 septembre 1994.

EU fugaces labuntur communitates

Qu'importe le nom?

C'est précisément au moment où la plupart des gens avaient cessé de parler du 'marché commun' pour enfin s'habituer à l'appeler la Communauté européenne, qu' arrive le traité de Maastricht pour sèmer la confusion par la création de quelque chose nommé l'Union européenne. Qu'est-ce que c'est, et pourquoi 'The Economist' aurait-il décidé à contrecoeur d'abandonner ce terme, déjà connu, de la CE en faveur de la UE, un nom beaucoup moins élégant et euphonique.

La viscosité de la réponse réflète celle du traité de M, qui est entré en vigueur le 1 novembre et qui a donné lieu à cette Union. Voici encore un chef d'oeuvre de faux-fuyants européens. La nouvelle union est identique à l'ancienne CE mais avec ceci de supplémentaire. D'abord, une politique étrangère et de securité en commun. Tout le reste de ce qu'est censé réaliser le traité de Maastricht — ouvrir la voie vers l'union économique et un système monétaire unique, renforcer le parlement européen, donner de nouveaux pouvoirs à Bruxelles en ce qui concerne la politique industrielle, les affaires de consommation, la santé et l'éducation — tout ceci reste bel et bien la responsabilité de la CE.

L'ensemble de l'infrastructure — la CE plus les politiques étrangère et de securité, plus la justice et la co-opération policière — constitute en son entier l'Union européenne. De l'autre côté, elle ne forme pas un processus unique de prise de décisions, mais trois processus individuels. Qui plus est, la UE n'a pas de persona juridique. Seule la CE et/ou les états membres peuvent conclure des accords internationaux, par exemple.

Autrement dit, c'est la confusion totale, surtout parmi les architectes de l'Union. Lors d'une conférence de presse suivant le sommet récent à Bruxelles, John Major a raté sa tentative d'explication de ce qu'est l'Union européenne et de ses raisons pour une utilisation peu fréquente de ce nom. Il a parlé enfin d'une 'union à trois piliers' dans le cadre de laquelle le travail de la CE continuerait comme avant, tandis qu'il incomberait à l'Union de s'occuper de tout ce qui toucherait à la justice ou à la police. La raison principale pour cette séparation serait la volonté de plusieurs pays, avec en tête la France et la Grande Bretagne, de soustraire autant que possible les additions à Maastricht des mains de la commission à Bruxelles et du parlement européen. Les officiels britanniques à Bruxelles affirment qu'ils tâcheront de maintenir cette distinction dans les affaires européennes quotidiennes.

38   *The Economist* est d'avis que ces efforts ne risquent pas de réussir.
39   Certains continueront de parler de la CE en dépit de toute exactitude
40   juridique, d'autres feront de plus en plus référence à l'Union dans tous
41   les contextes sauf ceux historiques. Nous avons décidé de choisir le
42   terme, l'Union, dans la conviction (erronée peut-être) qu'au fil des
43   années l'usage fera prévaloir ce terme.
44   Les autorités ne nous ont pas été d'un très grand secours dans la prise
45   de décision. Le 8 novembre, le Conseil des Ministres, l'organe principal
46   de décision de la Communauté, est devenu le 'Conseil des Ministres de
47   l'Union européenne'. Mais le 17 novembre la commission à Bruxelles a
48   esquivé le problème en se rebaptisant 'La Commission européenne',
49   nom que leur donnait déjà l'opinion publique. Les juges de la cour
50   européenne au Luxembourg, tous conservateurs sans exception, ont
51   décidé de garder le nom, 'Cour de Justice des communautés européen-
52   nes', ce qui rappelle l'existence continue de la Communauté du Charbon
53   et de l'Acier, et du Commissariat à l'Energie atomique.

De 'Notre Reporteur à Bruxelles', *The Economist*, le 20 novembre 1993.

La Grande Bretagne avec Eurotunnel?
C'est si facile!

Petit guide du voyageur Eurotunnel

1. La route intelligente vers la Grande-Bretagne

Quand ouvrira le tunnel?

Eurotunnel ouvrira son service de navettes aux voitures et aux poids-lourds à partir du 15 Juin 1993. Le transport des autocars et des caravanes sera assuré à partir de l'automne 1993. (Les services de trains directs de la SNCF et British Rail fonctionneront aussi à partir du 15 Juin 1993.)

Comment voyagera-t-on dans le tunnel?

Le Tunnel sous la Manche comprend deux tunnels ferroviaires à voie unique (un pour l'aller, l'autre pour le retour) et une galerie de service, entre la France et la Grande-Bretagne. Les navettes ferroviaires spéciales exploitées par Eurotunnel transporteront les véhicules routiers et leurs passagers dans le tunnel; les trains de voyageurs et de marchandises, exploités par les compagnies ferroviaires nationales, emprunteront aussi le tunnel.

Où se trouve Eurotunnel?

Le service de navettes Eurotunnel fonctionnera entre deux terminaux, l'un situé aux abords de Calais avec accès direct au réseau autoroutier (A26), et l'autre près de Folkestone, dans le Kent, relié à l'autoroute M20.

2. Une traversée rapide et facile

Conduira-t-on sa voiture dans le tunnel?

Non, il vous suffira de conduire votre véhicule dans une navette, qui vous transportera en toute sécurité. Les locomotives qui tireront les navettes sont électriques, ainsi l'air du tunnel ne sera pas pollué par les gaz d'échappement.

Qui pourra l'utiliser?

La plupart des véhicules routiers. Selon leur hauteur, les autocars, les voitures (avec caravane ou remorque) et les motocyclettes seront transportés dans les navettes simple-pont ou double-pont et la plupart des passagers voyageront dans leur véhicule. Les poids-lourds seront dirigés vers des navettes spéciales, comprenant un wagon séparé pour les chauffeurs. Les compagnies de chemin de fer, quant à elles, assureront tous les services habituels de trains de passagers et de marchandises.

37 *Combien de temps durera le trajet?*
38 Environ trente cinq minutes de quai à quai, et en moyenne un peu
39 plus d'une heure d'autoroute à autoroute.
40
41 *Comment saura-t-on s'il y a des embouteillages?*
42 Avec un départ de navette passagers toutes les 15 minutes en période
43 de pointe, les bouchons seront exceptionnels. En appelant le numéro
44 d'information d'Eurotunnel, ou en écoutant la radio Eurotunnel à l'ap-
45 proche du terminal, vous serez informé de la fréquence de départ des
46 navettes, du temps d'attente, ainsi que de la météo, des conditions de
47 circulation routière, ou de l'actualité.
48
49 *Comment les navettes traverseront-elles le tunnel?*
50 Deux locomotives électriques, une à chaque extrémité de la
51 navette, seront capables de tirer la navette à une vitesse allant jusqu'à
52 140km/h
53
54 **3. Pas de stress**
55 *Peut-il y avoir des fuites?*
56 Les tunnels sont creusés de 25 à 45 mètres sous le lit de la mer, dans
57 une couche de craie bleue imperméable. En outre, les parois du tunnel
58 forment un revêtement étanche. Les risques de fuites sont donc pratique-
59 ment inexistants.
60
61 *Que se passerait-t-il en cas d'incendie?*
62 Dans l'hypothèse exceptionnelle d'un feu dans un wagon, l'équipage
63 fera évacuer les passagers dans le wagon adjacent. Les membres d'équi-
64 page ainsi que des systèmes sophistiqués de détection et d'extinction
65 repèreront et éteindront tout feu, qui serait de toute façon contenu par
66 les portes coupe-feu étanches situées aux extrémités des wagons. Dans
67 la plupart des cas, la navette continuera son trajet jusqu'au terminal, où
68 des mesures complémentaires seront prises, si nécessaire.
69
70 *Faudra-t-il emporter son passport?*
71 Oui, vous serez soumis aux mêmes contrôles frontaliers que pour les
72 ferries ou l'aéroglisseur. Cependant, l'ouverture du marché unique
73 Européen aboutira à l'abolition des contrôles de passeports en Europe.
74
75 *En quoi consisteront les contrôles frontaliers?*
76 Bien que la frontière officielle se trouve au milieu de la Manche, vous
77 passerez les contrôles de douane et de police français et britanniques sur
78 le terminal de départ. Il n'y aura pas d'autres contrôles à l'arrivée.

79 *Pourra-t-on emmener des animaux dans le tunnel?*
80   Seulement si vous respectez la législation sur l'importation d'ani-
81 maux et la quarantaine. Des procédures strictes seront mises en place
82 pour assurer le respect de la loi britannique visant à empêcher l'intro-
83 duction accidentelle de la rage.
84
85 *Comment la propagation de la rage sera-t-elle évitée?*
86   Plusieurs types de barrières sont installés, sur le sol et sous-terre, pour
87 empêcher les animaux de circuler dans le tunnel, et la surveillance sur
88 les terminaux sera telle qu'il n'y aura pas plus de risque de voir des
89 animaux importés en fraude en Grande Bretagne qu'avec les autres
90 modes de transport trans-Manche.
91
92
93 **4. Pas de réservation, pas d'heure limite**
94   **A peine arrivé, aussitôt parti**
95 *Faudra-t-il réserver son passage?*
96   Non, aucune réservation ne sera nécessaire, mais vous pourrez
97 acheter vos billets à l'avance. Vous pourrez utiliser Eurotunnel à n'im-
98 porte quel moment; en période de pointe, il y aura jusqu'à quatre départs
99 de navettes passagers par heure. Les temps d'attente seront donc réduits.
100
101 *Combien de temps avant le départ faudra-t-il arriver au terminal?*
102   Il ne sera pas nécessaire d'arriver à une heure précise. Lorsque vous
103 arriverez au terminal, vous serez dirigé vers la prochaine navette dis-
104 ponible; vous ne risquerez donc pas de 'rater votre navette'.
105
.06 *Quel sera le prix du trajet?*
.07   Les prix seront comparables à ceux des ferries, avec une grille tarifaire
08 simple.
09
10 *Qu'est-il prévu pour les handicapés?*
11   Des mesures spéciales ont été prises pour leur rendre le voyage aussi
12 aisé que possible, et les membres d'équipage seront toujours présents
13 pour les aider.
14
15
16 **5. Ouvert 24 heures sur 24, 365 jours par an**
17 *Le tunnel sera-t-il ouvert la nuit?*
18   Oui, les navettes fonctionneront 24 heures sur 24, 365 jours par an,
19 avec au moins un départ par heure pour les passagers pendant les heures
20 creuses de la nuit.

121 *Comment arrivera-t-on aux terminaux?*
122   Les terminaux d'Eurotunnel seront fléchés à partir des autoroutes et
123 des autres routes d'accès, des deux côtés de la Manche. Dans les deux
124 terminaux, la signalisation sera en français et en anglais.
125
126 *Que trouvera-t-on sur les terminaux?*
127   Les deux terminaux offriront une gamme étendue de services aux
128 passagers (cafétérias, restaurants, toilettes, boutiques et bureaux de
129 change). Vous aurez le choix de vous y arrêter le temps que vous
130 souhaiterez ou d'aller directement vers la navette.
131
132 *Quels moyens de paiement pourra-t-on utiliser?*
133   Vous paierez votre billet au péage à l'entrée du terminal. Vous pour-
134 rez payer en espèces (Francs Français ou Livres Sterling), par chèque ou
135 avec la plupart des cartes de crédit et de paiement.
136
137 **6. Entrez, et coupez le contact**
138 *Comment conduira-t-on sa voiture dans la navette?*
139   Vous suivrez l'itinéraire fléché qui vous mènera du péage à votre
140 quai d'embarquement. L'équipage vous guidera pour l'embarque-
141 ment de votre véhicule dans la navette par un wagon de chargement.
142 Vous conduirez votre voiture dans la navette jusqu'à l'emplacement
143 qui vous sera indiqué, vous serrerez le frein à main et vous couperez
144 le contact.
145
146 *Combien de temps durera le chargement?*
147   Environ huit minutes si la navette est pleine.
148
149 *Que se passera-t-il si une voiture est en panne?*
150   Un service de dépannage sera disponible dans chaque terminal.
151
152 **7. Le confort en plus**
153 *Le trajet sera-t-il confortable?*
154   La voie ferrée a été spécialement conçue pour assurer un service
155 agréable, et vous n'aurez sûrement pas le mal de mer! Le niveau sonore
156 sera semblable à celui d'un train de grande ligne.
157
158 *Devra-t-on rester dans sa voiture?*
159   Vous voyagerez normalement à bord de votre voiture, où vous pour-
160 rez vous reposer, étudier votre itinéraire, écouter la radio Eurotunnel,
161 ou regarder les panneaux lumineux vous indiquant la progression du
162 voyage. Vous pourrez aussi sortir de votre véhicule pour parler à d'au-

3 tres passagers ou à un membre d'équipage, utiliser les toilettes, ou vous
4 dégourdir les jambes.
5
6 *Risquera-t-on de souffrir de claustrophobie?*
7   Les navettes seront climatisées et bien éclairées, et vous aurez la place
8 pour vous déplacer pendant le court voyage. Les navettes auront des
9 fenêtres de taille réduite.

Petit Guide du Voyageur Eurotunnel, pp. 1–3.

Peche lucrative dans les réserves de main-d'oeuvre étrangère

1 Une ordonnance de la Cour Européenne autorise les employeurs à
2 transférer des ouvriers immigrés n'importe où dans l'Union Européenne.
3 La responsabilité électorale sera la première à souffrir, écrit Alistair
4 McAlpine.

5 L'un des avantages principaux de l'Union Européenne — peut-être le
6 plus important — est la possibilité pour ses citoyens de rechercher un
7 emploi n'importe où entre ses frontières. Les habitants du reste du
8 monde doivent faire une demande de permis de travail auprès du
9 pays-membre où ils voudraient être employés. En tout cas, ceci était le
10 cas dans le passé. Mais une décision de la Cour Européenne a, depuis,
11 changé tout cela.

12 Un groupe de Marocains, employés par un entrepreneur belge dans
13 les services de démolition, voulaient travailler sous un contrat que
14 celui-ci s'est fait accorder par compétition en France. Les Officiels du
15 Service de l'Immigration Français ont insisté pour que ces ouvriers du
16 bâtiment marocains obtiennent un permis de travail, comme ils l'avaient
17 toujours fait dans le passé. La Cour en a décidé autrement: il semble
18 qu'un employeur peut maintenant transférer sa main-d'oeuvre immi-
19 grée n'importe où dans l'Union Européenne, sans égard aux frontières
20 nationales.

21 L'industrie du bâtiment emploie un grand nombre de main-d'oeuvres
22 non-qualifiées. La première exigence pour obtenir un emploi sur un
23 chantier est d'avoir de la force, puis de l'endurance. Les constructeurs
24 ont traditionnellement cherché des ouvriers non-qualifiés à l'étranger.
25 Les gouvernements des pays où travaillent ces constructeurs ont tou-
26 jours régulé le flux de cette main-d'oeuvre. L'industrie du bâtiment est
27 un monde très compétitif dans lequel la concurrence entre constructeurs
28 s'avère féroce. Cette nouvelle décision de la Cour Européenne a changé
29 les règles du jeu.

30 Le constructeur le plus compétitif n'est plus le mieux organisé ni le
31 plus expérimenté, mais celui qui a accès à la plus grande réserve de main
32 d'oeuvre la moins chère. Un constructeur italien, par exemple, négociera
33 avec le gouvernement italien pour obtenir des permis de travail pour,
34 disons, des ouvriers nord-africains qui travailleront pour lui sur des
35 chantiers qu'il aura peut-être obtenus en plein centre de Londres. Les
36 autorités officielles italiennes et, dans ce cas, leurs maîtres, les politiciens
37 italiens, auront peu d'intérêt à refuser ces permis, puisque les emplois

que prendront ces ouvriers immigrés d'Afrique du nord seront ceux d'ouvriers du bâtiment anglais qui n'ont pas le droit de vote aux élections italiennes.

De toute façon, les richesses créées par l'entrepreneur italien, bon marché mais prospère, reviendront en Italie, alors que les charges sociales de cette main d'oeuvre retomberont sur les contribuables britanniques. Les conséquences des décisions prises par un officiel italien ne toucheront pas du tout l'Italie.

Avec le temps, le besoin d'être compétitif fera que tous les ouvriers du bâtiment seront des immigrés. Les pressions sociales sur les pays dans lesquels ils travailleront seront intolérables.

Les gouvernements qui souffrent des conséquences des décisions prises par des officiels d'autres pays de l'Union Européenne peuvent rager autant qu'ils veulent: la loi stipule clairement que les ouvriers immigrés ont le droit de travailler dans n'importe quel pays de l'Union Européenne où leur employeur choisit de diriger ses affaires.

J'ai pris l'exemple de l'industrie du bâtiment parce qu'il est évident. Le principe peut être appliqué à l'industrie de production industrielle, au tourisme ou à tout autre secteur. Ne ressortiront de cette décision de la Cour que chaos et conflits.

Extrait d'un article de Alistair McAlpine, *The European*, 9–15 septembre 1994.

La cour de justice européenne confirme les droits des travailleurs

1 Hier soir une décision de la cour de justice européenne, qui aura des
2 conséquences non-négligeables pour les droits des millions de tra-
3 vailleurs britanniques, suivant le manque de volonté de la part de
4 gouvernement britannique de donner aux employés le droit de par-
5 ticiper aux décisions ayant un effet sur leur avenir, a poussé ce premier
6 à se mettre sur la défensive.
7   Dans une décision faisant l'objet des interprétations diverses, vue par
8 certains comme ayant porté un coup accablant au gouvernement, par
9 d'autres comme n'ayant que peu d'implications pratiques, la cour de
10 justice européenne a proclamé que les représentants ouvriers avaient le
11 droit à l'information et à la consultation en ce qui concernait les licencie-
12 ments en masse ou lors du transfert du contrôle d'une société, y compris
13 dans le cas de la privatisation.
14   La Commission européenne a constaté que la Grande Bretagne
15 devrait changer sa législation concernant les droits des travailleurs.
16 Selon Padraig Flynn, commissionnaire aux affaires sociales, 'Il ne fait pas
17 de doute que des changements devront s'effectuer afin de satisfaire à la
18 décision de la cour'.
19   M Flynn refusait d'exprimer son opinion quant à la possibilité de
20 l'ouverture, suite à cette décision, aux revendications de compensation
21 par les travailleurs dont les emplois ont passé du secteur public au
22 secteur privé pendant les années 80.
23   Hier soir, pourtant, M Jack Dromey, représentant du TGWU (syndicat
24 des travailleurs dans le secteur du transport et du secteur général), et
25 responsable des services publics, a fait appel au gouvernement, re-
26 vendiquant la négociation de la compensation pour tous ceux ayant
27 souffert en conséquence du système de soumissions concurrentielles
28 obligatoires; ou bien qu'ils se voient obligés de comparaître devant la
29 cour de justice pour se défendre contre les syndicats.
30   Il a affirmé d'ailleurs la détermination du TGWU de poursuivre une
31 action juridique contre toute autorité locale qui tenterait de refuser de
32 reconnaître l'autorité des syndicats. 'Nous sommes d'avis que cette
33 décision mettra fin au refus de reconnaître le rôle des syndicats dans les
34 services publics'.
35   Le Ministre pour l'Emploi, Michael Forsyth, a répondu que le gou-
36 vernement aurait à considérer ce jugement mais que les effets n'en
37 auraient qu'une portée extrêmement limitée. Les employeurs ne se ver-

38 raient pas obligés de reconnaître les syndicats lors des licenciements et
39 les transferts, mais que les employés eux-mêmes devraient être con-
40 sultés.

41   M John Hendy, QC, (Conseiller de la couronne) et président de
42 l'Institut des Droits au Travail, a dit que 'La signification de cette décision
43 ne réside pas en la possibilité de compensation mais en le progrès vers
44 une démocratie à l'endroit de travail qu'elle représente.'

45   La décision a donné lieu à une confrontation entre John Major et le
46 porte-parole travailliste sur l'environnement, M Jack Straw, lors de la
47 conférence de presse hier pour les élections européennes. M Major l'a
48 décrite comme étant basée sur une directive européenne approuvée par
49 le gouvernement travailliste en 1975.

50   Mais M Straw a insisté que cette décision se fondait sur une loi
51 approuvée par le gouvernement conservateur, il y 13 ans. 'Elle se fera
52 désormais implémenter afin d'accorder aux travailleurs britanniques les
53 mêmes droits que ceux dont bénéficient les travailleurs partout en
54 Europe.'

55   M John Monks, secrétaire général du TUC (Congrès des syndicats
56 ouvriers) a décrit cette décision comme un 'coup accablant' pour le
57 gouvernement. 'Une fois de plus, on a vu refuser aux travailleurs britan-
58 niques des droits qui sont inscrits dans les lois de tous les autres pays
59 membres de l'Union européenne.'

60   Les directives ont été prononcées lors de deux actions portées contre
61 le gouvernement britannique par la Commission européenne, pour ne
62 pas avoir implémenté correctement de la législation de la UE. La pre-
63 mière concernait la directive visant les droits acquis, connue en Grande
64 Bretagne comme la 'Tupe';[1] elle gouverne la protection des salaires et
65 des conditions des ouvriers lors de la vente ou du transfert du contrôle
66 de l'entreprise. La deuxième recouvre la législation visant la protection
67 des droits des travailleurs en cas de licenciements en masse. Les syndi-
68 cats britanniques se sont servis de cette 'Tupe' pour contester la pratique
69 de l'endommagement aux salaires et aux conditions de travail lors de la
70 privatisation des activités du secteur public.

Extrait d'un article de Keith Harper, Julie Wolf and Seumas Milne, *The
Guardian*, le 9 juin 1994, p. 2.

1. Transfer of Undertakings (Protection of Employment) — le transfert des
    garanties/engagements (la protection de l'emploi). Cette regulation britan-
    nique de 1981 vise la mise en oeuvre de la directive de la cour européenne
    des droits acquis, no. 77/187/CEE.

Les employeurs exigeants cherchent du personnel sachant travailler en équipe

Les affaires connaissent une hausse

1 *Un sondage peint en rose la vie dans le secteur tertiaire: reportage de Clive*
2 *Woodcock.*
3 En dépit de la récession et du taux élevé du chômage, les patrons
4 éprouvent toujours des problèmes à trouver du personnel aux aptitudes
5 voulues, selon un nouveau sondage sur l'emploi dans les petites entre-
6 prises du secteur tertiaire. Cette situation s'explique en partie par le
7 processus de sélection à l'embauche très exigeant. Il ne saurait être une
8 simple question des compétences requises; en effet, il faut aussi que le
9 nouvel employé soit capable de 's'intégrer'; voici l'avis des auteurs de
10 cette étude, du Centre de Recherches sur les petites entreprises de
11 l'université de Kingston.
12 Une petite entreprise doit se doter d' un effectif capable de collaborer
13 en équipe: dans un secteur où les employés entrent en contacte avec les
14 clients, ce qui est d'ailleurs fréquent dans le secteur tertiaire, il leur faut
15 aussi des compétences sociales en relations interpersonnelles. Les rela-
16 tions entre patrons et employés s'avéreraient plutôt sans conflits, selon
17 ce sondage. Les employés ont constaté que de manière générale les
18 patrons étaient équitables, et la surveillance ne s'est fait voir que rare-
19 ment comme étant trop minutieuse ou autoritaire. Qui plus est, les
20 relations entre les employés eux-mêmes se montraient somme toute
21 bonnes — ce qui est d'une importance capitale au bon fonctionnnement
22 d'une petite entreprise, comme le font remarquer les chercheurs.
23 La plupart des employés aussi bien que des patrons ne se rappellaient
24 que difficilement d'une dispute grave au sein de l'entreprise. Il n'y avait
25 non plus que peu d'évidence de l'existence des petites entreprises du
26 genre 'atelier exploiteur' ni même des mauvaises relations patron–
27 employés comme se sont tant fait reporter jadis dans les industries telles
28 que la restauration.
29 Plus de 270 patrons et employés ont été sondés: certaines des entre-
30 prises se trouvaient dans le secteur tertiaire traditionnel, tels les petits
31 garages et les petites entreprises de restauration, tandis que d'autres
32 travaillaient dans les services informatiques et dans les domaines en voie
33 d'expansion récente, tels les services-conseils d' affaires. Une proportion
34 importante des emplois étaient à mi-temps ou intérimaires, plutôt que
35 d'être des emplois à plein temps et permanents, tant caractéristiques du
36 passé. Un nombre significatif des emplois étaient occupés par des

37 femmes, autre caractéristique frappant des emplois dans ce secteur
38 tertiaire. Beaucoup de ces emplois se faisaient faire par des gens qui
39 cherchaient du travail à mi-temps ou temporaire, afin de s'accorder avec
40 les responsabilités à domicile ou aux exigences de l'éducation. Il n'y avait
41 guère d'employés ayant exercé précédemment un emploi à plein temps
42 qui faisaient du travail à temps partiel.

43   Selon les chercheurs, l'importance toujours croissante des services et
44 des petites entreprises au Royaume Uni exige une politique très forte de
45 recrutement dans ces types d'entreprises, si les syndicats ouvriers
46 veulent effectuer un renversement du déclin subi actuellement par ceux-
47 ci. Les entrevues avec les employeurs ont pourtant fait ressortir que les
48 syndicats risquaient de le trouver difficile de s'imposer/d'avoir un
49 impact quelconque. La plupart des employeurs étaient d'avis que les
50 syndicats n'avaient pas de rôle à jouer dans une petite entreprise. Tandis
51 que de nombreux employeurs s'opposaient à une représentation syndi-
52 cale des employés, une proportion surprenante se sont déclarés
53 favorable à la représentation par le syndicat si tel était le souhait des
54 employés.

55   L'on a tendance à considérer que le salaire et les compléments de
56 salaire sont moins favorables chez les petites entreprises qu'ils le sont
57 chez les grandes, ce qui s'est vu confirmer de façon générale par la
58 recherche, bien qu'elle ait découverte des variations sensibles entre les
59 sociétés dans des secteurs différents. Les employeurs étaient partisans
60 enthousiastes du principe de l'adaptation du salaire et d'autres avan-
61 tages selon l'employé individuel.

62   Les employeurs n'ont guère fait preuve d'enthousiasme envers une
63 formation plus soutenue ni pour les Conseils de Formation et d'Entre-
64 prise comme source de formation. Ils ont constaté l'existence d'un niveau
65 important de formation continue au sein même de l'entreprise, dont une
66 grande partie serait d'ordre informel, adaptée aux besoins de l'entreprise
67 elle-même. De leur part, les employées manquaient aussi d'enthousi-
68 asme pour un accroissement considérable du niveau de la formation.

*L'Emploi et les relations dans l'emploi aux petites entreprise du secteur tertiaire,
du Centre de Recherche pour les petites entreprises, Université de Kingston,
Surrey, £40 LS. [Employment and Employment Relations in the Services Sector
Small Enterprise, £ 40, from Small Business Research Centre, Kingston University, Kingston Hill, Surrey KT2 7LB.]*

Clive Woodcock, *The Guardian*, le 4 mai 1993.

Marks & Spencer

1 **1. Activités principales**

2   Marks & Spencer, détaillant international de renom, vend des articles
3 de confection et de la maison et des produits alimentaires sous la marque
4 'St Michael' au Royaume Uni, en République d'Irlande, en France,
5 Belgique, Espagne, Hollande et à Hong Kong.
6   En Amérique du Nord, au Canada en particulier, la société commer-
7 cialise une gamme de marchandise et d'articles de consommation
8 courante St Michael. Aux Etats-Unis et au Japon, les articles de confection
9 de qualité sont vendus sous l'enseigne de Brooks-Brothers, alors qu'aux
10 Etats-Unis les produits alimentaires sont diffusés sous celle de Kings
11 Super Markets.
12   La politique de Marks & Spencer est d'offrir à sa clientèle, dans le
13 monde entier, un rapport qualité-prix et un service irréprochables.

14

15 **2. Quelques chiffres (1991/92)**
16   – Le chiffre d'affaires excède £5.700 millions
17   – Le bénéfice fiscal dépasse £615 millions
18   – Plus de 690 magasins dans le monde entier
19   – 74.000 employés
20   – 15 millions de clients chaque semaine
21   – Degré de solvabilité AAA
22   – Les investissements dans des activités communautaires diverses
23   excèdent £5 millions.

24

25 **3. Europe**
26 *Royaume-Uni*
27   Au cours de deux dernières années, la société a ouvert 93.000m^2 de
28 surface de vente supplémentaire dans ses magasins du Royaume-Uni et
29 sa surface totale d'exploitation atteint environ 930.000m^2. Le programme
30 d'expansion de ses magasins installés en centre-ville et à la périphérie se
31 poursuivra pendant la période 1992/93.

32

33 **Europe Continentale**
34   La performance des 17 magasins de la société implantés en Europe
35 continentale a été excellente en 1991/92 avec une augmentation de 38%
36 des bénéfices d'exploitation. Après avoir ouvert des magasins, pour la
37 première fois en Espagne et en Hollande, la société projette de quadru-

88 pler sa surface de vente dans les pays d'Europe Continentale dans les
89 quatre années à venir.
40   Une expansion en Europe est également synonyme de débouchés
41 pour les universitaires les plus compétents.
42
43 **4. Débouchés pour les universitaires**
44   Des débouchés existent pour les diplômés de toutes les disciplines
45 dans les trois catégories de gestion des magasins suivantes:
46
47 *Direction commerciale*
48   Responsable de l'accroissement des ventes et de l'exploitation des
49 perspectives commerciales. La direction commerciale doit offrir à la clien-
50 tèle un service d'une qualité irréprochable, maximiser la productivité du
51 linéaire, contrôler les coûts et développer l'efficacité opérationelle.
52
53 *Direction du personnel*
54   Responsable de la rentabilité de la ressource la plus précieuse des
55 magasins: son personnel. La direction du personnel met en application
56 la politique de la société en établissant des programmes de recrutement,
57 de formation et de développement de la carrière tout en demeurant à
58 l'écoute des besoins de chacun et en continuant à résoudre les problèmes
59 d'ordre personnel et professionnel.
60
61 *Direction administrative*
62   Responsable du contrôle et de l'expansion des secteurs financier, de
63 l'information et des systèmes, domaines d'une importance vitale dans la
64 gestion rentable d'un magasin. Les responsables de la gestion adminis-
65 trative mettent en oeuvre et gèrent les systèmes informatiques,
66 surveillent les budgets et garantissent un contrôle rigoureux des coûts à
67 l'intérieur des magasins.
68   Un programme de formation structuré et une formulation du profil
69 de carrière basés sur les performances individuelles seront offerts à tous
70 les candidats sélectionnés. Les salaires de base sont compétitifs et
71 s'agrémentent d'avantages sociaux importants.
72
73 **5. Conditions requises pour l'embauche des diplômés universitaires**
74   Dans tous ses emplois la société accorde autant d'importance aux
75 qualités de l'individu qu'aux qualifications académiques.
76   Les candidats seront diplômés de l'enseignement supérieur et ceux
77 dont la candidature a été acceptée devront démontrer des aptitudes de
78 leader incontestées, un engagement certain et un intérêt réel pour le
79 commerce de détail.

80   Tous les candidats seront aptes à communiquer couramment en
81   langue anglaise et pour les postes à pourvoir en Europe occidentale, dans
82   l'une des langues suivantes: hollandais, flamand, français ou espagnol.
83   Si vous envisagez de faire une carrière chez Marks & Spencer et si
84   vous souhaitez obtenir des informations complémentaires, n'hésitez pas
85   à écrire à une des adresses ci-contre en expliquant la raison de votre choix
86   initial entre l'Europe occidentale et le Royaume-Uni.

European Graduates' Career Guide, 1993, EC, Brussels (guide à l'emploi
pour les diplômés universitaires, publié par la CE, Bruxelles).

Part 3:
Annotations

Welcome to Ouistreham

This relatively brief text is an example of a totally functional text type, its purpose being to give accurate information and instructions to future passengers. The text forms part of an information pack issued to customers on booking a ferry crossing to Ouistreham.

This rather different method of text analysis, where units of meaning are examined in chronological order of appearance in the text, is intended to act as a guideline for any initial reading of a text, to indicate the kind of think-aloud process that could be going on (whether aloud or silently) in the translator's head whilst reading the text for initial impressions

Heading:
Welcome to Ouistreham/Bienvenu à Ouistreham
- ST underlying structure is '(You are) welcome (i.e. welcome functions as an adjective).
- TT could either imply 'souhaiter la bienvenue à qn' hence noun form, or 'Vous êtes bienvenu' but not so obviously a direct address.

This is the procedure for vehicle embarkation at OUISTREHAM
Ceci est la procédure relative à l'embarquement des véhicules à OUISTREHAM
- Appropriate collocation: economy in ST: noun plus preposition only; TT: *procédure relative à.*
- ST compound noun, in which first noun functions as adjective, becomes TT: *l'embarquement des véhicules* (n + des + n) — note also TT plural vs ST singular for generalisation.
1. Embarkation of vehicles will commence approximately 45 minutes before time of departure.
1. L'embarquement des véhicules commencera environ 45 minutes avant l'heure de départ.
- ST zero article, for embarkation and time of departure (kind of telegraphese/economy of language).
- TT requires definite article — both use future tense for statement of fact.
2. If you are transporting animals please ensure you have all the relevant documentation and declare them to our Freight Office here in the Terminal Building.
2. Si vous transportez des animaux, assurez-vous que vous possédez tous les documents nécessaires et venez les déclarer à notre bureau frêt en Gare Maritime.
- ST Present Continuous, more immediate/situation specific; TT Present Simple.
- ST Imperative preceded by *please*; TT Imperative.
- ST have; TT *possédez* .
- ST singular mass noun — *documentation*; TT plural count noun — *documents.*
- ST has one imperative, *please ensure*, followed by two finite dependent verbs, *you have* and *declare*, where TT has two imperatives, *assurez-vous* and *venez*. Alternatively, the ST construction could be read as, *Please ensure you have*, and, (please) *declare.*
3. At car control you will have been given boarding cards. Any special attention

you may need (with disabilities, illness, vehicles, etc.) should have been requested at the car control desk. Please advise us now if you have not already done so.

3. Lors du contrôle de votre billet, il vous a été remis des cartes d'embarquement. Tous cas particuliers (incapacité, maladie, problème de voiture…) doivent être signalés au contrôle. Merci de nous en informer dans le cas où vous ne l'auriez pas fait.

- why does TT translate *car control* as *contrôle de votre billet*? Is this TL accepted jargon/norm for this situation/context?
- TT uses impersonal construction, *il vous a été remis*, whereas ST prefers more direct address, 2nd person plural.
- both TT and ST use passive voice for act of being given boarding cards — impersonal, agent unknown/unimportant.
- TT takes approach of declaring any specific problems; ST interprets this in a more customer-friendly approach by referring to *any attention you may need.*
- shift in emphasis involves shift from personalised need to impersonal event.
- shift in verb tense from ST modal perfect passive *should have been requested* to TT Present passive — *doivent être signalés.* Difference in tense implies difference in timing of action, could result in different sequence of actions on part of SL and TL passengers.
- where ST adopts the Present Perfect with *already*, note TT use of Conditional Perfect for hypothetical condition — TT thanks customer for doing so (more conciliatory, assumes co-operation), whereas ST asks customer to do so (gives instruction); ST also states urgency — *now.*

4. You will then be directed into the correct lane depending on vehicle categories. Loading will be prioritised where possible.

4. Nous vous indiquerons ensuite dans quelle file garer votre véhicule, ceci en fonction des catégories de voitures.

- ST uses passive for statement of fact/agent unimportant, stresses action/instruction.
- TT avoids passive by use of *nous*; TT uses *indiquer* — point out, less forceful than directed.
- *depending on/en fonction de*: equivalent meaning but different form.
- ST has extra item of information: *loading… possible* (loss in TT).

5. You will be advised by public address announcement to return to your vehicle immediately prior to vehicle embarkation.

5. Une annonce sera faite pour vous prévenir de regagner immédiatement votre voiture avant l'embarquement des véhicules.

- whereas ST prefers direct form of address, a form of indirect imperative, *you will be advised… to return* (cf. use of Future Simple to coerce, *you will* do it), here TT uses future passive for statement of fact which stresses action not agent — TT *une annonce* is contracted from ST form (more explicit): *public address announcement.*
- as in (1): ST compound noun, in which first noun functions as adjective; in the TT *l'embarquement des véhicules* (n + des + n).
- in ST *immediately* becomes adverb of exact time at which (intensifier): immediately prior to; in TT adverb *immédiatement* refers to *regagner* — time when to do something.

6. Please have your boarding cards and passports ready for inspection prior to embarkation.

6. Préparez vos cartes d'embarquement et vos passeports pour le contrôle précédant l'embarquement.
- again where ST introduces request with *please*, TT uses direct imperative.
- ST analytical construction, *have ready*, becomes TT verb *préparez*.
- TT *précédant* usual collocation in such contexts.

7. A large number of vehicles of differing sizes need to be loaded safely. This takes time so please wait patiently until you are called to board, even when you appear to be moving slowly.

7. Un grand nombre de véhicules de différentes tailles doit être embarqué sans risques. Cela prend du temps; merci d'attendre patiemment jusqu'à ce que vous soyez appelés pour embarquer, même si vous avez l'impression d'avancer lentement.
- ST prefers to make verb agree with sense of *nombre*, as present in *véhicules* (pl count noun) — *have to be loaded*; TT makes verb agree with *'nombre'* mass noun — ST adverb *safely* becomes TL adverbial expression *sans risques*.
- whereas ST links the two by use of conjunction *so* which introduces adverbial clause of reason (not result or purpose), TT breaks the second sentence into two parts.
- TT is more explicit in interpreting passenger's involvement / perceptions: *vous avez l'impression*; ST uses simple synthetic verb *'seem'* which is less precise, although the context makes the intended use clear (you feel as if, not, you look as if).
- SL less specific, *moving* is translated by TT *Avancer*; is this the TL norm for context?

8. Finally, remember your passport must be checked at the UK Immigration Control on board so take your passport and anything else you require during the crossing with you when you leave the car deck.

8. Enfin nous vous rappelons que votre passeport doit être contrôlé à bord, au bureau de l'immigration britannique. Aussi avant de quitter votre véhicule, asurez-vous que vous avez sur vous votre passeport et tout ce dont vous pourriez avoir besoin durant la traversée.
- ST uses direct form of imperative, *remember*; TT uses more gentle form of imperative introduced by *nous vous rappelons* (personalised appeal, the caring company) — again, ST uses *so*, as a reference to the explanatory nature of the preceding information, to introduce a further instruction.
- ST more general location of two events around the same time could appear to be simultaneous but in fact SL norms allow this use of *when*.
- TT *avant de quitter*, more specific sequencing of actions, one after the other.
- TT uses conditional for possibility of need (*pourriez avoir besoin*); SL uses Present Simple for fact of need (require). Why *require* rather than *need* — more forceful/essential?
- NB: When was this written? No mention of who has to go to passport control, does this assume that all passengers need to have passports checked? What about EC regulations, etc?

9. May we wish you a pleasant crossing and thank you for your co-operation.

9. Nous vous souhaitons une agréable traversée et vous remercions de votre collaboration.
- SL request, wish, *may we* (norms of ST style/address for travel, cr air travel), becomes TL fact, *nous vous souhaitons*.
- why does ST use *co-operation* (obeying instructions) whilst TT uses *collaboration*

(working as partners) — does this reflect cultural differences in the forms of manipulation of the masses/respect for the customer?

NOTE: this envelope contains documents you will need for your crossing.

NOTA: Cette enveloppe contient tous les document dont vous aurez besoin durant votre voyage.

- SL *note* (please); TT Latin *nota*/ST.
- SL more vague, not limiting, *documents* (not necessarily all); TT specific, *tous les documents*.
- ST *for*, implies in order to be able to make the trip, to start the crossing and during; TT *durant votre voyage* — literally, during, while it is going on.

Problems arising from any comparison of two texts

Where two texts in any given language pair are intended to convey the same information and fulfil the same function with regard to their respective target readers, the translator needs to undertake an initial translation-oriented text analysis (cf. Christiane Nord) in order to be able to answer the following questions, before tackling the exercise of interlingual transfer.

1. Which was the source language/which the target language, or are they parallel texts? How could we know/find out?
2. What is the text type and its intended function and effect on the reader?
3. Are there any predictable rules or norms for production of this text type? Have you seen similar texts?
4. Have the ST and the TT in fact respected the relevant rules for SL and TL for this text type?
5. Is the SL/TL consistent in its use of lexis/syntax/style with respect to these norms and to the initial part of the text (initial choices made)?
6. Are there any ambiguities or inaccuracies of information in the TT which need to be resolved for the TL reader, either when translating the TT to appear at same time or with benefit of hindsight if translating at a later date.
7. Given the text type and function, are there any inaccuracies in translation leading to misinformation and incorrect/undesired, undesirable effects on the TL reader (could be potentially dangerous, incur legal liability)?
8. If there are any inaccuracies or modifications of information given, implied or to be understood from TT choices, how have these arisen and how could they have been avoided?
   (i)   actual strategy used/to be used;
   (ii) presumed or possible reasons for the strategy used;
   (iii) reasons why the strategy used is or is not appropriate for text type/context/ target reader.
9. Do any of the strategies used constitute predictable generalisable rules for transformation? Could any of the strategies be used again elsewhere in a similar context and combination of ideas and units?
10. After translating: **Very important: how does the target text read as a sample of the target language, without reference to the source text?**

The Pedigree of Plain English

This text is composed of extracts from an address given by the author to the first National Plain English Conference, held in Cambridge. In this speech the author traces the evolution of the concept of a simplified form of expression which would be accessible to all readers. The play on the word 'plain' and its etymology form an essential element of this discussion, particularly in the extract chosen for translation. The text contains numerous references of a culture-specific nature, intended to illustrate comments and to involve the target audience by implicit recognition that they in fact possess the degree of education necessary to comprehend and appreciate such references. It is interesting to note that the terms used to describe the two approaches to the 'propagation of plain usage in public life' are also in fact terms used to describe approaches to the task of translating a given text (see preface to texts).

The author himself gives us the key to the level of language used, describing it as 'middle... not uniformly plain or low... because there are things that I want to say and effects that I want to produce that cannot be achieved in a really plain style'. The translator must take note of this when selecting or making choices, to ensure that he accurately reflects the author's stated intentions.

In view of the subject matter it is hardly surprising to find in this text the metalanguage of linguistics and linguistic analysis. The author combines some elements of direct address in a less formal register with an historical description of a more formal nature in terms of both syntax and lexis.

Sentence Structure

In keeping with the stated form of style, this is neither uniformly simple nor uniformly complex. The fact that this was originally intended as an oral address is reflected in the degree of subordination and embedded information, as well as in the use of dashes in the written text to indicate insertions or asides; there are clauses of contrast, concession, and other clauses of explanation, result and purpose. There is a strong degree of coherence and cohesion at the level of sentences and paragaphs, again to facilitate retention for the listener/audience. Most sentences take the form of a main clause followed by a relative or other subordinate clause, again facilitating differentiation between main and secondary information, although sometimes the subordinate clause is placed first, perhaps for emphasis: e.g. (57), *'le style dont je me sers'*. In some instances problems of lack of corresponding syntactical forms lead to the creation of additional subordinate clauses, increasing thereby the degree of complexity of the sentence structure:

- *Church-based... Church-linked* (16): compound adjectives are expanded to give relative clause introduced by past participle.
- *all-male* (17): this has to be expanded into a clause of reason — *puisque l'accès... était... limité au sexe masculin.*
- *media attention* (73): first noun, functioning as an adjective in the SL, becomes an adjective in form in the TL — *attention or intérêt mediatique.*
Sometimes a complex sentence in the SL is broken down into two sentences

in the TL, as in the last sentence of line 101 in TT, where the linking device is the relative pronoun, *chacun*.

Syntax

Passive voice in SL becomes pronominal or other construction (verb or noun) in TL:
- *the history of plain English is measured not in...* (1): *ne se calcule pas...*
- *was intended to explain...* (5): *visait l'explication de.*
- *was intended quite differently* (11): *l'intention était tout autre* — verb plus adverb becomes noun plus adjective.
- *that had formed* (19): *qui s'était formée:* note the use of the pronominal form in the TL.
- *which can be translated by* (40): *qui peut se traduire par* — another pronominal verb to avoid the passive.
- *it was used* (41): shift to an intransitive construction with introduction of noun as subject — *ce mot servait à définir.*
- *good orators... have been expected to be able to do...* (51): replaced by impersonal form — *on s'attendait à ce que... sachent le faire.*
- *in 1979 the... was founded* (73): here the year becomes the subject, and the passive verb becomes a noun object of a new verb — *l'année 1979 a vu la création de...*

Other verbs:
- *showed that he wanted to* (8): adverbial clause of result becomes an analytical verb construction followed by an abstract noun — *a fait preuve de sa volonté de*
- *cut off from* (14): phrasal verb becomes a synthetic verb in TL — *privées de.*
- *they lost out* (15): phrasal verb becomes present participle used adjectivally, *elles étaient perdantes.*
- *before there was* (33): in the TL the adverbial phrase *avant que + ne* requires the subjunctive form of the verb, here the past subjunctive.
- *I'm using... I'm not using* (46–47): the TL opts for the Present Simple here, since the sentence structure is complex enough without resorting to verbal constructions such as *être en train de.* It may appear to the SL reader that an element of emphasis is lost, but this implicitation is common in the TL. Could also insert an adverb of present time.
- *there is no* (52): stylistic variation gives — *il n'existe pas.*
- *especially avoiding* (61): this participle is translated by an infinitive of purpose.
- *take the initiative* (67): this becomes a noun phrase preceded by an impersonal construction — *implique une prise d'initiative.*
- *the tendency is* (71): the TL uses the conditional form for reporting possibility rather than statement of fact. The conditional is used again, for emphasis this time, in line 96 in TT.

Other syntax:
- *their men* (22): anaphoric reference: the reference contained in this pronoun, to the women, undergoes a shift of frame from women to class, and the meaning is made more explicit by expansion to read — *de cette classe.*
- *it grew larger* (74): insertion of demonstrative pronoun, *celle-ci,* to make anaphoric reference clearer.
- *things have improved* (25–26): substitution of specific singular noun, *la situation,* for more generalised plural noun.
- *above them both* (34): preposition of place is replaced by a comparative adjective to bring out meaning.

– *goes back further than Chaucer* (38–39): since this is a reference relative to sequences in time, the TL renders this more explicit by substituting an noun phrase in which the name Chaucer becomes an adjective describing an era — *l'époque chaucerienne*. This is a useful linguistic device not always available in the SL.

– *began to be interested in* (56): here the TL uses the Passé Composé since this is the text of a speech, delivered orally, rather than the Passé Simple which belongs to the written language medium.

Lexis
Title:
– in SL the term *pedigree* (symbol) is associated with pure-bred animals or perhaps also people, by extension. In the TL the dictionary offers *de pur race, arbre généalogique, origine* amongst others. The middle term was chosen as it could equally apply to animals, language and people in the same way as the SL term: index thus replaces symbol.

Collocations:
– *were on the borderline* (23): *franchir les limites*, not verb *to be.*
– *convoluted syntax* (62): *syntaxe complexe.*
– *awards (prizes)* (69): *décerner un prix.*
– *make changes* (73): *effectuer des changements.*
– *put pressure* (72): *exercer de la pression.*

Terminology:
– *top-down* (65)... *bottom-up* (71): these terms have to be expanded in the TL to give the sense of relational direction (of movement or focus of attention): index for icon.

Loan words:
– the term, *Plain English* (47), depends on the understanding of the Latin etymology of the adjective and so this effect must somehow be reproduced in the TL, even at the expense of accurate or stylistic collocation: index for symbol.
– *table alphabeticall* (5): it would be difficult to recreate medieval spelling of these two words in the TL and so their modern form is used, keeping the expression in inverted commas to show some kind of special use. Although the SL uses an inverted word order, having noun then adjective (probable interference from either Latin or French), given that the modern form of these words is used in the TL it was not deemed appropriate to operate a similar inversion of word order, which would have given, according to TL norms, *alphabétique table.*

Other:
– *sexist* (10): this is expanded in the TL to render more explicit the sense of prejudice against women.
– *layer of Latinity* (19): this quasi neologism is reproduced according to SL/TL conventions for -y endings (change to -é, e.g. *beauty — beauté*).
– *Plain English Awards* (74): this could be translated generically as *prix*, or given the name of a famous TL culture award, such as *'Les palmes d'or de l'anglais simple'.*
– *doublespeak* (69): an SL specific reference (icon) based on the meanings of the two words used to form this reference. Better to retain the SL form in inverted commas to show its origin, with a brief explanation in brackets.
– *the grassroots* (72): expanded to compensate for lack of direct single word equivalent: index for symbol.
– *two-way co-operation* (77): compound adjective of less formal register, replaced by single word, more formal register, bilatérale.

– *feedback* (81): although this word exists as a loan word in the TL the translator has chosen to find an explanatory paraphrase, perhaps because the text already contains several loan words of different origins: index for icon.

Stylistic Devices
Inversion for emphasis/stylistic effect:
– *the commanding heights of language* (14): this becomes a relative clause with inversion of subject and verb — *les avantages qu'apportent la compétence linguistique* (18).
– *then came* (43): in TL — *venait ensuite:* Imparfait for habit.
Alliteration:
– *layer of Latinity* (19): this alliteration is lost due to form of appropriate TL lexis — *couche.*
– *limited literacy* (24): also lost in TL.
– *communicate clearly* (60): the immediate juxtaposition is lost due to use of adverbial phrase.
– *Canterbury Tales* (30): alliteration created in TL.
Imagery:
– *leave people out in the linguistic cold* (28): expanded idiomatic expression: substitution of image in TL — *le désert* — loss of sensory effect but retention of sense of isolation.
Repetition:
– *'good' orators and writers* (51): adjective is repeated in TL for parallel form, balance.
Cultural references:
– *grammar schools* (17): although this is an SL specific cultural term, it is still placed in inverted commas in the SL to show its particular use in the more literal sense of the word 'grammar', as would have been relevant at the time of which the author is speaking. This term is thus translated literally into the TL, retaining the inverted commas to show a specific use in this context.
– *Canterbury Tales* (30): note different spelling of place name in TL.
– **names of historical personages:** *Robert Cawdrey* (4) — his function is explained sufficiently in the text not to require any further notes; *Elizabeth I* (12) — date of death can be deduced from date given in paragraph 1; *Chaucer* (29) — a similar use and explanation, although TL does insert adjective *anglais.*
– *Church-based, Church-linked* (16): here the use of *capitals* shows that the reference is to the Church as an institution, not to a specific building, and so should be repeated in the TL.
– *PEC* (73); obviously known to the SL target audience but needs explanation in TL.
Acronyms:
– *NCTE* (67): explained in brackets in the SL; the same approach can be used in the TL since this is a culture-specific reference with no direct TL equivalent.
– *PEC* (73: no expansion in SL but needed in TL — see above.

Punctuation
– names of languages require **capitals** (33–34) in SL even when used adjectivally, but not in TL.
– also title of works, e.g. *Contes de Cantorbéry* (30).
Inverted commas:
– to show special status of use *'grammaire'* (20 in TT).

- SL culture-specific origin — *'doublespeak'* (69); or loan words, in which case the word is also in italics *'planus'* (39).
- actual quotes *'hard usual words'* (5–6), *'good'* orators (51).
- historical nomenclature or title *'table alphabeticall'* (5).

Use of **colon**: similar in TT to ST.

Bless Thee Burgess, Thou Art Translated

This text was delivered at the Cheltenham Festival of Literature in 1993, and also published in a quality daily newspaper, whose editorial policy is one of intended objectivity in the presentation of information to its readers. The target audience would be professional, from the liberal professions or business-related occupations, probably having an educational level of degree standard or higher, concerned with factual information and looking for this to be presented without bias. There is however evidence in the text of personal bias on the part of the author towards the translation of literature [e.g.' literature cannot be translated' (23); when people praise a translatable book they are discounting the literary angle altogether' (32)]. This should be reflected in the TL choices of lexis and structure.

The text selected would not seem to contain any evidence of political or other bias, since the subject matter, that of the exercise of translation and the way in which it points to, enhances or otherwise affects the literary value of the work to be translated, is one of intellectual rather than political interest. The potential meaning of the word 'translation' offered by Burgess himself, in terms of the meaning of '*Übersetzung*' (13), is particularly interesting given Burgess' own background, with which the target reader would be expected to be familiar.

The text is written in the first person as it is an extract from an address given by the author, Burgess; it contains several quotes from different sources, including ones from Shakespeare whose TT version should be checked for authenticity. The author shows his experience in the world of literature, listing proper names of authors both contemporary and from the past, which will also require checking in the TL. There is a descriptive narrative section in lines 48–60. Generally the sentence structure reflects the oral delivery, with few complex sentences. The main problem for the translator will be the culture-specific references, including the play on the word 'translated' upon which the title depends.

As befits a discussion of literature and use of language, with concomitant relevance to the target audience, the language of the text is of a high standard of literacy, with appropriate stylistic devices and use of lexis intended to enhance the listener's enjoyment of this, whilst retaining the tone and style of a form of direct address. There are also, however, examples of a more colloquial form of address which contrast with those more literary turns of phrase and choice of lexis, a contrast to be reproduced in the TT.

There are so many points worthy of comment in this text — it is hoped that those selected will be representative of those not commented on directly.

Sentence Structure

As noted above, this is mainly designed to enable the listener to follow and appreciate both the arguments presented and the actual use of language of this presentation. As such, there are few lengthy complex sentences (except lines 16–20, 55–60). Many of the sentences follow the form of co-ordination of two points linked mostly by *and*, or else that of a main clause together with a subordinate adverbial clause of reason, linked by *because*.

208

In some cases sentences have been rephrased to bring out the underlying meaning, thus avoiding any clumsy attempts at paraphrase at the level of individual units of syntax: e.g.:
- *although I am translated I am not quite so multitudinously translated* (19–20): by anaphoric reference to an element of the preceeding sentence the TL aptly conveys the intended sense whilst avoiding the need for expansion of the word *multitudinously*.

There are also examples where the SL sentence structure of co-ordination with *and* is presented differently in the TL, whilst not altering the overall relationship between the two actions so linked:
- *forgets about words and gets on with the job* (33–34): here the TL links the two clauses with *pour* plus infinitive for the second verb, rendering more explicit the idea of purpose or intention.

Other changes include the breaking up of a long sentence linked by *and* into two sentences separated by a full stop.

Syntax
Title:
- *Bless Thee Burgess:* this apparent imperative is in fact only part of the structure, the rest, unstated, being 'May God... ' and so this will require a subjunctive in the TL. In some ways this is an iconic representation of meaning, a whole syntagm expressing a concept.
- *Thou art translated:* given the discussion which follows, and in view of the TL tendency to avoid the passive voice, it would appear more appropriate to render this by an active verb with an impersonal subject — *on*.
- *by translation I am beginning to think of a possible transmigration* (3–5): the TT rephrases this slightly, introducing *y voir* (different verb) and changing the adjective *possible* to a noun phrase, *la possibilité de*.
- *from a superficial angle* (15): note the different preposition to be used in the TL with angle (fixed expression — *sous un angle*) — see also *from an aesthetic angle* (80).

Use of passives:
- *I am expected to feel* (18–19): avoidance of — this first person passive form of the verb becomes an active verb using *devoir* in the TL.
- *because I am not translated* (19): explicitation by insertion — here the TL becomes more specific, taking as subject of the verb *translate* the actual, not the figurative, subject, namely, the works written by the author rather than the author himself, as in the ST.
- *to be translated is horrific* (20): rephrasing — the TL refers to the works, not the person; the verb becomes a noun, followed by a prepositional phrase referring to the object of the action and the adjective *horrific* is subjected to expansion for the purpose of stylistic expression — *est à redouter*.
- *to be turned into a film* (28): here the verb *faire* is used in conjunction with a pronominal verb.
- *I don't think that Babel will ever be unbuilt* (85–86): in the SL the past participle *unbuilt* is usually used in reference to something that has yet to be built, not to indicate an opposite action to that of the stem verb, *build*. In this case, the author uses *unbuilt* in the latter sense almost as a neologism and so the translator may be forgiven for adopting a similar strategy in the TT, perhaps with a pronominal construction.

Other verbs:
- *one may say* (27): since the author uses the conditional form, *could*, at the beginning of the next paragraph, this contrast in use of modals should be respected in the TL by the use of different tenses of the verb *pouvoir*.
- *I lived in a part of Rome* (48): here the TL could use either the Imparfait or the Passé Composé depending on the effect intended by the translator and the stress to be given, either to the aspect of duration over time or to the simple description of a completed past action.
- *a means of inaugurating* (73): this construction of noun plus gerund in the SL has to become a noun plus infinitive in the TL.

Lexis
Title:
- *translated:* since the author himself proceeds to give an explanation of how this word can be of relevance in the title and in relation to the subject of the address, it would appear appropriate to retain this same word in its usual TL form, since the most overt aspect of meaning referred to here is indeed that of translation from one language to another.
- *translation* (1): even though the TL word *traduction* is not polysemous in the same way as this word, the text will in fact explain the various meanings attributed by the author to this word in this context and so the comment above *(translated)* would seem relevant. A problem at the level of indexical correspondence.

Semantic fields:
- of spiritual dimensions to literature and translation: *a very dark end* (3); *transmigration or elevation* (4)... *a new life* (5)... *spiritual dimension* (6)... *bishops...* (7).
- Literary terms of lexis: *yearn* (27); *quail before* (66), *scatology* (64), *advent* (66).

Collocations to consider:
- *get the meaning right* (9): in this context, the expression *le mot juste* would seem particularly appropriate; *do a minimal job* (25) — if the word *fonction* is used here, the correct verb collocation should also be used: *exorcise the curse* (88).
- *übersetzung* (13): this loan word should be retained in the TT in its German form, as it is explained in the text anyway.

Fixed expression:
- *strictly speaking* (22): this can be substituted for in the TL by a Latin expression, *stricto sensu* — representation at the level of icon for icon.
- *the point is* (42): in the TL this becomes, *l'important, c'est que.*

Stylistic Devices
- *Bless Thee Burgess, Thou art translated* (title): this archaic form of the second person singular reinforces the tone created by the use of the subjunctive, *Bless thee,* as well as creating a feeling of sacrosanctitude, of an untouchable aspect of the writer's work, in contrast with what happens to his work when it is translated into another language. This is also reinforced by the use of the term *new connotation* in paragraph one, referring to the concept of passing from one place to another, for Burgess, from one plane of existence to another.
- *asinine* (12): play on words, reinforcing the reference to the ass's head and also allowing the author's attitude towards translation of literature to be conveyed.
- *if a book is yearning for the ultimate translation* (27): this collocation of the verb

yearning with an inanimate noun *book* as its subject serves to personify that noun and make it seem as if the book has gone beyond the control of its author to become a living entity, as exemplified in the reference to the cinema and the play of characters. The word *oeuvre* is also inserted in paragraphs 6 and 8 to give greater explicitness.

– *(feel we know foreign literature because) so much it has been translated: un si grand nombre d'oeuvres...* (50)
– *Belli has never been translated: on n' jamais traduit les oeuvres de Belli* (62).

Contraction:
– *in a dialect that nobody not Roman can possibly know* (54): *connu par les seuls Romains.*

Rhetorical questions:
– paragraph 7 (52) is the only one in which an example occurs, perhaps because the author is attempting to give a more factual tone to his address, which in some ways resembles a lecture talk, in that he is trying to inform and present a point of view, rather than to evoke any emotive response in his listener.

Repetition: which contributes to the cohesion of the message as a whole:
– *one may say* (27), *you could say* (35): although the SL changes subject from *one* to *you*, the TL has used the same subject, *on*, for parallelism of structure to refer anaphorically and cataphorically one to the other. This impersonal subject is used throughout the text to translate various references to *people* and *they* (38).
– of the word *translation*, as a noun, active verb, past participle.
– of the word *great* — *great writers* (1, 15, 20); *a translation becomes greater than the original* (35, 36, 61).
– of the word *revivify* (70, 71) to create the impression of a close link between language and culture.
– of the word *confusion* and *confused* (83, 84, 86) to play on the polysemy of the word in order to establish a link between two different occurrences: *confusion of tongues = multiplicity of languages* — TL lexis here will entail a certain loss of ambiguity, since *langue* can be both *tongue* and *language*: *confusion of civilised endeavour* could almost mean the *rendering impossible* of such effort. Probably the best way to deal with this is to retain the same lexical form in the TL and hope that the TL reader will perceive the same play on words, with perhaps some degree of explicitation to facilitate the reader's task.

Alliteration: to be recreated wherever possible:
– *defend dubbing* (81).

Less formal **register**: this contrast is sometimes difficult to recreate in the TL, particularly where the SL uses phrasal verbs:
– *gets on with the job* (34): *it's* (contracted form of spoken language) *what the Romans speak* (56).

Cultural References

– *Burgess* (title): the man was more latterly perhaps more well-known for other activities than the literary field. It may be considered politically incorrect, however, to append any information about him for the TL reader.
– *Shakespeare* (9): although the name is known internationally, each play will have its own official title and translation in each target language and this must be verified, as must the TL form of the name, *Arabian Nights* (41). Similarly, the names of *Dickens* (38) and *Schlegel* (71) should require no explanation.

Because of the extent to which the authors are known, these names will not change form in the TL.

- *Red Sea* (14): the geographical name exists as a direct translation in the TL, *la mer rouge*: the Biblical connotation of crossing an impassable obstacle by divine intervention should also be accessible to the TL reader, given his background in a Christian civilisation, albeit in a country in which the education system is overtly secular in orientation. This reference also reinforces the concepts of new life, new planes of existence and also the reference to the spiritual dimension as represented by the comment regarding bishops. See also the reference to *Babel* (85) which should be known to most TL readers for its Biblical connotation, but should also recall for the initiated the work of Steiner, *After Babel*, on the subject of translation.
- *Lord Archer* (32): although he should be known to the TL reader it may be helpful to add a brief translator's note here.
- *Upper Stobovia and Middle Ruritania* (17–18): two fictitious countries from the world of the theatre, requiring a translator's note to this effect. Their form may be naturalised to an appropriate TL form, but their function in the text should be apparent and require no further explanation.
- *Don Quixote and Sancho Panza* (37), *Rimski-Korsakov* (40), *Sheherazade* (40): whilst these names may not require explanation as they refer to well-known figures of classical literature or music, the form of the names themselves should be checked in the TL.
- references to *Rome* (48) in paragraph seven include contemporary place names which could justifiably be left in their Italian form, taking care however with the adjective *Petrarchan* (58) which, as a name from classical antiquity, should have its own naturalised TL form.

Punctuation

- '*translation*' (1): when first used ths word appears in inverted commas to show that it is polysemous; the TL should also reflect this.
- *übersetzung* (13): this is in italics in the ST to show its German origin and should remain so in the TL in its original form, followed by a translation (in the TL this time, for the non-German TL reader) in inverted commas as in the ST.
- '*translated in several languages... Ruritanian*' (17): this is intended to be a quote from a book cover and should remain in the same form, in inverted commas, in the TT.

Preaching Community

This article appeared in a publication whose target readers will be of professional status, probably middle and senior management. They will be interested in the background, context and possible motivation for any event or occurrence relating to the political or business worlds, in order to evaluate possible outcomes and how this may affect their professional activity. Given its Europe-wide publication, it would not be unreasonable to expect *The Economist* to seek to avoid particular country-specific political affiliations and adopt a fairly objective stance when presenting contentious issues. This is the case for the subject of this article, which attempts to present a fairly balanced view of what the term 'community' might mean to the two main political parties and why each seems to have adopted this term as a key concept in their political propaganda.

It could be argued that the author has tried to make much of a single concept, giving detailed references and descriptions which could give an appearance of serious reflection. Also it has to be said, he rather seems to have enjoyed the descriptions of past idylls in lines 30–40, the length of which could almost be taken to indicate a certain tongue-in-cheek approach to the whole issue, deliberately playing on the rose-tinted glasses view of the past. His description of contemporary society certainly leaves no illusions as to his views on this, and the translator will have to think carefully about how to render both the tone and the snappy terseness coupled with exaggeration of effect as afforded here by the SL facility for the accumulation of preceding compound adjectives.

The references and descriptions make mention of some very culture-specific institutions and concepts, which will require paraphrase or translator's notes or both for the TL reader. Familiarity with the political or business institutions of a culture does not automatically endow the TL reader with an insight into aspects of more mundane daily life, such as meals on wheels; the community spirit as embodied in the image of mothers popping in and out of terraced houses borrowing a cup of sugar; volunteers doing service in the community; not even the idea of the 'bobby on the beat' and his role in the community. The TT will no doubt suffer some loss of impact as a result of any attempt to explain such references for the TL reader; the translator's task will be to minimise this loss of impact by explanation, expansion or compensation.

Sentence Structure

In view of the stated objective of presenting two different interpretations or viewpoints, it would be reasonable to expect many and varied mechanisms for comparison and also for contrast. The author seems to have chosen to develop one view in one sentence followed by the view of the other party in the following sentence, with subordinate clauses having introductory phrases and conjunctions such as *du côté de...* (17); *une cause... un autre facteur* (32): *pour... par contre...* (37, 46); *considérons... considérons également* (101, 105). There are also phrases designed to highlight similarities: *même le parti Libéral* (22); *les deux côtés...* (56); as well as contrasts: *néanmoins* (101)... *cependant* (116).

The translator may well find it helpful in several instances to invert the order of presentation of subordinate and main clauses, especially where the TT is seeking to compensate for loss of impact in one part of the sentence through careful positioning of another part.

Syntax

− *laments that* (4): TL uses *regretter que* in order to avoid a more complex pronominal construction with *se lamente de ce que.*
− *is every political thinker's…* (1): the TT has sought a variation on the simple verb *to be,* choosing instead an idiomatic expression, *fait figure de.* This also occurs in line 113 with … *charm… is…* where the TL uses the verb *réside dans* plus noun.
− *(puts) it (at the centre of)…* (2): this pronoun serves as anaphoric reference to the term *'community'* of the first sentence: the TL prefers to use a more specific form of reference, inserting the noun concept instead of simply using the pronoun *le,* which could also refer to the *homme politique* (whereas this confusion could not arise in the SL, as the latter would be refered to as *he,* differentiating this pronoun from *it,* the pronoun used to refer to inanimate objects.
− *the challenge facing* (9): here subject becomes object and vice versa, due to the TL verb chosen, whether *faire face à* or *confronter.*
− *the race is on* (12): where the SL uses a preposition in conjunction with the verb *to be* to form a phrasal verb having a specific meaning, the TL prefers a past participle, *partie,* which describes the action, not having such a phrasal verb at its disposal.
− *not that there is* (13): this negative form for emphasis is reproduced in the TL, *non pas que* followed by the subjunctive mood to express possibility of doubt.
− *that he thought were the secrets* (15): the TL structure requires an infinitive instead of the second finite verb *were.*
− *it can be traced to* (16): this passive voice is replaced by an active intransitive verb, *il remonte à.*
− *though… this meant…* (19): *bien que* takes a past subjunctive form of the verb here.
− *be surprised* (21): again the passive can be avoided, this time by a pronominal construction with *laisser.*
− *community politics* (18): this becomes a singular mass noun in the TL, *la politique communautaire.*
− *a widespread cynicism* (25): the SL term here contains two different units of meaning combined to give a single item of lexis: the TL uses an adverb to modify a past participle, the two functioning adjectivally to qualify *cynisme.*
− *there are differences between the two sides as to…* (41): this impersonal form is rendered in the TL by a more personalised construction, *les deux côtés proposent des explications différents de la cause des…*
− *they (i.e. the discontents) (stem from)* (42): it would be preferable to repeat the noun in the TL, *ces sentiments* to avoid possible ambiguity of reference.
− *the State imposed* (6): the TL concept of sequence of tenses is better served here by a Plus Que Parfait (idea of *déjà*) than by a Passé Composé.
− *put people off serving* (53): this phrasal verb followed by a gerund can be translated economically with no loss of meaning by a synthetic verb *décourager* followed by a noun phrase incorporating the concept of the verb *serve,* in the sense of *participate* in offering a service.

- *when historians turn to* (57): TL requires a future tense after *quand*.
- *argued* (59): here the TL uses the Imparfait.
- *Mr Blair... may dislike. Mr Willetts may complain...* (68–69): the SL modal auxiliary has to be translated through use of the verb *pouvoir*, remembering the difference in likelihood or probability as indicated by the different SL use of *may* and *might*.
- *he can argue for* (73): here the TL uses a pronominal to bring out the full intent of the modal *can*.
- *consider... and consider...* (76, 79): the TL prefers to use the first person plural form of address to give an example.

Lexis
- *leader in waiting* (2): this SL phrase can be translated more economically by a single TL word: index for index.
- *Thatcherite philosopher* (5–6): the TL has expanded the adjective derived from an SL name in order to convey the meaning: icon for icon.
- *significant* (6): the TL has selected the lexis closest in intent.
- *in politics* (13–14): the TL expands this into a noun plus adjective — *la vie politique*.
- *taxation* (62): the TL includes the adjective *fiscale* for greater precision.
- *the essence...* (70): the SL term is a noun whose adjective has a different form, whereas in this context the TL uses the adjective with a definite article to create a noun.

Collocations:
- *there must be a role* (11);*... doit jouer un rôle*.
- *very good reasons* (40): *des raisons entièrement valables*.
- *drains the life-blood* (50): shift of sense but no loss of meaning — *saigner la force vitale*.

Idiomatic expressions:
- *work all hours* (78): can be replaced with a TL expression of equivalent impact but not quite the same form — *24 heures sur 24*: icon for icon.
  rather **archaic** use of **lexis**, lending an air of distance in time:
- *stultifying* (34); *over-arching* (49): *for the common weal* (81): this lexical effect may be difficult to reproduce in the TL, other than by the criterion of dynamic rather than lexical equivalence, i.e. icon for index where index for index is not possible.
More familiar **register**: *clipping delinquents' ears* (32): an expression of similar register is used in the TL — *filer des claques à (petits) délinquents* — since the bobby would presumably only clip the ears of young offenders.

Stylistic Devices
Metaphor:
- *borrowing cups of sugar* (31): a metaphor for the sense of community spirit and reciprocal help and support as practised, as legend would have it, by the working classes living in close propinquity to each other in their terraced houses. The reference would have no meaning and therefore no concomitant connotation for the TL reader and so requires a translator's note to avoid puzzlement: symbol for symbol, were such an equivalent symbol to exist, would have been the best way to achieve equivalent impact.
- *new-born welfare state* (33): the connotative significance of this in the post-war years will be more widely appreciated by the SL reader than by the TL reader, but there will not be total loss of impact: icon for symbol.

Imagery:
- *drains the life-blood* (50): the TL substitutes an idiomatic expression of similar intent and impact whose difference lies solely in the frame of reference, *la force vitale*, which symbolises life-blood rather than stating so explicitly — even so, the reference to blood is maintained in the verb *saigner* which is used in collocation with this: icon for icon.

Simile:
- *shines like a beacon* (28): the TL uses a simile of like construction.

Alliteration: an important guide to the authorial voice in this particular article:
- *bobbies on bikes* (32): this can be recreated in the TL only thanks to the device of retaining the SL term in inverted commas, becoming indexical rather than symbolic in form of reference.
- *present pains* (39): although there is some loss of impact due to loss of polysemy of the SL term, this alliteration is preserved in the TL by opting for a term which by denoting mental (albeit rather than physical) anguish does thereby reflect one of the potential meanings of pain.
- *disappointing tub thumper's premise* (88): there is a loss of impact from the lexical connotation of tub thumper as a type of politician, but this is compensated for by the impact of the TL alliteration: *devis décevant du démagogue*, which conveys a similar kind of contempt or lack of respect.
- *social sacrifices* (66): the TL can easily accommodate this alliteration.
- *practical task of formulating policies* (87): the TL creates an alliteration operating a referential shift, linking *practical* to *policies* rather than to *task*, with no real shift in underlying meaning.

Personification — shift from or to:
- *a new pamphlet... laments* (3): in the TT the author becomes the subject of the verb rather than the agent or publication.
- *there must be a role for* (11): here the inanimate attribute becomes the subject of a new verb, *jouer*, collocate of *rôle*.
- *contradictions* (76): in the TL this becomes a more impersonal construction, *il existe des...*

Emphasis:
- *not that there is* (13): this negative form in an initial position in the sentence, for emphasis, is reproduced in the TL. This is further reinforced in line 21, *nor should anyone — personne ne devrait non plus*.

Explicitation:
- *the British are not... a happy people... one reason is... another reason for unhappiness* (22): the concept of not being happy/unhappiness is used initially and the explanation is expanded to give: *une des causes de ce mécontentement... un autre facteur...*

Parallel structures: for textual /thematic cohesion:
- *Mr Blair may dislike... Mr Willetts may complain* (68–69): recreated in the TL for stylistic effect.
- *consider... and consider...* (76, 79): also recreated in the TL for similar impact.

Cultural references

Names: of which there are several
- of political parties (1, 14, 16, 30, 35) and throughout the text: the three main political parties do have official TL forms which must be respected.
- of politicians and other persons (1) (3) (5) (14) (16) (18) (42) (58) (68): these

should either be known to the TL reader, e.g. John Major, or else are already explained in the text in terms of their function and relevance in this context, thus requiring no further explanation by the translator.

- of other institutions or organisation (8): *the Social Market Foundation*: it may seem elementary, but the translator must take care to have agreement of the adjective social with the appropriate noun — this precision is of course not required by SL syntax.

Other culture-specific references:

- *crumpets; squire; kindly vicar; (afternoon) tea* (36–37): these all recall shades of Jane Austen but should not be completely unfamiliar in their essence to the TL reader. However, the TT has chosen to retain the word *'crumpet'* in its SL form, in inverted commas, giving a translator's note, rather than lose impact of the very Englishness of the reference by attempting to find a TL near equivalent. As for the word *'vicar'*, a partial cultural equivalent has been used in the form of the phrase *de paroisse*: to use the word *prêtre* may not be appropriate given the difference in religious affinity.

- *for tea* (37): this has been expanded to reflect the TL cultural form of reference to the SL culture-specific connation of this word.

- *new-born welfare state* (33): the effect of this reference has to relate to SL reader awareness of its timing in relation to the description of *past Edens* and to the expectations of and attitudes towards these changes as felt by the population at that time, projecting what is seen to have been, at that time, a rosy view of future (which gives a further cynical contrast with the comments that follow). A TL cultural near equivalent can be found to preserve much of this implied tone and intention.

Punctuation
Use of inverted commas:

- *'community'* (1): because the author wishes to define this term he presents it in inverted commas, and so this is repeated in the TL.

- **titles**: of a pamphlet (7): of a book (58): both are also in inverted commas in the SL and so in the TL.

- **direct quotes** (4–5); (15); (18–19); (59–67) the same applies for these.

- **culture specific terms** having no direct dynamic equivalent: *'bobbies'* (32), *'crumpets'* (37): given the lack of a dynamic equivalent for these in the TL culture, the TT has retained these SL terms to highlight their culture specificity, giving explanations in a translator's note so as not to impede the flow of the text. It could be argued that there should at least be a near equivalent TL term included in brackets immediately following these to ensure no gap in TL reader comprehension at the level of connotative and descriptive impact.

- upper case for *Big Idea* (1); (86) thereby recreating the effect of a proper noun, something specific rather than generic.

Defining a European Immigration Policy

Just as for the text 'Jobs and Competitiveness' this extract from a much longer paper is taken from a publication by the Philip Morris Institute for Public Policy Research, of Brussels. With as its target readers academics and professionals interested in issue of political and social relevance in contemporary Europe, these publications are released simultaneously in different languages including English and French. It would seem reasonable to assume once again, given the apparent nationality of the author as could perhaps be deduced from his name if from nothing else, that this extract was originally written in English.

As for 'Jobs', this publication is intended to inform the reader by presenting a wide range of views, expressed by authors of different nationalities, on a given theme which links all the papers in a particular issue, the theme in question being 'Towards a European Immigration Policy'.

The role of the author (as Director with Responsibility for Co-operation in the fields of Justice and Home Affairs in the Secretariat General of the European Commission) would lead the reader to expect a pan-European view of the problem (as in the EU and to be differentiated from the Europe of the Atlantic to the Urals as also described by the author), based on the provisions of the treaty of Maastricht. Indeed, this is clearly stated as one of the objectives of such a policy on Immigration, which are listed in the form of an 'executive summary' directly below a photograph of Sir Adrian and his job description. The summary states that 'the EC should take advantage of the Maastricht Treaty to formulate a determined and organized policy on immigration. Such a policy would...'(there follows a list of objectives).

This pan-European view should, then, attempt to examine causes and effects without reference to national partisan views, other than to describe these in order to explain them and seek solutions. There should not therefore be such overt bias towards a particular national approach as can be found from the extract relating to jobs. Indeed, the author seeks to be as factual and objective as possible, attempting to give clear definitions of the key terms used in his discussion at the outset of the paper. This intention necessitates the organisation of the text into points of information, marked by asterisks and introduced by rhetorical questions intended to lead to explanations in response to these questions. The register would appear to be quasi-legal in its search for clarity of definition but this is counterbalanced by the existence of modal auxiliaries indicating doubt or possibility, resulting from the attempt at definition coming from one person rather than being the object of consensus.

Sentence Structure

Sentences contain in general two main segments for consideration or information, presented in the form of hypotheses linked by conditional verb forms and introduced by *if*, or else in the form of attempts to justify by concession, limitation and explanation an initial definition, again resulting in a two-part structure to the sentence. There is much description relating to key terms or concepts, which gives many examples of direct or implied relative clauses, and

sub-headings take the form of a list of nouns or noun equivalents, corresponding to the list of terms to be defined. Some sentences are broken down into two parts in the TT by the introduction of a colon and the omission of the conjunction, e.g.:
– *factors, namely wars…* (62): becomes *facteurs… : les guerres.*

Syntax

– *frustratingly elusive* (1–2): this adjective defined by an adverb of intensity is rendered in the TT by a simple adjective *pénible*, resulting thereby in a loss of impact.
– *it would be impossibly so…* (2): this clause relies on anaphoric reference to the subject introduced in the previous sentence, the search, and its qualifying adjective, *elusive*, through use of the elliptic *so* following the conditional form. The TL has developed this reference by the insertion of a more explicit attribute to the TL adjective (instead of adverb) *impossible*, which explains the reference as being to *une telle opération*.
– *in the title* (3): takes a different form, *du titre*, not *dans le titre*.
– *for the purpose of* (5): an apparently more neutral adverbial expression in the TL, *dans le cadre de*, but one giving a more explicit translation of the intended use of the word *purpose* in this context.
– *without first attempting* (2): here the SL has a preposition followed by a gerund, translated by a preposition followed by an infinitive, and a single-word adverb translated by an adverbial expression, *au préalable*.
– *European* (5): this adjective has to agree in gender and number with its referent, this being the word *Immigration* in the name of the policy to be developed (the same use and reference is found in line 9). In the next sentence we find:
– *'European' can also be used* — an apparent contradiction of rules for agreement, but here the adjective *utilisé* does agree in number and gender with its referent, this being the word *adjectif* as introduced in the first sentence.
– *a collective attempt jointly to define* (7–8): in the TL this rather redundant repetition of a noun qualified by an adjective, and then by a verb phrase comprising infinitive and adverb, is translated more economically by a simple verb modified by an adverb, *tenté collectivement*, the only loss being perhaps one of emphasis but not of meaning.
– **omission or use of articles**: following the questions *'what is'* (5, 13, 22) the SL uses two nouns without articles, to indicate their precise use in the title quoted, whereas the TL introduces a definite article with *immigration* to give the same generalised reference, but then has to use an indefinite article with the noun *politique*. This is because of the polysemy of this word in the TL, which, when used with a definite article, would refer to politics, whereas when used as a count noun *policy*, as here, in a general sense and without definition (e.g. *la politique d'immigration du gouvernement*) must have an indefinite article to indicate this different use in context.
– *the whole examination… would look very different* (11): here the TL rephrases this information, moving the adjective *whole* to refer adverbially instead to another adjective, by using an analytical verb construction *prendrait un air*, with *air* qualified by an adverbial expression of intensity, *tout à fait*.
– *by limiting* (13): here the **gerund** is avoided by use of an impersonal conditional construction, *si on limite… à* which also allows removes the need to select an appropriate term for *to mean*.

- *being considered* (16): becomes a simple past participle, losing the continuous aspect of the SL.
- *the wider subject* (19–20): here the TL introduces a deictic *ce* for greater explicitness.
- *some generosity is needed* (22): the concept of generosity is somewhat lost through its shift to the adjective *large* — unless the TL reader had seen the SL he might not make the link between *large* and *largesse* which may have been in the mind of the translator when selecting the expression *au sens plus large*, although there is in fact no loss of actual information content, rather an attempt to bring out the implied meaning of generosity in this context.
- *only the huge geographical spaces* (28): this **adverb** is used adjectivally to agree with the plural noun in the TL to give stylistic effect with no loss of meaning.
- *moves made by EC Member States* (39): there would appear to be an **omission of agreement** for preceeding direct object in the TL version here, *les action que les Etats membres... ont entrepris* (*sic*).
- *ultimately* (57): this single word adverb becomes an adverbial expression in the TT, *en fin de compte.*
- *is widely felt* (59): this **passive construction** is replaced by a causative pronominal in the TL.
- *important distorting factors* (61–62): this construction (of adj + adj/gerundive + n) becomes in the TL n + prep + n + adj.
- *policies to control* (67): **shift in construction** from n + infinitive of purpose to compund noun (n + [prep + n — adjectival function).
- *unplanned* (69): the TL cannot make the **opposite** here by adding a suffix to form a single word; instead it uses a negative particle, *non.*
- *were searching for* (96): the TL manages to reproduce the **continuous aspect** by the use of an analytical verb form incorporating the Imparfait of *être: étaient à la recherche de.*
- *moyens pour garantir* (96): it may be that the translator used *pour* to indicate purpose, and this is perfectly correct, although the word *moyen* is more usually followed by the preposition *de.*
- *would be as reliable as* (97): here the intended sense is more that of subjunctive (wish/hope) than of conditional or future in the past, and so the TL could quite easily have used this mood, or a modal form, instead of a conditional form which mimics the SL form but loses some of its intent.
- *would be losing* (97–98): this time the translator has recognised that the auxiliary *would* does not carry a conditional sense and so the TL has rendered this in the sense of incompleted past action, using the Imparfait.

Lexis

- *three words in the title* (3): the word *terme* is used in the TL as being a more **precise** object of definition than *mot*, although this word is used in 1c in the TL, perhaps for stylistic variation following the use of *terme* in the preceeding clause.
- *migration issues* (11): beware the **faux ami** here, not *issus* (adjective in TL) but *questions* or *problèmes:* index for index but requiring analysis of use.
- *to make sense of* (38): it is to be queried whether the SL analytical verb phrase *donner un certain contenu à* successfully conveys the intent of this SL phrasal verb or whether it implies something specific but different (adding to the bare bones of something, perhaps), whilst the SL construction could have been interpreted as meaning 'to explain or give a definition of': icon for icon.

- *what has led* (45): *led* becomes *poussé*.
- *the break-up* (53): this **noun formed from a phrasal verb** is replaced in the TL by a single-word noun, also derived from a verb, *la dissolution*, but having a possibly more neutral, less informal register. Similarly:
- *the slowing down* (73): becomes *le ralentissement*.
- *overlain* (61): it is to be queried whether the TL term *ajourné* actually gives the same implication as the SL word.
- *peacetime* (62): to note equivalent fixed expression — *en temps de paix:* icon for icon.
- *shift* (69): the SL term implies movement and may not actually be the most appropriate in this context, whereas the TL term is more contextually accurate as it refers to a change of nature or state.
- *European immigration to the New World* (73): the SL text does not differentiate between *emigration* and *immigration* but the TL text does.
- *berate* (79): an uncommon term to use in an article of this kind, matched by an equally uncommon TL word.
- *aspiration* (84): this SL word gives the implication of wish or ambition, somewhat different in nuance from the TL term *volonté*, a more explicit expression of intention.
- *frontier-free Community* (90): the TL brings out in more explicit manner the underlying meaning, i.e. *sans frontières internes*.
- *it has meant* (91): a difficult word for which to find a dynamic equivalent, but again, the TL brings out in more explicit manner the underlying meaning by the use of *entraîner*.
- *reliable* (97) the translator has chosen to bring out the intended meaning here rather than choosing a more usual dictionary equivalent for this SL adjective.

Collocations:
- *sustained economic growth* (65): note collocation, *développement économique soutenu*.
- *(as unemployment figures began to) rise* (67): TL *grimper*.
- *calls for* (67): expanded to give *des demandes pressantes*.
- *the collapse (of the Iron Curtain)* (77): *la chute*.

Stylistic Devices

Parallel structure/form:
- in lines 5, 13, 22, there is the **repetition** of the **rhetorical question**, '*What is…*' used to introduce each key term and definition, as well as giving coherence to the text structure through the use of this parallel mechanism.
- *to grope now and collectively* (45–46): here a more neutral verb is used — *chercher*, thus allowing the translator to use two adverbial expressions to express the SL intent — *à tâtons* and *de manière collective*.
- *aspiration* (84, 90): the same TL term *volonté* is used to create a similar cohesive device.

Elegant variation:
- the form of the question differs in the TL, either framed as '*qu'est-ce que*' (5), or as '*que signifie*' (13), whereas in the SL the form is identical in all instances, '*what is*' (22).
- note the use of *également* instead of *aussi*, for *also* (14) and of *notamment* instead of *surtout* (59).

Loss of personification:
- *this article will use* (39): is translated by a passive construction, *dans cet article l'expression sera utilisée*.

Metaphor:
- *entry doors... exit doors* (81–82): a similar image is used in the TL: icon for icon.
- *welcome mats* (89): the idea of coming home is implicit in this figurative reference, but translated in the TL by a fixed expression recalling warnings and prohibitions as found, for example, in the underground railway system — *accès interdit* — a more official form of expression which loses the imagery of the SL.

Cultural References
Place names:
- *from the Atlantic to the Urals* (10): in the TL the spelling of the latter place name is naturalised and takes a singular form.
- *Western European* (14): this adjective (a + a) becomes a place name in the TL (n + a), *Europe occidentale*.
- the New World... the Americas and Australasia (29) and *ex-Yugoslavia, Soviet Union, Czechoslovakia* (52–54): these names have a naturalised form in the TL.
- *the Iron Curtain* (77): icon for icon: note use of lower case. The TL form is a transparent translation of this but this may not always be the case for references to international phenomena or even for place names (cf. *The Channel Isles = Les Iles anglo-normandes*) — much depends on the origin of the term and its initial use.
- *Ireland* (75): is it sufficiently clear to translate this in the TL as *Irelande* — probably yes, given the presumed background knowledge of the TL reader, although the distinction is easier to make in the SL because of the availability of two different names for North and South.

Punctuation
- *simply to happen* (47): this is given greater emphasis in the TT by the use of **inverted commas** around *'se produire'*.
- all terms to be defined are enclosed in **inverted commas** when forming part of a question concerning their precise signficance.
- *'temporary' immigration* (69) in the SL implies a fixed name or term of reference, whereas the omission of **inverted commas** in the TL gives a more generic, less specific use of the adjective. However, *'permanent'* receives similar treatment in both SL and TL — an oversight on the part of the translator or even of the typist, perhaps?
- **asterisks** (5, 13, 22, 50, 61, 69, 73, 77) are used to indicate or draw attention to bullet points and give structure to the discussion.
- *European Immigration Policy* (38–39): this is given in **italics** in the ST but not in the TT, where it takes on the function of a definition rather than that of a proper name as indicated by its ST form — perhaps not a significant **loss** of content but a **shift** in information content and referential nuance all the same.
- *imperceptible (and unplanned) shift* (69): **brackets** are used in the ST to indicate an interjection, where this information is quite simply incorporated in to the main TL text.
- *frontier free Community* (90): here *Community* commences with an **upper case** letter to refer to the EC: the upper case is used in both SL and TL in the preceeding reference to the EC (83) and the following one in the same sentence.

Jobs and Competitiveness: The UK Approach

This text is taken from a publication by the Philip Morris Institute for Public Policy Research, of Brussels, whose quarterly publications have as their target readers academics and professionals interested in issues of political and social relevance in the contemporary Europe going beyond the borders of the European Union to include the wider geographical boundaries of the continent. These publications are released simultaneously in different languages including English and French. It would seem reasonable to assume, in view of the nationality of the author, that this article, or rather extract, was originally written in English.

This publication is intended to inform the reader by presenting a wide range of views, expressed by authors of different nationalities, on a given theme which links all the papers in a particular issue. The theme of this article is evident from the title; the fact that the author was, at the time of writing, the UK Secretary of State for Employment points to the necessarily nationalist view that will be presented in the article promising, in view of the title, a positive view of the UK policy on employment. This positive tone can be clearly identified through the use of lexis and syntax, as well as through the selection of information and the examples given. The extract below is only part of a much longer article, and as such constitutes the introductory section.

Sentence Structure

In the spirit of informativity, the sentence structure often reflects a co-ordination or contrast of events and ideas, at the level of description (adjectives and nouns) as much as at the level of clauses linked by *and* or *but* or similar conjunctions.

In several instances the translator has chosen to invert the order of information in the sentence, either to avoid a passive verb — *has been exploded* (5) — or to prioritise the main clause by giving it initial position in the sentence — *il y a actuellement... là où...* (6–7). See also *En accroissant... le commerce...* (30–31) and *notre approche repose sur...* (66).

Longer sentences in the ST are broken down into two shorter sentences in the TT to give greater emphasis:
- ... *inacceptable. Aucun pays...* (10): perhaps also to avoid excessive repetition of *and*.
- *the painful truth that there are...* (11): by insertion of a colon this becomes, in the TL, *la triste réalité: il n'existe* (13).

Towards the end of the extract it would appear that the translator has adopted a far freer approach to the sequence of presentation of information, so that, whilst there is no loss of basic tone or information, it becomes difficult to compare sections between the ST and TT. Paragraphs 13, 14 and 15 of the TT are a paraphrastic composite of paragraph 13 of the ST, and part of the information contained in paragraph 16 of the TT is also to be found in para 13 of the TT, while para 17 of the TT corresponds to para 16 of the ST. The only dangers here are those of (i) possible shift in orientation, tone or intent, whether minimal or significant and (ii) possible omission of information which, whilst not essential, still contributes to the overall impact and effect of the message.

Syntax

- *for 30 years* (2): verb tense shift: the translator has remembered the **formula**, changing SL Present Perfect with for to TL Present Tense with *depuis*.
- *countries have seen income rising* (3): the problem of the **gerund** in the SL is dealt with by a change in verb to *connaissent* (Present Tense after *depuis*) which then requires a noun as object, *une croissance*.
- *the G7 jobs (conference)* (13): this preceeding compound adjective has to be **expanded** in the TL.
- *search for* (10): this SL phrasal verb can be translated by a single word, synthetic verb form in the TL.
- *common ground* (21): this singular mass noun in the SL becomes a plural count noun in the TL due to choice of lexis to render the concept of *ground*.
- *in which businesses can flourish* (24): this indirect relative clause, referring to conditions, and having a new subject of a new verb, becomes a direct clause with *conditions* as the subject — *qui*... This shift also leads to the **insertion** of a different verb, *favorisent*, whilst the SL verb becomes a verbal noun, *le développement*, as the object of the new verb.
- *we... face...* (34): this **synthetic SL verb becomes an analytical verb** in the TL: *être confronté à*. Similarly we find:
- *damage* (100): becomes *aller à l'encontre de*.
- *the UK approach* (54): the SL technique of using a noun to function adjectivally preceeding a second noun undergoes a shift in the TL, where the noun UK is substituted for by the adjective *britannique*, with the term Great Britain obviously considered by the translator to be synonymous with United Kingdom. Later we find — *Britain's system* (96): also translated as *le système britannique* (124).
- *we are committed* (55): this present **tense,** passive voice in the SL becomes a Present Perfect Passive in the TL, *nous nous sommes engagés*, altering the emphasis slightly to give greater stress to the action rather than to the state of affairs — an inverse transformation to what might be expected from English to French.
- *making the labour market more efficient* (71); the gerund here becomes an infinitive. A similar strategy is used to translate: *increasing... enhancing... encouraging...* (74–76).
- *step by step* (72): SL adverbial expression becomes one of equivalent meaning, but not of form, *peu à peu*.
- *focus on* (73): synthetic verb becomes an analytical one in the TL, *mettre l'accent sur*.
- *through (strikes)* (78): this single-word adverb becomes an adverbial expression — *pour cause de (grèves)*.
- *we have left employers and employees free to* (79): here the adjective *free* becomes a noun (object of the verb) — *la liberté* (followed by *de* not *à*), making *employers and employees* the indirect object in the TL.
- *a more effective jobs market* (87): the TL renders this by an adverb of intensity — *véritablement* — rather than by a comparative construction. Whilst not affecting the overall message, the nuance of intent has been changed.
- *there is a balance to be struck* (94): note the avoidance of the passive voice by the use of the impersonal *il faut trouver un équilibre*.
- *opportunities available* (101); a shift here from active sense to a passive verb introduced by a relative pronoun, *leur sont offertes*, probably **expansion** in order to render the TT more **explicit**.

— *lesson to be learned* (99): avoidance of the passive voice by use of *à* plus *infinitive*.

Lexis
Collocations:
— *human costs* (8): becomes *les coûts sociaux*, giving a shift to a less specific context of reference: icon for icon.
— *high unemployment* (8): becomes *chômage (aussi) important*.
— *painful truth* (11): *la triste réalité* — a degree of *loss of intensity* here.
— *achieve low inflation on a permanent basis* (25): is expressed more economically with an appropriate collocate: *endiguer l'inflation*.
— *sound public finances* (25–26): this noun phrase is expanded to bring out the meaning, as well as including the appropriate collocate — *la saine gestion des finances publiques* .
— *promote free trade* (27): becomes *favoriser le libre-échange*.
— *what to do about this crisis* (38): the collocate here also requires a change of preposition.
— *the labour market is very special* (61): the translator has chosen to use *particulier, not spécial*.
— *we fully intend* (97): there is also a shift here, from active verb to verb *to be* plus past participle attribute functioning adjectivally and requiring a particular preposition to follow: *nous sommes fermement décidés de*.
— *we also have* (98): becomes *nous disposons de*.
Other:
— *conference* (2): TL has *conférence*: would *colloque* have been more appropriate?
— *hand in hand with* (3): index for icon: this **idiomatic expression** in the SL is replaced with a single-word adjective, *simultanée*, of a more neutral register, referring to the new noun, *croissance*, but with no loss of meaning.
— *both incalculable and unacceptable* (9): the single-word adverb *both* is rendered in the TL by a fixed adverbial expression, *à la fois*.
— *again consider* (18): the TL prefers a fixed expression, *à nouveau*, to a single word here.
— *immune* (10): this single word adjective is rendered in the TL by an explanatory expanded prepositional phrase, *à l'abri de ce problème*, losing thereby the medical image and substituting a more neutral one.
— *of course* (22): this fixed expression meaning, *it goes without saying / everyone knows*, is replaced in the TL by a more restrictive fixed expression, *selon toute évidence*, which could be said to detract somewhat from the definitive tone and intent of the SL expression.
— *ensure that* (27): becomes *garantir que* (note, plus subjunctive) rather than *assurer que*, slightly altering the mode of action from positive steps to be taken in order for something to happen, to one which seems to imply promise of state of affairs, stressing the promise rather than the action to be taken.
— *trade works to everyone's benefit* (28): rather than using the verb which first springs to mind for *work* — *travailler*, a more appropriate term here is *oeuvrer*.
— *all that is valuable* (34): the translator has chosen, correctly, to interpret this adjective in the sense of *significant* rather than in terms of financial value — TL *important*.
— *on a sustainable basis* (55): there is a **loss of polysemy** here, as the term chosen by the translator — *durable* — only incorporates the time element of the

implied meaning of *sustainable*, ignoring the aspect of *being possible for this to be continued*.
- *a market which concerns* (62): there could be said to be a shift in meaning here, with the TL giving *conditionne* for concerns, which is used in the ST in the sense of *to affect* or *x is an issue*.
- *unnecessary regulations* (82): does *inutile* give the quite the same meaning as *unnecessary*?
- *opportunities* (101): beware of the potential **faux ami** — the translator has, correctly, chosen to use *possibilités* here.

Stylistic Devices
- *therefore* (13): **stylistic variation:** rendered in the TL by a more elegant form — *par conséquent* — perhaps to avoid the rather inelegant *donc*. This change in form also gains emphasis by being placed in the initial position at the opening of the sentence and also of the paragraph, providing thereby a more overt linking mechanism to the preceeding paragraph.
- Several **short sentences** throughout the text give extra **emphasis** to authorial comments; these are often to be identified by the use of the first person plural pronoun, *we* and can be similarly tagged in the TT.

Personification:
There is an element of **depersonalisation** at work in the TT, where, for example:
- due to selection of correct collocation, *human costs* (8): becomes *les coûts sociaux*.
- *everyone's benefit* (28–29) becomes *l'intérêt général*.
- *what we have to do* (38): becomes more impersonal — *comment remédier à*: and similarly:
- *knowing what we have to do* (44): becomes *savoir ce qu'il convient de faire* and also:
- *we must ensure* (41) becomes *il convient de préserver* and:
- we had too many obstacles (67) gives *il y avait trop d'obstacles*.

However, in lines 72–101 of the TT the aspect of use of the first person plural pronoun *we* has been repeated in the TT, giving a certain inconsistency of style.

Repetition:
- of the verb *favoriser* in TT 26/TT 29, creating thereby a linking mechanism at the level of lexis between the points discussed in these paragraphs.
- of the key word *jobs* — and of the related concept of *unemployment* (2, 24, 29, 36).
- *too many obstacles, too little incentive* (67–68): similarly in the TL — *trop de... trop peu de*.

Alliteration:
- major industrialised countries (22–23): the translator has managed to create an example of alliteration through selection of the appropriate collocation, *les principaux pays*.

Expansion:
- *Britain in 1979 was little different* (67): the TT develops this to give — *en 1979, la situation en Grande Bretagne était peu différente*.
- *over the... we have worked to change that* (72): the TL inserts a noun to replace the deictic *that* and render this anaphoric reference more explicit: similarly, the verb change is translated by one giving more precise reference to the nature of the change — *inverser cette situation*.

Contraction/loss:
- **omission**: of the description — *labour market (reforms)* (73) — and of the

noun — (aspects of) *performance* (73–74): these concepts could be said to be implied by the preceeding sentences but could just as easily have been translated for greater fidelity to the ST information content. There appears no valid reason for their omission, other than perhaps the fact that the translator has adopted a freer approach in general to the sequencing and presentation of information in this section of the extract and this may have led to inadvertent omission, which should have been noted when revising and checking for accuracy.

- *does not discriminate against* (84): there is a loss of intensity in the TL, which merely states *n'écarte pas*, a more neutral concept.
- *the hard lesson to be learned* (99): the adjective *hard* is not translated, resulting in a **loss** of inflection in the TT.

Accumulation:
- of gerunds: *increasing... enhancing... encouraging...* (74–76)

Co-ordination: there are numerous examples of co-ordination — of adjectives: *incalculable and unacceptable* (9); of nouns — *unemployment and human misery* (4–5), *no easy answers and no magic solutions* (11–12); of clauses: *each country must promote... and ensure...* (27)

Cultural References
- *G7* (1, 13): rendered in the TL by the same form: symbol for symbol.
- *Naples* (18): although the pronounciation differs, the TL form is the same. This is not always the case for names of cities.
- *GATT agreements* (29): having been the subject of much controversy in France, the GATT talks are known to the informed TL reader both in the SL form — *GATT* — and in the TL form *AGETAC*. The translator has chosen to keep the TL form.
- *the Single Market* (31): following TL syntax the appropriate collocate for *single — unique —* is commenced by a lower case letter.
- *The European Council... Brussels* (39): the correct TL forms are used in the TT, with the adjective European being commenced by a lower case letter.
- *EU* (40): here, although the acronym contains an adjective convention has accepted *UE* as an appropriate TL form.
- *OECD* (45): the translator has given the TL acronym here.
- *United Kingdom* (77): is translated, but in TT para 14, by *Royaume Uni*.
- *a strong welfare state* (87): this political concept/term is translated by a more neutral term in the TL — *système de protection sociale*, although the term *Etat provident* does exist in the TL.
- *benefit help* (90): this would be immediately understood by the SL reader as referring to social security benefits to those on low income. To avoid the necessity for translator's notes, the translator has chosen to follow a policy of **expansion,** giving a more detailed explanation of this in the TL by describing it as *des allocations pour les travailleurs à faible revenu qui ont une famille.*
- *health and safety at work* (96): index/indices for icon. This is a fixed phrase in the SL referring to a particular act of parliament, but is translated in generic terms in the TL, with no loss of meaning.

Punctuation
- where the ST has additional information between dashes — *increasing... jobs —* (29), the TT incorporates this into the main body of the sentence.
- the acronym *GATT* (29) is retained in capitals in the TT, as are *G7/G-7* (13)

(note the hyphen in the TL), *UE* (40) for *EU* and *OCDE* (45) for *OECD*. Similarly, since it forms a name, the *Group of Seven* in the first sentence, although the word *Seven* could also be said to be functioning as a number, in that it is followed by a plural count noun — *major industrial countries /principaux pays industrialisés*.

- dates are also written as numbers in both ST and TT, noting of course that the names of months are written with a lower case initial letter in the TL, as opposed to upper case in the SL, as are adjectives of nationality.
- *the Community* (42): clearly refers to the EC and so retains the initial upper case letter in the TL — *la Communauté*.

Law & Disorder

This text is an extract of approximately half the length of an article published in *Computer Shopper*, a dedicated magazine giving information about new and old products, software and hardware, as well as articles describing events of more general interest to all those who use computers whether professionally or privately. Sections of the article are flagged by sub-headings in bold type, and this lay-out should be respected in the TT.

As such, the articles tend to adopt a less formal register than the standard news magazine, often with extensive use of idiomatic expressions as well as, of course, the terminology of the 'trade' and sometimes introducing new terms, or terms in the process of becoming institutionalised within the specialist domain if not yet in the wider lexicon of the language. In the context of translation, such texts are mainly likely to pose problems on the level of lexis rather than syntax, and whilst some terms may be institutionalised and recorded in a specialised dictionary, more recent introductions may not be found in these sources.

The problem with this use of computer terminology, for the translator at least, is that the language or jargon of such a specialised sub-culture is in a constant state of flux, with terms appearing and disappearing with alarming rapidity, so that it is difficult to keep abreast of developments in the mother tongue. The only way to do so is one which is equally valid for either mother tongue or second language, namely to read dedicated magazines on a regular basis and to seek the advice of those engaged in professional activity within the field. Whilst magazines reflect current usage, they may also be the source of neologisms, which is why the advice of the practitioner is so helpful in determining the extent of acceptance of new terms. When in doubt and when sources are consulted to no avail, the translator may have to invent a new term or else, if he feels unable or unwilling to do this where there is a certain play on SL word formation, phonetics and polysemy, he may have to use the same term as a loan word and put it in inverted commas with an explanation in brackets following this. The translator must also be aware that competing software manufacturers may have opted, in the TL, for different terms to refer to the same SL concept or unit of lexis, and he must be consistent in his use of a term.

Finally, the article contains many references to culture-specific institutions sometimes having no direct equivalent in the target culture nor any recognised translation. Here there must be some degree of explication and paraphrase to render the sense as well as the form of the name.

Sentence Structure

Given the more informal style of such articles, as reflected here in the use of the contracted verb forms (it's, isn't, that's) and the use of dashes, one would not expect to find a high degree of subordination in sentences. Rather like computer language itelf, the style tends to be factual, aiming for an informative presentation of details rather than an emotive or descriptive approach which might necessitate subordination and accumulation. Most sentences therefore consist of one main clause and one subordinate clause.

In this particular article there seems to be repeated use of dashes as a way of inserting additional, subordinate information, rather than more formal puntuation. This will actually lend itself well to translation within TL conventions, although it would be equally appropriate to include these in the main body of the sentence as a relative clause:

- *hours or days — a recipe for anarchy?* (6).
- *number of individuals — known as phreakers —* (20).
- *motivation that drove them — and still drives the modern-day hacker —* (36).

Syntax

- *public misconception* (4): this is a construction based on two nouns, including *the public*, not on the fact of the transparency of the misconception. The TL renders this relationship explicit by use of a relative clause, *qu'a le public*.
- *left without its phone system* (5–6): in the TL the past participle is omitted, the preposition *sans* carrying the meaning.
- *it almost happened to...* (7): the impersonal element is created in the TL by a use of a relative clause linked to the preceding one by anaphoric reference, *c'est ce qui* together with a verbal construction to convey the concept of *almost — a failli se passer*.
- *resources were deployed checking* (12): here the gerund is translated by a clause of purpose, *pour vérifier*.
- *has its roots in* (18): the TL avoids the problem of the correct verb to collocate with *roots* by substituting a different image having the same meaning — *est né*.
- *by sending* (24): here the gerund is one of manner which can by rendered by the preposition *en* plus present participle *envoyant*.
- *happened to give away* (28): in the TL this has to be rendered by an impersonal expression plus a subordinate clause, *il s'est trouvé que*.
- *whistle up a free phone call* (31): this phrasal verb is expanded into a verb plus object and followed by a clause of purpose, *donner un coup de sifflet pour obtenir...*
- *set about cracking access* (35): in the TL the gerund *cracking* becomes part of an infinitive construction, *se mettre à* plus *infinitive*.
- *they do tend to leave clues* (40): *shadowy hacker organisations do exist* (89): this use of the Present tense of the verb *to do* as an emphatic auxiliary is specific to the SL and the emphasis should be recreated in the TL by other means. Here the translator has chosen to ignore this stylistic element but could have used some kind of expression such as *en effet, effectivement, il est vrai que*.
- *it's akin to the graffiti artist tagging property* (41): here the gerund is translated by means of a relative clause in the TL.
- *hacking into computer systems isn't all that difficult* (45): the phrasal verb in the gerund becomes a single-word infinitive, *pirater*.
- *these controls can be circumvented* (47): the passive voice is also used in the TL, since only the action is important.
- *the usual approach... is to...* (49): here the TL uses the same construction as the SL, although a pronominal *ce* could have been used, giving *c'est de*.
- *the user would be denied... if no identity code... were supplied... the problem was finally resolved...* (57–58): these passive verbs are treated differently, possibly for stylistic variation, so that we find: *se voyait refuser l'accès* (a useful and stylistic form of avoidance of the passive construction); *n'était donné-*; and *fut finalement résolu —* again the translator reverts to the simple passive voice to

stress action with no agent, perhaps thus differentiating involvement of a user/person from that of simple fact referring to abstract nouns.

- *for some years* (62): here the word some is a quantifier implying *several* in the sense of a signficant number, not in the more indeterminate sense; the translator is aware of this and has chosen *plusieurs*.
- *while any password* (64): here the intention is one of contrast, not concurrent events.
- *prosecute an individual for gaining...* (67): here the gerund is translated by a relative clause with a verb in the Passé Composé in order to respect rules governing sequence of tenses.
- *we had to wait* (71): becomes an impersonal expression in the TL with *falloir*.
- *in this country* (74): here the translator has to make the reference more explicit in the TL to avoid confusion. The deictic *this* should be replaced by the name of the country referred to, as this will not be the country of the TL. Although the author refers earlier to the US government, the more immediate preceding reference is one to the UK and is followed by reference to British Telecom; this should enable the translator to decide which country is being referred to here.
- *running a business* (85–86): this gerund is translated by a present participle.
- *excitement of beating the system* (87): here the gerund becomes an infinitive following the preposition *de*.

Lexis
Information technology terminology, for which the appropriate TL accepted and most commonly used equivalent must be sought:
- *logic bombs* — a neologism in the SL, hence perhaps to be used similarly in the TL: icon for icon (9); *software* — often used in the TL in its SL form, so index for index (13); *hacking* — the TL term borrows from a bygone era. In fact the SL uses the same term but in the sense of illegal copying, not illegal access: indices for icon(18).
- *phreakers* (20) — this is perhaps the most difficult term, since it relies on a play of graphic representation of the phonetic sound [f] giving a play on the word 'freak'and including reference to telephones by the use of the initial [ph] instead of [f] — it may not be possible to invent a term having similar effect and, anyway, the term has become a name, which may well be known to computer buffs in the TL, given the degree to which loan words, usually from English, are used in information technology in France, despite the recent loi Toubon, for the practical purpose of being able to use software as it is originally produced, without having to resort to costly and time-consuming translation of such software.

Other terms to be checked:
- *billing equipment* (23); *blue box* (26); *personal computers and modems* (34); *operators* (41); *unauthorised access* (47); *identity code and password* (50); *VAX mainframe, VAX/VMS operating system* (53–55); *press Return at each prompt* (59); *system software* (63); *mail box; pirate bulletin boards* (77, 93); *digital burglars* (90).

Collocations: (which also reflect an idiomatic use of language)
- *disaster didn't happen* (11): here the subject necessitates the use of a reflexive verb, *se produire*. Compare this idea of *taking place* (as in line 11, *happened*) with the different meaning of chance occurrence in *happened to give away* (28).
- *massive resources were deployed* (12): there are two collocations to consider here: *massive resources*, and *resources were deployed*.

- *plant (logic) bombs* (9): not *planter*, but *installer* (in the computer).
- *by sending a tone* (24): same verb — *envoyer* but *signal*, not *ton*.
- *cracking access* (35): TL has *forcer l'accès* but this may not include the connotation of 'safecracking', i.e. finding the correct code by trial and error. There may be a more appropriate term which also includes this aspect of meaning.
- *wilful damage* (40): here the translator has selected one aspect of meaning, *prémédité*.
- *perform a security check* (55): *exécuter un contrôle de passe*.
- *prosecuted on a fraud charge... acquit* (82): in the TL the construction is changed to give, *le dossier est allé*, which loses the syntactic balance of reference to the same subject between *prosecute* and *acquit*.

Idiomatic or fixed expressions:
- *crime wave* (1)(introduction): a similar expression is used in the TL — *vague de crimes* (note the plural noun): icon for icon.
- *beat the system* (38): *contourner le système*.
- *a fatal flaw* (56): loss of impact through expansion and loss of alliteration — *un inconvénient qui lui est fatal*.
- *all well and good* (58): this has been interpreted rather than looking for a TL fixed expression: index for icon.
- *are well versed in* (65): again, the meaning has been brought out but by a different expression, *des maîtres de*.
- *poacher turned gamekeeper* (85): the same image is used in the TL: icon for icon.
- *for fun* (87): the TL uses *exaltation*, which may seem more extreme or intense than the SL *fun*.

Other:
- *white collar* (3): the TL has a more generic term, *employés de bureau:* index for symbol.
- *a recipe for anarchy* (6): here recipe becomes *secret*.
- *spotted the attack* (11): *repéré*.
- *graffiti artist tagging property* (41–42): here the word *tag* is used in its sense of *label*, translated by *marquer* (also appropriate in the purely linguistic sense as used in text concordancing).
- *issue users* (49): a potential **faux ami** here.
- *shadowy hacker organisations* (89): the TL uses *fantômes*.

Stylistic Devices
Of which there are few, the emphasis being on terminology and information.
Rhetorical questions: surprisingly few of these are used, the main objective being to inform rather than to stimulate a response:
- *a recipe for anarchy?* (6)
Word order:
- *Attacks against businesses in an attempt to gain money are rare* (88): the delayed verb and complement give greater emphasis to both subject/noun and adjective. The TL retains the same sentence structure.
Alliteration: is created in the TL by the adoption of the term *pirates* for hackers: *attended by* (94) becomes a relative clause, *auxquelles participent des pirates*.

Cultural References
Place names:
- *the cities of Atlanta, Georgia; Denver, Colorado; and Newark, New Jersey* (7–8): the

translator has respected the TL convention of using a preposition to indicate the relationship between city and state, where the SL uses simple juxtaposition.

Other:
- *American West Coast culture of the late 60s and early 70s* (18–19): it is to be expected that the target reader will be aware of the significance of this reference in terms of computing and information technology: symbol for symbol.
- *breakfast cereal manufacturer… give away a children's toy whistle* (28); although this may be considered a culture-specific practice the implications are clearly explained in the text: index for symbol.
- *access all areas* (44): may appear to be assonance at the level of graphics but at the level of phonetics this is found not to be the case.
- *fatal flaw* (56): this fixed collocation is also an example of alliteration which will probably be lost due to the need for the appropriate TL collocation — in fact the translator has resorted to paraphrase through a relative clause.
- *US Congress* (69): the word *congress* is translated by identical form transparent terms, making a *calque* in the TL, the noun *US* becoming an adjective, *américain*, thus retaining its function but in a changed, although TL conventionally appropriate, form: index for icon.
- *the Computer Fraud and Abuse Act 1986* (70)… *1990 Computer Misuse Act* (71–72): these refer to specific acts in the SL culture and can only be translated in such a way as to bring out the underlying meaning, which may result in expansion, since juxtaposition of nouns in the TL to imitate the SL may result in a potentially inaccurate interpretation of meaning.
- *private member's bill* (72): not a culture-specific concept, so there should be an equivalent TL term.
- *British Telecom's Prestel service* (76): *British Telecom* is a culture-specific name whose function should be evident from its composition: the name *Prestel* may also be known to the specific TL reader but may also require explanation.
- *Prince Philip* (77): the TT simply says, *de Prince Philip*, assuming target reader familiarity with the persona. It may have been more syntactically accurate to say *du* rather than *de*, remembering the need for the definite article with honorific titles in the TL.
- *The Legion of Doom in the US and the Chaos Computer Club in Germany.* (91–92): here the translator has chosen to translate the names of these organisations into TL equivalent terms, another example of the process of calque where there is no standardised or official equivalent, perhaps because the referent does not exist in the target culture.

Punctuation
- the use of the *&* instead of the word '*and* ' in the title reflects the desire for economy as well as adding to attention-seeking impact.

Use of inverted commas:
- '*logic*' *bombs* (9): obviously a new concept and a new use of the word logic as a descriptor in conjunction with bomb — the inverted commas indicate the neologicity.
- '*phreakers*' (20): also a neologism.
- '*tagging*' *property* (42): again, a neologism.

- *the £/$ rate* (79): note the economy achieved by the use of signs instead of words, which the TT does not recreate, preferring instead to use the full word for each currency.
- for comments on the use of dashes, refer to sentence structure.

Doctor on Screen

Taken from the Health Section of the daily supplement to *The Guardian* (quality daily) newspaper, this article has for its primary function that of informing the public about new developments in the integration of information technology into on-going health care. It takes the form of a report based on the production of an interactive video, supported by comments from experts and patients alike. As such, the general level of language used contains a mixture of medical terms and direct speech, the terms used being ones relating to widely publicised health problems of which the general readership of this newspaper would be aware. In fact, it could be said that the level of inclusion of direct quotes leads to a use of a less complex sentence structure and more informal register than might otherwise be expected from *The Guardian*. The rather journalistic, more informal style will obviously have an effect on the selection of appropriate TL lexis as well as on TL style and syntax, although the norms for this text type in the TL must also be taken into consideration, so that the TL may appear to be of a less informal register.

Sentence Structure
The approach adopted would seem to be influenced by the presence of so many direct quotes, in that the author too seems to be talking directly to the reader, describing and explaining, using co-ordination of themes; this approach is reflected in a sentence structure where relative clauses explain new points and contrasting information develops the intial point by offering an explanatory or opposite view; for example:
- *to them... but to patients* (20–21).
- *it put my mind at rest and helped me decide* (27).
- *I do not have to... so I've decided to wait* (44).
- *it is too early... but the first findings...* (73).
- *our aim is to... because our research shows* (85).
- *emphasising... and* (67): here the TL has shifted the emphasis from co-ordination to contrast by substituting *mais* for *and*, influenced perhaps by the theme of contrast to the point of altering (however subtly) the relationship between the two parts of the sentence.
- *was unusual in seeing* (56): here the TL breaks this down by insertion of a colon to separate two different statements: *n'est pas un exemple type: il a consulté...*
- *sit down and explain everything* (78): here the TL brings out the underlying concept of purpose by the use of an adverbial clause, *pour plus infinitive.*

Syntax
Passives:
- *he was given access* (5): description, not indirect speech, so TL opts for an active verb, *il a eu accès.*
- *they will be sent a date* (11): although this is indirect speech, the passive verb becomes active, *ils recevront*, perhaps because to do otherwise would necessitate the introduction of another impersonal subject, *on.*

235

- *one of whom had surgery* (39): becomes a passive form in the TL.
- *they were never warned* (80): here the passive form is part of reported speech and so is retained in the TL for accuracy of quotation.

Analytical to synthetic verb forms:
- *gets larger* (8): *grossit.*
- *I would sooner wait* (48): the concept of preference is replaced by one of advisability, in another analytical verb form, *je ferais mieux d'attendre.*

Other:
- *he knew as much about... as about...* (2): the TL requires the insertion of *en — il en savait...*
- *the night before the operation* (12): SL adverb becomes TL present participle, *précédant l'opération.*
- *usual warning given* (13): it is interesting to note here that the past participle in the SL has to be part of a passive verbal construction, because of its position following the noun warning, which is seen as the subject of the passive verb; whereas in the TL the past participle precedes the noun, implying thereby that it is part of an active verbal construction of which the noun, *warning*, is the object. This may well reflect actual practice or else established conventions for the writing of information on patients' medical records.
- *prostate operations are routine but to patients they are not* (20): the TL conveys the need to repeat the adjective routine by substituting a pronoun in the form of the direct article: *ils ne le sont pas.*
- *I found it very useful... it helped me...* (26–28): here the it refers to the video, and there must be appropriate agreement in both past participle (preceding direct object) and pronoun subject of the verb.
- *when it starts* (29): adverbial clause becomes adverbial phrase — *au début.*
- *so that the information shown is relevant to...* (32): in the TL the verb form here needs to be in the subjunctive mood following an adverbial phrase of purpose.
- *did not want an operation* (43): shift from want to prefer. Also use of passive instead of noun.
- *at an early stage* (44): again replacement of noun by negative verb, *ne viennent que de commencer.*
- *risks... small* (46): the positive form of the adjective becomes a superlative in the TL, *minimaux.*
- *it took an hour to watch* (52): shift from an impersonal verb form to replace passive in SL becomes a personalised form, *j'ai passé une heure à regarder...*
- *the response has been to turn people away from* (62): where the subject of the SL sentence is implied (the video) the subject of the TL sentence is the patient.
- *than they need* (69): personalised clause becomes impersonal in TL, *que besoin n'en fait.*
- *the pressures on us* (78): expanded to give a relative clause with a passive verb having pressures as subject.
- *a small proportion of patients have difficulties* (76): in the SL and in the TL the correct form of the verb is the plural, to reflect the concept of numbers not of mass quantity.
- *we have patients come back* (79–80): relative clause in SL without relative pronoun becomes infinitive construction in TL, *nous avons vu des patients revenir.*
- *research-based* (86): compound adjective becomes relative clause *basées*, with preposition *sur.*

Lexis

Medical terminology, for most of which there will be an accepted direct equivalent in TL terminolgy: *prostate, hypothalamus, hip replacement* (2–4); *urination* (8); *watchful waiting — attente surveillée* (17); *side-effects — effets secondaires* (52); *drug treatments — here, médicaux,* to contrast with *la chirurgie* (50): *BPH — HBP* (57); — *health maintenance organisations — organisations médico-sociales* (70): *the operation... work:* TL uses *marcher,* for the idea of success — still index for index (80–81).

- *(make) an informed decision* (19): this TL specific noun phrase refers to a very specific concept. There does not appear to be a TL direct equivalent unit to refer to the same concept and so the translator has expanded it into a clause bringing out the implied meaning: *décider sur la base de l'information reçue,* i.e. icon for index.

- *a junior doctor* (12): the adjective here relates to professional status and level of training (any doctor below the status of consultant), whereas in the TL the adjective *jeune* refers more specifically to physical age and gives no indication of level of training: index for symbol.

IT terminology, for which there will again be fixed accepted TL equivalents: *inter-active video* (16); *laser disc player; touch sensitive screen, print-out* (30–36); *'learn more' section on the screen* (35–36).

Acronyms:

- *UWG* (13): this is a short form used amongst the medical profession, probably not known to the SL reader, hence the explanation in the text, with the capital letters showing the origin of the acronym. A similar approach has been adopted in the TL, but with the addition of inverted commas to show that this is a direct quote. Note also the use of the passive voice for economy.

- *BPH* (57): this abbreviation of a medical condition is given in brackets for extra information rather than constituting the primary form of reference. The TL adopts a similar tactic.

Other:

- *realise* (1): *réalisé:* strictly speaking this is a **faux ami** but one which is now being used quite unselfconsciously in the TL media; the correct form should be *se rendre compte de ce que + verb/de + noun.*

- *outlines* (16): becomes *souligne* in the TL, incurring a shift from description to emphasis.

- *patient* (21): this is now accepted in the TL but would appear to have originated as an SL loan word. The dictionary only offers *le malade.*

- *programmed* (31): here the TL uses the SL word as a loan word but adapted to TL syntax.

- *which affects* (57): *qui touche.*

- *risk-adverse (to surgery)* (64): a form of medical speak, achieving economy through unusual collocation, having a noun plus adjective where one would normally expected to find *patients are adverse to the risks of.* Also an unusual adjective, more commonly collocated with *conditions, results, effect.*

- *dearth* (87): a rather less common noun, whose TL equivalent should be equally uncommon (for this register).

Collocations:

- *risks and benefits* (20): this has been expanded to give *des risques possibles et des avantages,* showing polysemy of TL term, *avantages.* See also *the risks* (12) — *les risques encourus* (15).

- *pros and cons* (6): *avantages et inconvénients:* a different pair of collocatives used

here, intead of the Latin loan words in SL, which are often rendered in the TL as *les pour et contre*.
- *common* (61): *courant* is used here in TL, and also in line 21 to convey the concept of *routine*, although *routine* in the context of surgery means *with minimal risks* as well as *common, often repeated* — i.e. different polysemy of TL word means loss of SL information.
- *surgery carried out* (72): note the shift to a plural TL noun, the noun *chirurgerie* being reserved for the skill or practice, not for individual cases: *opérations effectuées*.
- *the American pattern* (74): *le modèle américain*.
- *amount of information* (85): *le volume des informations*.
- *makes it clear* (82): *insiste sur le fait que*.

Stylistic Devices
Since the text consists of a mixture of reporting and direct quotes there is not much scope for deliberate use of rhetorical devices on the part of the author.
Alliteration:
- *in later life* (8): loss of alliteration but compensation, as this becomes assonance in the TL: *à un âge avancé*.
- *watchful waiting* (17): a medical jargon neologism obviously coined in the TL for its alliterative value; this is lost in the SL.
- *severity of symptoms* (31): a usual medical collocate which is more memorable for its alliterative quality, lost in TL in order to respect TL collocate.
- *the most telling evidence* (38): gain of alliteration by collocation, *la preuve la plus parlante*.
- *first findings* (74): loss in TL.
Assonance:
- *important implications* — *implications importantes* (66): lost in the TL but could have been reproduced by use of equivalent TL forms, although perhaps not so appropriate in context.

Cultural References
- *in Middlesex* (23): according to literary tradition, references to a county have to be preceded by a definite article.
- *12 inch laser disc player* (30): measurements need to be converted to TL norms.
- *the King's Fund* (25, 64): this may require a footnote, or at least a note in brackets in the SL to explain the function.
- *research nurse* (75): the TL loses the concept of being attached to the research project, keeping simply the noun, *l'infirmière*.

Punctuation
Inverted commas:
- *inter-active video* (16): this word is placed in inverted commas as if to signal a neologism or new invention, although this is surprising, given the degree of familiarity amongst the educated general public with such videos, through the recent intensive advertising of CD interactive computer games and programmes by companies such as Philips; unless it is the use of the word video which is here intended to describe the visual (hence resembling a video) form of the programme rather than the medium by which it is stored

and accessed (probably a compact disc). The TL thus reproduces this effect by a similar use.
- inverted commas are, of course used to signal direct speech in both SL and TL (26–28, 43–55, 64–65, 76–81, 85–87).
- also used to indicate the name of the project (84).

Other:
- *he or she* (34): this attempt at political correctness is conveyed in the TL by a simple slash: *il/elle.*
- *use of dashes for the insertion of information* (59): in the TL these are replaced by commas, integrating the information into the main body of the text. However, in (86 in TT), the opposite happens, with dashes being introduced in the TL — *environ quatre pour cent.*

The Inhumanity of Medicine

This is the first part of a text which appeared in *The British Medical Journal*, a weekly publication for all doctors (senior and junior, in hospitals and general practice) which offers a selection of more in-depth articles combined with brief reports, letters, reviews, short snippets and a separate section for jobs. Together with *The Lancet*, it probably reaches the widest medical audience and lays no claim to specialist status, every specialisation having its own specialist publication.

It is important to note the timing of this article, in the week before Christmas, a time when people are perhaps wont to reflect on aspects of life and work in a more philosophical vein. This is especially true for this article, published at the time of year when the emphasis is on 'goodwill to all men'. It serves as a mirror to reflect what is good in the relationships between doctors and their patients, but also what is not so good, taking a historical perspective which echoes the commonly held belief that things were much tougher a few decades ago. Modern technological developments are examined in the light of their effect on the patient, the target 'consumer' in medicine, and both the spirit of the time of year and the earnest desire to address colleagues on a matter not directly related to types of treatment and medical knowledge have led the author to adopt a more direct form of address, combined with a more emotive lexical content than would generally be found in this journal, whose usual style is that of the medical or scientific report, with its concomitant conventions of objective comment, lack of authorial presence and absence of emotive content.

Sentence Structure

With the above comments in mind, the translator could expect to find a more subjective approach, with a greater degree of accumulation and complexity of subordination, reflecting the thought processes of the author rather than aiming at clarity of reporting through brevity of the sentence. This is indeed the case, e.g.:
- *The diagnosis and prognosis were discussed... next patient* (22).
- *and in the frenetic, reorganised NHS... part of doctors* (61).

These longer and more complex sentences contrast with shorter ones consisting of a single clause, to give increased impact through contrast:
- *such behaviour was common during my student days* (25).
- *yet this kind of relationship is all too rarely available to them* (49).

There is also greater scope in an article of this kind for reformulation of the order of presentation of information so as to conform to TL stylistic norms, as can be seen, for example, in the way in which the translator has rewritten the introductory quote at the head of the article.

Syntax

- *in the past few months* (1): in accordance with TL conventions, the TT omits the preposition, stating simply, *ces derniers mois*.
- *I have been made aware* (1): here the TT retains the passive construction, since there is no subject of the main verb. The translator could just as readily have used an impersonal construction with *on*.

- *how to behave* (4): this verbal syntagm is expanded in the TT to include a noun from the SL verb plus an appropriate TL verb to collocate with this noun.
- *newsworthy* (9): this compound adjective formed from noun plus adjective cannot be rendered in such an economic way in the TL and is replaced by an expanded verbal syntagm, *valent la peine d'être publiées*, which brings out the underlying aspects of meaning of the two elements of this compound.
- *vividly remember* (16): this single-word adverb has been expanded into an adverbial clause of manner, *comme si j'y étais*.
- *pomposity, inhumanity and cruelty* (27): in this list of abstract nouns there is some expansion in the TL, so that for the first two nouns the SL noun becomes an adjective describing a kind of quality or behaviour — this explicitation conforms to TL stylistic conventions.
- *is highlighting* (34): following the use of *aucun doute*, the TL has a simple form of the subjunctive here, with no attempt to bring out the continuous aspect.
- *I know of no evidence* (14): here the emphatic *no* is rendered in the TL by the standard construction, *rien + ne*, with the difference that in the TL the construction is impersonal, the subject of the SL clause becoming the indirect object of the TL clause, giving perhaps a greater degree of objectivity to the statement.
- *we may look back on this in the same light as we do on… today* (38): the verb becomes a noun in the TL, allowing the use of the adjective *même* to carry the intended comparison between past and future. The modal of the ST is rendered by *peut-être* in the TT.
- *not unreasonably* (67): this single-word SL adverb becomes an adverbial phrase in the TL, *non sans raison*.
- *more demanding than they used to be* (66): here the implied negative aspect of the comparison requires explicitation in the TL by use of a negative construction and insertion of an anaphoric reference — the pronoun, *le*.
- *few would disagree* (82): the SL stresses the small number of dissenters through use of a negative quantifier, *few*. The TL version would seem to lose impact by its use of *beaucoup*, which underlines the degree of consensus rather than lack of resistance.
- *two years spent…* (83); this SL past participle is transformed into an infinitive (having the function of a gerund, as could have been used in the SL).
- *distressed people* (85): this past participle becomes a relative clause in the TL.

Lexis
Terminology of the medical world: to be researched and checked with a TL culture professional:
- *consultants — médécins spécialistes* (2); *general practitioners — praticiens généralistes* (3): *teaching rounds — visite d'enseignement* (16): *inoperable lung cancer — cancer du poumon non-opérable* (18): *the senior physician — le chef de clinique* (18): *diagnosis and prognosis — les diagnostic et pronostic* (22): *protocols (of chemotherapy) — protocoles de chimiothérapie* (36): *bleeding and cupping — les saignées et les ventouses* (39) *chronic or terminal illness — maladies chroniques, dans leur phase terminale* (46): *the quality of life — la qualité de vie* (43): *rotating — tournent dans des programmes de formation différentes* (icon for icon, not index for index) (54): *junior grades — jeunes médecins* (icon for index — not precise correspondence

in terms of hierarchy) (57): *general practice — consultation des généralistes* (icon for symbol) (58): *family doctor — médecin de famille* (59): *rapid turnover of patients — un défile incroyable des malades* (64) (here we find, in true NHS reform style, a business term applied to the medical world, causing a shift in indexical use through neologism of collocation).

Collocations:

- *disturbing questions* (8): the translator has chosen *dérangeantes*, although this may be considered insufficiently intense, of a lesser degree of emotive content than the word *disturbing*.
- *uncaring* (11): the translator has chosen to expand this adjective, for lack of a direct equivalent single word, into a relative clause. Perhaps the same effect could have been achieved with greater economy through the use of an adverbial expression comprising *sans* plus an appropriate noun.
- *historical perspective* (14): a potential **faux ami**, as *perspective* relates more to future possibilities, the appropriate TL term here being *contexte*.
- *a huddle of American football players* (21): this descriptive noun for a group of players needs an appropriate TL collocation.
- *problems are compounded* (44): appropriate collocate is used here, *aggravés*.
- *systems… geared to* (45): becomes *adaptés à*.
- *a pattern of care that spills over into* (58): there are two collocates here, one being *pattern* with *care* (commonly used), and one being *pattern* with *spills over into* (less common) — the phrasal or analytical SL verb construction of the second being replaced by a TL analytical verb form.
- *criticisms levelled at* (71): becomes *critiques formulées à l'encontre de*.
- *poor track record* (77): here the translator has substituted a different item of lexis with its appropriate collocation, *maigres résultats*.

Fixed expressions:

- *in a similar vein* (7): this fixed expression takes advantage of the inherent medical term, *vein*, to add to the cohesive effect of the main themes. The TL does not offer this opportunity, relying instead on a more neutral expression, *d'un esprit similaire*.
- *the Christmas season* (8): becomes *la période de Noël*.
- *the excuse that* (9): expansion is required here to conform to TL norms: *l'excuse selon laquelle*.
- *death's door* (37): a similar expression is used in the TL but in the plural: *aux portes de la mort*.
- *hopes and fears* (48): again, a similar construction in the TL, *espoirs et craintes*.
- *(reflect) a caring attitude* (65): this could be described as a collocation but has by virtue of use almost become a fixed expression (icon); the TL fails to render this other than descriptively, thereby losing the element of *attitude* and concentrating on the concept of *care*. This in fact alters the meaning of that part of the sentence and is thus inaccurate and untrue to the ST message.
- *along these lines* (78): becomes a more specific but more neutral anaphoric reference, *de ce type*.

Interpretation:

- *encompass* (10): in the SL context this verb has the meaning of: to include, to cover, to bring into its sphere of influence. The TL verb *contiennent* could be said not to cover all of these meanings and to focus more on the immediate dictionary definition. Whilst not incorrect, it fails to respect the nuance of

encompass, which is more descriptive for being more precise. Perhaps *renfermer* or a synonym of this would have been more appropriate.
- *handling their patients* (15): this synthetic verb is replaced by an analytical expression in the TL, since the direct equivalents, *manier* or *manipuler*, cannot be used with such a collocate in such a context.
- *eradicate* (37): this is translated by *supprimer* in the TT — is this really the most appropriate collocation with *tumeur*?
- *final illness* (51): this has been interpreted as *phase finale de leur maladie*, which may be considered more specific than the ST, as it implies only chronic, not also recurring or new illnesses.
- *rotating* (54): this is a very specific use of this verb in a medical context of training correctly rendered by expansion in the TT (icon for index).

Faux amis:
- *perspective* (14): not *perspective* but *contexte*.
- *effective* (40): not *effective* but *efficace*.

Stylistic Devices
- The form of **direct approach** is most apparent in the series of rhetorical questions towards the end of this first half of the article, as the author extends his own process of enquiry to include his reader, serving either to summarise a point already made or to introduce a new concept:
- *are they new?* (14).
- the **introduction of the article** (1–5) by a quote from a letter serves both to outline the problems to be discussed in the article and to give extra credibility to the author's comments by showing that his views are shared, as well as almost allowing him to disclaim responsibility for the rather more emotive concepts discussed therein, as if he were responding to a need, not creating a new debate. The nature of this quote should remain the same in the TT.
- *cupping and bleeding* (39): reference to practices of the past carry a pejorative intent in this comparison.

Alliteration:
- *patch up practice... patients are pushed* (41): lost in both cases in the TL, although the second could have been retained by using *patients* instead of *malades*.
- *patients' problems* (44): the same applies here as in the previous example.
- *deficiences that have dogged us* (68): lost in the TL.
- *radical revisions* (78): lost in TL although it may have been possible to recreate.

Assonance:
  extremes of endurance (42): lost by use of *résistance*.

Imagery:
- *patch up* (42): the reference to the sewing metaphor is recreated through *racommodage*, used almost as a neologism in the TL.

Cultural References
The medical world:
- the whole of this article is based on a detailed knowledge of how the NHS works, what current issues are being discussed, both openly in the press and more discreetly within the ranks; also on an awareness of how things used to be. To anyone not initiated into this subculture, for example, the wider British public, many of the references in this particular article will be fairly readily understandable, given the press coverage of NHS problems and reforms in

recent years. To the Target reader, however educated, such references will be more problematic, as even those in the profession in the target culture may not be aware of all the implications of the comments made with regard to the NHS. The underlying concept of doctor–patient relations, whilst not perhaps assuming the same degree of priority in the target culture, may be seen as a universal concern for anyone practising medicine, at least in the West, and as such should strike a chord in the TL reader, be he a professional or a member of the general public.

- one aspect of the need for detailed knowledge of the system relates to the names of the various types of medical practice and the terms used to designate the status of different doctors within the hierarchy, e.g. *consultant, general practitioner, junior grades, teaching round (including the significance of ward rounds and the stereotypical view of how these are conducted)*. Thus we find the substitution of index for icon or symbol, the explication of SL inherent concepts for which there is no direct TL corresponding icon or symbol, and even when there is an apparently equivalent unit at the level of index, it may not cover the same conceptual spectrum, thus offering at best a 'fuzzy match' (see Conceptual Framework chapter)
- the reference (59) to not always being able to see their own family doctor should really be accompanied in the TT by a note regarding the role of the family doctor, the way these are sometimes organised in group practices, and the use of locums for out of hours cover.
- *the frenetic, reorganised NHS* (61) presumes familiarity with the complaints of increased bureacracy making more demands on the time of those primarily designated as providers of medical care, who are required to undertaken more and more administrative functions thereby detracting from the time available to see to patients.

Other:
- the reference to *Alan Bennett* (28) and his play may require explanation for the TL reader. In the light of subsequent events, writing with the benefit of further information, the translator may also wish to add a note relating to the film produced from this play and released in 1995.

Punctuation
- the dots (1) in the introductory quotation have a definite function, namely to show the omission of a segment of text; as such they must be retained in the TT.
- the name of the play (29) by Bennett is written in italics in the SL and also in the TL.
- the concept of *patch up practice* (41) is seen by the translator to be an unfamiliar collocation forming a new concept to the TL reader and so *racommodage* is placed in inverted commas.

Black Death

This extract is from an article taken from *Mensa Magazine* and is quite representative of the kind of article one might find in this magazine. Written by members themselves, they reflect the wide range of interests of Mensa members, who are drawn from all social and professional groups of society, their shared attributes including an often eclectic passion for knowledge and intellectual stimulus in any shape or form. Articles thus tend to cover almost anything and everything. It would be difficult to describe in more detail the typical Mensa profile, and the style of the article, as well as its subject, would make it difficult to determine its source, were this latter not known.

This article is written in a rather descriptive, sometimes dramatic style, attempting to bring to life an aspect of the past through evocation of more emotive details than the pure (often dry) facts of the traditional school history book. This style is perhaps a reflection of the professional experience of the author, who also uses quotes from a contemporary author to add colour to his narrative. However, he also gives a lot of useful explanation and supplementary background details which would be of particular interest to the TL reader keen to develop his knowledge of the origins of some aspects of SL culture.

Sentence Structure

Given the wish to render the text more interesting to the reader, the author uses the mechanism of contrasting longer, more detailed lists of facts and actions, with more dramatically effective, mainly short sentences to drive home a particular point:

- *they brought cargoes from the Far East. They brought something else as well. The Black Death* (4–5).
- *Still no-one knew why* (24).
- *children sang about it* (60).
- *they still are* (67).

In keeping with the dramatic style, there are many conjunctions and other linking words or phrases to bring out the relationships between sentences or parts of a sentence and this effect should be reproduced, e.g. *as well; but; yet; still; such was; and; indeed; broadly speaking; by now; then.*

Syntax

- *limped into harbour* (3): in keeping with TL conventions, verbs of types of movement are often translated by a generic verb plus an adverbial phrase of manner. This is the case here, the translator using *regagner* plus *tant bien que mal*, bringing out the meaning but losing the figurative use of a mode of ambulation which is an acceptable collocate with *ship* in the SL but not in the TL.
- *walk throught infected areas* (39): a similar strategy is found here, with the verb of movement incorporating the preposition of direction, *traverser*, and an adverbial phrase of manner, *à pied*.
- *half the population of a continent* (9): the TL prefers to be more specific, using

the definite article as anaphoric reference to Europe, named in the first part of the same sentence.

– *it took until… to* (20): a fixed expression replaced by an equivalent form of impersonal expression with a more explicit statement of obligation, *il fallut attendre… pour.*

– *limped into — regagnèrent* (3); *were brought ashore — furent portés* (7): these are but two examples of the use of the Past Historic tense (Passé Simple) in keeping with the conventions of narrative discourse in the TL. It is important to be aware of the use of different tenses in the SL — Past Simple, Imperfect for continuing action, Imperfect for implied condition or repeated habit — in order to preserve the dramative impact in the TT.

– *crossing the Channel to London* (22): the TL inserts a verb to be more explicit, *pour atteindre.*

– *a man with a bell* (27): the TT changes this prepositional phrase into a relative clause, using a verb which is an appropriate collocate with *bell*, i.e. *sonner.*

– *people… would run* (35): this is used in the sense of repeated past habit, not part of a conditional sentence.

– *when they came to bury others and found them there they were…* (36): this SL use of the third person plural pronoun to refer to two different subjects in the same sentence could be confusing, and is especially so in the TL, where it would have been preferable to adopt a demonstrative pronoun, repeat one of the two nouns or use the impersonal form *on* to avoid confusion.

– *women with long noses for…* (38): the same procedure is adopted here, creating a relative clause.

– *stood a watchman to prevent people getting out* (44): the idea of purpose is lost in the TL which simply describes what happened in a relative clause, *qui empêchait…* followed by an infiniitve, *de sortir*, according to TL conventions (*prevent someone from* plus *gerund, empecher de* plus *infinitive*).

– *abated* (51): becomes an analytical verb construction, *pris moins d'importance.*

– *were largely excused the flames* (57): the passive verb in the SL implies active choice on the part of an unknown agent (a vengeful God, the spirit of the plague?), whereas the TL active verb, *avaient évité* implies choice on the part of the parishes. The single-word adverb becomes a fixed adverbial expression, *en grande partie.*

– *broadly speaking* (56): this fixed adverbial expression is replaced by a similar fixed expression in the TL, although the two may not be seen to cover exactly the same conceptual territory.

– *by now* (60): dramatic present, becomes an adverb of past time in the TL, *alors.*

– *children sang about it* (60): here the TT inserts a pronoun, *la*, to evoke the idea of the plague being commemorated in a song; both nouns being feminine, *la peste, la chanson*, the pronoun conveniently covers both by a single reference.

– *which caused bubonic plague to spread* (78): here the SL infinitive following the verb *caused* becomes a noun, *la propagation*, also following the verb *causaient.*

Lexis

– *sailing ships* (3): this compound noun is translated by a single word in the TL, incorporating both aspects of description.

– *flared up* (21): the TL verb conveys the suddenness of the spread but perhaps not its medical connotation. *Eclater* is also used in line 54 for *broke out* to refer to the Great Fire, which shows its polyvalence.

- *scythed through* (22): the same term of reference is used in the TL, thus preserving the dramatic effect in keeping with practices of the period for cutting a way through a field or harvesting a crop.
- *corpses* (29): although *corps* is correct, perhaps *cadavres* would have been more evocative here.
- *daubed* (42): the TL choice conveys the same aspects of meaning, of being a broad stroke, done in a hurry, with a lot of paint, making perhaps a mess.
- *poses, buboes* (65–66): the vocabulary of the plague is described in the SL, immediately following the rhyme, thus making both rhyme and terms easier to explain in the TL.

Fixed expressions:
- the onomatopoeia of *Atishoo* (61) is transcribed into the TL conventional form of representation, *Atchoum*.

Collocations:
- *fanciful theory* (80): the TL has kept the kernel of fantasy plus the derogatory connotation through the suffix *-iste: fantaisiste.*
- *blatant attacks* (81): this is somewhat modified in tone in the TL, where the adjective *blatant* (*overt, visible* — factual comment with some emotive connotation) becomes and adverb (*injustement* — more clearly emotive).
- *convoluted peregrinations* (83): this is almost a tautology but both terms contribute to an overall effect and so are retained in the TL, *pérégrinations circonvolues.*

Interpretation:
- *culprits who caused bubonic plague to spread* (8): in the TT the translator has chosen to bring out the sense of physically bringing the infection to the country, rather than stressing the aspect of causality. This could be argued as being a shift in authorial intention, but is not necessarily a serious shift, since there is no real loss of information or change in overall effect.
- *one of the biggest lies...* (30–31): here the TL has *gît*, normally found on tombstones, perhaps a deliberate choice to recall this association, rather than a more neutral expression such as *se trouve*. This could be an example of indexical correspondence which also requires consideration of the role of collocation.
- *curtailment* (55): it could be queried whether *extinction* is the appropriate term here, given the introductory statement to the effect that the plague still exists, as well as in the light of semantic analysis of the word *curtailment*. Perhaps here an inaccurate indexical correlation.
- *was limping into...* (58): it could be argued that *disparaissait tranquillement* does not convey the concept of petering out, losing force — the TL choice is more benign in tone.
- *the miasmatists... the contagionists* (72–73): here the TL opts for greater explicitness; instead of using the suffix *-ists*, it inserts the words, *les tenants du...* , hence a more iconic use of the unit of meaning.

Stylistic Devices
Imagery:
- *entrenched* (60): recalls the mass graves, whereas the TL *ancré*, as well as being appropriate for the context, recalls the *voiliers.*

Repetition:
- *half the population... half a century* (9) due to TL use of different words for *half*

to collocate with the two different nouns, this repetition of form is lost, but not that of meaning.

- *no-one could stop... no-one could cure... no-one knew why* (18–19): this effect, used for intensity of emphasis here, is reproduced in the TT.
- *no-one knew why* (18); *still no-one knew why* (24); *still didn't know why* (71); *now they knew why* (85); this effect is used here as a device to lend coherence to the overall structure of the text and as such is important to its impact.

Exclamations/Rhetorical questions:
- *what a London it became* (25): here the translator has used a rhetorical question, changing the emphasis from stressing a result to seeking an answer. A shift in orientation, but not a serious one.

Alliteration:
- *lingering popular belief* (53): the translator manages to create an alliterative effect in the TL, *populaires persistentes*, contributing thereby to the overall literary stylistic effect.
- *poorer parishes* (56): intensified in the TL by the form of the superlative, *paroisses les plus pauvres* — note the shift here from comparative to superlative form, quite a common shift.

Word order:
- *much derided were the fools who...* (76): this inversion of verb and subject is intended for emphasis. The TT cannot copy this order but achieves the same effect by splitting the main clause, inserting relative clause, and leaving the emotive passive construction, *tournés en ridicule*, until the end of the sentence.

Contrast:
- *the nearest... far short* (80–81): this is retained in the TL by *plus proche... loin*

Cultural References
- *the Far East* (5): there is sometimes a difficulty in deciding on the appropriate terms to use for the East in the TL; for example, the TL uses *proche Orient* where the SL uses *Middle East*. Here the SL has *Far* East, for which the translated has used *Moyen Orient*, although Harraps standard does give *l'extrême orient*. This may be then a case of the translator overcompensating in the light of awareness of the differences in representation of the Middle East and extending this by analogy. Here we find icon being substituted for icon, depending on the way in which geographical boundaries and locations are described in the two languages.
- *Genoa* (1): note the use of the TL form of this city, probably because it is well-known in the TL it has a naturalised form; were it not so well known, it may have been necessary to use the form of the original language, Italian, as in fact does the SL.
- *the City* (56): perhaps the translator has assumed that the TL reader will know of this particular contemporary use of the word city with a capital C in referring to London. However, it would be advisable to add a note to explain this specific reference, which could otherwise be misinterpreted.
- *Ring a Roses* (61): the way the rhyme is set typographically does not help to make clear that this is a song, but the use of the verb *sing* goes some way towards this. It may be useful to append a translator's note to explain when and how this song is sung (sociocultural context). This is a case where SL symbol finds no corresponding TL symbol.

- *Yersenia pestis* (85): since medical diseases are given Latin names, this should be appropriate in its SL form in the TL. Hence index for index substitution:

Punctuation

- *they brought... they brought something else. The Black Death* (4–6): where the SL uses three consecutive short sentences for impact, the TL attempts to do the same by combining two of these through the use of a colon.
- note the use of capital letters for *the Great Fire, the Great Plague* (53, 55), retained in the TL to show the use of names, not generic descriptors.
- capital letters are also used in the TL for the names of the two theories of propagation, *le Miasme* and *la Contagion* (83) — this may be a result of translator idiolect rather than TL conventions, influenced also perhaps by a more medieval style of naming personified elements of a story.
- the word *why* is used in italics for emphasis in the TT as in the ST (19, 24, 71, 86).

Our Children's Education — The Updated Parent's Charter

This text is an extract from a parent's charter published by the Department for Education in 1994 within the context of a government drive to be seen to be maintaining or improving standards and as part of a series of charters intended to provide a detailed framework by which the citizen could judge and assess performance in the public sector. As such, the structure is one based on promises of service (on the part of the government) and statements of rights (on the part of the parent).

This charter is therefore destined to reach the wider general public — in fact, we are told that the document was sent to every home in the country — so that clarity of expression is essential in order for the content to be easily accessible to all socio-educational and socio-professional groups, to allow no apparent ambiguity of intent which could lead to misrepresentation or inaccurate expectations. One of the devices adopted to facilitate communication is the use of a more direct form of address in the second person where the document lists promises of performance, whilst aims and achievements are summed up in the third person, making of the promises a statement of fact. Another device is to shift attention from the government as provider to lay responsibility for performance with those involved in delivering the service, be they governors, teachers, schools, inspection teams or other. Where promises are seen to be of great importance, underlining actions to be taken by these others on behalf of the government, the actions are presented as obligations, so that the government appears to act as a regulating body rather than as provider. Modals also modify or introduce rights claimed by the provider, and conditional clauses inform of further rights of the consumer.

Since the document refers to a national education system, it is clear that there will be many correspondences of aim/concept/approach in the TL culture. But equally clearly, there will be many SL culture specific references, some of which may be matched by equivalent or near-equivalent concepts in the TL, whilst others may find no analogy and thus require explanation or expansion. The translator will have to beware the temptation to use apparently similar terms (form, spelling) in the TL to those in the SL without first checking that they have the same denotative and/or connotative value in the TL — e.g. the word/function of [school] governor.

Sentence Structure

There is some degree of **listing** within a sentence, to stress points for action or related promises:

- *you need to keep track of your child's progress, to find out how the school is being run and to compare all local schools* (30): accumulaton of clauses of purpose;
- *the school will keep records about your child's attendance, behaviour and achievements* (57): accumulation of nouns;

but generally a minimal degree of subordination, new sentences being started in preference to the insertion of additional information, giving one main item of information per sentence. Although the tendency in the TL may be to link these

clauses, consideration must be given to the overall text type conventions in the TL and to the communicative function of the text:
- *You will receive a written report on your child's progress at least once a year. It will tell you about...* (39).
- *the people who lead inspection teams have to be approved by OFSTED. OFSTED regularly checks that they are doing a thorough job* (75).

Given the need for transparency, many of the subordinate clauses are introduced by interrogatives, as if in answer to questions — hence an element of reported speech in terms of achievements and promises relating to the child's performance, as seen in subordinate clauses introduced by interrogatives:
- *that is why we have* (19).
- *to find out how the school is being run* (30).
- *what your child has achieved* (47).
- *explain what they have done* (96).

The TT has also, in places, broken down one SL clause into two in the TL, perhaps due to syntactical requirements but also remaining true to the overall ST structure:
- *this updated Parents' Charter tells you* (15): becomes *Cette Charte Parentale a été mise à jour et vous donne.*

Where there is co-ordination in the SL this is maintained in the TL:
- *to keep track... to know... and to compare...* (30–31).

Syntax

As stated in the introduction, much use is made of verb tenses and modal auxiliaries to differentiate between promises, rights and obligations:

Past achievements — present perfect: retained in TT by use of Passé Composé
- *schools have changed... standards have improved... teachers, governors and parents have all played their part; they have brought* (1–5).
- *the governing body must explain what they have done* (96).

Promises — future simple: also retained in the TL:
- *you will receive a written report about your child; it will tell you about... ; the school will keep records* (39); *your child... will receive* (60–61).

Conditional sentences to imply promises:
- *if you ask the school they will let you look* (58): note use of first conditional type of sentence to imply certainty of occurrence in main clause.
- *if a school is failing to give..., special measures will apply* (90).

Obligations: the translator has used the same verb to preserve the effect of coherence and reinforcement through repetition:
- *the people who lead inspection teams have to be approved* (75): *devoir.*
- *they must hold a meeting...* (82): *devoir.*
- *the inspectors must publish the report... the school must act on the report* (84): *devoir.*
- *the governing body must explain* (96): *devoir.*

Rights: of the parent as consumer:
- *you should get all the information...* (29): conditional of *devoir.*
- *you have a right to... ; if you ask the school they will let you look at...* (58)

Rights: of the providers:
- *the school may charge for this* (91): *il se peut que* plus subjunctive.
- *he may close the school if...* (103); *ce dernier peut fermer l'école si...*: here there is potential polysemy and therefore possible ambiguity of interpretation as *peut* may be taken to refer to what is allowed/functional capacity as well as to the

possibility that something might/may happen. However, neither interpretation would result in serious changes to the overall message.

Impersonal observations distancing the government from direct involvement:
- *standards have improved* (1): present perfect for achievements.
- *a new independent organisation monitors standards* (68): present simple for facts.
- *the Office for Standards in Education is led by...* (69): passive to emphasise action by a different agent, retained in the TT.
- *all state schools are inspected* (74): passive to stress action, changes to a noun in the TT, *l'inspection*, following introductory statement, *se traduit par*.
- *these are designed to tackle... if necessary the school will be managed* (100): again, stress on action, distancing of government from direct involvement. TT uses two different constructions — avoiding the passive in the first case, *ont pour but*, but retaining it in the second, *sera dirigé par*.
- *special measures will apply* (99): this intransitive use of the verb becomes a kind of passive (deep) structure, but not form, in the TL — *mesures... seront applicables*.

Other:
- *on standards... on choice* (6, 11): in the TL the preposition changes to *pour*.
- *updated... Charter tells you* (15): becomes two separate clauses/verbs in the TT, *a été mise à jour et vous donne*.
- *the key to making* (18): this gerund is rendered by a relative clause with finite verb, *le facteur-clé qui rendra*.
- *the right to know* (22): in the SL the same preposition can precede noun or verb, whilst the TL requires *à* plus noun or *de* plus infinitive.
- *under the government's reforms* (29): preposition here becomes *selon*.
- *progress* (30): this singular SL noun becomes plural in the TL.
- *important for raising standards* (33): as often happens, the gerund here becomes a TL noun derived from the verb. This happens again in:
- *publishing tables...* (34): this also becomes a noun derived from the verb, *la publication*.
- *a report about your child* (38): the preposition changes to *sur*.
- *the new arrangements mean that...* (73): to note that although the syntax of each point in section seven of the ST is a logical syntactical development from the introductory sentence, this is not the case in the TT. Perhaps further reflexion could have produced either a different form of introductory sentence or different syntax to introduce each point, in order to preserve this stylistic and syntactic coherence of the ST.
- *so you can compare... ask the school for a copy... the school may charge for this...* (90–92): note the use of the subjunctive in the TL where SL indicates purpose or possibility.
- *these are designed to* (100): becomes *ont pour but de*.

Lexis
Collocations:
- *played their part* (3): *jouer un rôle*.
- *making the country more competitive* (18): the verb *rendre* is to be used here.
- *take a (hard) look* (35): phrasal verb (verb plus noun qualified by adjective) becomes verb plus adverb — *sérieusment étudier*.
- *a thorough job* (77): becomes *un travail en profondeur* — other collocations could also have been used, such as *conscientieux, approfondi, compréhensif*.
- *act on the report* (85): *se conformer au rapport*.

- *strengths and weaknesses* (87): icon for icon — fixed expression, *points forts et points faibles.*
- *(what they have done to) carry out plans* (96): *plans... ont été suivis.*

Domain specific terminology:
- *children with special needs* (14): this euphemism for handicapped children or those with various problems (often called learning difficulties) has become a fixed term in the SL but is adopted into the TL via calque (direct translation) implying that there is no TL specific match for this term: index for icon.
- *National Curriculum; names of examinations* (42, 44–46) (see Cultural References).
- *state schools* (74): to note appropriate TL equivalent is *école publique,* not *d'état.*
- *the governing body* (94): by translating this word for word in the TL the translator may have lost the effect of domain-specific terminology and culture-specific reference: icon for icon.

Other:
- to note that *home* (19) is translated by *foyer,* not *domicile* or *maison,* helping to stress the involvment of the whole family.
- *attendance record* (50): note the different stress created in the TL by the shift from positive *attendance record* to negative *taux d'absentéisme,* through use of equivalent TL term.
- *brought in by the Secretary of State* (103): the connotations (possibly not deliberate but would be understood by the alert SL reader) attached to State intervention in a system which is effectively governed at local level are likely to be lost here without an explanatory footnote, but omission of such a note will not affect the overall message. Perhaps in this context *nommé* would serve better than *choisi.*

Stylistic Devices
Alliteration:
- *played their part* (3): alliteration through appropriate collocation in SL, lost in TL through similar need for collocation.

Ambiguity: in this text this effect is probably accidental, due to inaccuracy of style, rather than deliberate; however it does exist in this text despite an obvious desire for clarity:
- *wider choice* (2): possible ambiguity here, which can only be resolved by background knowledge of the issue of parental right to choose the school they wish their child to attend.
- *new targets of school* (12): even with background knowledge of SL culture this is difficult to interpret for the SL reader, could refer to types of school to be opened or developed, targets to be achieved at the level of the school as performer, range of choice to be offered or even schools to be targetted to improve intake levels by becoming first choice for more parents. The translator has opted for the aspect of types of school, which may not be the most likely interpretation but is a logical one in the context.
- *improvements for parents of children with special needs* (13): one has to assume that *improvements* refers to rights as mentioned in the preceding clause, but since this is not absolutely certain the TT is right to preserve the same element of openness to different interpretations by not expanding or making the reference more specific.

Expansion for explicitation:
- *tells you all about these improvements* (15): *vous donne toutes les informations concernant ces améliorations.*
- *the key to making* (18): key is expanded to give: *le facteur-clé:* icon for index.
- *it will tell you about* (40): insertion of demonstrative *ce* plus noun *rapport* to give clearer anaphoric reference than SL *it.*
- *results in the national tests* (42): expanded into a relative clause with insertion of appropriate verbal collocate, *passer (examen, test).*

Repetition: for emphasis and to give coherence:
- of syntactical forms: *to keep track... to find out... to compare* (29): this is recreated in the TL using *pour.*
- of modal verbs for obligation — *must, should* (84); effect also recreated in the TL, but through different tenses, forms of verb *devoir* (104).
- of lexis: for example, the words: *rights* (13), *improvements* (13), *better* (8): also repeated in TT.

Cultural References

- *wider choice* (2): an icon in the SL, even perhaps a symbol, there is possible ambiguity here (see above). The translator has misinterpreted this reference, as is evident by the insertion of the possessive pronoun *leur*, which has to refer to *les écoles* in the first sentence, since there is no other preceding plural noun and since the preceding singular noun, *niveau*, is also qualified by *leur*, referring to schools.
- *teachers, governors and parents* (3): the reference to governors has a particular connotation for the SL culture. It is to be queried whether the term *directeur d'école* actually refers to this particular function, which would seem to be SL culture specific. However, there is no loss of essential connotative or denotative information which would obscure the message: index for icon.
- *Citizen's Charter... Parents' Charter* (4): TT has — *la charte des citoyens... la charte parentale.* Names of charters could perhaps have been given parallel forms in the TL; since they are culture specific the names could reflect SL construction.
- *the right to know* (22): icon for icon; again, this is almost a slogan in the SL but can be translated word-for-word in the TL as a corresponding analogy exists with expressions such as *le droit à la différence, le droit d'asile.*
- *National Curriculum* (42): translated as *Programme d'Enseignement National,* a TL calque of the SL term but one which is comprehensible within the TL culture/education system.
- *GCSE, A levels, GNVQ's* (45): symbol for symbol; TL cultural equivalents are given in brackets following these names of SL culture-specific examinations.
- *OFSTED* (69): acronym is first presented through its component terms then used alone in the SL. In the TT the translator has given the TL translation followed by the SL words plus acronym in brackets, so that this acronym can also be used alone in the second occurrence of the name, albeit accompanied by a definite article in accordance with TL conventions: index for symbol.
- *the Secretary of State* (103): there is no problem here, the TL having a similar term/function.

Punctuation

- *Citizen's Charter... Parents' Charter* (4): the TT chooses not to reproduce the capital letters, following TL conventions, but again the SL conventions could

have been followed since the names are SL specific. This procedure was in fact followed in the TT in the case of *National Targets for Education and Training*.
– *'an outside' view* (81): inverted commas are used here to show the (probable) use of a quotation or perhaps something considered to be a neologism. The TT does not adopt the same procedure preferring to use a more neutral term, *personne non-concernée*.
– use of capital letters for acronyms of public examinations, *GCSE, A levels, GNVQ* (44), retained in TT, also for acronym *OFSTED*.
– SL uses capital letters for title, *Secretary of State* (103), so does TL.

Charter 88

This text takes the form of a declaration, similar to that of a political tract or manifesto. The source and indeed the day of publication (Sunday) would tend to indicate that the text is intended for the general public, albeit of a certain level of education, given that it appears in the Colour Supplement of *The Observer Magazine* from the Sunday newspaper. The day and nature of the publication presumes a public with time to read and reflect on issues presented. Despite what might be considered as an invitation to leisure reading, the style does not, however, violate the linguistic coventions of a document dealing with matters relating to the constitution and the rights of the citizen, so that the register is somewhat formal and there are several terms or expressions from the semantic field pertaining to such matters.

The text adopts a distinctive approach, using the first person plural form of address, which immediately makes clear its nature and excludes it from the domain of genuine legal documents, to which the title might seem to attribute it. The style seems to alternate between a factual, impersonal approach, 'a process is underway', one in which some statements are presented almost as rules or eternal truths, 'By taking these rights from some, the government puts them at risk for all' (25), to a more personalised form, 'we have been brought up' (1). The document in fact relates to a particular movement (also called Charter 88) but knowledge of this would not in fact seem essential to an accurate interpretation of the message of the text by either translator or target reader. Information about the background to the title and text could, however, be included in a translator's note for the target reader.

The structure of the final paragraph, with one main idea or statement per sentence, resembles a list of points in a manifesto, summing up the key themes of the text and pointing to its aim, to make the reader aware of the danger of an unquestioning belief in tradition. The choice of lexis reflects the intended tone.

Sentence Structure

The sentence structure tends in some ways to reflect the complexity of a legal document, especially through the comprehensive listing of both clauses (1–7) and noun groups (21–24). Three paragraphs commence with a brief single clause statement (33, 58, 91) which gains in impact due to the contrast with other, longer sentences. It may prove easier to introduce semi-colons instead of commas wherever there are lists, since none of the elements of these lists consist of a single word.
– it was felt more appropriate to reformulate the sentence beginning *Our freedoms* (35) in order to facilitate the process of anaphoric reference in the TL. The correct agreement for number and gender is essential to the successful decoding of such references.

Syntax
Passive voice:
– *we have been brought up* (1): TL tends to try to avoid use of direct form of passive, through pronominal structure or, as here, impersonal use of *on*.

- *are being curtailed* (14): another example of the need to find a stylistic variation for avoidance of the passive voice: TT suggests the use of *se voir imposer des limites*.
- *Scotland is governed... from Whitehall* (19): another passive construction in the SL which is transformed into a pronominal one in the TT, *L'Ecosse se fait gouverner*. It should be noted that the name *Whitehall* functions in the ST as a place name, not as a metonym for the Civil Service or for a Ministry, and so has been translated as such in the TT, introduced by the prepositional phrase, *à partir de*.
- *our press is brave* (6): it is stylistically more interesting to substitue another verb or verbal expression for a simple form of the verb *to be*, where possible — see TL *fait preuve de* plus two nouns instead of adjectives.
- *our liberty is the envy of the world* (2): another example of where the TL would tend prefer a more specific verb than the verb to be, one which forms an appropriate collocation with 'envy'.
- *a process is underway* (17): note the shift in the TT from the personnification of process as subject of the verb *to be* to an impersonal structure, *il existe... un processus*.
- *the rights to* (21): the translator will need to recall here the difference in syntax between *le droit de* with the infinitive, and *le droit à* plus noun; also to remember to repeat the definite article with each noun listed and dependent on '*le droit à*'.
- *by taking these rights... the government puts them at risk* (24): the ST uses a gerund with the preposition *by* to indicate the manner or means of doing something. This intent is rendered in the TT by the adverbial phrase, *à force de*, plus infinitive.
- *considered in isolation* (28): here is an example of a reversal of the usual shift (from TL adverbial phrase to SL single-word adverb); it is more appropriate to use a single-word adverb in the TL here, as *isolation* designates sound-proofing or insulation in the TL.
- *the events of 1688 only shifted* (31): here the TL has used a negative construction, *n'ont fait que de* plus infinitive to give more emphasis to the adverb.
- *we have had less freedom than we believe* (34): the idea of negative comparison has to be reinforced in the TL by the insertion of the definite article, *que nous ne le croyions*. The TL has also taken into account the sequence of tenses and occurrence of events by its use of l'Imparfait, *croyions*.
- *to make real* (37): although this appears to be a simple infinitive there is in fact an element of ellipsis, requiring explicitation in the TL through the use of an adverbial phrase of purpose, *afin de*.

Lexis
- *Charter 88* (title): there exists here a potential for selection of an inappropriate term due to interference and inaccurate analogy. The word charter is polysemous in the SL, with possible meanings including a document of conditions to be agreed or a declaration granting rights or status; also, a private hire of a means of transport, usually with the word *plane*. In the TL, the first meaning is translated by *charte*, the second by *charter* (from English) for planes but *contrat d'affrètement* for boats.
- *fair* (3) and *impartial* (5): it should not be difficult to avoid repetition of the word *juste* by the use of synonyms such as *équitable* or *impartial*.

- *legal control* (5): here there is the need for analysis of meaning to ascertain which is the appropriate TL term, whether *juridique* (from Latin *ius, iuris* — right, duty, law) relating to actual laws or rules regulating the behaviour of citizens; or *judiciaire* (from Latin *iudex, iudicis* — judge) relating to the system, the means through and by which the laws are applied and enforced, the *pouvoir judiciaire*; or *légal* (*lex, legis* — law) referring to that which is allowed or demanded by the law.
- *is the mother of democracy* (2): index for symbol: a fixed expression in the SL by analogy with 'the mother of parliaments'. It may be possible to adopt a literal translation, since the intended meaning should be transparent, but it is also possible, given the lack of an equivalent expressive form in the TL, to substitute a different unit which will convey the meaning but without the force of a fixed expression.
- *habeas corpus* (21): index for index: a Latin loan term used in legal jargon as it appears in the text, referring to a particular right, that of protecttion against wrongful detention. The same term is used in the TL for the same concept.
- *the rights to* (21): the rights listed are those accepted within the EC as civil rights and as such there should be an officially recognised translation for each in the TL, so that the translator must not simply translate the separate elements of each unit of meaning on a word-for-word basis.
- *take for granted* (38): icon for icon: a fixed expression in the SL corresponding to *considérer comme admis (comme allant de soi)* in the TL.
- *to make real* (37): this overworked verb in the SL should be replaced by a more specific and appropriate collocation in the TL.
- *to take* (39): another overused verb which is rendered more explicitly in the TT, *saisir*.

Stylistic Devices
Personification:
- *Parliament is the mother of democracy* (2).
- *a process is underway which endangers* (17).

Metaphor:
- *the gap... has widened* (8): this is further reinforced by the use of *erode*.
- *the government has eroded* (20): the TT picks up this reference cataphorically by its use of *érosion en partie involontaire*.

Metonymy:
- *our liberty... our system of justice... the guardians of our safety... our civil service... our cities... our press* (2–7): here there is the use of the whole, the hyponym, to represent each individual aspect. This is a stylistic device which should present no problem with regard to recreation in the TT.
- *Whitehall* (19): similarly, the name is used to represent both the place and the official bodies to be found there, thus, by implication, the functions exercised by those bodies. This may require a note for the TL reader.

Ellipsis:
- *to make real* (37): as commented in **Syntax**, although this appears to be a simple infinitive there is in fact an element of ellipsis, requiring explicitation in the TL.

Cultural References
- *our Parliament* (2): indexical use in TL of symbol in SL: whilst a word having

a similar form exists in the TL it must be remembered that the functions of this
body in the target culture may be similar in intent to those of the source culture
institution, but the manner of election and the nature of its composition are
different. This knowledge, or lack of it, should not however impinge on the
transfer of the impact of the sign to the extent of requiring a translator's note.
- *The United Kingdom's sovereign formula* (12): the SL reader is expected to
  understand the cultural implications of this signification, especially given the
  play on the word sovereign, with its two meanings of (a) literally, based on
  the existence of a sovereign or monarch and upheld by that monarch and (b)
  in the figurative sense of being of the highest order, of the highest power. The
  TL reader may or may not perceive this play on words, but the polysemy does
  exist for the TL equivalent sign, *souverain*.
- *'Glorious Revolution'* (11): index for symbol: this clearly refers to an actual event
  in British history, as evidenced by the use of quotation marks and the accompanying date, but while the SL reader would, hopefully, recall that this refers
  to the bloodless passing of power to William and Mary, the TL reader may
  not be expected to do so and it would be of help to add a brief note here.
- *Whitehall* (29): it would be helpful to append a note here to explain the
  significance of *Whitehall* in this metonymic use.

Punctuation
The use of quotation marks to denote different ways of interpreting the
information thus enclosed:
- *'unwritten constitution'* (9): this term is used as a name, a unit of meaing and
  description of a concept so-named by consensus but not to be found as a single
  unit or sign in a dictionary.
- *'Glorious Revolution'* (11): this indicates the actual name given to the event by
  history.
- *'issue'* (28): this is probably meant to indicate that the word is in fact a quote
  or direct report of a sign used by many to denote this question or similar ones.
  In this context there is an underlying connotation of associated disagreement
  or discontent which will need to be similarly conveyed in the TL.

The NHS Reforms and You

This is an extract from a document published by the Department of Health in the same context as the extract from the Parent's Charter, namely to make available to the general public information concerning the way in which reforms to be effected in the Health Service would affect the target 'consumer', to offer explanation and reassurance in response to criticisms being aired in the media and by those involved in the delivery of health care. The view of the patient as consumer is only part of a new approach to health care which adopts the principles of business, looking for efficiency and cost-effectiveness in the name of better delivery of care to the patient in order to ensure a better quality of life, with equal emphasis on prevention as well as on care. Central to this extract is the concept of the GP as the first point of contact for primary health care, prevention and referral for further specialist treatment.

The document clearly seeks to give this information in a register and level of language which will be easily accessible to the public, avoiding any overuse of jargon or specialist terminology and opting for concise sentences with minimal subordination, as this might cause information overload or obscure the tone of the message. Information is again conveyed through the device of giving answers to anticipated questions before proceeding to give greater detail of information about each aspect of the changes. Simplicity of presentation conveys an impression of simplicity and logic to be associated with the subject matter, i.e. the reforms, and simplicity can be reassuring to the lay-person whose main concern is the effect on him- or herself in time of need. In fact, the document uses the very same word 'quite simply, the answer to all these questions is Yes'. The relevance of such reassurance and advice may not be so obvious to the TL reader who may be unaware of the public fears and possible negative reaction as a result of the proposed changes.

As for the Parent's Charter, the document adopts a direct form of address when talking about rights, resorting to the third person to describe those responsible for delivering the changes and what the new service will offer. Since the document refers to a particular health-care system, although general principles and aims will correspond to those of the target culture health-care system, details of organisation and demarcation of responsibilities may differ. At times the different functions of roles or services may be sufficiently clear from the immediate context, at others the translator may have to decide whether or not the information/different denotative or connotative reference is integral to the overall message yet so unclear to the TL reader as to necessitate an explanatory note. To some extent the need for notes may increase in direct proportion to the level of specialisation of the target reader, so that the average layman may need less information about the system than might a medical or other health-care professional in the target culture. It is appropriate for the purpose of this exercise to assume that the TT target reader will be a member of the general public, as for the ST.

Sentence Structure

As commented above, sentence structure is one way in which the message can be made more accessible, by avoidance of complex sentences involving a high

level of subordination. Demonstrative pronouns help to give coherence and by avoiding repetition of compound subjects help to reduce the appearance of density of information:
- *there have also been changes... Others are planned... These changes* (2–4).
- *regular life-style check-ups will be available. These will be offered to you...* (51).

Information is also organised in the format of introductory paragraphs followed by points in the form of a list. Listing also occurs within a sentence, giving the impression of comprehensiveness of cover and information:
- *clinics giving detailed advice on diet, blood pressure, giving up smoking, diabetes, heart disease, alcohol control and stress management* (65).

Syntax
Possible avenues of access to care and potential limitations are given in the form of **conditional sentence**s:
- *if my family doctor has... will I still get* (23).
- *if you prefer... you may choose... if that GP is willing* (75).

Also encouragement, advice, through **implied conditional:**
- *for the sake of... I would strongly urge you* (46).

Because of the target reader much use is made of the less formal verbal form, the **phrasal verb**: in the TL this is often, but not always, rendered by a single-word, synthetic verb form. There is no rule, the translator can only learn individual examples from experience:
- *bring about — introduire* (1–2); *be open to — rester ouvert à* (12); *have a choice about — choisir; have a baby — accoucher* (26); *be emphasis on — l'accent sera... mis sur* (35); *come from —* whole sentence is reformulated to introduce an anonymous subject, *on* (42); *to make use of — profiter de* (45); *look out for — guetter* (48); *carry out — passer des examens* (note shift from anonymous subject who conducts test to patient undergoing tests) (56); *look after — prendre soin de* (60).

Other:
- *they are designed to* (5): passive verb becomes active: *ils visent à.*
- *is treating* (11): continuous aspect of verb not available in TL, so TT uses present simple but loses emphasis on immediacy.
- *as now* (12): this adverbial phrase of comparison has become an adverbial clause of restricted time in the TL, *pour le moment*, effectively changing the whole intent and potential impact of the sentence to confirm rather than allay fears by implying that there will be more changes on this particular aspect. The translator has not checked his/her TT against the ST for shifts in orientation. There is another significant omission in the second half of the same sentence, again of an adverb, *largely*, which also affects the meaning of that statement.
- *continue to get* (21): the same concept is rendered through different form: *j'obtiendrai toujours.*
- *what services should you look out for* (48): advice is given through use of modal in SL, conditional form of *devoir* in TL.
- *the purpose of these check-ups is* (53): *ces bilans... ont pour but de*: shift from subject to object.
- *when you first register* (52): TL requires *lorsque* or *quand* plus future tense.
- *this may include recommending* (61): this gerund becomes a finite verb with the subject being repeated from the previous sentence, *il peut... vous recommander.*

Lexis
Domain-specific terminology: index for index: most of this should be familiar to the average target reader in the SL culture and care should be taken either to find TL culture matches in terms of form, role and function or else to expand the term in order to bring these out for the TL reader:
- *Community Care... family doctor service...* (1–3): *National Health Service... quality of life* (8–9); *general taxation... free at the point of use* (a major difference from TL culture system and a founding tenet of the NHS) (13–14): *get prescriptions even if medicines are expensive... practice fund... self-governing NHS trusts...* (21, 23, 27) *GP...* (33): *quality of life* (47): *life-style check-ups* (51): *blood pressure* (57): *heart disease, stress management* (65–67)... *family planning* (71)... *well-person clinics* (67)... *health authority family clinics...* (72).

Collocations:
- *bring about changes* (1): *introduire des changements.*
- *caring service* (2): *services médico-sociaux — a more explicit term.*
- *self-governing* (27): *autonome.*
- *promotion of good health* (35): this is expanded to become *la campagne pour la bonne santé.*
- *active prevention* (35): loss of term *active, la médecine préventive.*
- *the (wider) range of services* (34): *la sélection (plus étendue) des services* (could have used *la gamme*).
- *reduce the risk of illness* (44): similar terms in TL, *réduire le risque.*
- *treat an illness* (39): *soigner.*
- *fit and well* (40): *en forme et en bonne santé.*
- *strongly urge* (46): *recommander vivement.*
- *provide an opportunity* (56): to note here the potential **faux ami** of opportunity — see below.
- *carry out tests* (56): shift of subject makes patient the actor — *passer des examens.*
- *check blood pressure* (57): *prendre la tension.*

Fixed expressions:
- *prevention is better than cure* (42): icon for icon; a TL expression exists stating the same sentiments in similar terms.
- *it is up to you whether...* (45): TL almost as SL but insertion of implied verb, *c'est à vous de décider si.*
- *life-style* (51): the TL uses a calque from the SL, *style de vie.*
- *family planning (advice)* (70): noun plus noun becomes noun plus adjective: note use of SL term *planning* in TL.
- *in other words* (60): *pour résumer.*
- *healthy living* (63): *un style de vie sain* (sounds like a calque from the SL term)
- *stress management* (67): no fixed TL term — we find *gérer son niveau de stress.*

Faux amis (potential):
- *medicines* (21): *médicaments* not *médecine* (the profession).
- *opportunity* (56): not yet officially accepted use of *opportunité*, despite contemporary media usage: TL *occasion* or *possibilité* (TL *opportunité* is the noun corresponding to the SL concept of something being opportune, happening at the appropriate or suitable time).

Stylistic Devices
Accumulation:
- *These may include clinics giving detailed advice on diet, blood pressure, giving up*

smoking, diabetes, heart disease, alcohol control and stress management (65): list of problems repeated in TL: index for index.

Repetition:
- *will my doctor... will I... can I still have* (16–27): the form of the inverted question in the SL has to vary according to the modal or auxiliary used. However, in the TL the use of the introductory interrogative *est-ce que* gives greater appearance of cohesion through uniformity of structure in the initial position in the sentence.

Expansion for explicitation or interpretation:
- *also known as* (33): *connus sous le nom de*: icon for icon
- *advice if needed on such matters as* (58): *sur des sujets qui vous touchent tels que...*
- *diet* (58): this is expanded into *faire un régime* but in fact the two are not near matches, the SL term being a more general reference to overall type/constitution of food intake, the TL term making specific reference to an act of deliberate limitation of intake.

Cultural References

Aspects of the workings of the British health-care system which may or may not be deemed worth of a footnote (refer also to domain-specific terminology in Lexis). When in doubt, extensive reference should be made to native speakers or to sources describing the TL culture system, but the translator should also and firstly ensure that he/she is aware of the frame of reference of each term within the SL:
- *The National Health Service and Community Care Act 1990* (1): can only be translated term for term (a calque).
- *family doctor service* (3): the idea of being attached to a single General Practitioner for all primary diagnosis and subsequent referral. See also: *when you first register with a doctor* — the culture-specific information is not adequately covered by the TL — *irez* (52); *a GP other than your own family doctor if that GP is willing to accept you* (76).
- *largely free at the point of use* (14): this makes implicit reference to the differences between medical, dental and eye care.
- *will my doctor be able to spend as much time with me* (20): concept of limited time for consultations due to number of patients to be seen per session; not part of TL cultural experience in quite the same form.
- *get prescriptions even if medicines are expensive* (21): the concept of practice budgets and fears of being struck off a doctor's list if suffering from chronic illness or one which is expensive to treat.
- *treatment at a local hospital* (25): the concept of GPs as purchasers looking for the cheapest place to obtain a particular treatment for a patient, which may not always be the local hospital. Also the idea of shipping patients to hospitals in other areas in order to cut waiting lists in problem areas.
- *practice fund, self-governing NHS trust* (23, 27): a quite different concept of funding to that of the TL system — the first reference becomes in the TL, *reçoit des fonds extérieurs*, which shows that the translator either does not know what this concept involves or else did not manage to find an appropriate way to express this in the TT without recourse to footnotes. The concept of the second phrase is more aptly rendered, *unité financière autonome*.
- *Chief Medical Officer* (41): a government appointment, for which the equivalent or lack of equivalent in the TL culture must be checked.

Punctuation

Use of **capital letters** for:

Role titles: *Chief Medical Officer* (41): repeated in TL.

Acronyms: *GP* (33) — full reference used, acronym omitted in TT: *NHS* (10) — translated as calque and used in full form in TT.

Use of **inverted commas** in TT as in ST:

– *'More information for patients'* (78): names of section of document.

– *'Prevention is... do so'* (42): reported speech.

The Wrong Way to Defend a Culture

This text is taken from *Eurobusiness*. Its target customers are mainly senior executives and financial officers, mainly throughout the European Union but also in Japan and the USA. The magazine professes to no particular political tendency, aiming instead for a more objective and analytical approach to issues of pan-European interest. This particular article was written at a time when the GATT talks were causing great public concern, in France perhaps even more so than in certain other European countries. Many French journalists and politicians were writing on issues relating to these discussions, in which the question of culture and in particular the 'American invasion' played a major part, in view of the on-going concern in France about the influence of American films and music on the French language, especially for French youth, and the result of this market share on the French music and film industry. As such, this article could very well be of interest to a wider group of readers in France than may be the case for the publication as a whole.

Given the target readership, it would be reasonable to expect the article to be concerned with economic aspects of the question, rather that problems of identity, and this is the case. The semantic field is that of the audio-visual media, this being the primary topic discussed in the article. The register is factual and free from any emotive lexical terms, with points being expressed in a formal register. Aspects which lend coherence to the text include the repetition of key concepts, and the sentence structure does not give rise to extensive subordination, thereby increasing the clarity of expression and facility of access to the points being made. This lack of subordination also gives rise to an appearance of economy of expression, reinforcing the factual nature of the article.

Sentence Structure
As stated above, this tends not to rely on extensive subordination but rather to contain one major idea which either stands alone as a single clause sentence (18, 27) or is developed thorough a subordinate clause, e.g. relative (4, 20, 31); contrast (but — 31) (while — 48). Sentences are also divided by the use of a colon or commas which replace the relative pronoun or other link word (3, 11, 23).

Syntax
- *you cannot defend values militarily* (1): index for index; the TT expands this statement: firstly, by transforming the adverb *militarily* into a new noun which defines the underlying concept, this noun being qualified by the adjective derived from the SL adverb, to give *l'option militaire*; secondly by using a form of syntax and lexis often used to emphasise impossibility or inadmissibility, of which the new noun becomes the subject: *ne saurait*.
- *the maverick politician* (1): TL does not use the definite article, in case Enoch Powell does not enjoy the same notoriety for the target language reader. Instead, the TT uses the indefinite form in apposition to denote a function or role.
- *the EU has yet to grasp* (2–3): the TL opts for a more synthetic verb form, *tarde à*.
- *you cannot defend* (1, 3): when this formula is repeated, in order to give some

kind of syntactic cohesion, the TT looks to a more impersonal construction, having already translated this statement by a shift to a third person construction the first time of use, so that we find *on ne saurait*.

- *designed to keep... off... screens* (4): there is a shift in the TL from past participle (relative construction) plus infinitive to present participle *visant*, acting as a relative construction, followed by a noun; the whole clause is rephrased on this basis, to bring out the underlying meaning by looking at the problem from the opposite point of view, which would probably echo the feelings of the anti-American TL reader — *la protection de l'accès aux écrans*.
- *misleadingly named* (8): this adjectival phrase consisting of an adverb modifying a past participle is transformed in the TL into a noun phrase — *au nom trompeur*. It could be argued that this results in a shift in emphasis, from the action of naming to the force or effect of the name itself, although both interpretations could be extracted from the TL unit used.
- *with certain exceptions* (11): this fixed expression contains a past participle in the TL, not a preposition, *certaines exceptions faites*.
- *ensure that* (12): TL expands this to give *veiller à ce que*.
- *few more blatant examples... can be conceived* (9): here the TL uses a singular form following the negative verb, which is expressed in an active rather than passive voice through the use of the impersonal construction with *on*.
- *it is worth asking* (22): the TL is more explicit, inserting a pronominal form, *se demander*, since there is no obvious direct object of *ask*.
- *market for film and television* (16): the TL requires repetition of the partitive *de* and definite article (different for each noun).
- *doubts are not hard to find* (26): the TL adopts the opposite meaning to the adverb and rephrases the sentence around this, using a pronominal form to convey the underlying passive sense: *se laissent facilement identifier*.
- *if this hope proves groundless the... will come under* (45): here the TL reverts to a construction which implies a greater degree of doubt, by the use of the Imperfect, *devait s'avérer* followed by the conditional, *subirait*. To note also, the use of a sythetic verb in the TL instead of a phrasal verb in the SL.
- *admits that controlling* (40): the SL gerund becomes a TL noun.
- *be penalised financially* (47): this passive contruction is replaced by an active one, *doivent subir des peines financières*, with expansion through the transfer of the idea of penalty to the noun *peines* in collocation with the verb *subir*, and a shift from the adverb, *financially*, to an adjective qualifying the noun *peines*.
- *within* (46): this preposition is translated by a prepositional phrase in the TL.

Lexis

- *legislative fiat* (3): a rather rare example of the SL using a Latin term, from the framework of legal and political terminology — TL uses *décret*.
- *the maverick politician* (1): index for symbol: this term is taken from the US lexicon of cattle farming, evoking a particular connotative value in politics, but finds no indexical correspondent in the TL.
- *non-European* (4); negative form of adjective of nationality, becomes expanded in TL to include *d'origine*.
- *bone of contention* (6): icon for icon: this fixed SL expression/image is translated by a much more elegant reference to classical mythology inherent in the TL expression of equivalent intent: *la pomme de discorde*.
- *come into force* (5): could sometimes be translated as *entrer en vigueur*, but here

the TL has chosen to use the single word, synthetic verb *introduire* in order to give a tighter structure to the whole sentence and make it easier to keep the subject close to the main verb, unlike the ST format.

– *global trade liberalisation* (7): the translator has to decide whether the adjective *global* refers to the concept of a compound noun, trade liberalisation, i.e. the juxtaposition of the two nouns implies a subordination in the sense of an indication of the nature of the second noun through the juxtaposition of the first) or else, that the word *global* applies only to the word *trade*, and that liberalisation applies to this unit as a whole. In the SL this ambiguity created by the juxtaposition of two nouns does not need to be resolved, but with agreement for gender in the TL this becomes a necessity, giving either *la libéralisation globale du commerce* or *la libéralisation du commerce global*.

Collocations:
– *redress the balance* (23): *redresser l'équilibre*, note the avoidance of the **faux ami** *la balance*, which can however appear in fixed economic collocations such as *la balance des paiements*.
– *formidable frontiers* (9): loss of alliteration in the TL but also avoidance of a faux ami, not *formidable* but *redoutable*.
– *blatant examples* (9): the TL seeks to bring out the apparent pejorative or critical tone of this item of lexis.
– *before the… rule begins to* (32): note that TL syntax requires *avant que* followed by *ne* and the subjunctive mood of the verb.
– *the Commission expects* (38): another expected subjunctive here, following *s'attend à ce que*, but one which could be avoided by use of the Future tense.
– *if this hope proves groundless* (45): the TL adopts here the extremely useful pronominal verb, *s'avérer*, instead of the SL intransitive verb.
– *high-cost* (98): compound adjective can be rendered by a single word in the TL, *coûteux*.
– technical vocabulary: index for index, to be confirmed in the TL — *beaming programmes* (37): *terrestrial channels* (34): *satellite channels* (36).
– business vocabulary: *overheads* (17); *recoup production costs* (18); *pay their way* (21).

Stylistic Devices
– in the first sentence, there is an **inversion** of presentation of information; the TT presents the name of the person quoted first, and the main information, the quoted comment, last, in order to highlight and emphasise this.
– *the European Union's fear* (1,5): this form of **personification** is lost in the TT by the introduction of a past participle, functioning adjectivally, to render more explicit the reference to fear, *la crainte ressentie par*.

Direct address to the reader:
– rhetorical question at the end of paragraph five (23–25) allows the author to lead into a discussion of two possible problems — this is reproduced in the TL.
– this is further reinforced in the TL by the invitation to the reader to join the author in this consideration — *considérons d'abord*.

Expansion/explication:
– *the… fear… has its roots in economics* (15): *a pour base des soucis d'ordre économique*: the TL introduces a noun phrase in order to render more explicit the reference to economics.
– *in this direction* (30): becomes more explicit in the TL, *vers une telle politique*.

- *the European Commission's divison for* (40): the TL inserts a relative clause here with the adjective, *responsable (de)*.
- *through which* (44): becomes, *par l'intermédiaire de laquelle.*

Parallel form/structure:
- *feasible... desirable* (24–25): this parallel use of adjective formed by suffixation of root with -able can be reproduced in the TL.
- loss of **alliteration** through selection of appropriate TL terms; *formidable frontiers* (9); *transmission time* (13); *far faster* (34); *serious strain* (46).

Cultural References:
- *Mr Enoch Powell* (2): this name requires no translator's note since a description is included in the ST which suffices to explain for the TL reader the significance of the quote by the person named. The TL reader may, however, miss the associative response to this mention which may be experienced by the SL reader old enough to remember the more extremist views of this politician and to wonder why the author has chosen to quote this particular person; more specifically, whether the choice of quote was dependent on the key word, *culture* — which is highly likely — or whether the selection of this politician carries some underlying political comment — which is less likely, given the stated apolitical intentions of the publication. However, this possible ambiguity of intention will most probably be lost to the TL reader albeit without any significant effect on the overall accessibility of the message.
- *GATT talks* (7): the TL does sometimes use GATT, depending on the target reader, and since in this case the reader will be from Senior Management it is quite likely that he will know and may even expect to find the English form. However, the French acronym is included in brackets.
- *DGX* (39): this acronym is explained in terms of its function in the ST without any reference to the individual words making up the name, so the same procedure is adopted in the TT as it is clearly not essential for the reader to know the full name.
- the acronym *EU* (9), has its direct equivalent, *UE*.

Punctuation
- use of colon to indicate separation of sentence into main and subordinate information, the second expanding on and explaining the first. This form of punctuation is retained in the TL.
- use of quotation marks: this is generally repeated in the TT, for the same reasons as regulate their use in the ST: for example, around names generally used to describe a concept, whether by analogy: *'television without frontiers'*(3), or by coinage of a new term throught the combination of two known items of lexis 'Fortress Europe': also to indicate direct quotation: first sentence of text; *Member States shall* (11), *progressively* (30), *where practicable* (29) — (quotes from the directive); *Very difficult* (41) — direct quote of the words of an official.

We Are...

This text forms part of an article published in *Contact Bulletin*, a publication of the European Bureau for Lesser Used Languages. Although it was published in 1983, it still has relevance in the context of the on-going debate over the use of minority languages and the rights of their users. The other part of the article consisted of an extract from the resolution passed by the European Parliament with regard to a charter of rights. Given the pan-European nature of the Bureau and the time elapsed since publication, it was not possible to confirm the source language, but since the two versions, English and French, exist in parallel, they offer nonetheless excellent scope for comparison of the strategies adopted. The text could be expected to have been published in the main working languages of the Community and possibly also in some of the lesser used ones. The article also lists addresses in Ireland, France, Italy and the Netherlands, amongst others, for national Chairmen and Chairwomen of the Bureau.

The bulletin could be expected to be of interest to a wide audience across the EU (then EC), having certain level of education and interest in European affairs, comprising pressure groups for minority languages, speakers of these languages, academics and others interested in the survival, protection and development of these languages; probably also government departments responsible for the co-ordination of policy in this area.

Although the document commences in an apparently less formal tone, with its heading 'We are', followed by three rhetorical questions, in fact the rest of the text resembles a more formal use of language appropriate to a report intended for international information. The lexis is that of the specific domain of language use and language minorities but is not inaccessible to the non-specialised reader; there is also an element of EC terminology, again not unfamiliar to the non-specialised but educated reader. The apparent desire for objectivity of reporting of information and the creation for the text of an air of official authority will lead the reader to expect a degree of impersonal constructions and distancing of the agent through the use of passive constructions which focus on the action, not the agent.

Sentence Structure
Given the need to state basic facts which are then elaborated on or described, there is a not-unexpected level of relative clauses throughout the text, these clauses constituting the main form of subordination, whether introduced by a relative pronoun:
- *Arfe report which the European Parliament had adopted* (6).
- *there are only two countries... that do not have* (21).
- *a large number of people... who do not enjoy* (33).
- *communities who speak...* (42).

or by the use of a present participle:
- *human rights ensuing from...* (4); here the TT also uses a present participle, *découlant de*.
- *a motion demanding... all centering on... a document encompassing* (59): the TT

269

actually inserts an extra present participle here, substituting *parlant* for *speakers (of such languages)* and using for the other three verbs: *exigeant… portant… comprenant.*

There is also subordination through clauses of reason, condition and purpose, introduced by various conjunctions or other link words. Sentence structure in generally not complex, with one main idea per sentence in most cases, reflecting the need for clarity and intelligibility. There should be no element of ambiguity in such text types.

Syntax
Adverbs: usually a single word in the SL:
- *essentially* (15): *essentiellement.*
- *internally different* (22): becomes two adjectives — *(communauté) interne différente.*
- *widely spoken* (40): *largement parlée.*
- *so efficiently* (67): expansion in the TL gives, *d'une manière si efficace que…*

Impersonal constructions:
- *there exists… il existe; there are only… il n'y a que* (19); *that is to say that — ceci signifie que* (27); *there are over… il y a plus de* (31); *this means that there exists… ceci veut dire que* (33); *one may add… on pourrait ajouter* (45); *it cannot be denied… il est indéniable que* (49); *there is strong evidence… tout semble indiquer* (52); *one might well ask… on peut se demander si…* (50); *this is no longer the case — cela n'en est plus le cas* (57).

Passive voice: given the text type it should be expected that this form of the verb can be retained in the TL:
- *it cannot be denied* (49): passive voice, impersonal construction — although the TT has, *il est indéniable que…* there is another very useful TL construction of equivalent intent, mood and impersonality: *l'on ne saurait contester/nier.*
- *once some basic facts are acknowledged* (53): the TT adopts a similar construction.
- *if they have been ignored* (56): TT has a passive construction but a different verb in the negative, *prendre en considération* — no shift in meaning, merely in form and possibly extra emphasis.
- *motions were tabled… were discussed* (62–63): also passive in the TT — *furent mises à l'ordre du jour… furent discutées.*
- *Gaetano Arfe… was requested to…* (65): *fut prié de.*
- *now known as…* (68): TT also uses a past participle, but it would have read better with expansion, to give — *connu sous le (nom du) Rapport Arfe.*

Verbal nouns having a passive impact — also used in the TT:
- *the establishment* (9): *la mise en place.*
- *the adoption* (67): *l'adoption.*
- *the building (has begun)* (73): replaced in the TL by a more personalised subject, *nous avons commencé à bâtir.*

Other:
- *majority language speaker* (35): TL has expansion, giving a relative clause — *ceux parlant un langue majoritaire.* The SL compound noun comprises noun plus noun plus noun, where the first two nouns form a compound which qualifies the third. The same economy through juxtaposition is possible in the TL.
- *do not enjoy… as do…* (34): this use of the auxiliary for avoidance of repetition of the main verb in the second element of a comparitive sentence will require the insertion of an object pronoun, definite article, in the TL.

- *less widely-spoken languages* (36): *ces langues moins parlées*: there is a loss in the TL of the adverb, *widely*.
- *one might well ask* (50): this SL modal has to be conveyed in the TL but the use of *on peut se demander*, in the present tense, loses the extent of likelihood or unlikelihood as conveyed by the conditional in the SL.
- **error in the TL:** *si elles n'ont pas été pris en considération* (57–58): following the rule that past participles in passive constructions have to agree with the subject, agreement should be made here for feminine plural, *prises*.

Lexis
EC terminology: index for index: to be checked according to the official terms at the time of publication of the ST. If, for any reason, the official version of any given term has changed over the years, the translator may prefer to use the term currently in use at the time of publication of the TT, in order to make the maximum quantity of information readily accessible to the target reader, depending on the intended function of the TT and the target reader profile.
- *human rights… movement of peoples* (4–5), *Council of Europe* (11), *member states* (13), *European communities* (13); *nation-states, European Community* (15); *official working languages, treaty language, the Treaties* (25); *a charter of rights* (70).

Minority Language terms: index for index:
- *identity, ethnicity, 'small peoples', autochthonous languages* (4–14); *majority language speaker* (35); *less widely spoken languages* (36); *extra-territorial minorites* (46).

Collocations: as used in this text, but may not always be exactly the same in different contexts:
- *a viable future* (53): *un futur viable*.
- *supportive measures* (60): *mesures en leur faveur*.
- *basic facts* (53); *basically a charter of rights* (70); *basic foundation* (71): in each case the adjective *fondamental* is used in the TL.
- *express support* (9): *exprimer leur solution* in the TL does not appear to translate quite the same intention.
- *carry authority* (28): *avoir autorité*.
- *enjoy… linguistic status* (34): *jouir du même status linguistique*.
- *put forward a motion* (59): *proposer une motion*.
- *table a motion* (62): *mettre à l'ordre du jour*.
- *draw up a document* (65): *rédiger*.
- *perform a function* (66): *s'acquitter d'un tâche*.

Fixed expressions:
- *in a sense — d'une certaine manière* (3); *in the accepted sense of that term — dans l'usage accepté de ce terme* (43): icon for icon.

Faux ami:
- *if they have been in ignored* (56): not *ignorer*, although this is increasingly common in modern journalistic use; the TT uses a negative construction with *prendre en considération*.

Stylistic Devices
Given the factual and semi-legal nature of the text there are very few examples of a carefully crafted style, the important thing being to avoid potential ambiguity. However, there are a few points on which to comment:

Rhetorical questions:

Three such questions are used as an introduction to the subject, that of the Bureau, its aims and its achievements.

Repetition:

- *their own language and their own particular identity* (20): repeated in the TT.
- *basic facts — faits fondamentaux* (53); *basic rights — droits fondamentaux* (60); *basic foundation — une base fondamentale* (71); a reiteration of the tenets of the Bureau and an implication of the unquestionable nature of these.
- *future... future* (51–52); *futur* is used both times in the TT.

Coherence is assured through the use of link words and phrases:

- *however, in so far as, in fact, that is to say,*
- and through **anaphoric reference:**
- by use of pronouns: *it — the Bureau* (2, 5, 11); *a most viable one* (53).
- by use of deictics and other qualifiers: *such internally different communities* (22); *speakers of such languages* — here the TL actually creates ambiguity by its translation of such by the parititive — *des langues* (60) *This function* (66); *this Report* (70).

Personalisation of the Bureau:

- *we are* (introductory heading); also retained in TL but expanded for TL syntax — *ce que nous sommes.*
- *the building has begun* (73); here the TT attempts to give equilibrium to the overall shape of the message by ending as it begins, with the first person plural form of reference: *nous avons commencé à bâtir.*

Emphasis:

- *are not without their problems* (50): use of the negative form of the verb *to be* plus *without*, for emphasis (i.e. *do have*). Also used in the TL, *ne sont pas sans problèmes.*

Cultural References

Names of institutions (see above for EC) places and peoples which may or may not have a different TL form:

- *the European Bureau for Lesser Used Languages* — see below (1).
- *the Arfe report* (6): this is explained later in the text so the translator can adopt the same procedure as in the SL but according to TL conventions, i.e. placing the name of the author of the report after the noun.
- *the EC, the Council of Europe* (11): *la CEE* (note that at the time of publication the shorter form, EC, had not yet been widely adopted), *le Conseil de l'Europe.*
- *Welsh, Bretons, Frisians... Ladins* (38): *les Gallois, les Bretons, les Frisons, les Ladins.*
- *Schleswig-Holstein, Val d'Aosta* (48): minimal difference in the TL — *Schleswig-Holstein, Val d'Aoste:* note that it it easier to 'franciser' a name from another Latin language than one from a Germanic root.
- *Northern Ireland* (59): *l'Irlande du nord.*

Punctuation

- *the European Bureau for Lesser Used Languages* (1): capital/upper case letters are used for each word of the name except the definite article and the preposition. The translator has chosen not to reproduce this in the TL; although this could have been done according to current usage, to preserve the indication of a proper name, perhaps this procedure was not so widely used at the time of publication. However the result is that the TL form looks like a descriptive translation of the function of the Bureau rather than a calque of its actual name.

- *'the roots phenomenon'* (3): inverted commas are used here to describe a concept which may still, at that time, have had a relatively neologistic use or nature.
- *'small peoples'* (8): another example of inverted commas, probably for a quote from an official document.
- *'to preserve and promote... associated cultures'* (12): this is clearly a direct quote from the constitution fo the EC.
- *European Communities* (13): to note the difference in nuance or emphasis of meaning between the plural form and *European Community* (14), singular. It might have been more appropriate in the SL to use a lower case for the plural form and an upper case for the singular, since the latter refers to a proper name.
- *the 19th century* (17): the translator has preferred to use Roman numerals here to indicate the date, followed by the lower case letter *e* which is the abbreviation for the ordinal number.
- *French, English, German, Italian...* (26): to note also, that the TL uses lower case for names of languages, not upper case as in the SL — *the Treaties* (4); here the use of the upper case indicates that this refers to specific (named) treaties, namely those establishing different stages of development of the EC, not just a generic type of agreement.
- *'a treaty language'* (27): another quote from the treaty, an official term.
- *defines this general aim* — *'to preserve...'* (12): note the use of a dash instead of the insertion of some kind of linking word, phrase or verbal syntagm (a form of economy through juxtaposition).
- *this Report* (70): the use of the capital letter R for *Report* for the first time in the text appears to have an anaphoric function; the omission of the name *Arfe* is compensated for and simultaneously recalled through this device.

Unhappy Families

This text is an extract from a longer article, published in *The Economist* following a speech by the then Secretary for Social Security which looked at the growth of family breakdown, echoing a speech made the previous month by the Health Secretary, Virginia Bottomley. These speeches are further confirmed in their assessment by another paper appearing on the same day as this article, so that the three lend credibility and justification to the writing of the article.

Appearing in *The Economist*, the growth of family breakdown may not necessarily seem of immediate interest to the usual target reader of this publication, namely those in professional and business-related occupations. The article appears under a general section heading of 'Britain' and is flanked by articles on the privatisation of British Rail and one concerning the planned publication of a White Paper on pensions, so it could be considered as the 'human interest story'. It is only in the closing paragraph that we find the true link between the target reader and the subject matter, perhaps having a greater effect thereby through the invitation to read an apparently non-economic article, with a kind of sting in the tail in terms of recommendations for action or thought on the part of those likely to be involved in the consequences of such action.

Given the source of publication one would expect to find a formal level of use of lexis, with uncomplicated syntax and sentence structure to facilitate access to important and relevant information, with minimal emotive or affective use of language and few instances of deliberate stylistic effect beyond that which is to be expected from an article written for the educated and informed reader. The immediate situation giving rise to the article is a report, and so one can expect to find a significant proportion of the article dealing with reported facts, possibly statements, from different sources, hence a degree of impersonality in order to highlight the information being given and distance the author from any element of personal comment or involvement. His role is to present facts, which will, of themselves, provoke discussion and further reflection, without any bias, although it could be said that the last sentence would appear, by virtue of its juxtaposition with what is clearly a quote from Mr Lilley, to be a summing up of the situation by the author himself, giving an insight into his own views through the metaphor of the fairy tale.

Sentence Structure

The presentation of information seems to be bi-partite, with subordinate clauses either contrasting or comparing with the main clause:
- *while death disrupted the Victorian household, today's families are shaped by...* (22);
- *children in the 'reordered' families were more likely to suffer from... than children whose parents stayed married* (31);
- *the more changes... children experience, the more miserable they were* (36);
or else some shorter sentences interspersed with longer, more explanatory ones, with the apparent function of underlining a key point:
- *Mr Lilley may also be right to worry about the trend of family breakdown* (16);
- *the British family is more diverse than it has ever been* (20);

– *it will take a generation, he believes* (55).
Clearly the relative clause plays an important role in defining key participants in the debate:
– *most of the children who now live…* (23).
– *children who live with both natural parents* (50).
– *Mr Lilley, who links family breakdown…* (53).
The longest sentence would seem to be the central one of paragraph 5, also approximately in the centre or mid-point of the article. This sentence, with its list of three main points, sums up the key effects observed by different studies:
– *preliminary results… children whose parents stayed married* (30).
There seems no reason to reformulate such sentences, since the TL allows similar structures thereby preserving a similar effect.

Syntax
Single-word adverbs: variation for stylistic effect or according to TL usage:
– *obsessively* (1): translated by a noun phrase — *en désaccord obsessif:* icon for index.
– *deeply disturbing… manifestly* (3–4): the first adverb is translated as such, the second adverb becomes an adjective in the TL and the order of presentation is reversed, giving the longer attribute second, thus we find: *la cause manifeste et profondément troublante.*
– *roughly four times as likely* (49): this adverb is translated by a fixed expression of quantity, *à peu près.*
– *physically abused* (50): the TT has the same structure, *physiquement abusés.*
Discussion of probability and speculation:
– *children in reordered families were more likely to suffer… their children were more likely to suffer* (31): *avaient plus de chances de… avaient de plus grandes chances de* — the translator could have used *risquer de*, thus avoiding possible more favourable connotations of *chances.*
– *children who live only with… are four times as likely to be physically abused… and between six and ten times as likely if…* (49): *ont à peu près quatre fois plus de chances… voient leurs chances multipliées par six ou dix.* Obviously the translator wishes to use the same structure each time, perhaps to mirror the ST.
– *one reason why children… may be unhappy* (43): this modal is lost in the TL, which has *sont malheureux.* The translator could have used the conditional form here in its journalistic sense of reported but unconfirmed fact.
Reporting of comments and opinions:
– *Peter Lilley described* (3): *décrit* — Past Simple used in TL.
– *a speech… which argued* (5–6): *un discours prononcé par… qui soutenait:* expansion and slight shift in intent.
– *Mr Lilley agreed his speech with…* (9): *accorda son discours avec celui de…* Has the TT really brought out the use of agree in this context, which would seem to imply consultation with a view to getting official approval of the content? Deliberate alignment of content of the two speeches would seem to be contradicted by the comment (4) stating that *'this seemed to contradict a speech last month by Virginia Bottomley'.* Perhaps *faire approuver/agréer* would be more accurate here?
– *Mrs Bottomley is right that* (10): here the TL introduces a modal of possibility where the SL has statement of fact — *Mme Bottomley pourrait avoir raison lorsqu'elle explique* — note also the insertion in the TL of a verb of reporting, in accordance with TL norms.

- *according to an article* (12): *selon un article de* — no problems here.
- *recent research suggests that* — *des recherches récentes suggèrent que* (note plural for *research* in TL (17); *preliminary results suggest that* — *les premiers résultats suggèrent que*... (30).
- *according to a study by*... (27): *selon une étude de*... note different preposition.
- *Mr Whelan argues* (48): ... *soutient* — same verb used for *argue* as in para 1.
- *Mr Lilley sees the cure as*... *he believes* (53–54): *pense que la solution se trouve dans*... *il pense qu'il faudra*... note use of a more explicit verb of location.

Other:
- *are arguing* (1): Present continous aspect of the verb — the ongoing nature of the debate is represented in the TL by the use of the verb *to be* plus a noun phrase, *sont en désaccord obsessif*.
- *commitment to raising children* (15): the gerund in the SL is replaced by an infinitive in the TL.
- *this summer's Population Trends* (13): the time of publication is omitted in the TT.
- *half of whom had seen their natural parents' marriage collapse* (29): *avaient vu le mariage de leurs parents s'effondrer* — the translator has correctly interpreted the syntax of the sentence to show that *collapse* here is a verb — had it been a noun there would have been a different word order plus the possessive '*of'*.
- *children whose parents split up* (36): this finite phrasal verb becomes a past participle, *séparés*, indicating the event as already having occurred, therefore a state of being, rather than an action. Perhaps not important in this kind of article but in a document having greater legal force, greater precision of reference should be achieved.
- *more likely to suffer such problems than the children of happy marriages; but much less likely than children whose parents split up* (34): the use of contrast *more/less* plus adjective is maintained by *plus grandes chances, moins de chances*.
- *Mr Lilley who links*... (53): the TL shifts from verb to collocation of verb plus noun, *établit un lien*.
- *It will take a generation* (55): *il faudra une génération pour que ceci soit mis en place*. Here the noun *generation*, in conjunction with the verb *take*, is an indicator of time passing, not a description of a synchronous state. The translator has maintained the same degree of lack of explicitness, but the insertion of an adverbial clause of purpose should indicate more explicitly the intended meaning — *pour que ceci soit mis en place*.

Lexis
Of social problems: to verify equivalent terms in the TL. The concepts will probably exist, but the means of description or reference may not correspond to a calque translation in all cases:
- *Social Security Secretary* — *secrétaire d'Etat à la Sécurité sociale* (2); *growth of family breakdown* — *l'effondrement croissant de la Famille* (3); *Health Secretary* — *ministre de la Santé* (5) — why *ministre* when the SL has the same noun, *Secretary*?; *spokesperson* — *porte-parole* is less clumsy since it already encompasses both genders (6).
- *step-child situation* (14): expansion in order to ensure political correctness gives *situation de beau-fils ou de belle-fille*. To note, the potential ambiguity here due to polysemy of the two terms, *beau-fils*... *belle-fille* (*step relations* or *relations in law*, e.g. *stepson / son-in-law*).
- *Victorian counterparts* — *homologues de l'ère Victorienne* (25): indexical descrip-

tion of symbolic reference; note insertion of *ère* to qualify time, not likeness to the person, and capital letter to indicate proper name.
- *natural parent — parent naturel* (21).
- *marriage... collapse — s'effondrer... le marriage* (30).
- *domestic arrangements (euphemism)* (38): index for symbol: *changements dans leur vie famiale* — expansion here gives greater explicitness to intended, not surface meaning.
- *frequent rows* (34): note the register of rows as opposed to arguments: TL avoids the question by substituting a verb plus adverb — *se disputaient régulièrement.*
- *battered children and broken homes* (44): *enfants battus et foyers brisés:* index for index.
- *think-tank* (46); *'puits de pensées'* — perhaps this is in inverted commas to indicate a loan concept, a social neologism in the process of being adopted
- *social benefits* (55): *prestations sociales.*
- *absent parent* (41): *celui de leurs parents qui était absent:* index for symbol: does this paraphrase have quite the same connotative value as in the SL culture where there is a fixed term to describe a recognised concept?
- *'reordered' families — familles 'réorganisées'* (43): use of inverted commas denotes neologism.

Collocations:
- *raising children* (15): *élever les enfants.*
- *marriage collapse — s'effondrer... le marriage* (30).
- *less likely to enjoy the support* (41): *apprécier le soutient:* this is perhaps not the most appropriate TL verb, since the idea of *enjoy* here is *to benefit from, have available,* not *appreciate.*

Fixed expressions:
- *sees the cure in terms of* (54): *pense que la solution se trouve dans* — a different way of presenting the same information/intent.

Stylistic Devices
Objectivity:
- *a speech... which argued* (5–6).
- *the British family is more diverse* (20): *death disrupted the Victoran household, today's families are shaped by a different attitude* (22–23); a kind of personification of states of being or causes, to give a greater appearance of factuality.

Alliteration:
- *death disrupted* (22): possibly deliberate, since *disrupt* does not have quite the intensity of effect one would associate with the noun *death*. The TL retains the sense of disrupt at the expense of the alliterative effect.

Repetition for emphasis:
- of syntax: *the more changes in their domestic arrangements children experienced, the more miserable they were* (38).

Also:
- *children in reordered families were more likely to suffer... their children were more likely to suffer* (31): see notes in Syntax above.

Cultural References
- *social-security secretary... health secretary* (2, 5): both are culture-specific government titles having a similar corresponding function in the TL culture, although, as discussed above, the latter title seems to have been mistranslated.

- *Population Trends* (13): written in italics in the SL to indicate the name of a journal, according to bibliographical conventions. No italics used in TL.
- *a 'golden age' of the family* (7): this reference to a time of mythical classical antiquity is common to both cultures and presents no problem, although the use of inverted commas in the SL would suggest that it is less common in the SL culture.
- *the Victorian household... Victorian counterparts* (22): TT has expansion to achieve explicitation of this SL culture specific reference — in both instances the TL inserts a noun, *l'ère*, to indicate the function of the adjective *Victorian*.
- *Department of Child Health* (27): the TL has a calque translation here, perhaps because there is no direct equivalent department in the TL culture, but the function will be clear from the nouns composing and describing its name.
- *Joseph Rowntree Foundation* (31): the name of the sweet manufacturer will be immediately recognisable to the SL reader although perhaps not to the TL reader. The term *foundation* indicates a charitable body and so it should not be necessary to add a footnote regarding the name.
- *Institute for Economic Affairs* (46): again, a calque translation will make the function/role of this culture-specific organisation evident.
- *the National Society for the Prevention of Cruelty to Children* (47): the same applies to this name.
- *as unhappy as Cinderella* (56); this reference to an SL culture fairytale as metaphor for the suffering of the children described will also be recognisable to the TL reader for whom the same story forms part of his or her cultural baggage.

Punctuation

- *l'effondrement croissant de la Famille* (3): capital letter used in the TT for *Famille*, perhaps to represent a concept..
- *'reordered' families* (43): use of inverted commas indicates neologism of this term
- *a 'golden age' of the family* (7): see comment in Cultural References.
- *Population Trends* (13): written in italics to indicate name of a publication — see above.

Age of Stress Dawns for the Middle Class

This is an extract from a text published in *The Independent*, a quality daily paper targeting professionals and business executives whilst, as the name states, attempting to present an unbiased view of contemporary events in order to inform and to suggest possible causes and effects of these events. Whilst some of the developments and aspects of the scenario described here are of specific relevance to the source culture, the general problem under discussion is one that could very well develop or be developing in the target culture.

The stimulus for this article was a presentation by a leading psychologist at a conference of the British Psychological Society, so that many of the statements are presented in the form of Reported Speech with all the concomitant stylistic and linguistic mechanisms. In fact, these are partly what gives coherence to the text. There are also some instances of direct quotes, for stylistic variation and impact, and the lexis used is as readily accessible to the layman as to the professional who may have attended the meeting. Given the fact that the article is a construct of reported statements, there is less scope for stylistic innovation or display of competence on the part of the SL author, therefore less analysis is required of the translator prior to translation. The main point to remember in a text of this nature is the rules of sequence of tenses and of tense shifts from direct to indirect speech, as well as the need for consistency in the tense shift to be operated, in order to increase readability and overall coherence of the text, source or target. This may sometimes require the translator to improve on the ST, especially where TL norms necessitate greater attention to such aspects of syntax than may be required by the SL.

Sentence Structure

The first thing to note is the revision of the introductory sub-heading which precedes the main title, where significant expansion was deemed necessary to explain a more economical but possibly more ambiguous SL form; for example, *job* might be read as the object of *warn*, rather than as the first of two nouns which form a new compound noun, *job insecurity*. Also, *will take its toll*, gives no indication of the object of the action.

Given the form of the text as reporting comments and points made by a speaker, with some direct quotations included, the TT has in several instances resorted to a reformulation of the sentence, preferring to indicate the fact of reporting comments by placing the subject in an initial rather than final position:
- *the middle classes are entering... according to a leading psychologist* (1): becomes *selon un pyschologue de premier ordre, les classes moyennes...*
- *while the new work environment... Professor Gary Cooper told...* (4): becomes *le Professeur Gary Cooper a annoncé...*
- *the new working patterns... Professor Cooper said* (25): *le Professeur Cooper a expliqué*

Where there is no introductory verb of indirect discourse, this function being fulfilled through appropriate verb tenses, the sentence structure and order of presentation of information remains as for the ST:
- *The cost to employers...* (31): remains *le coût subi par les employeurs*.

Each new point is the subject of a new sentence, with minimal levels of subordination, mainly emphasising results, coordinating elements of equal importance:
- *success and a permanent job* (8); *companies routinely contracted out... and were increasingly employing* (14); *a social work manager who... and who...* (32).

Syntax

Verbs of introduction of indirect discourse are somewhat more varied in the TT than in the ST:
- *told* — *a annoncé a* (6); *said* — *a expliqué* (11): *said* — *dit*: note the use of the Present tense here, not the Passé Composé as for other verbs in this list; *said* — *a expliqué* (27); *said* — *a indiqué* (45); *said* — *il a ajouté que* (53).

Continuous aspect of a verb for immediacy, emphasis: can only be translated by a simple form of the verb in the TL but should really be accompanied by an adverb of time where the emphasis of continuity or immediacy is particularly important:
- *middle classes are entering* — *entrent* (1); *were increasingly employing* — *il était... courant de... et d'employer* (15); *was already costing* — here the TL has the Present Simple: see discussion of tenses (27).

Single-word adverbs: these usually involve expansion from SL to TL:
- *be simply unavailable* (12): the position of the adverb might be misread by a non-native speaker of limited fluency as referring to the manner in which one is unavailable rather than as a separate statement of degree — *quite simply, tout simplement* — however the TL omits this adverb, using instead a negative particle, *ne... plus*, which may give a slight shift in frame of reference; *routinely* — *il était déjà courant* (14); *increasingly* — *omitted in TT* (15); *deeply worried* — *j'ai bien peur que* (23) — there may be a shift in register here as well as a loss of intensity; *increasingly* — *de plus en plus* (47).

Tenses:
- *people would have to learn* (43): Future tense in direct speech becomes conditional in reported speech — the translator has ignored the rules for sequences of tenses, using the Present tense and the Future Simple throughout this paragraph. This shifting from reporting using Past tense sequences (see paragraphs 3, 4, 5,) to Present and Future (paragraphs 7, 8, 9) in fact does not give coherence or balance to the overall text and should be avoided.
- *were now working* (46): a present continuous tense, translated by a Present tense in the TL (see previous note). It should however be noted that the TL gives the exact opposite information to that given in the SL, since the SL has an affirmative statement, *were now working*, whereas the TT gives a negative statement, *ne travaillent pas*, a claim which would not make sense in the immediate microcontext.

Other
- *work environment* (4): description through juxtaposition, indication of place as well as nature, requires preposition of place in TL — *environnement au travail;* also found in *at the workplace,* becomes simply — *au travail* (25). Also, in the title, job insecurity becomes *l'insécurité au travail,* recalling the polysemy of the TL term *travail,* which can be used as a mass or count noun.
- *at its most fundamental* (5): this stylistic form of expression using the possessive pronoun is replaced in the TL by a more neutral phrase, *(sera) encore plus fondamental.*

- *that's no longer the case* (8): a similar form of expression exists in the TL — *ce n'est plus le cas.*
- *on a project by project basis* (16): here SL sense is that of the isolation of the work into separate, unconnected tasks, each constituting a contract in itself rather than forming part of an on-going contract. The TT appears to misinterpret this as referring to one of the criteria for initial employment, giving a potential for misunderstanding of the author's intention.
- *keynote address* (16): this compound noun is formed of two nouns, the first being itself a composite of two nouns: the TL does not permit this form of collocation, requiring instead an extended paraphrase. Whilst the TT gives, *la note dominante de son discours,* as does the dictionary for *keynote ideas,* but here is no collocate indicated for the actual use of *keynote address* in its function as an intrroductory presentation intended to outline the key issues to be addressed at a conference, so perhaps a more appropriate strategy might be to expand into a relative clause, *son discours au cours duquel il a souligné les thèmes principaux du colloque,* or something similar.
- *absence throught sickness* (27): in the SL *through* has a causative function; in the TL a compound noun does the same job more economically due to permitted combinations, although the TL term may be more directly linked to sick-leave than to the concept of absence as a quantifiable construct (number of absences).
- *sickness rates* (28): compound noun becomes *taux de maladie,* following TL construction norms.
- *The cost to employers...* (31): this is expanded to include a semi-relative clause by the use of the past participle in place of the preposition *to* — *le coût subi par les employeurs.*
- *was likely to* (31): the translator could have chosen to use the verb *risquer de,* or the impersonal expression, *il était fort possible que* — in fact the TL has *était susceptible de.*
- *some companies might be tempted* (36): this reported modal (conditional form) is correctly translated by a conditional of *pouvoir* in the TL.
- *went without holidays* (39): this SL phrasal verb becomes a pronominal verb in the TL, *se passer de.*
- *(in case) the work dried up* (40): this phrasal verb is replaced in the TL by an expanded impersonal adverbial clause of condition, *juste au cas où il venait à manquer de travail.*
- *working as a freelance* (40): a gerund *working* becomes an infinitive, *travailler;* a noun from an adjective: *a freelance* becomes an expanded noun phrase in order to bring out the meaning since there is no single equivalent TL term, giving *collaborateur indépendant.*
- *to work from home* (43): the use of the preposition *from* should have alerted the translator to the difference in meaning between *from* and *at* in collocation with work and home, especially in the microcontext of the discussion of information technology and freelance work. The two prepositions may well mean the same thing in terms of the place where the work is done, but not in terms of the nature of the form of employment.

Lexis
- *age* (title): time, not person, becomes *ère,* not *âge.*
- *on a freelance basis* (2): index for icon: *en tant que collaborateurs indépendants* —

the TL lacks a single-word equivalent, and the translation shifts from the basis for the work to the nature of the role of the translator.

- *a leading psychologist* (3): again the adjective is expanded into a noun phrase, *de premier ordre*.
- *a ticket to...* (8): index for symbol: this idiomatic expression is replaced in the TL by a simple verb, *garantir*.
- *'feel bad factor'* (11): index for icon: the use of inverted commas shows that this neologism is still in the process of being institutionalised. The TL has no equivalent form of expression, so opts for a more generic descriptive expression which has no neologicity and so loses the inverted commas.
- *blue-collar, white-collar workers* (19–20): index for symbol: fixed terms having meaning by usage and consensus in the SL, become *ouvriers, employés de bureau* (loss of parallel forms).
- *the end of the millenium* (18): this loan word is also used in the TL, not forgetting that the TL form requires an accent.
- *the entrepreneur* (21): since this is a loan word in the SL taken from the TL the same word is used.
- *cope with* (23): this phrasal verb is replaced by a similar construction in the TL, equivalent in nature but not in form — *faire face à*.
- *fundamental shift* (24): here *shift* means movement in the sense of change, so the TT uses *changement*.
- *stress-related* (28): index for icon: this compound adjective is expanded into a form of relative clause, *dûs au stress* (note the loan word *stress* used in the TL.
- *'a duty of care'* (35): index for icon: not a neologism but an official term in the SL, translated generically in the TL to give the meaning, but not having the same value of official sanction — *il est maintenant du devoir des employeurs de prendre soin de...* (expansion involving loss of economy).
- *contract workers* (38): here again the TL expands into a noun phrasee, *sous contrat à durée déterminée* — loss of economy.
- *marketing expertise* (43): note that the TL has the same loan word, *marketing*, despite the loi Toubon of 1994.
- *ill-equipped* (45): the TT has *n'était pas prête*, which gives the same idea but in less specific terms.

Collocations:

- *age of stress dawns* (title): here the TL uses *naissance* to collocate with *ère*.
- *to contract out (services)* (14): *sous-traiter (leur service du personnel)*.
- *costs... soar* (31): *monter en flèche*.
- *suffer a nervous breakdown* (33): the TL simply states, *qui a eu*; perhaps a more interesting collocation could have been found, even the same term, such as *souffrir* which generally collocates with *une maladie*.
- *took on jobs* (39): phrasal verb becomes a synthetic verb form, to collocate with *emplois — acceptent*.
- *possess skills* (41): the TL uses the same verb, *posseder*, but prefers *connaissances* to collocate with list given rather than *compétences*.

Stylistic Devices

These are almost non-existent in this text, given the nature of its shape and content. The main stylistic effect seems to be one of **expansion** in order to bring out an underlying meaning conveyed by a more economical SL construction whose form cannot be mimicked or recreated in the TL, notably with regard to compound nouns.

Alliteration

Only one example was found in the SL, probably a result of collocation rather than choice:

– *the production process* (19): this is contracted to simply — *la production.*

Cultural References

– *the British Pyschologial Society* (6): a culture-specific institution, so the name needs to be translated as a calque, word-for-word but following TL norms of order, syntax etc.
– *Warwick University* (7), *University of Manchester Institute of Science and Technology* (3): proper names follow the same rule as above.
– *Northumberland County Council* (34): another culture-specific proper name for a service.
– *Professor Cooper* (6): potential problem due to TL polysemy but given the context, it would be expected that this title would be understood to refer to a *Professeur* as in senior academic, not *professeur* as in teacher.

Punctuation

Use of inverted commas:

– *'age of uncertainty'* (1): a quote, not retained as such in TT although it should/could have been.
– *' a good education… case'* (7): this direct quote is retained as such in the TT.
– *' feel bad factor'* (11): this fixed expression/neologism does not appear to exist in the TL so a generic interpretation is given, without inverted commas.
– *'duty of care'* (35): this may be a quote from an official document or judgement, but is rendered in the TT by a descriptive predicate, impersonal construction, no inverted commas.

Use of numbers to give ages of people (46): this is repeated in the TT.

Use of capital letters:

– *British industry* becomes *l'industrie Britannique* (27): it should be remembered that where the word *British* functions as an adjective it should be written with a lower case *b* in the TL — capitals are only used for nouns/persons of nationality.

Deliver Us from Motor Hell, Dr Mawhinney

This is an extract from a longer article published in *The Independent*, whose starting point is a report due to be published on the same day on the state of transport and travel in the UK, which advocates a significant improvement in public transport. Although the target reader would expect this publication to aim for objectivity of presentation, there is nonetheless a clear bias in the tone of the article. This bias does not, however, reflect any political tendency, rather the opinion of the author on what he describes as a fundamental social issue.

The title is a personalised address or appeal to the Minister for Transport of the time, Dr Brian Mawhinney, and the text itself is a mixture of factual report and personalised comment, using the form of the first person plural to imply representativity of the wider readership, not just the opinions of the author of the article. Progress is charted since the arrival in office of Dr Mawhinney, adopting an encouraging tone, and the problem is then widened out to pose the greater philosophical question 'what sort of a society do we want to live in?', closing with a statement of authorial opinion as to the real nature of the problem, which would appear to be different to that posed initially by the introducing heading and summary linked to the name of the author.

The language of the text thus reflects this mixture of practicality and more lofty aims; the first part of the extract deals with practicalities, the last paragraph, containing the real issues for reflection, deals with more abstract concepts. The choice of lexis and rhetorical questions confirm the author's attitude (e.g. *misguided thinking... fatally flawed* (11–14): the choice of quotations in lines 36–44).

Sentence Structure

The main objective being clarity of information in order to allow the reader to make up his mind, the sentence structure has no ambitions of complexity requiring attentive reading in order to deconstruct the various constituent units of information. There is, however, a clear authorial opinion in evidence, even in the introductory header, and so there is a certain degree of subordination of information in order to reinforce the viewpoint which the author wishes to convey to the reader. Thus sentences tend to have one main clause and one subordinate clause, introducing a point and expanding on it, although the first paragraph contains a greater degree of subordination, given its role as introduction to the key issues. This is done through relative or other clauses of different constructions, whose underlying tone or intent it should be possible to recreate in the TT, if not the actual form:

- *a paper... saying that...* (3): *qui annonce que* — a direct relative clause replaces the present participle.
- *most solutions put forward by governments* (38): *la plupart des solutions proposées* — the TL uses a past participle, as does the SL.
- *those new to car ownership* (50): an economic form of relative clause without a verb, requiring expansion or reformulation in the TL, although the solution chosen may not be the most stylistically pleasing — *les gens qui ont une voiture pour la première fois*.

284

- or through contrast: *energy use for travel to work... while in London... there was...* (7): here the TT has *alors que*, but could also have chosen *tandis que*.
- and comparison: *the anti-roads lobby can be just as facile and wrong-headed as its opponents* (40): the TT also avoids the use of a verb in the second half of the comparison, *aussi facile et entêté que son opposant* (see lexis for note on *facile*).
- through explanation/result: *the solutions are so difficult that is must be tempting* (33): the TL shifts from explanation to pure statement of effect — *ne font que frôler.*

Syntax

Present Perfect: for assessing or listing actions and achievements to date — this corresponds to the Passé Composé in this aspect, and contrasts in the text with the use of the Passé Simple (Past Historic) where the SL uses Past Simple for a single, completed event in the past with no relation to the present:
- *where good public transport systems have survived* (9): *ont subsisté.*
- *thinking that has steered...* (11): *qui a guidé.*
- *there have been concrete signs* (23): *on a déjà noté.*
- *road schemes have been scrapped...* (24): *des projets... ont été abandonnés: cars have made it much easier... for people to visit* (47): the TT simplifies this construction, losing the impersonal form by using (a) a single verb *faciliter,* with *car* as its subject, instead of the phrasal, analytical verb, *make easier;* (b) a noun, *visite,* instead of the verb and avoiding thereby the need to introduce a second subject — *people: les voitures ont facilité les visites* (47).

Personalised/Impersonal constructions:
- *energy use... had increased... while in London... there was little increase* (7): in the TT both verbs have named subjects, *ont subsisté... l'augmentation a été,* so the impersonal tone of the second clause is perhaps less obvious.
- *how should we go about replacing* (21): this direct address also invites consideration of the phrasal verb, *go about* — TT uses a simple verb form, *que devrions nous faire,* which is less informal in register; and of its dependent gerund, *replacing* — TT norms follow *faire* with another infinitive of purpose, *pour remplacer.*
- *take leisure* (47): this imperative form of the verb in the SL is almost incongruous, except that the direct form of address has already been established by the use of the first person plural. The TT has *Prenez,* which probably has the same effect in the TL.

Reporting comments: the comments above regarding tenses do not obtain here, and differences in use of tenses should be noted:
- *the researchers found that...* (7): gives — *les chercheurs ont découvert que* and *a report by... which found that... qui annonçait que* (19–20).
- *as David Mackenzie... put it* (35): gives — *comme l'expliqua* — *as Dr Mawhinney pointed out* (40): *comme le souligna.* Both examples are more precise in the TT, there is also stylistic variation.

Gerunds and participles:
- *a paper... saying that* (3): *une étude qui annonce que* — the TL cannot offer this use of the Continuous form in a finite verb; although it could have used the Present Participle, the relative clause form is more stylistically appropriate.
- *introducing high charges* (49): this gerund becomes a noun based on the verb, *l'introduction.*

- *it must be tempting* (33): the TT keeps the same construction, *il doit être tentant*, although this appears to be more an example of SL interference than TL style.
- *to keep industry moving* (43): the inherent concept of purpose is rendered in the TT by *pour* plus infinitive: *pour faire avancer l'industrie*.

Other:
- *is revealed as fatally flawed* (14): passive verb plus a second passive in the form of a past participle — the first is replaced in the TL by a pronominal form, *s'est révélé*; the second by a simple adjective, *fatalement imparfait*: no loss of tone or message content.
- *made the previous policy appear* (17): loss of indirect reference in the TL, and the use of the deictic, *cette politique* instead of *previous* means that the reader has to reread the preceding paragraph — *more is being spent... £3m is being spent* (25): Present Continuous Passive.
- *no easy votes to be won* (31): this SL passive infinitive becomes a past participle in the TL. It may have been more accurate to use *à remporter*, which implies future action, than *remportés*, which could be read as a completed past action thus losing the concept of futurity.
- *those new to car ownership* (51): the TT has opted for paraphrase and expansion here — *les gens qui ont une voiture pour la première fois*, but there could well be a more economic and stylistically attractive way of expressing the concept.

Lexis
Different registers: the balance and contrast should be preserved where possible:
More **formal:**
- *central tenet* (12): index for index: the TL choice *principe de base* does not have quite the same degree of formality.
- *entrenched positions* (28): *positions très arrêtées*.
- *ideological obsession* (32): becomes adverb plus verb *to be* and past participle — *idéologiquement obsédés*.

More **informal:**
- *giving it a go* (23): *s'y essaie*.
- *scrapped* (24): the TT choice is less colloquial, more neutral — *des projets... ont été abandonnés*.
- *Dr Mawhinney is hamstrung by* (32): icon for icon: here the TL substitutes an idiomatic expression of equivalent impact, if somewhat less economic in form — *se trouve pieds et poings liés*.
- *nibbling at the edges of the problem* (39): the TL attempts to compensate for the lack of a similarly connotative verb by the introduction of alliteration *ne font que frôler le problème*.
- *will stump up* (51): icon for icon: recalling perhaps the terminology of cricket, this idiom cannot be replaced in the TL by one of similar origin. The TL uses *les conducteurs casqueront*, which is at least idiomatic and introduces, again, an example of litany or rhythm through the use of alliteration.

Collocations:
- *massive investment* (5): *un investissement très important*.
- *an explosive increase* (6): *considérablement augmenté* may not give the same degree of intensity as the SL *explosive*.
- *increased dramatically* (8): the TL uses here *augmenté proportionnellement au nombre d'emplois*, which is not quite the same as the SL subtext, which

intended to explain that more travelling was done in other areas of the country, in connection with each job, than would be done within London, not that more jobs meant proportionately more travelling, as this would imply that each job, wherever it may be, generates the same amount of travelling.

- *thinking that has steered roads policy* (11): *l'idée... qui a guidé...*
- *new roads generate extra traffic* (20): indirect discourse gives *de nouvelles routes créaient davantage de circulation.*
- *entrenched positions* (28): *positions arrêtées.*
- *set objectives* (45): *établir des objectifs* — TL could also use *fixer des objectifs.*

Compound nouns — a desire for economy leads to the use of compound nouns to describes issues of contemporary concern. These terms have for the most part become accepted by social consensus to the point of forming part of the domain-specific jargon of social issues which are common to most developed nations if not to all, and so may be expected to have equivalent recognised terms in the TL. Compound nouns will usually require the prepositions *à* or *de* in the TL, depending on the function of the term:

- *energy use* (7): *la consommation d'énergie.*
- *roads policy* (12): TL has expansion, *la politique d'aménagement des routes*, by analogy with *aménagement du territoire..*
- *out of town shopping centres* (17): *centres commerciaux situés en dehors des villes*
- *a road building policy* (21): *politique d'aménagement des routes.*
- *a transport policy* (22): *une politique des transports.*
- *pro-roaders* (30): compound noun formed by use of Latin suffix *pro-* plus noun. The noun is formed by analogy with other nouns in the SL through the addition of *-er* to either noun or verb, mainly the latter (especially from USA, life — *lifer* or *pro-lifer*: also (n) *prison — prisoner*, (v) *sing — singer*). In the TL this has to become a noun phrase —*les partisans de la construction routière* — which, in fact, brings out only one of the possible underlying meanings. This is one of the risks of expansion, which allows a greater degree of explicitness but also sometimes incurs an element of loss of polysemy.
- *the transport debate* (29): *le débat sur le transport.*
- *transport problems* (36): *les problèmes de transport.*
- *the anti-roads lobby* (40): *le lobby anti-routes* — here the translator has created a term by analogy with the SL form, using the Latin prefix *anti* as does the SL and a loan term, *lobby*. In the spirit of the loi Toubon of 1994, the translator may prefer to use a term such as *groupe de pression.*

Other:
- *per job* (9): should be *pour chaque emploi*, not, as in TT, *proportionnellement au nombre d'emplois.*
- *bus lanes... cycle networks* (24–25): two terms from the jargon of traffic control, *les voies réservées aux bus et... réseau de pistes cyclables.* The second term has been correctly interpreted in the TL, although its structure in the SL would lend itself to more than one possible interpretation.
- *a sensible transport policy* (37): potential **faux ami**, not *sensible* but *raisonnable*, although the TT has *simple,* which is not quite the same thing.
- *facile* (41): also potential faux ami, requires analysis of meaning content in order to select most appropriate TL adjective. TL uses *facile*, but the sense is more that of *superficiel, sans raisonnement approfondi.*
- *areas of outstanding natural beauty* (48): a fixed expression in the SL for descrip-

tion of a type of area, TL offers *une beauté hors commun*, not a fixed expression but a paraphrase.

- *with bad grace* (51): fixed expression in SL: TL gives a similar expression, *de mauvaise grâce*.
- *issue* (52): potential faux ami, since *issu* means *sorti de* (past participle) and *issue* (noun) is, in TL, *question, problème, sujet*.

Stylistic Devices

Rhetorical Questions are used to create a sense of solidarity with the reader as well as to invite reflection. They also convey key points of the article and reflect the author's attitude:
- *how should we go about replacing...* (21).
- *what sort of society do we want to live in* (46).

Imagery — overt or implied:
- the direct comparison of life with the motor car to a kind of living hell (title).
- *the minister must be brave* (1) and *nibbling at the edges of the problem* (39): the use of the first adjective suggests the contextual interpretation of implied timidity through the potential collocative association with a mouse (traditionally timid) as suggested by the verb *nibble*.
- *throw up their hands in the air* (34): an SL image for despair, rendered in the TL by the opposite in terms of movement, but an equivalent in terms of fixed expression although it may not fulfil the same function — *baisser les bras* is more the sense of resignation, inactivity.

Ambiguity:
- *Motor Hell* (title): given that the introductory header states, *'only radical change can save Britain from the car'*, we have to assume that *motor* in this context refers to the motor car. However, this title could still be interpreted in several ways, to suggest a hell for drivers of motor cars (for whatever reason); a hell involving motor cars, presumably on the roads; even a hell to which motor cars should be consigned; or in a more abstract sense, the hell created for society by its dependence on the motor car.

Accumulation: the text uses the rhythm of three to reinforce its message:
- *road schemes have been scrapped, more is being spent... £3m is being spent...* (24).

Alliteration: probably not deliberate, but still having a visual and phonic effect of memorability:
- *fatally flawed* (14): loss of effect — *fatalement imparfaite*.
- *previous policy* (17): becomes *cette politique* — loss of alliteration.
- *constant cries* (41): careful selection of lexis and syntax has allowed the translator to retain this effect — *pleurer en permanence*.
- *profound political and social question* (52): *question politico-sociale plus approfondie* — the plosives are still there [p] although not quite as immediately obvious.

Repetition for reinforcement and dramatic effect:
- *no easy answers and no easy votes to be won* (31): although roughly parallel in construction for both points, the TL loses in impact by not having an equivalent single word negative qualifier, *no* — *il n'existe pas de... ou de...*

Cultural References

Numbers and money:
- *£3m is being spent* (25) is written in full in the TL.

- *1,220 mile cycle network* (25): this measurement has been converted in to kilometres for the TL reader.
- *Institute of British Geographers* (3): a culture-specific body whose name can only be translated as a calque to explain its role.
- *Manchester, West Midlands, London* (8): the TL reader may not be aware of the importance of geographical location and associated population size/ wealth/industrial activity. Would a note be helpful here?
- *Royal Commission on Environmental Pollution* (15): another culture-specific name, to be translated word-for-word to explain its role.
- *Department of Transport* (19) and *Transport Secretary* (22): to be translated literally unless the translator is convinced that this government office corresponds directly in all its functions to a transport office in the TL culture.
- *Transmark* (35): the proper name of a company whose function is described in the text.

Punctuation

This relates mainly to the use of inverted commas for direct quotes (31–53) and to the use of dashes for insertion of additional information (27–39), which the TT has reproduced in some places but not in others.

Also, attention should be paid to correct TL use of capital letters in the translation of names of bodies and organisations. The translator has also chosen to use capital letters for certain key concepts such as *les Transports* (39) and *la Voiture* (42).

Deaths Linked to London Smog

This text appeared in *The New Scientist*, immediately prior to a report due to be presented on the subject of the article, thereby drawing readers' attention to its existence. In view of the type of publication, readers could reasonably be expected not only to have an interest in the information content of the article but also to possess a general level of awareness of the implication of the different statistics and measurements quoted. However, the publication and therefore the article may also be expected to be of interest to the non-specialist in this particular field and so clarity of meaning should be sought after, to the extent of rendering more explicit any implied information where this is considered necessary.

The format of the article itself resembles that of a report, in that each point is dealt with in a separate paragraph, although not numbered or presented as points. This gives a rather disjointed effect to the text, which appears to lack devices to ensure a smooth progression from one point to the next. This would tend to indicate that the information content takes priority over the manner of presentation, and may suggest to the translator a lesser need for attention to coherence of style and structure than would be the case for other texts. However, the Target Text has endeavoured to reproduce this format, since it may be integral to the Target reader's ability to apprehend the information to be conveyed.

Sentence Structure

The Source Text varies in sentence structure, between initial presentation of the main point and initial presentation of the manner of arriving at a particular discovery. In some cases the Target Text has reordered this presentation to stress the main clause, as conveyor of the main idea of the sentence, rather than appear to stress subordinate clauses. There is some degree of subordination, where all relevant aspects of information pertaining to a given point are included in the same sentence. The sentence structure has been preserved in the TT, using commas and colons as in the ST. The SL will offer greater possibilities for explicitation and clear anaphoric reference, as well as requiring these.

Syntax

- There are many **third person constructions** with the focus of the sentence as subject, which is consistent with the linguistic norms of report-writing (e.g. *the figures suggest* [3]; *the episode presents* [4]; *results have convinced* [15]). This will only prove problematic when the main verb relating to these subjects is in the Passive Voice, thereby having a potential for the need to find a way of avoiding this form of the verb whilst still retaining the emphasis on the noun in question by keeping it as the subject of the verb.
- *results suggest that an increased mortality occurred* (42): this is an example of the previous comment, where the pronominal form will allow the word *mortality* to remain as subject of the verb *occurred*, rather than having recourse to an impersonal construction such as *il y a eu*.
- *direct evidence of deaths* (4): shift from adjective to adverb, *directement*.

- *deaths from air pollution* (4): shift from preposition for cause to prepositional phrase introduced by *attribuables (à)*.
- *air pollution* (5): compound noun where the first noun qualifies the type or nature of the second noun; also indicates something done to the first noun. Can be paraphrased in SL as *pollution of the air*, not by the air. NB: *car travel* = travel by (in a) car; *road works* = work being done to the road; *board meeting* = meeting of (the members of) the board. Remember to bring out this relationship by appropriate choice of TL structure; also to note that this is a feature of more scientific language seeking economy of expression through the use of compound nouns, which is not always easy to reproduce in the TL, since it does not possess an analogous facility for economy. Similarly — *air quality guidelines* (1, 16) — *la politique de contrôle de* (7): *les directives réglant* (19) *la qualité de l'air; government figures* (33): *les chiffres gouvernementaux* (n + adj); *the episode week* (43): *la semaine de cet épisode* (43).
- *the smog, which built up from* (7): in the TL this is rendered by a conditional form to imply that this is one of the conclusions of the report.
- *many of those... had probably been suffering* (9): the TT operates a shift in syntax here, introducing an impersonal construction, *il est probable que*, at the beginning of the sentence, followed by an Imperfect form of the verb accompanied by *déjà* to suggest existence of the condition prior to the smog, as is conveyed in the SL by the use of the Past Perfect tense.
- *convinced the... to act* (15): the TL introduces a noun as the object of convince, to render a more explicit construction.
- *convinced* (15): expansion to bring out inherent concept of success: *ont déjà su convaincre*. This construction is used again, but in a negative form to heighten emphasis (10): *cannot prove: ne saurait apporter la preuve définitive*.
- *until winds cleared the air* (20): here the emphasis is shifted to make the wind (in the singular) the agent and fog the object of the action: *il fût dissipé par le vent*. Note here the use of the subjunctive mood after *jusqu'à ce que*.
- *cannot prove* (40): *ne saurait apporter la preuve définitive*: this example also illustrates a shift from an synthetic SL verb, *prove*, to an analytical TL construction.
- *people died* (9, 25, 35, 39): this concept is rendered in a more economic form in the TL by focusing on the event, since that is what is recorded, and using a single noun, *décès*. This avoids awkward constructions using the Passive, such as *people were registered dead* (33), and conforms to TL statistical usage.
- *(new regulations) intended to reduce* (46): here the TT operates a shift from past participle to present participle and as a consequence of this shift, another from verb to noun dependent on that participle: *visant la réduction*.
- *if the same weather* (47): here the TL uses *dans* plus a conditional tense to imply a similar relationship between the two events described. This also avoids the problem posed by the mixing of tenses in the SL (Future and Conditional instead of Imperfect or Subjunctive — *happened / were to happen* — and Conditional).
- *if the same weather happens again* (47): the TL achieves greater economy here by summarising: *dans de pareilles conditions météorologiques*, without any loss of meaning or information content.

Lexis
- *presents the first evidence* (4): the TL selects a different verb to bring out the underlying meaning: *révèle*.

- *windless* (7): adjective comprising noun plus suffix, rendered in TL by *sans* plus noun.
- *a summary of his results* (13): expansion to bring out meaning through a shift from SL — noun (N1) + *of* + noun (N2): to TL — noun (N2) qualified by an adjective derived from N1: *un rapport sommaire des résultats obtenus.*
- *people who actually died* (29): this potential faux ami, *actually*, is dealt with correctly by translating it as an adverb, *effectivement* (not *actuellement*, which means *currently*) followed by a past participle referring to the noun *décès* used to describe the concept of people who died.

Collocations:
- *smog... enveloped London* (1): TL uses a different verb.
- *peaked at* (22): this synthetic construction is transformed into an analytical one in the TL, *a atteint le plus haut niveau.*
- *14 per cent higher* (39): *plus élevé que prévu...* Note the particular collocate, *élevé*, for measurement of increase of quantity in this context. In a desire for precision, this sentence repeats the *que prévu* of the previous sentence, where the ST does not, relying on the reader to supply this.

Terminology:
- *episodes as bad as* (45): here the meaning of *bad* is one of severity, not in contrast with goodness or good behaviour, nor even with suitability, hence the use of the TL term *sévère.*
- terms of reference to pollutants and the way in which their presence in the air is calculated. To be checked for accuracy of use in the TL: *nitrogen dioxide, particulates, parts per billion* (22).
- medical terms (37): *respiratory diseases, asthma, lung disease, cardiovascular disease* — functioning at the level of indexical correspondence.

Meaning:
- *latter-day smog* (1): *smog* — can be used in the TL, index for index; *latter-day*: index for index/symbol — what is meant by this term, which is not often found outside of the religious context, e.g. latter-day saint? The TL attempts to render the meaning by the word *contemporain.*

Stylistic Devices

As stated in the introduction these will be few in number given the factual style and informative function of the text. There is an example where the TL has used the device of inversion of noun and verb or adjective and noun to heighten emphasis:
- *episodes... are rare* (45): *rare sont les épisodes.*

Culture-specific references

- *London Smog* (title, 1, 45): the word *smog* actually appears in the dictionary (Harraps) but it would still have greater connotative significance for the SL reader. This is why the translator has chosen to use the word *brouillard* in the title, and then revert to the word *smog* once the concept has been established, to avoid the accusation of overreliance on a loan word which may not be part of the non-specialist TL reader's vocabulary. The TT takes advantage of the facility offered by the TL to create an adjective from a place name, referring instead to *le brouillard londonien*. Similarly *hôpital sud-londonien* for *Hospital in South London* (12).
- *Department of Health* (3): a similar department exists in the Target culture and

so this term can be transferred by the process of *calque*, translating word-for-word, rather than using the exact TL term, which may not cover quite the same range of activities.

- *Oxfordshire* (45): literary conventions in the TL require this to be translated as *dans le* + county name.
- *National Environment Technology Centre* (44): this name is transparent with regard to its function and so can be translated directly into TL terms in the main body of the text. In case the TL reader may wish to write for further details, the SL name can be appended in a footnote. To note, *environmental technology* (adj + noun) becomes a compound noun, *la Technologie de l'Environnement*.
- *British Thoracic Society* (13): the same applies to this name as to the one above.

One-Stop Quality

This text is taken from a publication supplement intended for nurses, a newsletter produced by the Royal College of Nursing Dynamic Quality Improvement Programme and the Foundation of Nursing Studies, in association with the *Nursing Standard*. Its cover page proclaims that this newsletter is intended to be 'An authoritative guide to European issues in quality assurance and standard setting'. According to the publication, Euroquan is the European Nursing Quality Network, which was launched in March 1992 for the promotion of high standards of nursing care through the dissemination of research findings and the application of this knowledge in practice. Euroquan has representatives in most European countries (EC and non-EC), and is circulated in English only, although according to the representative in London in 1995, there are plans for each country to be allowed to produce and circulate its own target language version.

Given the objectives of this magazine as stated above, as one might expect, the newsletter contains a range of types of article, from the purely factual, reporting on meetings and workshops to more detailed descriptions of particularly important events (such as the subject of this article), case study reports from different centres usually written in the first person, reviews of procedures for action on quality in different countries and book reviews. The emphasis is on the informative function, with little emotive or affective use of language, denotative rather than connotative, and as such would not be expected to have been the object of much painstaking attention to rhetorical devices. Those that are present are likely to relate to economy of expression, to coherence and cohesion rather than serve any purpose of elegance of expression, particularly in view of the target audience who are trained to look for facts and demonstrable truths, and to convey these in a very precise and economic style.

Sentence Structure

As befits the style of a factual report, the information content is very dense, and sentences mainly consist of key words or concepts linked as economically as possible by syntactical units. Thus the dominant pattern would seem to be either a single clause, often with the verb *to be*:
- *the other teams to reach the finals were...* (17): this entire paragraph consists of a list of teams with their countries of origin, all depending on the verb *were*.
- sometimes we find another appropriate collocation for the main noun/subject, or else a main clause with a single second clause, either a relative clause: *in addition, the Leicester Royal Infirmary set themselves a set of targets, which included* (31): (followed by a list of points) — note that the rather clumsy repetition of the polysemous word set is avoided in the TL.
- or a co-ordinating clause: *only 50 per cent... were seen... and only 93 per cent... were available...* (46)

There is some attempt at impact through the use of contrasting shorter sentences in which the information content is limited to a single statement, to highlight this statement. Such sentences are the initial sentences of a new

paragraph and serve as anaphoric reference in the form of a summary of preceding points or comments as well as pointing to a subsequent explanation of
the statement, thus contributing to the coherence of the text:
- *these targets contrast with the initial project baseline* (43): also a short sentence in
  the TT.
- *the team achieved all quality targets* (51): again, a short sentence in the TT.
  Sometimes emphasis is also achieved through a less usual word or clause
order (see Rhetorical Devices).

Syntax
- *a team from the UK's Royal Leicester Infirmary beat finalists* (1): the SL uses the
  Past Simple tense here for a simple statement of fact about an past event, a
  completed action with no reference to the present. However, given that the
  next reference to the victory (see below) uses the Present Perfect tense for
  dramatic immediacy, it could be argued that the SL could have used the
  Present Perfect tense here as well. In both cases, the TL will need to use the
  Passé Composé since the Passé Simple belongs to a different register and style
  which would be inappropriate here.
- *the UK entry... has won the 1994 competition* (4): note the use of the Present
  Perfect tense here in the SL (see above).
- *held in Geneva in June, the Award finals featured...* (6): here the use of the Past
  Simple is justified in the SL by the inclusion of the actual time at which the
  action took place, and again will be translated by a Passé Composé in the TL.
- *measurably raised standards* (13): this single-word adverb is replaced by an
  adverbial expression in the TL, *d'une manière quantitative*.
- *this is achieved through completing the entire process...* (25): the verb *achieve*
  requires a gerund or a noun to follow the preposition *through*. In the TL this
  construction is replaced by a slightly different one, still making anaphoric
  reference by use of the deictic but changing the verb from *achieve* (action) to
  consiste en (nature/state) followed by a new noun qualified by an adjective
  combining the meanings of both the SL verb and the SL adjective — *un
  déroulement complet*.
- *100 per cent of appropriate patients to have finished... all patients to be seen... all
  expected patients to attend... 100 per cent of GP's to receive a full report* (34): all of
  these infinitives are dependent on the introductory statement, *a set of strict
  quality targets, which included...* although it may have been syntactically more
  correct to follow the noun *target* with the preposition *of* and a gerund form.
  The translator should not therefore attempt to reproduce the infinitive form
  in the TL without first considering the syntax of his translation of the introductory statement preceding the list of targets. In fact the TL shifts the syntax
  to make the list of points into ones introduced by a noun subject, which will
  be qualified by a past participle or by adjectives, in order better to preserve a
  sense of parallel structure, coherence and patterned regularity which will
  identify these as being grouped together and all dependent on the same
  structure.
- *this can be achieved* — becomes *celle-ci* (anaphoric reference to *une méthode de
  prise en charge*) with *consiste en* — which actually loses the emphasis of method
  to focus on nature, state or result (25); *all patients to be seen* — in the TL the
  passive voice is rendered by a past participle, again focusing more on result
  than intention (38); *it was subsequently changed* — *il fut transformé* — this use of

the Passé Simple is inconsistent with the use of the Passé Composé throughout the text (4); *patients were seen — des malades voyaient le médecin* — the loss of passive voice indicates or causes a shift of emphasis from the doctor as instigator of the interaction at the time of appointment to the patient as consumer (46); *not only can patient need for medical or other treatment now be promptly and accurately determined — peut être défini...* passive retained in TL (51) *but the time spent travelling... is greatly reduced — sont grandement réduits* (53); also to be noted, TL requires a plural verb since the noun *time* is repeated by use of the demonstrative, *celui*, thus splitting one SL concept into two defined aspects or occurrences (53); all of these passive verb forms serve to present the actual action without reference to any acting subject, since what is important here is results, not agents.

- *the time spent at and travelling to...* (53): the gerund here is replaced in the TL by a noun, *le temps passé à l'hopîtal et celui du voyage pour s'y rendre*. Note the insertion of the demonstrative, *celui*, required by TL style for greater precision, and the expansion by means of a clause of purpose to bring out the SL intended meaning — loss of economy.
- *promptly and accurately determined* (52): these two single-word adverbs are translated by two similar adverbs in the TL.

Lexis

Obviously mainly **terminology** from the field of quality assessment relating to patient care in the context of the medical world; items of lexis from both fields are used in conjunction. None of the terms used could be considered eclectic or highly profession-specific and all should be accessible to the non-specialised reade. Most terms of lexis will come into the area of indexicality, where a concept/term in L1 will find an equivalent or near-equivalent term in L2. Any case where there is a lack of indexical correspondence will probably result in expansion or paraphrase to explicate the meaning of the unit or term:

- *a quality service for outpatients — un service de qualité aux malades non-hospitalisés* (3).
- *a healthcare institution — l'institution de la Santé* (14): it is interesting to note here that the TL has not only shifted from the indefinite *a* to the definite article, *l'*, thereby changing the import of this unit of the message, but has also used a capital letter for *Santé* as if by analogy with *la Sécu* (for *Sécurité sociale*) where the service takes on a persona and the term almost becomes considered as a proper name.
- *quality improvement project* (13): *projet d'amélioration de la qualité* — again, the TL makes the qualifying noun definite rather than indefinite, partially due to the requirements of syntax in the case of compound nouns.
- *neurology outpatients* (23): *le service spécialisé en neurologie... auquel s'adressent les malades non-hospitalisés* — the lack of economy of description could be due to more than one reason, perhaps that the practice of outpatient treatment is not so advanced in the TL culture so there is no specific jargon term for this kind of care; or else that the TL inability to create compound nouns by juxtaposition will always result in some degree of expansion and/or paraphrase.
- *initial consultation with a specialist* (27): *première consultation du malade par un médecin-spécialiste:* it is interesting that in the TL the roles are almost reversed, in that the consultation is seen to be done by the specialist towards the patient, thus indicating in fact a different interpretation in the socio-cultural commu-

nities of this apparently equivalent term having the same linguistic form in both languages.

- *complex investigations* (27): *examens medicaux complexes* — the SL term is replaced by a two-word TL term which specifies what kind of investigations, whereas in the SL the context is held to render this explication unnecessary.
- *a follow-up session* (28): *une séance de suivi*: index for index: for once the TL has an equivalent term, substituting a single-word noun (based on a verb and preceded by a qualifying preposition *de*) for an SL phrasal verb.
- *treatment options* (29): *choix du traitement* — although the end message of this segment is the same, the manner of arriving there is slightly different, with the SL emphasising range only and the TL using the polysemy of *choix* to imply both range and process of selection — a gain in the TT.
- *quality targets* (32): *un ensemble d'objectifs de qualité*.
- *diagnostic investigations* (35): this is summed up in a single mass noun for the abstract notion of the overall process, *un diagnostic*.

Collocations — some will be generally applicable, some context-specific. Collocations can generally be thought of in terms of indexical links, in that a given term evokes a corresponding co-occurring term for each of the two languages:

- *provide a service* (3): *fournir un service*.
- *promote an awareness* (11): *promouvoir une reconnaissance*.
- *raise standards* (13): *relever les normes* — this collocation may only hold in this particular context where previous comments make it clear to what *les normes* refers.
- *set oneself a target* (32): *se fixer un objectif*.
- *implement a project* (44): *mettre en place un projet*.
- *attend a clinic* (49): *voyaient effectivement quelqu'un à la clinique*: the TL has shifted the emphasis from attendence, which is the important point of the TL unit in terms of increased efficiency and reduction of time-wasting by patients, to a comment which implies the same activity on the part of the medical staff instead. An inaccurate formulation which gives the wrong information.
- *achieve a target* (51): *atteindre un objectif*.

Stylistic Devices

As described above, the use of a short sentence, having an anaphoric function, at the beginning of a paragraph increases its effect in term of impact and memorability.

Word/clause order:

- *set up in 1991 and sponsored and co-ordinated... , the Award exists...* (10): this device of placing in initial position the subordinate relative clauses (with three past participles following the rule of three for memorability) gives greater importance to the delayed subject when it finally appears.
- *not only can patient need... but the time...* (51): inversion after *not only* adds to impact.

Parallel or contrasting structure for coherence:

- *in the list of targets* (34–42): there is an attempt at coherence through parallel structure by use of the infinitive in the SL; however, this is not consistently adopted, giving rise to some lack of clarity and continuity and making the dependence of all points on the introductory statement less obvious.
- *more convenient and less stressful* (25): here we find two opposite forms of the comparative, for impact through contrast of intent within similarity of form.

Cultural References

These may be SL culture specific, relating to the world of healthcare and the process of this care:

- *Leicester Royal Infirmary NHS Trust* (4–5): the translator has paraphrased the name but omitted any reference to the status of the hospital as an NHS Trust hospital. In this particular text, the additional information may have been quite important to the subject of quality control, given that Trust hospitals are driven by similar concerns to industry, i.e. those of customer service, performance indicators and cost-effectiveness more so than the non-Trust hospital. It would have been helpful to add a translator's note here. The financial domain use of this unit of information could be described as indexical in the context of interlingual transfer, with a corresponding concept and term existing in the TL, but the neologistic use within the context of healthcare makes this unit a culture-specific symbol in this case.

- *Golden Helix award* (4): it is not clear where this originated (although probably in the SL culture) nor whether there is an official translation of this name in the different languages of participating countries. Since no sources were able to confirm a particular translation, the SL name has been retained in inverted commas in the TT, although it would have been helpful to append a translator's note or else given a TL translation in brackets after the SL form. This could be described as iconic, in that the name of the award describes the physical shape of the object conferred as an award.

References also relate to the participants in the competition, in which case the reference is to a list of names of countries and cities, for which the TL form should be checked, e.g.:

- *Geneva, Denmark, Netherlands, Spain* (6–7).

- *the EV. Waldkrankenhaus Spanau, Germany; UCL 9 Reggio Emilia Italy…* (17–22): It is to be noted that the SL has used the source culture specific form of the name for each hospital, and so the TL should do likewise.

- *Minister of State for Social Affairs* (15): also to be noted is that the SL has in fact translated as a calque from the TL the title of the position of Simone Veil at the time of writing.

- *GP's* (40): although translating this as *médecin généraliste* covers the broad function in comparison with the role of the specialist, without specific SL cultural knowledge of the Health Service much connotative value is lost without an explanatory translator's note for the TL reader as to the role of the family doctor.

Punctuation

Inverted commas are used:

- *Prix Hospitalier Européen 'Golden Helix'* (2): since the actual name appears untranslated, even though there is expansion to define its function, the name itself is included in inverted commas to signify this quality as a foreign name.

Chaos Theory — Achieving a Balance

This text would seem to refer to a rather specialised, or semi-specialised subject area, that of a sub-specialisation of physics, namely non-linear dynamics. One might wonder about the relevance or interest of this field to the average reader of *The Economist* who would be expected to have more concern for the state of world markets and exchange rates, economic policies and related issues. But in fact the principle described through the theory elaborated in the text is of relevance to and will have implications for any area of activity, hence the appearance of the article in this publication. It may be of trivial interest to note the date of publication, at a time when the film, '*Jurassic Park*' was enjoying a sweeping success across the Western world: chaos theory (with its implications of inherent instability and unpredictability) underpins the prediction of disaster for the prehistoric park by the expert mathematician invited to give his opinion on the venture prior to its opening.

The most important task for the translator is to ensure an overall understanding of the principle features of the theory and its nature as described in the text. The general level of language used is appropriate to the expected level of education of the target reader, relatively formal and dependent on a good level of education; although none of the items of lexis used, should in themselves be unfamiliar to the reader in their more general usage, the fact of their appearance as part of a given semantic field within a specific context and domain may give rise to some difficulty in interpretation of their precise signification in this context. Hence the need for consultation in order to achieve correct interpretation and a clear overview of the subject area.

The layout is quite clear, with each new idea forming the subject of a new paragraph, and the longest paragraph being the introductory one. Two quotes also serve as sub-headings to summarise and point to the subject matter.

Sentence Structure

In general the sentences tend not to be complex in their information content, very often consisting of a single main clause modified, explained or exemplified by a subordinate (often relative) clause (3–9). Sometimes there is an initial noun to introduce the relative clause, repeating or referring to a preceding noun (40, *pendulum, a system which*). Contrasting with these sentences are shorter, single clause statements intended by means of this contrast to have greater impact (para 1, last sentence, para 2 first sentence).

Where there is insertion of additional information using dashes, this has been maintained to preserve the style of the text type, since this device is also common in the TL (paras 1, 3, 5).

Syntax

— *all sorts of bizarrely fluctuating things* (7): to avoid word-order problems and expansion in the TL arising from a pre-positioned adverb in the SL, the TT has opted for a different structure, that of apposition of a relative clause where the verbal action is implied by the adjective '*sujets*'.

- *for people studying* (9): implied relative clause in SL needs to be made explicit in TL. Also to be noted, loss of aspect of continuity through use of simple form of verb in relative clause.
- *endlessly looping round* (42): ST takes full advantage of the *-ing* form to imply continuity, lack of completion. TL can use the same form, or can substitute a relative clause with a finite verb. The suggested TT has done so, presenting the meaning of *'looping'* in the form of a noun introduced by an appropriate collocation (verb). Also, the single-word adverb *endlessly* has been subjected to transformation into an adverbial phrase, *sans fin*.
- *consider a simple pendulum* (28): SL uses second personal plural imperative form, whereas TL would tend to use first person plural when citing an example.
- *one provides... the other records* (30): note SL use of *one* as numerative, requiring definite article to introduce the second part of the equation, whereas TL requires the use of the definite article with both contrasting or complementary elements.
- *the pendulum has a given velocity* (33): note that the varying use of *'have'* in the SL is not reflected in TL usage, which prefers to use a more explicit verb according to context and collocative use: e.g. *prendre une douche, recevoir des visiteurs*.
- *inherent in the system* (14): requires appropriate preposition following adjective in TL.
- *back and forth motion... is a perfect circle* (34): where SL uses verb *to be* for description, TL prefers a more explicit verb, dependent on signification within context: perhaps *'dessine'*.
- *much of chaos theory* (37): here the adverb *much* is used in terms of extent, not quantity, and the TL will require a more specific partitive, perhaps *'une grande partie'*.

Lexis
Collocations:
- *sexily rechristened* (3): index for icon: the lack of a direct equivalent term to translate this rather bizarre collocation of physical attraction and religious consecration necessitates an analysis of the constitutent meanings of the word *'sexily'* in order to select the most appropriate TL term *attrayant* conveying the more important aspect of physical attraction, which alternative term *provocateur* may not suffice to evoke.
- *a mixed blessing* (4): index for icon: fixed expression/collocation in SL, recalling the metaphor of consecration and religious fervour. The lack of an expression of equivalent effect in the TL necessitates either expansion in order to bring out the underlying meaning or else substitution of a different colloctional pair intended to achieve the same effect.
- *right conditions* (5): need to find appropriate collocation for *conditions* in TL, necessitating analysis of possible signfications of the word *right* — possibly *favorables* or *bonnes* but not *justes* or *exactes*.
Fixed expressions:
- *left to themselves* (16): SL uses specific collocation, not primary dictionary translation of verb *to leave*: *livrés à eux-mêmes*.
- *just a phase...* (22): note the possible play on signification by use of this expression: either the technical meaning relevant to the subject domain, or else the citation of what has become a cliché expression used by parents about

growing and developing offspring (hence the relevance to the subject matter): *phase* in the sense of a *transient stage of development*. This is the justification for the choice of the adapted form of the sub-heading, to bring out the underlying meaning of an SL-specific expression.

Mathematical/physics/other terminology:
- *non-linear dynamics* (3): note existence of technical term of equivalent form in TL, subject, of course, to TL rules for order of occurrence of adjectives within a noun group.
- *phenomena* (9): note SL use of Latin plural, more likely to be used in TL adapted form, *'phénomènes'*.
- *chaos theory* (3): this term has to be checked in an up-to-date bilingual diction-ary of physics terms or with an expert in the field in order to confirm the appropriateness of the intuitive response of translating this according to TL rules governing the translation of a compound noun consisting of two nouns where one noun, the first, describes the exact nature of the second: e.g. *entrance door, porte d'entrée; bus ticket, billet d'autobus; business man, homme d'affaires.*
- *phase space* (26): as with the term *chaos theory* this technical term has to be checked in an up-to-date bilingual dictionary of physics terms or with an expert in the field.

Other terms or items of lexis:
- *chaos theory says that* (16): note appropriate use of verbs of reporting for pseudo-scientif report: SL use of *say* for statement of scientific fact. Translator need to substitute an appropriate TL verb, not *'dire'*.
- *back and forth motion…* (34): icon for icon: a fixed expression in the SL can be conveyed by an equivalent fixed expression in the TL, which, however, uses verbs instead of adverbs: *le va-et-vient.*

Stylistic Devices

Given the source of publication and the semi-scientific nature of this text one would not expect to find many stylistic devices. However, there are some attempts to create a kind of stylistic effect, perhaps in order to create added interest in the text as a piece of writing as well as in its function as a semi-spe-cialised article.

Inversion:
- *no longer can they hope* (12): TL loss of impact of initial position of *no longer*.

Alliteration:
- *flames of industrial furnaces* (24): this alliteration can be reproduced in the TL.

Simile:
- *like tangled skeins of wool* (42): the same image can be used in the TL.

Cultural References
- note the use of a quotation (1–2) from Marx as the introduction to the subject matter. The translator should attempt to find the accepted translation of this in the TL, but given constraints of time and the lack of any reference to the source of the quote, this may prove unfeasible and the translator may have to devise his or her own translation into the TL.

Punctuation
- As stated above (Sentence Structure), in cases of insertion of additional information using dashes, these dashes have been retained (6, 26, 37).

- where there are lists of actions linked by colons in the SL (24) or commas (7–9) these have also been used in the TT.

Great Expectations for Optical Card Trial

This text is taken from a publication whose target readership includes professionals both of the scientific world and those having a lay interest in this field. The subject of the article is one of on-going discussion and interest, likely to be of relevance to the non-specialised reader for whom the study points to possible implications of future use, as well as to those engaged in health care at a non-medical or semi-specialised level.

Given the technological nature of the object of the article, the optical card, and the format of a report on a subject of technical interest in this kind of publication, one would expect to find mainly very objective and factual reporting, according to the norms expected for this text type. However, given also the wider appeal of the subject matter, this factual reporting is interspersed with direct quotes, adding human interest and a more personal perspective to the report. There is of necessity a certain amount of technical vocabulary but none which is inaccessible to the target reader of the magazine, whose general level of education should equip him or her to read this level of report with complete understanding.

True to the function or *skopos* of the article, to inform and report, there is an element of summary of the nature of the report, the methodology of the trial and technical data relating to the card and its use, as well as consideration of wider implications. All these key aspects are presented in separate paragraphs, making it easier to see the progression from one point to the next.

The general level of language is educated and semi-specialised, with no particular difficulties of interpretation being caused by a use of over-complex syntax, since this would contradict the need for clarity in order to render the information accessible, and that of economy, in order to concentrate on relevant information rather than extraneous and redundant stylistic use of language.

Sentence Structure

In order to facilitate a more economical form of expression whilst giving further details of each new point introduced, there is quite a high incidence of relative clauses, which give the impression of listing points or supplementary information. Other information is also embedded in the sentence by the use of dashes (12–13, 20–21, 37–39).

Syntax

- *incentive for* (2): look for correct collocation pronoun for TL — *impulsion à*.
- *patient records held on memory cards* (2): icons for icons: problem of compound nouns: for the first, TL requires possessive *de* — *fichier du malade* — plus preposition *à* for the second compound noun, *carte à mémoire*.
- *beginning this autumn* (4): the rest of the sentence indicates that this has not yet taken place (will be given) and so suggests to the translator the need for a future verb, or one of obligation, as part of a relative clause.
- *has been under way for eight years* (10): a clear case here for the patterned shift using *depuis* plus present tense. A different verb, one more specific than the

verb *to be*, could incorporate the idea of *underway* into a synthetic single word verb.

– *difficulties in finding and paying for* (14): these SL gerunds can be rendered by nouns in the TL.

– *which is very common* (23): the TL looks for a more precise term, *arrive*, followed by an adverb formed from the SL adjective.

– *if a woman says* (25): this is translated by the concept of future possibility using *devoir* in the Imparfait; the second verb of the conditional sentence, *we can*, then also becomes conditional.

– *here* (24): this adverb of place is replaced by a more specific reference to the name of the country.

– *the rising tide... could provide* (1); *growing number* (41): here it is the *number* which is the subject of the verb and not the noun it is quantifying, therefore the translator needs to use a singular verb.

– *if it comes to court* (44): icon for icon: this can be expressed more economically in the TL without a verb, *en cas de*.

– *what advice was given* (43): singular mass noun becomes plural count noun in the TL, followed by a simple past participle (with correct agreement for number and gender) instead of a passive verb.

– *arguing over whether a text was carried out and what the results were* (44): these two co-ordinated noun clauses can be translated by simple co-ordinated noun phrases comprising noun plus past participle, introduced by *une dispute au sujet de...*

– *the TV picture is already...* (49): here the TL is more precise in its use of a Future tense.

Lexis

– *rising tide (1):* index for symbol: shift of terms of reference results in loss of image due to TL lack of direct equivalent form, *le flot toujours accroissant*.

– *owned by* (3): this raises the question of who owns a patient's records and really refers to who holds these. The TL can therefore be more specific, but this may require expansion.

– *'Clinicard'* (7): this is a proper name and a neologism in the SL, as is indicated by the use of inverted commas. Since this is likely to be a new technological invention, it would be well to check whether the TL has a similar concept and a neologism to label it. If this is not the case, it may be appropriate to naturalise the name, which would give the same degree of transparency to the main root of the new lexeme whilst preserving the prefix, *clini-* or perhaps substituting *medi-* for *clini-*.

– *hold* (7): to convey this concept of storing information in computer technology the TL actually uses an SL word — *stock* — not used in this domain in the SL; this is naturalised to form a TL infinitive or noun with appropriate endings (*-er/-age*). This SL word appears again in lines 59 and 62 — the translator can decide whether to repeat the first TL term or to vary it, according to TL domain specific use.

– *trial* (12): index for index, but the translator must take care to select the appropriate term for the context, since the SL term is polysemous and there exist different terms in the TL for different SL meanings.

– *offshoot* (15): index for symbol; this rather horticultural image in its figurative sense needs to be translated by the appropriate business term in the TL, thereby incurring the loss of this image.

- *the principal benefit... should be that* (17): TL can find a more specific collocation appropriate to context avoiding the verb *to be* and introducing the noun clause with *dans ce que.*
- *this has implications* (22): again, the TL seeks to find a more specific verb than the verb *to have,* an appropriate collocate for implications.
- *a woman says* (25): here the SL implies, 'makes the claim that', and this underlying meaning should be brought out in the TL lexis selected.
- *tests to administer* (32): another appropriate collocate must be found to go with the term chosen to translate tests in this context. A different TL term may be needed in line 26, for *given a test for it,* where the passive form of a verb may be more appropriate.
- *in traditional paper systems* (34): the translator must decide whether *traditional* refers to paper or to systems in order to make the correct adjectival agreement for number in the TL.
- *squeezed into* (47): this verb reinforces the concept of compressed: the TL uses a term from the semantic field of storage, giving greater lexical cohesion.

Technical vocabulary, which must be checked for accuracy of use in this context:
- *ultrasound scans* (6); *X-Rays* (6); *Megabytes* (27); *formatted data* (27); *burning microscopic pits* (28); *read the data* (29); *software* (31); *audit trail* (42); *digital scans* (46): i.e. indices for indices.

Medical vocabulary: which must also be checked for accuracy of use in this context:
- *clinical trial* (4); *antenatal care* (5); *medical records* (7); *malpractice case* (23) *malpractice suits* (41); *tests* (18).

Stylistic Devices
Emphasis:
- *the women will receive all the tests* (18): TL repeats *toutes* to give parallel structure plus stress; also in TL, expansion and explication.
- *studies a few years ago* (18): the TL inserts a past participle to collocate with studies.
- *that should halve* (30): the TL uses a pronominal verb with an adverbial construction.
- *with mass production* (30): becomes more precisely, *à la suite de,* bringing out a more accurate representation of the sequence of events.
- *to their condition* (18): TL is more specific in its term of reference whilst more general in its scope of reference — *à la maternité* — as the word *condition* is polysemous and could be translated by several different terms according to context (*état, circonstance, situation, condition*).
- *alerting doctors to allergies* (37): the underlying implication is more clearly stated in the TL, *à la possibilité des réactions allerqiques.*
- *compression technique for this* (49): the TL is more precise: *technique pour le compactage de tels renseignements.*
- the TL attempts to vary the form of introduction to a direct quote, avoiding the repeated use of *says,* to give more of a *variation élégante* of style (21, 36, 45).

Cultural References
- *Chelsea and Westminster Hospital* (5): again, as a proper name this should not be translated — note that this refers to one hospital, not two; its function is transparent in the name, although it may be considered helpful to indicate the

geographical location of this by the insertion of the adjective, *londonien*, a very economical function of the TL being that it allows this mechanism rather than having to use *de* or *à* plus the name of the city.

– *British Telecom* (11): this is the name of a public service which has a more or less equivalent function to that of the *PTT*, which term will be adequate for the purposes of this text, since there is no further need to be aware of the differences in scope and function between the two. The translator can retain the SL name and insert a brief note in brackets in the text of the TL acronym.

– *BT Tallis* (15): this is also a proper name, whose function is explained in the text and requires no further note.

– *Nippon Conlux* (31): this proper name can remain the same; the context makes it clear that this is a company and no further note is required.

Punctuation

– As stated in the introduction, dashes (12–13, 20–21, 37–39) are used to insert supplementary information immediately following the referent and this use is recreated in the TT.

– Inverted commas (7) are also used to indicate either neologisms or direct quotes, as in the SL.

Britain Under Siege

This text gives a review of the current state of affairs in Ireland, taking as its starting point a massacre in a pub and offering a brief explanation of the aims and fears of both sides. It supposes a certain background knowledge of the on-going conflict and an interest in the affairs of Ireland.

The target readers of *The Economist*, professional, probably management and senior management, will have just such interests, being keen to understand the context and possible motivation for any event or occurrence, in order to evaluate possible outcomes and how this may affect their professional activity. Given its Europe-wide publication, it would not be unreasonable to expect *The Economist* to seek to avoid particular country-specific political affiliations and adopt a fairly objective stance when presenting such contentious issues.

In order to promote this semblance of objectivity this particular texts adopts the tactic of appearing to report facts and views with no overt or clearly discernible editorial stance. However, the form of use of descriptive terms in relation to the Protestants might seem to imply some kind of sympathy, as does the attempt to present the question from their point of view, stressing the fears of these towards the Catholic community but not attempting to explain the feelings of the latter towards the former. Fortunately, the introduction to the article explains that this forms part of a series intended to look at both sides of the question, starting with the Protestant viewpoint.

Sentence Structure

There is a sense of drama throughout the text, created by the construction of somewhat complex sentences which contain one or more subordinate clauses, with much additional information offered to explain and clarify the main point of the sentence. The idea of comparison is introduced in the first sentence by the adverb *'while'* and as could be expected in a comparison of viewpoints, there are several clauses of opposition introduced by *'but'*. There is further indication of the idea of sides through the introduction of different groups of supporters by means of a parallel construction, *'for those in the Republic'* (8), *'for English fans'* (9). The author also makes use of dashes to insert additional information. There are also several instances of placing the subordinate clause in initial position to heighten the sense of drama and the impression of victimisation. In paragraph 2, the first sentence is divided into two sentences to heighten the sense of drama through shorter clauses.

- *covert steps towards shared sovereignty with the government...* (49): here the TL inserts a past participle to qualify the noun steps and make the translated text more precise, resulting in a relative clause being formed and changing the structure of the sentence by the insertion of this clause between commas following the qualified noun, *shared sovereignty*

Syntax

- *while the British and Irish governments* (1): here the *while* could be taken to imply one or both of two potential meanings, those of simultaneity of occurrence

307

and of contrast between two actions. Due to a lack of a similarly polysemous conjunction, the TL will force the translator to choose to prioritise one of these two.

- *in Northern Ireland* (2): a feminine country name requires *en*.
- *underlying* (4): this present participle becomes a relative clause in the TT.
- *pubs were full* (6): in the TT the word *pub* becomes part of a prepositional phrase of place, thereby removing the effect of stress on the place towards a stress on the people; an impersonal subject is introduced, changing the noun drinker to a verb, *on buvait*.
- *coached by* (10): referring to the noun *équipe* this verbal construction, in the form of a past participle replacing a relative clause, undergoes a transformation in the TT to become a noun phrase introduced by a preposition, *avec son entraîneur*.
- *for those in the Republic of Ireland* (8): it is not immediately clear from the syntax of this sentence who this anaphoric reference relates to; careful consideration will show that the referent is in fact the noun, *drinkers*, but since this noun has been replaced in the TT by a verbal construction with an anonymous subject, *on*, it would be helpful to introduce a new noun referent here in the TL.
- *the cheering* (14): this gerund is transformed into a verbal noun in the TL, in plural form to conform to usage: *les applaudissements*.
- *claimed it had carried out the attack* (17): this is simplified in the TL to give the idea of claiming responsibility for, rather than claiming to have done, an action, thus stressing the source rather than the action.
- *it chose* (18): the impersonal pronoun refers to the UVF but it would seem more stylistically appropriate to use a plural pronoun *ils* to include the two men who were the actual agents of the action as well as the group as a single entity.
- *was faced with* (20): this passive construction in the SL becomes an active one in the TL with N. Ireland as the subject of the verb.
- *have a hand in* (22): this analytical construction in the SL becomes a synthetic one in the TL using the verb *participer*.
- *done in their name* (23): this past participle is expanded to become a relative clause with an impersonal subject, *que l'on fait*.
- *do not feel as strongly* (32): there is a shift in the TT from *feel* as verb to the noun, *sentiments*, introduced by the verb *partager*, which brings out the underlying meaning of the SL construction albeit in a different surface structure.
- *the claimed Britishness* (37): the TL does not have such flexibility in coining nouns by the addition of the suffix *-ness* (although sometimes the suffix *-icité* can be used. Here it may help to expand the single word into a noun phrase, with an inserted noun qualified by the adjective *British*.
- *union with Britain which they cherish* (38): conversely to the previous point, the TL here allows for economy through the adjectival use of a past participle qualifying the noun *union* to replace the SL relative clause.
- *take part in negotiating* (40): the SL phrasal verb can be replaced here by a synthetic TL verb, which must be followed either by an infinitive or by a noun, depending on the verb chosen and given the lack of gerund form in the TL.
- *subvert any such goal* (44): the TL here requires a plural noun.
- *brutal random killings* (45): to avoid the problem of two preceeding adjectives, the TT sets these in apposition to the noun, following this and placed between commas, for greater emphasis.
- *predominantly Catholic united Ireland* (51): similarly, the TT here divides the

noun phrase into two parts, inserting the phrase *de tendance (majoritaire catholique)* in apposition to *Irelande unie.*
- *meant to soften them up* (50): this phrasal verb in the SL can become a synthetic one in the TL.

Lexis
- *'the troubles'* (4): index for symbol: to use the TL equivalent form might mean a shift in meaning towards a more specifically emotive rather than generally disruptive sense. A more appropriate item of lexis should be sought to cover this more general application.

Collocations:
- *articles describing the attitudes* (introduction): in the TL the usual collocate here would be *traiter.*
- *cheering on* (7): following the shift of the noun *drinkers* to verb, *buvait*, the concept of cheering on is rendered by an appropriate collocation expression linked to the verb, *on buvait au succès éventuelle.*
- *English fans* (9): this actually means fans of the English football team, not just fans who happen to be of English nationality; this meaning has to be clearly brought out by means of expansion in the TT.

Faux amis:
- *containing* (10): the appropriate TL term would not derive from the verb *contenir*, which is not appropriate for this aspect of meaning of *contain*, but rather from the construction, *être composé de.*
- *fuel a conflict* (25): unless an appropriate single-word collocate can be found, the verb here may require expansion in the TL to bring out the intended meaning.
- *to do a deal* (49): remember, the TL does not say *faire un accord.*
- *latest round of secret contacts* (46): the TL will have a different contextual collocation for the word *round*; the translator must take care to select one suitable for the intended reference.

Other:
- *proxy* (11): index for index: this term has the meaning, amongst others, of *stand-in*, and this would seem to be best conveyed by the TL noun *substitut.*
- *fail to qualify* (12): this is rendered in the TL by a negative verbal construction which brings out the unstated but implied negative meaning of not managing to do something.
- *the Britishness... the Irishness* (37, 41): here these two nouns, created by the suffix *-ness*, will require insertion of a more specific noun, qualified by the adjective of nationality, for the TL — perhaps the word *'identité'* would be appropriate in this context.
- *cross-border institutions* (42): the TL needs to bring out the underlying implication of this, i.e. that these institutions be shared by and common to both North and South.
- *eventual absorption* (51): two points to note here: (a) the potential faux ami in *eventual* and (b) the potential problem with *absorption* — perhaps *intégration* would be more appropriate, although this may lose some of the effect of the implied take over of one by the other.

Stylistic Devices
- *walked into the pub* (15): in an attempt at economy, the TL adopts a more simple,

general term, *entrer,* in order to avoid having to insert an adverbial phrase of manner which would detract from the impact created by such a brief clause.
- *they describe their political allegiance as...* (30): in the interests of economy this becomes, *ils affirment une allégiance.*

Imagery:
- *underdog team* (7): index for icon/also symbol: an idiomatic use of description which may have to be lost through use of a more neutral form of description in the TL.

Personification:
- *union... is slipping away* (39): this can be recreated in the TL.
- *covert steps* (49): can be recreated in same figurative sense.

Cultural References
- underpinning any potential interpretation of this text there has to be at the very least an awareness of the fundamental issues at stake in Northern Ireland. This could be presumed to hold true for the TL reader, given his or her professional status and level of education.
- *'the troubles'* (4): this noun has taken on the status of a proper name in the SL, requiring no further definition. A similar noun needs to be found in the TL, used in inverted commas to indicate its status.
- *Ulster Volunteer Force* (16): since this is a culture specific name of an organisation, the translator will need to give a translation in the text, perhaps giving the SL name in a footnote; the text itself supplies a descriptive explanation of the nature of the group, so no further notes would be necessary.
- *describe their political allegiance as unionist* (30): a brief note here could recall the dates of Union between GB and Ireland and the date of the founding of Eire, to set this remark in context, although the translator may decide this is not necessary.
- *mainland Britain* (30): it is not very often that the SL needs to make such a distinction, unlike the TL which has to differentiate between French *départements* and those overseas possessions designated either as *départements* or *territoires;* the concept will not thus be unfamiliar to the TL reader.
- *Albert Reynolds* (43): again, this name requires no note as there is a reference to the man's political role immediately following the name.
- *'Loyalist' paramilitaries* (44): translation may give the effect of index for symbol: it may be helpful to add an explanatory reminder note here.

Punctuation
- *'the troubles'* (4): the use of quotation marks shows that this term, although widely used, is in a way a neologistic and very specifically referential use of an item of lexis having an existing, broader sense.
- *'Loyalist' paramilitaries* (44): the word Loyalist should be reproduced in the TT in inverted commas to show that adjective has the force of a proper name, given the context and the use of capital letters.
- *'peace process'* (47): the same is true for this noun phrase, which has a neologistic use as a proper noun, although both elements of the phrase can exist and be used independently of each other.

The Policy Paper that caused the Storm

This text from *The European* appeared a week after the same newspaper had published details of Germany's 'blueprint for a hard core of European states'. The text appeared on page two, accompanied by discussion articles evaluating the proposals, with titles such as 'Why some can't be more equal', and 'Uproar over hard-core blueprint', which illustrate the polemic nature of the document, starting on the front page and continuing onto page two. The text itself is described as 'fuller extracts from the blueprint for a hard core of European states', a document published by the ruling party in the German Parliament at that time, the Christian Democrats. The actual text given here is the complete extract published except for the omission of the final two paragraphs relating to the Franco-German axis and the need to preserve the sovereign status of the member states through reinforcement of external security.

Target readers will include professionals and those involved in international, pan-European business. They will be keen to know the document on which discussions and protests have been based in order to evaluate the potential impact of the proposals on a national and personal (business) level.

It is of interest to the translator to query whether this text was produced simultaneously in different EU languages by a trained team of translators, or whether there was a source text in German which was then translated into other EU languages for the various member states. The document uses EU terminology in referring to the institutions and constitution of the union. Since this is an extract from a political document seeking clarity of use of terms and avoiding potential ambiguity of interpretation, there is a structure of cause and effect, the statement of obligations and a certain admonitory tone. Economy of use of language relies on consensus as to the 'meaning' of terms and through SL linguistic devices, such as the creation of compound adjectives, e.g. *community spirited* (44).

Sentence Structure

There is a tendency to state the main point of each sentence first, followed by a subordinate clause to qualify, modify or extend this information.
- in paragraphs 2 and 3 the first word is in fact the predicate of the sentence at the end of para 1, *the main causes include...* (8)
- *all existing institutions...* (17).
- *the task of the hard core is* (41).

Sometimes the main clause is introduced by a link phrase (*with regard to*), prepositional phrase (*in the monetary field*) or adverbial clause (*to achieve this*); this is because further subordinate clauses are also dependent on the main clause and for the sake of clarity of expression it becomes necessary for the main clause to precede these latter.
- embedding of supplementary information is achieved through the use of brackets (46) or dashes (17).
- important points consist of a single sentence which in turn constitutes a paragraph (25, 41, 43).

Syntax

- *caused the storm* (title): note the use of the definite article to indicate a specific storm, namely the one referred to in other articles accompanying this text.
- *if no solution... is found, the Union... will... become* (3): the TL has a different tense sequence to imply future possibility of non-occurrence, resulting in a mix of tenses, l'Imparfait and the Future.
- *no solution is found* (3): here the TL introduces an anonymous subject, *on*, to avoid the passive voice, and the negative determinant shifts from the noun in the SL to the verb in the TL, *n'arrivait pas à trouver*.
- *loosely-knit grouping* (6): this compound adjective consisting of adverb plus past participle becomes a single past participle in the TL, *décousu*. The SL term implies unity in place of a previous lack of unity, but as yet not rendered more solid, not yet completely drawn together; the TL term, with its prefix *dé-* implies that a pre-existing unity is being fragmented, undergoing a break-down — i.e. a contradictory image.
- *the main causes include* (7): shift due to use of verb *figurer* involves use of *parmi*.
- *all things national* (14): introduction of a relative clause here in the TT.
- *changes must be geared to* (19): just as in the NHS document, the translator has used an active verb form instead of passive, and the synthetic form *viser* for the SL phrasal verb.
- *take on the features* (23): the TL substitutes an active verb for one of passive deep structure, *se verra doter de*, giving a shift in emphasis as to the originator of the change, from the Commission to external forces.
- *existing* (17): present participle used adjectivally becomes a simple adjective, *actuelles*.
- *must be reformed. (doivent être réformés); must be geared (doivent viser)* (18); *should be sanctioned (devrait être approuvé); it must be decided (il faut ainsi décider); should be replaced (devrait être remplacé); no country should be allowed (il est esssentiel qu'aucun pays ne puisse)* (37); all of these express both wish and command, using the passive voice to emphasis action by an external force on the object of the action (subject of the passive verb); the TL opts for different mechanisms to render these underlying intentions, perhaps in the interest of stylistic variation as much as for reasons of clarity of syntax.
- *means striking a better balance* (25): this gerund is omitted in the TL, as the use of the verb *exiger* plus noun renders the verbal aspect of *striking* redundant here.
- *this approach might well encourage* (33): the TL uses the conditional form of *risquer* here in a conditional clause introduced by *sinon*.
- *yet to be more specified* (37): here the TL resorts to an impersonal expression, *qu'il resterait à préciser* (note the use of *à* plus infinitive to avoid the passsive voice) apparently using the conditional form in the journalistic style of reporting an as yet unconfirmed fact.
- *use its right of veto* (38): the possessive pronoun is replaced in the TL by a definite article.
- *recognisably more community spirited* (44): expansion of the adverb, *recognisably*, plus the comparative element, *more*, into *un degré d'esprit communautaire qui sera plus élevé et plus évident*.
- *institutional overhaul... multispeed Europe* (16, 30): where the SL uses juxtaposition to imply a relationship between a noun and an adjective derived from another noun, the TL requires insertion of a partitive *des* or an article *une*.

- *to counteract* (42): for a change, the TL introduces an analytical verbal construction where the SL has a single verb, albeit composed of verb plus prefix.
- *the task of the hard core is, by giving... to counteract* (41): here the TL turns this clause of manner into one of purpose, *de donner afin de faire...* , making *donner* the verb linked to task, instead of *faire equilibre* — a shift in syntactical relationships within the sentence which slightly modifies the description of of the task and the explanation of its purpose, but not so significantly as to alter the overall impact.
- *is emerging* (46): here the translator has deliberately recreated the continous aspect of the SL verb through the use of the expression *en voie de* plus noun (derived from a verb — *émerger*).
- *as believed in Germany* (49): this passive construction becomes an impersonal active one in the TL with the verb requiring the insertion of an object pronoun, *comme on le croît...*
- *is the cornerstone* (49): the TL prefers a more descriptive verb than the verb *to be* — *constitue.*
- *alongside* (50): useful stylistic expression in the TL, *va de pair avec.*

Lexis

As stated in the introduction, there are several examples of **EU/EC terminology** whose appropriate and officially recognised TL equivalents (index for index) must be used. These terms include:

- *unification* — the TT has *union* — does this actually refer to the same conceptual content, or does it shift the frame of reference from the process to the existing body? (2); *the Council, the Commission* (17); *member states* (26); *multi-speed approach* — a compound is coined in the TL, *multivitesse* possibly by analogy with *à 2 vitesses* (31); *the principle of unanamity* (36).

Also more **general terms relating to politics and government**: (index for index):

- *policy paper* (title); *nation-state* (14); *law-making body* — note *organe de législation; a second Chamber* translated as *assemblée* to evoke TL concept here (20); *democratisation* (25); *quorum* — Latin loan word used in TL as in SL (37); *use its right of veto to block* (38); *integration* (50).

Collocations:

- *caused the storm* (title): here an appropriate collocate is used, one which has greater explicitness and intensity than the more neutral verb, *cause.*
- *a critical juncture* (2): becomes *étape décisive,* collocating also with *développement.*
- *closer association* (5): *association plus étroite.*
- *regressive nationalism* (12): translated in the TL as a calque, this term is part of political discourse. It is not clear why the term appears in inverted commas unless it had been frequently quoted at the time of publication of the article.
- *assume the functions* (22): this is reformulated to give a passive construction, *se verra doter de.*
- *perform tasks* (22): *s'acquitter des tâches.*
- *intensify... cooperation and deepen integration* (39).
- *hard core* (41): a calque in the TL, *noyau dur.*
- *joint action* (44); note that this becomes a plural noun in the TL, *actions collaboratives.*
- *strong signs* (45): *de fortes indications.*
- *meet convergence criteria* (47): *remplir les critères de convergence.*

– *additional element* (50): *élément supplémentaire.*

Other:
– *problem* (2): sometimes we are told to avoid the use of *problème* in the TL and look for alternatives such as *question, sujet,* although *problème* seems most appropriate here.
– *subgroupings of states* (7): use of the suffix *-uscule* gives a single word, hence also greater economy and extended impact, this suffix often being used in a derogatory sense (see Larousse dictionnaire).
– *over-extension* (9): creation of a term of greater degree/intensity in the SL by use of a prefix — this prefix is paralleled in the TL by *surextension,* the difference being that the SL still regards the term as a not yet conventionalised compound of two elements as signalled by the use of the hyphen, although this may also just be an example of idiosyncratic use of the hyphen.
– *originally set up for* (9): in the TL this phrasal verb becomes a single word, synthetic form, *prévus.* The use of this TL verb seems more appropriate here than in TT line 54.
– *laid down in* (36): is also translated by *prévu.*
– *stipulated in* (48): becomes *prévus dans,* where we find the same syntactic function (past participle) but perhaps a slight shift in emphasis from obligation to 'making provision for, prescribing' (as seen in line 8) but not necessarily making a rule or requirement? — an example of polyvalency of a TL term?
– *cater for a membership* (10): expansion through insertion of the word *exigences,* gives *pourvoir à.*
– *genuine* (20): here the TL chooses *vrai,* opposite of *faux* (not *authentique* as opposed to *copie*).
– *democratisation means* (25): here the TL selects a verb which brings out the true contextual intent of this catch-all verb, *to mean* — i.e. *to require* — by use of *exigera.*

Stylistic Devices
Alliteration:
– *better balance* (25): lost in TL.
– *strong signs* (45): lost in TL.
– *convergence criteria* (47): retained in TL by use of similar forms/terms.
Expansion:
– *all things national* (14): *tout ce qui a rapport aux interêts nationaux.*
– *to achieve this* (31): *afin de réaliser tout ceci* — ensures broader application of anaphoric reference to all preceding recommendations, not just to the last one to be mentioned.
– *to intensify cooperation and deepen integration* (39): the TL inserts a noun, using a demostrative pronoun for the second TL required occurrence of that noun, *le niveau de... et celui de...*
Imagery
– *the cornerstone of...* (49): in the SL this recalls the metaphor of the building of Europe, whereas in the TL a more neutral expression is used, *le facteur-clé.*
Accumulation for emphasis — to be retained in TT:
– *the Council, the Commission, the presidency and the European parliament* (17).
Creating a balance:
– *if not, then at least* (13); *on the one hand, on the other* (26–28).

Cultural References
Not many to comment on here.
- *The Maastricht Treaty* (5): known to TL reader.
- *a 'Europe à la carte'* (34): the ST uses the French expression quite justifiably to convey a particular concept, as this use is common in the SL. By retaining this expression in its TL form as used in the SL, there will be some loss of exoticism in the TL but no loss of meaning or impact.
- *Ireland* (46): which Ireland is meant here, i.e. which part of Ireland has an independent membership of the EU?

Punctuation
- *a second Chamber* (23); SL capital letter, TL lower case — why?
- *article N* (36): capital letter also in TL, probably because the common source for SL and TL is the actual treaty.
- *'regressive nationalism'* (12): is this a neologism or a quote?
- *'variable geometry'* or *'multispeed approach'* (31): judging by the use of inverted commas here, these must be new terms still in the process of being adopted. This may mean that there is as yet no consensus in the TL as to the equivalent terms/forms.
- *'Europe à la carte'* (34); inverted commas signal use of loan words but also of a fixed expression expected to be known to the reader through other connotations, i.e. eating out.

EU Fugaces Labuntur Communitates

This text (from *The Economist*) takes as its subject the change of name of the European Union and attempts to unravel the mystery of the defining characteristics of this new Union, noting where it differs in the scope of its responsibilities from the former EC. The question of who is responsible for what in Brussels will be of interest to *Economist* readers, mainly businessmen and women, students of business and professional people in general. There is a tendency to assume an appeal to a certain élite, namely those who will be in a position, thanks to their level of education, to understand the Latin title, or at least to recognise its origin. It may be that more TL readers will actually share this understanding than those of the SL article. Even the subject for discussion is somewhat pedantic in nature, attempting to unravel precise definitions for those interested in linguistic and terminological precision as part of their understanding of the overall picture, with a clever play on national characteristics to add a humourous note.

Sentence Structure
The text is divided into clear paragraphs, each dealing with a particular aspect requiring explanation. As befits a complex subject, the sentences tend to have at least one subordinate clause in addition to the main clause; often several subordinate clauses are listed (12–15, *ouvrir, renforcer, donner*) in a desire for comprehensive inclusion of information or examples.

Syntax
– *pour enfin s'habituer* (1–2): in the ST there is a co-ordinating construction implying equal value to both verbs, *stop* and *become*. In the TT the verb *become* is subordinated to the verb *stop*, the second action being expressed as the result of the first, in order to bring out in a more explicit manner the relationship between the two actions.
Adverbial expressions:
– *reluctantly* (4): *a contrecoeur*.
– *in time* (38) *au fil des années*.
– *we have not had much help* (40): the TT changes the syntax of the sentence, making the authorities the subject of the verb and *we* the indirect object.
– *increasingly* (37) *de plus en plus*.
Verbs:
– *now familiar* (5): becomes adverb plus past participle, *déjà connu*.
– *bringing the union with it* (8): the TL opts for a second, parallel relative clause construction to mirror that of *which came into force*.
– *be Union business* (29): the TL prefers a more specific term than the verb *to be*: *incomberait*.
– *anything to do with* (28): the SL avoids the repetition of *business*, but the concept is the same. The TL does likewise, using *tout ce qui toucherait*, with the Conditional form implying lack of specific definition and possibility or doubt (the concept of reporting rumour or possibility rather than fact).

- *why he would be using the name sparingly* (26): here the TL substitutes a noun, *l'utilisation*, for the verb *use*, and therefore an adjective for the adverb.
- *led by Britain and France* (30): the concept of *led* is conveyed by an adverbial phrase, *avec en tête*, as *mené* would seem to imply active leading or incitement to act, rather than being in the forefront of those voicing an opinion.
- *believing* (38): *dans la conviction que* — present participle becomes a (verbal) noun phrase. As a result of this decision, the adverbial phrase *perhaps wrongly* (38) has to be transformed into an adjective, *erronée* (referring to the noun *belief*) plus adverb *peut-être*.
- *a reminder that* (48): beomes a verb in the TL with subject *ce qui*.

Deictics:
- *abandon the now familiar EC* (5): the TL inserts a noun to specify the nature of the acronym *EC — abandonner… ce terme, de la CE*.
- *historical ones* (37): *ceux historiques*.
- *confusion reigns* (23): shift from verb to noun with *introducer — c'est la confusion totale*.
- *a reminder that… still exist* (48): TL inverts noun and verb forms, to give *ce qui rappelle l'existence*.

Lexis
- *something-between-a-sigh-and-an-expletive* (5–6): the use of hyphens to link all the words of this extended compound adjective indicates that the whole is intended to function almost as a single unit of meaning or lexeme. The SL is making a play on the onomatopoeia of the sound produced by the combination of the letters *e* and *u*. This particular combination of phonemes gives, in the TL, the effect of hesitation in the middle of an utterance, so at this level the two phonemes can still convey some connotative value of relevance to the subject matter of the text. However, they do not function as a sigh or as an expletive and so it may be more appropriate to create a descriptive phrase which brings out the underlying meaning rather than aiming to recreate the phonic and associative values.
- *what Maastricht is supposed to do* (2): where the SL uses a more general term for action, *do* (usually, as a point of style one avoids *do* and *make* in the TL), the TL prefers a more specific verb of action, *réaliser*.
- *Euro-fudge* (9): index for index: the SL constructs a compound noun using the prefix *Euro* — and a term of idiomatic expression, *fudge*. One aspect of the polysemy of the word *fudge* (literally, sticky soft toffee; figuratively, bluff, avoiding the issue) is reflected in the use of the word *viscosity*, which also has the concept of being sticky as one of its constituent elements of meaning.
- *the viscosity of the answer* (7): TL can use a similar term taken from semantic field of biology.
- *come into force* (8): *entrer en vigueur*.
- *four-square within the EC* (15): icon for icon, with equivalent meaning but different form, *reste bel et bien la responsabilité de la CE*.
- *the whole construction* (17): symbol for symbol: this rather general term from the semantic field of building (recalling the metaphor of 'building Europe', is replaced in the TL by a term describing the abstract rather than concrete nature of the administrative set-up.
- *single decision-taking process* (19): single can have several meanings in the SL (single person, single room, game of singles in tennis, the single most impor-

tant issue) and the translator must select the appropriate term for this context and collocation.

- *legal* (20): the word legal in the SL can be translated by different terms in the TL depending on which aspect of legality is intended: *légale* — permitted by law; *juridique* — according to/pertaining to the law or laws themselves; *judiciare* — pertaining to the system which implements these laws. See also line 36, *legal accuracy*.
- *persona* (21): index for index: this Latin term can also be used in the TL legal jargon.
- *John Major fluffed his attempt* (25): an idiomatic use of the word *fluff*, usually found as a noun. The TL opts for a slightly more neutral register with a word which conveys the meaning of failure, which is one aspect of meaning of *fluff* in this context.
- *sparingly* (26): this adverb can have different collocations but the underlying meaning is one of careful use, not excessive. In this context, the TL adopts as the guiding signification the concept of frequency of use in the choice of translation equivalent.

Fixed expressions:
- *in other words* (23): *autrement dit*: icon for icon.
- *day-to-day affairs* (33): TL single word, *quotidien*.
- *to a man* (46): icon for icon: but in the TL this becomes more generic adverbial phrase, *sans exception*.

Stylistic Devices
Emphasis:
- *c'est précisément… qu'arrive* (1): this introductory construction, *c'est* plus extended adverbial clause of time with embedded clause of result, followed by *que* and main clause, serves to highlight the irony of this particular incidence and co-incidental timing of the two events. This is also an example of stylistic inversion.

Imagery:
- *'a three-pillared union'* (27): symbol for symbol: this image is retained in the TL as this is one generally used in reference to this European concept. This usage is indicated by the quotation marks surrounding the image, indicating that this is indeed a quote of a (probably still quite new) term.
- *rebaptising itself* (44): this metaphor of birth and new beginnings can be retained in the TL.

Expansion:
- *the new Union is the old Community with two additions* (9): the TL insers an adjective to bring out the implied meaning, *est identique à*.
- *with two additions* (10): stylistic expansion, changing the noun *addition* to an adjectival phrase defining a deictic pronoun, *avec ceci de supplémentaire*.

Cultural References
- *EU Fugaces labuntur Communitates* (title): this title could be said to be both iconic, in terms of use of component words, and symbolic, in its connotative value on two levels. There are thus to be found problems of lexis and problems of cultural reference. The fact of it being in Latin stands for a certain level of complexity, and evokes the obscurity of legal jargon, since it is unlikely that many of the readers of *The Economist* will in fact have studied Latin to a level

which would enable them to understand the meaning, not to mention recognise the quote. The use of Latin also implies a traditional background with training in the classics, and indirectly recalls the earlier and different confederations of European states, that of the Holy Roman Empire and that of the Roman Empire. It is also somewhat surprising to find such a quote in an article from this source, and it would be interesting to find out how and why the author used this. However, whilst much of the essence will be lost, some of the superficial meaning should be transparent, namely the acronym EU and the word *Communitates*. In fact this is a quote from Horace (*Carmina* 2, 14, 2): *Eu fugaces labuntur anni*, an expression of regret at the passing of time (*Eu* — alas; *fugaces* — fleeting, swift: *labuntur* — slip, pass, elapse, be lost: *anni* — years).

The question for the translator to resolve is whether to imitate the ST author and use the same quote, especially since the TL reader could be expected to be more likely to have studied some Latin during his school years. If not, the translator must at least ensure that he is aware of the meaning of the title, in order to formulate some kind of descriptive title which encapsulates that meaning. What would be interesting from a stylistic point of view would be to find a suitable quote in the SL which could express similar sentiments and reasonably be expected to exist in translation. One possibility would be to select a quote from Shakespeare, for example, taking the question of which name to use, one could look for the TL equivalent of 'What's in a name — (a rose by any other name would smell as sweet)?' (*Romeo and Juliet*).

Terms relating to Europe, all of which should be familiar to the target reader in both countries, with an official form in each language:
- EU (title, 6): EC (5); the Maastricht treaty (7); the Common Market (1); the European Parliament (13); The Council of Ministers (41); The European Coal and Steel Community and the Atomic Energy Community (48).
- also to note, the place name '*Brussels*' (14) has its own form in the TL.

Punctuation
- '*a three-pillared union*' (27): note the use of inverted commas, as discussed above (Stylistic Devices: Imagery).
- there is the question of when to use capital or lower-case letters in the TL to translate terms such as the EC and EU (5–6). Usage will dictate this rather than rules of syntax.
- use of dashes to insert additional information (12–16, 17–19): this is retained in the TT.

Q. Europe by Eurotunnel?
A. The Easy Way to Go!

This is the text of a publicity brochure produced by Eurotunnel to advertise its services under the pretext of giving information to potential passengers prior to the opening. Information is presented in the form of question and answer, to establish a sense of dialogue between the passenger and the company, also perhaps to give the company a more personalised image. Although Eurotunnel information is sometimes produced in France and then translated into other languages where local information is required, in the case of this text it is clear that the SL is English, since the heading states 'Europe by Eurotunnel' which can only be targeting the UK mainland. Further confirmation comes in the second sub-section of part one, where we read about the tunnels which *link Britain and continental Europe*. The first heading, *Europe by Eurotunnel* also confirms this.

Given the need for specific travel information there will be some content of culture-specific information such as place names, but also a degree of cross-cultural content where the actual services on offer are being described. Since the questions are ones which could be expected to be of relevance to all passengers regardless of language of origin, there should be no problems of conceptual transfer, although the translator has to be aware that given the text type, the overriding aim has to be acceptability of style and register in conformity with TL norms for this text type and in relation to the target reader. This may often lead to rephrasing, reformulation and substitution of images in order to create for the TT an effect similar to that of the ST.

However, the layout and format of the text will also impose constraints in terms of order of presentation of information and selection of units to express that information, especially if the translator is working to a pre-established format in terms of space available and typographical use of that space. Certain devices permitting economy in the SL may require careful consideration and selection of corresponding TL units in order to respect these constraints.

Despite the personalised approach and the use of first and second persons of the verb, factual information is conveyed through the use of different verbs (Future tense) in the Passive voice; perhaps since the agent is known, this tactic avoids the frequent repetition of the company name.

Sentence Structure
In view of its informative function, the need for simplicity and clarity is paramount. Each sentence contains one point, expanded and developed by supplementary information which is often presented in the form of two co-ordinated items:
- *road vehicles will be carried... and through trains will carry...* (13).

Sentences are sometimes formulated as a short answer to a question, giving information but not having a main verb:
- *about thirty-five minutes from platform to platform with twenty-five minutes in the tunnel itself* (39).
- *only if you comply with...* (79): this answer contains the second half of a first

conditional sentence, the first part being the implied repetition in affirmative form (*you can take*) of the actual question, *can I take my pet?*
- *about eight minutes, if it is completely full* (141); this is another example of half of a first conditional sentence, the main verb here being the implied repeated auxiliary (*it will take...*).

Syntax
- Use of the **Future tense** to describe the facts, perhaps because this brochure came out with the introduction of the service — see the first sentence, *from June 1993*. Subsequent brochures may well shift to the Present Simple for fact. The TL has adopted the same tense.
- *when will Eurotunnel open...* (4): *quand ouvrira...*
- *queues will be rare* (96): *les bouchons seront exceptionnels.*
- *there will be no further controls on arrival* (75): *il n'y aura pas d'autres contrôles...*
- **Passive verb** forms are used in the ST to describe services and benefits offered, stressing thereby the ease of access and use for the passenger by avoidance of active verbs which might imply significant effort. However, given the lack of enthusiasm for repeated use of the Passive Voice in the TL, there is an attempt at stylistic variation through the use of various other constructions.
- *Euroshuttles are scheduled to carry cars* (5): *Eurotunnel ouvrira son service de navettes aux voitures...* Loss of passive through personnalisation of the company.
- *through-train services are also scheduled to run* (7): again, there is nominalisation, but this time the passive voice is retained: *le transport des autocars... sera assuré.*
- *cars... will be directed to... heavy goods vehicles will be carried* (24): in the TL there is an inversion of two verbs, so that *directed* becomes *seront transportés*, whereas the verb *carried* is translated by *seront dirigés vers*. Since there is no essential alteration to the meaning, this reversal is not significant. Note, however, the use of *transporter* for *carry* in collocation with *vehicles.*
- *heavy goods vehicles will be carried* (27): passive voice is retained in the TL.
- *terminals... will be well-equipped* (29): the TL paraphrases this to give the same message, *assureront tous les services habituels,* although the omission of the concept of 'well' detracts from the emphasis on (implied) superiority.
- *the air will not be polluted* (36): again, the TL retains the passive voice.
- *strict security procedures will be used* (81): passive in the TT — *des procédures strictes seront mises en places.*
- *terminals will be well-signposted* (119): passive again, but the TL again omits the adverb, *well*, giving only *les terminaux seront fléchés.*
- Use of **gerunds and present participles**:
- *as all the railway and shuttle locomotives using the tunnel...* (35): SL present participle is transformed into a relative clause which is also reformulated without any change in information effect — *les locomotives qui tireront les navettes...*
- *with passenger shuttles leaving...* (43): SL gerund following a preposition becomes a noun in the TL, *avec un départ de navettes passagers.*
- *by telephoning... or listening* (44): here the SL gerund also follows a preposition, but this particular preposition use has a corresponding form in the TL — *en* plus present participle.
- *in the event of fire breaking out* (60): gerund (the fact of something happening) used to form a conditional sentence instead of the imperfect form of the verb,

linked with the conditional form in the SL to imply the hypothetical, less probable nature of the event. The TL creates the same effect by use of the adverbial phrase, *dans l'hypothèse exceptionnelle d'un feu* together with the Future tense, which, by contravening expectation, may appear more definitive and therefore more reassuring.

- *to prevent animals (from) straying… to prevent accidental import of rabies* (86): this gerund follows the preposition *from*, which is an obligatory use after the verb *to prevent* used in conjunction with another verb in the SL. In the TL, however, *empêcher* is preceded by *pour* and followed by the preposition *de* plus an infinitive — *pour empêcher les animaux de circuler* (note the shift in emphasis from preventing access to preventing presence in the tunnel). In the second example the verb *prevent* is followed by a noun (here one created from a verb) — *l'introduction*.

Other:
- *find out* (46): this phrasal verb implying action on the part of the passenger becomes a passive verb in the TL implying instead effort on the part of the service-provider, *vous serez informé*.
- *extinguish any fire* (62): the SL indefinite article, in conjunction with the use of the 2nd form of conditional sentence, adds to the concept of minimal likelihood. The same effect is created in the TL by the use of an adverbial phrase, *dans l'hypothèse exceptionnelle d'un feu… éteindront tout feu*.
- *there is no slot to miss if you are unexpectedly delayed* (101): another first conditional sentence, with a different first part to the condition; where there would normally be a Future tense we find a Present Simple for habitual fact. The TL paraphrases this to bring out the same meaning — *vous ne risquerez donc pas de 'rater votre navette'*.
- *as you drive in to the terminals* (121): this is an adverbial clause of time, not concession or comparison. However the TL omits this extra description of actions, simply stating that *dans les deux terminaux la signalisation sera…*
- *what happens if my car breaks down* (143): the use of the first conditional sentence form here implies that this event is more likely than that of a fire breaking out (see gerunds above). The TT distances the passenger from this event by talking in more general terms of *si une voiture est en panne*. This is because the form of the TL questions is that of the third person singular, a more impersonal and factual approach, not personalised as in the SL.
- *until directed to stop* (137): emphasis shifts again from action, *stop*, to service and result, *jusqu'à l'emplacement qui vous sera indiqué*.
- *the ride will be smoother than on a normal train journey* (148): *the ride* — noun from verb, becomes more general, *un service agréable* — this could be said to constitute an omission of detail. Also the implied negative comparison, which would normally require insertion of an object pronoun in the TL, is thus avoided.
- *you may choose* (154): this modal verb contrasts with Future Simple for fact, indicating possibility in the sense of a choice from a permitted range of activities. In the TL, the modal *pourrez* is used in the Future tense but the verb *choose* is not translated, the concept of choice being found only implicitly in the listing of possible activities.

Lexis
Terminology of cross-Channel travel and transport, some of which will already exist in both languages and some of which will have been developed or created

in both SL and TL culture at more or less the same time, so there should be no problem in finding the appropriate terms, verbs and collocations:

- *Euroshuttles* (5) — the SL has a greater facility for neologism by the combination of the prefix Euro- with other nouns than has the TL, which simpy describes this as *service de navettes*.
- *through-train services* (14): index for icon: the concept of a through-train is somewhat unclear in this text, unless it is meant to be similar to that of the roll-on roll-off ferry. The TT avoids any decisions by simply describing these as *trains de voyageurs et de marchandises*. The resulting loss of information is not significant, since the same details are also given in section 6.
- *Eurotunnel* (4, 13): this trade name is used in both SL and TL.
- *freight vehicles* (5): index for index: this is supposed in the TL to refer to *heavy goods vehicles* which are mentioned later in the same section — *les poids lourds*.
- *single track railway tunnels* (11): this is another example of economy through combination and juxtaposition, requiring the insertion of a preposition in the TL to show purpose of use *tunnels ferroviaires à voie unique*.
- *road vehicles* (12) *véhicules routiers*.
- *shuttles* (13) *navettes; single-deck or double-deck shuttles — navettes simple pont ou double pont*: index for index.
- *frontier controls* (72): *contrôles frontaliers* — the TL adjective is formed in a similar fashion to *routier — cross-Channel routes* (88): here the TL is more specific in referring to *modes de transport trans-Manche*, since what is being compared is not the routes taken but the different forms of travel available to cross the Channel.
- *approach road* (120): *route d'accès*.
- *tollbooth* (128): *le péage*.

Lexis of safety (3):
- *will the tunnels leak: peut-il y avoir des fuites* (120). This use of an impersonal nominalised construction helps to make the event seem less threatening, by avoiding the mention of the word *tunnel*.
- *water impermeable chalk marl: craie bleue impérméable* (56).
- *concrete tunnel lining* (56): the TT omits the information that the lining is of concrete, simply citing *les parois du tunnel*. It may be that for some this information would have given further reassurance, which is this aim of this section.
- *waterproof seal: un revêtement étanché* (57) refers back to the concept of *lining*, but omits any specific mention of the word *seal*, obviously believing this to be implicit in the word *étanché*.
- *evacuate: évacuer; fire detection and suppression systems: systèmes... de détection et d'extinction; extinguish any fire: éteindront tout feu; sealed and fire-resistant doors: portes coupe-feu étanches* (60).

Collocations:
- *services are scheduled to run* (7): *le transport... sera assuré*.
- *cars... will be directed to... heavy goods vehicles will be carried* (24): as stated above, the two verbs are reversed, and the TL uses *transporter* for *carried*, choosing a more specific verb which is appropriate to the context.
- *fire... breaking out* (60): there is no verb in the TL, this being replaced by an adverbial clause, so no need for an appropriate collocation.
- *extinguish a fire* (62): *éteindre*.

- *board the shuttle* (75): again, TT avoids collocation by paraphrase, *sur le terminal de départ.*
- *comply with regulations* (79): *respecter la législation sur…*
- *will have extensive passenger facilities* (123): *(offriront) une gamme étendue de services aux passagers.*
- *put the handbrake on, switch off the engine* (138): *serrer le frein à main, couper le contact.*

Other:
- *the Smart Route to Europe* (3): index for symbol: by analogy with such terms as 'smart cards', this implies a link with the computer age and defies anyone to challenge its supremacy in terms of speed and ease of access/use.
- *a separate passenger coach for their drivers* (28): a train coach, thus *un wagon séparé.*
- *disabled passengers* (29): the TL uses a more specific, less euphemistic or politically correct term, *handicapés.*
- *exhaust fumes* (36): *gaz d'échappement.*
- *a queue* (96): the TL has *embouteillages* and *bouchon* here, which is perhaps not quite the same thing in this context.
- *sophisticated fire-detection and suppression systems* (61): a single noun, *systems,* qualified by three adjectives, two of which are compound, with *fire-* being the first part of both the latter compound adjectives *(fire-detection, fire-suppression).*
- *whenever it suits you* (95): this fixed expression could have been translated by a similar expression in the TL, but here the TL has *à n'importe quel moment,* which is not so specifically directed to convenience.
- *peak periods* (95): icon for icon: *en période de pointe.*
- *twenty four hours a day, 365 days a year* (115): the SL has two parallel structures to express frequency, using the indefinite article. The TL, however, requires different prepositions, *24 heures sur 24, 365 jours par an.*
- *feel seasick* (150): *avoir le mal de mer.*
- *room to walk around and stretch your legs* (159): icon for icon: here there is an example of economy through compression but without loss: these two concepts are rendered by one expression in the TL, *vous dégourdir les jambes.*
- *how long will the journey take* (38); *short journey* (160): in the first case the term used is *trajet,* meaning *trip* or *crossing,* but in the second case, the TL uses *voyage,* perhaps for stylistic variation.

Stylistic Devices
- as stated in the introduction, the text makes use of the technique of **question and answer,** with first and second person pronouns, to lend an appearance of simplicity as well as to create a sense of rapport between the potential passenger and the company, thus mimicking a telephone conversation. However, in the TL the translator has opted for a more impersonal form of question using the third person singular to highlight facts rather than the second person to create rapport and a personalised approach. Rather incongrously, however, we find questions asked in the third person and answered in the second person:
- *pourra-t-on emmener des animaux… seulement si vous respectez…* (78–80)

In the TL as in the SL the **second person form** *vous* can be used for either singular or plural, but any adjectives or past participles will have to agree for number and gender, so that the translator has to know, or to decide, whether the

dialogue is between Eurotunnel and an imaginary customer in the singular or all potential customers. Given that the question is asked in the first person singular, it would be reasonable to assume a singular addressee for the response, which is what the TT has done, as we find:
- *vous serez informé* (45); *à peine arrivé* (94).

Questions begin either with question words, *when, who, where, how...* or with auxiliaries which indicate fact, habit, obligation, necessity or permission:
- *do I drive my car through the tunnel* (33): TL has no such interrogative auxiliary — *conduira-t-on*.
- *will the tunnels leak* (54): *peut-il avoir des fuites* — the use of the modal reinforces the concept of probability where the SL appears more factual.
- *can I take my pet* (78): *pourra-t-on*, note use of Future tense to conform to other questions.
- *do I need to book* (93): *faudra-t-il réserver* — the TL questions being in the third person singular, this allows the use of the impersonal verb *falloir.*
- *how do I pay/find the terminals* (118, 127): *comment arrivera-t-on aux terminaux.*

The above technique seems to dominate to the extent of no other rhetorical device being immediately obvious, apart from that of expansion. This explicitation occurs wherever there may be underlying assumptions based on culture-specific knowledge:
- *what about rabies* (84): the translator makes this question more explicit to reflect for the TL reader the underlying reasoning and assumptions of the SL reader — *comment la propagation de la rage sera-t-elle évitée.*

Cultural References
- *British Rail and SNCF* (6–7): it is interesting to note that the acronym *SNCF* is not explained in the SL, nor is the reference to British Rail in the TL probably because the SL and TL readers are expected to have seen sufficient media coverage on the Tunnel to be aware of what these refer to.
- *continental Europe* (12): icon for symbol: this way of describing Europe is particularly pertinent to the SL reader, and it attempts to remind the reader that Britain is actually part of Europe, hence the more specific definition.
- *direct access from the M20* (19): here the TL inserts the noun *autoroute* to make this reference more explicit.
- *links to the continental motorway system* (20): here the TL is more specific, referring to the actual motorway number which is expected to imply the same information for the TL reader — *réseau autoroutier (A26).*
- *with the coming of the single European market... passport controls within Europe* (69): this requires no explanation and becomes *l'ouverture du marché unique... contrôles de passeports.*
- *can I take my pet* (78): the SL reader should be more aware than the TL reader of the regulations concerning transport of animals in and out of the UK, so perhaps this question is of greater importance in the TL.

Punctuation
Use of inverted commas for neologism of use, not of form:
- *'slot'* (101): frequently used in the sense of space or time allowed within a programme or schedule.
- *'roadway'* (137): a neologism of use since what is referred to is a ramp inside a shuttle wagon.

Measurements:
- *80 mph* (51) is converted to *140km/h.*
- *80–150 feet below the sea-bed* (55) becomes *25–45 mètres sous le lit de la mer.*

Lucrative Fishing in Foreign Labour Pools

This text is an extract consisting of about two thirds of a complete article published in *The European*, the title of which may well draw inspiration from on-going battles either between countries of the EU or between EU and non EU countries over fishing rights in territorial waters. It reflects contemporary anxieties over possible problems arising from the implementation of the Maastricht treaty with regard to freedom of movement of people and goods.

The European is a quality paper whose target reader will be of professional status, possibly in the world of business but definitely someone who takes an active interest in pan-European socio-economic issues, of a certain level of education and who can therefore be presumed to possess a certain amount of background knowledge. The aim is to inform without bias, to be factual and comprehensive. In the case of this article, however, there is a certain element of evidence of authorial opinion, given that the subject under discussion is one which poses a potential threat to Britain and to British industry, although the author also attempts to indicate the wider implications for all EU nations.

Sentences which carry emotive or important points to emphasise consist mainly of a single clause, in contrast with longer sentences where subordination is necessary, primarily in order to explain reasons for actions. Different rhetorical devices contribute to the effect of authorial tone and critical approach, as does the selection of key concepts or terms likely to highlight the nature of the perceived threat. Authorial presence is also noted through the use of idiomatic expressions, and the use of the Present Perfect and Future tenses adds to the sense of immediacy of reporting.

Sentence Structure
Short, single main clause, for impact:
- *but a ruling... changed all this* (8): commencing with a conjunction, this could have been expected to introduce a subordinate clause of opposition. The fact of turning it into a separate sentence serves to highlight the statement by contradicting expectations.
- *the court ruled otherwise* (13): simple statement of fact, four words, very brief, therefore stands out.
- *nothing but chaos...* (50): negative pronoun in initial position gives emphasis to pessimism of this firm statement, where the use of the Future Simple has the value of an indisputable fact or truth.

Longer for explanation:
- *it seems that... national boundaries* (14): the rule of three has been used to good effect here: *can now... anywhere... regardless of...*
- *the Italian officials... elections* (30): this sentence contains the essence of the argument, hence the degree of subordination used to present the key factors.
- *the governments who suffer... conduct his business* (43): this sentence is in fact the only one in paragraph 8. By its complexity we understand the thoroughness with which the author explains the dilemma; by its occurrence as a complete

327

paragraph we understand its role, to counterbalance the statement of fact in paragraph 5 concerning the rights of employers (27).

Syntax
Verb tenses:
Present Perfect for previous practice, contrasting with new developments:
- *a ruling... has since changed all this* (8): recent development — note TT order: *a, depuis, changé* — is this stylistically appropriate?
- *builders have traditionally sought* (19): habit until now.
- *these contractors have regulated the flow of this labour* (21): past habit until now.

Future Simple to describe potential results as future fact.
- *electoral accountability will be the first casualty* (2).
- *the employment taken... will be the jobs of...* (32).
- *the wealth created... will find its way back to...* (35).
- *Nothing but chaos and strife will come...* (50).

Passives, where the object of the action is to be stressed, not the agent or actor:
- *where they wish to be employed* (7): TT also has passive.
- *can negotiate to be given* (28): there is no passive infinitive in form, merely in concept (*se faire donner*); the translator has chosen to use an active infinitive, *negocier pour obtenir*, thereby losing the concept of an external agent being in control.
- *employment taken by...* (32): becomes a relative clause, *les emplois que prendront...*
- *consequences... will be totally detached from Italy* (38): avoidance of passive by use of an active verb, the subject of which is the same as the subject of the SL passive form.
- *the principle can be applied* (49): passive construction is used here, no agent involved, simple statement of action.

Phrasal verbs:
- *find its way back to* (36): becomes a synthetic verb, *reviendront*, losing the concept of the homing instinct of the money itself, also the irony achieved by making *money* the subject of a verb which implies deliberate action and even perhaps success against the odds.
- *chaos and strife will come from* (50): again, the phrasal verb becomes a synthetic verb of outcome, *ressortir*, although an impersonal expression could have been created with *il ne résultera... que.*

Gerunds:
- *little interest in refusing* (31): SL gerund after preposition *in*, becomes TL *intérêt à* plus infinitive, following TL norms.

Use of superlatives:
- *most competitive builder, best organised, most experienced, largest pool, cheapest foreign labour* (25): stylistic and syntactic device recreated in the TL.

Single word adverbs:
As intensifiers in conjunction with an adjective or past participle:
- *a highly competitive world* (22): loss of variety/emphasis/degree of intensity in the TL by the use of *très.*
- *totally detached* (38): the passive verb has become an active one, with the adverb being rendered by *pas du tout* — again, loss of impact here.

To modify a verb:

- *compete ferociously* (23): the verb becomes a noun and the adverb becomes an adjective qualifying this noun.
- *have traditionally sought* (19): single-word adverb in TL as well
- *clearly says* (45): again, single-word adverb in TL.

Other:
- *their master, Italian politicians* (31): in the TL there is a more logical attempt to link these two nouns by making them both plural.
- *the need to compete* (40): the verb *compete* is transformed into the verb *to be* plus adjective, *être compétitif*.
- *the right to work* (46): not noun, but verb in the ST, thus *le droit de travailler*, not *le droit au travail* (cf. polysemy of SL word, *work*).
- *this court's decision* (51): may require insertion of past participle to collocate with *decision*.
- *nothing but chaos and strife* (50): emphasis through use of negative pronoun in initial position. TT simply uses negative verb in initial position, losing some of impact of *nothing*.

Lexis
EU terminology to be checked, verified with official usage: *a ruling* (1); *the European Court* (1); *electoral accountability* (2): *European Union* (4); *boundaries* (6); *member state...* (7).

Terminology referring to a (foreign) workforce: again there should be equivalent terms (index for index) commonly used in the TL for this topic, given its relevance to TL culture: *immigrant workers* (1); *work permits* (6); *building workers* (13); *unskilled labour, labourer, building site, the flow of labour, the construction industry* (17, 18, 21, 22); *pool of labour, migrant workers, construction workers* (26, 32, 33); *social costs, workforce* (36, 37).

Collocations:
- *seek employment* (5): TL — *chercher un emploi*.
- *how the matter used to stand* (8): *ceci était le cas* (a fixed expression).
- *apply for work permits* (6): *faire une demande de permis de travail*.
- *regulate the flow of labour* (21): TT has *réguler la circulation*, but could also perhaps have used *le flux* by analogy with *le flux migratoire*.
- *win a contract* (11, 29): 11 —*s'est fait accorder* — semi-passive construction; 29 — the translator seems to prefer *obtenir des chantiers*, choosing a term which is specific to the context rather than a more generic term.
- *have an interest in* (plus verb, i.e. gerund) (31): *avoir intérêt à plus infinitive*.
- *be a charge on* (37): reformulation gives *les charges sociales retomberont* — point of style, avoidance of verb *to be*, using a more specific verb.
- *the law now clearly states* (45): *la loi stipule clairement*.
- *conduct business* (47): *diriger les affaires*.

Fixed expression:
- *as had always been their practice* (12): index for icon: *comme ils l'avaient toujours fait dans le passé* (note the extra object pronoun required).
- *(immigrant workers) in his employ* (15): becomes contracted, *sa main d'oeuvre immigré*, effectively avoiding having to deal with the fixed expression.
- *huff and puff* (44): TL index for what is both index and symbol in the SL: since this expression as it stands does not form part of TL folklore the translator has chosen to contract these two similar sounding verbs into one which give the same underlying meaning, but perhaps with greater intensity — *rager*. It may

be that this is the term used when recounting the same story — *Three Little Pigs* — in the TL (see below)

- *(suffer) at second hand* (43): loss of icon: in a way the translator has avoided any direct transfer of implication, preferring to use a more general term, *conséquences*, which does not quite convey the same nuance of meaning.

Other:

- *from overseas* (20): *à l'étranger*: the TL reader would immediately relate this to the concept of employing workers from former colonies rather than just another country? Related issues are ones of ease of entry; unskilled/single or married immigrant workers (depending on country and decade) — all these may be queries raised in the mind of the TL reader to whom such questions form part of on-going national debate, but none are essential to the understanding of the overall intended message.
- *the taxpayer* (57): *le contribuable* — no similarity of form, a term which must be known, can't be guessed or translated by a calque.
- *social costs* (36): euphemism for increased health care etc., becomes, *les charges sociales*, not *les coûts*.
- *social strains* (41): problems of immigration and integration, asylum by the back door, resentment from natives of the country thus affected; the TL has *pressions sociales*, equally general as the SL.

Stylistic Devices

Imagery:

- *fishing… pool, pool… labour* (title): this not only gives the idea of the wider market for labour force and the element of skill of judgement and choice, as well as chance. It also recalls recent problems at the time of publication with regard to fishing rights in territorial waters, thereby evoking the concept of national boundaries and territorial rights, i.e. national sovereignty and national interests being threatened or overridden by wider EU/EC rulings. It could also be seen as irony, mocking those who take lightly/make fun of/make a sport/gain out of other people's misfortunes without realising the serious consequences of their actions.
- *ball game* (24): index for icon: this fixed expression is also an image imported from another anglophone culture and relates not only to rules of a game, but also to conditions surrounding and regulating actions, thus here to new socio-economic and socio-cultural parameters within the construction industry, if not also within the wider world of employement as a whole.
- *the first casualty* (3): instead of a single noun, the TL expands, explains, *la première à souffrir* — loss of impact here.
- *huff and puff* (44): euphony of sound adds to the impression of mockery, trivialisation. See note below (Cultural References) for connotative meanings/associations.

Role of position within a sentence:

- *strength,… stamina* (19): in apposition to requirements, final position in sentence gives emphasis through delayed appearance.
- *as had always been their practice* (12): stylistic emphasis through inversion of subject verb, lost in TL.

Attempted objectivity through syntax:

- *it seems that* (14): *il semble que*.
- *the law now clearly states* (45): *la loi stipule clairement*.

- *nothing but… will come from…* (50): statement of fact — emphatic effect of initial position of negative pronoun plus positive verb, slight shift and therefore loss of emphasis in TL, which simply uses negative particles *ne… que* in initial position.
- *the principle… can be applied* (49): anaphoric reference to preceding account of new ruling (i.e. to whole text) — initial position indicates summative function.

Alliteration — not really a feature of this text:
- *strength and stamina* (19): lost in TL.

Repetition:

Lexis: *a highly competitive world where builders compete ferociously — concurrence, compétitif* (22); *competitive builder — compétitif* (25): not completely recreated in TL due to variety in syntax and lexis.

- *immigrant worker, migrant worker* (1, 32): the two concepts are somewhat blurred in the SL to the point of appearing to be synonyms; the TL therefore uses the same term for both — *immigrés*.
- *contractor, contract* (10, 11): two different terms are used, *entrepreneur and contrat*.
- *construction industry — l'industrie du bâtiment* (22); *construction worker — l'ouvrier du bâtiment* (40).
- *labour (immigrant — 15, unskilled — 17, foreign — 27): main d'oeuvre immigré; main d'oeuvre non-qualifiée; main d'oeuvre moins chère — foreign* is omitted in the TT.

Syntax: adverbial phrases/clauses of place:
- *anywhere in the Union — n'importe où* (4); *anywhere within its boundaries — n'importe où entre ses frontières* (6); *anywhere within the EU — n'importe où* (15); *in any country of the EU where their employer chooses to conduct his business — n'importe quel pays* (46).

Cultural References

- *the European Court* (1), *the European Union* (4): official bodies having a single authorised translation in each language.
- *the City of London* (30): in fact this does not refer to the capital city, but to the financial centre of London, often referred to as The City. A difficult concept to translate without either footnote or expansion, perhaps it would not really affect the overall TL message to leave it as a literal translation, ignoring the connotative value of the proper name.
- *Moroccans* (13), *North African workers* (29): more connotations/socio-cultural implications for TL reader than even for SL reader.
- *the British taxpayer* (37) i.e. the reader of the SL article, everyone who should be interested in the topic.
- *huff and puff* (44): this reference recalls a fairy tale, the story of the three little pigs and the pompousness of the wolf who is outwitted in the end by skill — does the author wish the reader to become like the third little pig and take precautions, or are those employers who take advantage of the ruling being credited with this degree of cunning? Either way, there is an implicit warning transmitted through this reference, which may be lost to the TL reader.

Punctuation

- *European Union, European Court* (1, 4): capital letters for institutions are also used in TL.

- *Moroccans* (13): noun of nationality requires capital letter in TL.
- *British taxpayer, Italian officials, North African workers* (37, 38): capital letters for adjective of nationality will not be used in the TL.
- *City of London* (30): as discussed above, the shift to generic rather than proper name involves the use of lower case for *la ville*.

Euro-Court Extends UK Workers' Rights

This text is taken from *The Guardian*, a quality daily publication which could be expected to present just such an article in which the concerns of the workers in Britain are seen to be overridden or ignored by the government, to the point that the European Court has to be called on to uphold the rights of these members of the population.

The Guardian, typing mistakes apart, tends to deal in 'straight talk', no convoluted or complex sentence structures, but often a degree of irony or sarcasm is brought to bear in defence of a matter of principle. Basically informative, reporting on a ruling by the European Court, quotations are used from different sections of the political spectrum in order to give an appearance of breadth and objectivity of reporting, supplemented in the final paragraph by background information. Direct quotations are intermixed with reported comments and explanations by the authors of the article. Although different people are named, their functions and the relevance of their contributions is apparent from the text, so lack of familiarity with the individuals concerned on the part of the TL reader should not prove an obstacle to accessing the message. The general level of lexis, although drawing on quasi- or semi-legal terms, is also not so domain-specific as to impede comprehension, most of the terms forming part of a general awareness of matters relating to workers' rights. The text consists of several brief paragraphs, each presenting one item of information, reflecting the content of the article with its references to different reactions and comments.

Sentence Structure

Although sentences are not on the whole excessively complex in structure, there is a degree of embedding of information designed to describe an event and place it in its context by expansion to include background information, results or implications, in order to achieve maximum informativity. In many cases one sentence comprises a complete, brief paragraph (1–3, 13–15). Other paragraphs consist of two sentences, except the last, which contains four. Subordination of information is achieved through **relative clauses** introduced in different ways:

- *a far-reaching European Court directive affecting the rights...* (1): here, by a present participle.
- *whose jobs were switched* (14): remember the correct word order and relative pronoun here; also the need for the insertion of a definite article.
- *who had suffered* (18): relative pronoun, subject — animate: this becomes a participle without relative pronoun: *ceux ayant souffert*.
- *which tried to derecognise unions* (22): relative pronoun, subject inanimate.
- *which protects workers' wages and conditions* (47): again, relative pronoun used as introducer.
- *two cases brought by...* (44): past participle used here to introduce relative clause.
- *the first concerning* (46): this could either become a relative clause, following the general pattern for dealing with present participles if a TL participle is not used, or else could be replaced by a finite verb (see Stylistc Devices below).

Adverbial clauses of time:
- *when a business was transferred... including when it was privatised* (8): this is also a reported question form.

Adverbial clauses of opposition:
- *employers would not have to... but workers would have to be consulted* (26).
- *the significance of the decision is not the question of... but* (implied, *the question of*).
- *a step towards* (30–31): no verb here.
- *Mr Major said... (34); But Mr Straw insisted* (36): as a kind of linking mechanism the authors commence a new paragraph with a subordinate clause of opposition following on from a main clause ending the previous paragraph.

Syntax

Verbs of reporting: not much attempt at stylistic or lexical variation in the SL but the translator should aim for greater diversity in the TL:
- said: *a proclamé* (6); *a constaté* (11); *il a affirmé* (21); *a répondu que* (24); *a dit que* (30); *l'a décrite comme* (34); called on: *a fait appel au gouvernement* (17); insisted: *insisté que* (36); described... *as: a décrit... comme* (40).

Passive Voice for reporting with emphasis on actions or events, not agents, conferring thereby a degree of impersonality or factuality of comment:
- *variously interpreted as...* (4): in the TL this is paraphrased to give *faisant l'objet des interprétations diverses.*
- *a right to be informed and consulted* (6): by analogy with other rights enshrined in various EC treaties, we find *le droit à l'information et à la consultation:* two verbal nouns replace the SL verbs. Note *le droit à* plus noun, but *le droit de* plus infinitive. Note also that the SL indefinite article becomes a TL definite article.
- *when a business was transferred... including when it was privatised* (7): another example of substitution of nouns for passive verbs — *lors du transfert... y compris dans le cas de la privatisation.*
- *changes will have to be put in place* (11): here a pronominal verb form avoids the use of passive, *des changements devront s'effectuer.*
- *whose jobs were switched...* (14): the TL turns this into a relative clause with an active verb, *dont les emplois ont passé* — same meaning but loss of emphasis on change by an external factor.
- *workers would have to be consulted* (27): the Passive form is retained here.
- *was based on* (34, 36): in para 9, a change of verb form allows the use of a present participle, *l'a décrite comme étant basée sur* and in para 10, another active verb form is used, *se fondait sur.*
- *it is now going to be enforced* (37): the TL prefers the Future Simple here for statement of fact/intention, and again avoids the passive by a nominalised construction with *faire* plus infinitive — *se fera... implémenter.*
- *British workers have been shown to be denied rights that are accepted in law...* (41): this becomes a more impersonal construction in the TT, losing the first passive verb and changing the second into a past participle introducing a relative clause: *on a vu refuser aux travailleurs... des droits qui sont inscrits dans les lois...*
- *when public services are transferred to the private sector* (50): note the use of the SL Present Simple here for repeated occurrence, habit or fact. In the TT we find another example of nominalisation, with a noun formed from the SL verb and paraphrase — *lors de la privatisation des activités du secteur public.*

Adverbs:
- *variously interpreted as...* (4): *faisant l'objet des interprétations diverses*: the SL verb plus adverb become a TL noun plus adjective.
- *for incorrectly implementing* (45): the TL requires the use of *pour* plus infinitive here where the SL has *for* plus gerund: also, the TL is more precise in its use of the Perfect infinitive for a completed action. In order to convey the intention of the adverb, the TL uses the device of a negative verb, *ne pas avoir implémenté* plus the positive form of the adverb, *correctement*.

Impersonal forms:
- *there is no question that* (11): *il ne fait pas de doute que...* : both are fixed expressions
- use of passive voice — see above.

Other:
- *failure to give* (3): this is expanded to give — *suivant le manque de volonté... de donner.*

Lexis
EC jargon and other jargon relating to (workers') rights: (index for index):
- *a European Court decision* (1, 35); *ruling* (4, 13, 36); *rulings* (44); *judgement* (25); all of the preceding terms are used in the text to describe the same concept. There is also the term — *directive* (35) and *the acquired rights directive* (46) to differentiate the decision in question from wider issues.
- *compulsory competitive tendering* (19): *soumissions concurrentielles obligatoires.*
- *derecognition* (23): this presumes an awareness of the particular use of recognise, in connection with trade unions, and by extension, of the significance of the suffix *de*, in this context, meaning to take away a recognition that has already been awarded, to reverse an action already implemented (cf. regulation, deregulation); we also find *recognise* in line 26. In the TL we find *refuser de reconnaître*, which is not quite the same effect as *derecognition*, since the TL choice implies that this recognition has not yet taken place. In other circumstances this could be misleading, but may not be overly important in this particular case, where the use of the term has no legal accountability *vis à vis* the TL reader, serving a purely informative function.
- *collective redundancies* (49): *licenciements en masse.*
- *Tupe* (46): index for icon: there is no note to explain this in the SL, so presumably the target reader is expected to know what this reference is. However, a conscientious translator should find out what the acronym stands for, in order to make this information explicitly available to the TL reader who may not necessarily be familiar with SL specific jargon. In fact, *Tupe* stands for *Transfer of Undertakings (protection of employment)* and is enshrined in Regulation 1981 of the amended employment legislation in the UK, which is intended to implement the EC 'acquired rights directive' 77/187/EEC (information obtained from the local Industrial Tribunal). See punctuation below for note on form.

Fixed expressions:
- *throw on the defensive* (2): *a poussé... a se mettre sur la défensive*: almost the same form, but a reflexive verb.
- *give employees a voice in* (3): *donner... le droit de participer aux décisions*: a paraphrase to bring out the meaning — no fixed expression.
- *of little (practical) consequence* (5): *n'ayant que peu d'implications pratiques*: the TL is more explicit here.

– *put an end to* (22): *mettre fin à.*

Collocations:

– *A far-reaching European Court decision* (1): this is expanded in the TT to give *décision qui aura des conséquences non-négligeables.* Alternatively a fixed expression could have been used with an appropriate collocate — *d'une portée considérable.*

– *changes will have to be put in place* (11); this passive verb becomes an active pronominal form in collocation with *changes* — *devront s'effectuer.*

– *satisfy the court ruling* (12): the TL uses the same verb — note the construction, *satisfaire à...*

– *open the way to compensation claims* (13): the basic collocate is *ouvrir* with *la voie*, but the TL paraphrases to introduce a noun, *l'ouverture*, following *son opinion quant à la possibilité de.* Relying on recognition of this fixed collocation, the TL then omits *la voie.*

– *enforce a law* (36–37): *implémenter une loi.*

– *the same rights as those enjoyed by...* (38): *bénéficier d'un droit.*

– *a devastating blow* (41): *un coup accablant.*

– *workers' wages and conditions* (47): *les salaires et les conditions des ouvriers.* Note the use of *salaire.* One could have expected to find expansion here, giving *des conditions de travail*, since the TL generally prefers to be more explicit.

– *cases brought... against...* (44): *deux actions portées contre.*

Stylistic Devices

Assonance:

– *incorrectly implementing* (45): this is lost due to paraphrase in the TL.

Alliteration: probably accidental due to choice of lexis, rather than deliberate, given the factual tone of the article:

– *compulsory competitive tendering* (19): lost in the TL.

– *described the decision* (40): this is retained in the TL.

Anaphoric reference:

– *the first... the second* (46, 48): these ordinals refer to the noun *cases* and as such have to be in the masculine singular form.

Ellipsis: not a good example of this technique, as the use of ordinals implies a balance between two parallel constructions, which is not borne out by the omission of the verb:

– *the first concerning...* (46): there is no main verb in this sentence, which takes the form of a relative clause following the ordinal used as pronoun, *the first.* the second half of this construction, introduced by *the second* forms another sentence, this time with a finite verb, and the translator may wish to link the two together in one sentence, or else introduce a finite verb in place of the present participle.

Cultural References

– *European Court of Justice* (5): familiar to TL readers.

– *the European Commission* (9): ditto.

– *Padraig Flynn, the social affairs commissioner* (10): the function is transparent and so is the TL equivalent.

– *Jack Dromey, the Transport and General Workers Union official* (16): here the translator has used the acronym first for economy with accompanying translation in brackets of what the acronym stands for.

- *TGWU* (21): icon for icon: the TL has the same acronym, since this has been explained in the preceding paragraph.
- *The Employment Minister* (24): this is a function having a similar role in the TL culture, which is translated using the TL word order with *pour*.
- *John Hendy QC* (29): QC is a culture-specific title requiring explanation in the TL; the translator might also have tried to indicate a similar function in the TL cultural system.
- *The Institute of Employment Rights* (29): an SL culture specific body, this can be translated by a calque without a note, since its function is clear from its name.
- *Labour's environment spokesman* (32): again, a TL equivalent role exists, with similar word order as for the preceding example, plus *pour*. Note the use of the specific term for the Labour party, used adjectivally so no capital letter.
- *Labour government* (35): again, the use of the specific adjective.
- *TUC* (40): again, the acronym is used in the TT with explanation in brackets: icon plus index for icon.

Punctuation
- use of capital G for *the Government* (1, 4, 17, 24, 37, 41, 45) to show that this refers to a particular government, the one in power at the time of writing. The TL has to make this reference clear by insertion of the adjective of nationality, and using a lower case *g*.
- *Tupe* (46): it is interesting to note that this acronym is treated in the SL like a single unit/noun, hence the initial capital letter to indicate a name followed by lower case letters. Since this does not exist in exactly the same form in the TL the SL form can be retained accompanied by a note. Since this is a culture specific term to the SL, it is used in the TL in quotation marks.
- use of quotation marks for direct speech is retained in the TL (11–12, 22–23, 30–31, 37–39, 41–43).

Choosy Employers Search for Skilful Team Players

This text comes from the business section of *The Guardian* and as such can be expected to be of more specific interest to a certain target group. However, the general use of lexis is not particularly specialised, and the subject of the article, being a review of recently published research concerning qualities looked for in employees and employer–employee relations, could be said to be of relevance to almost anyone employed or seeking employment in the kind of environment described in the article. The reference to the source of the report is also aimed at the more interested reader wishing to follow up any points discussed in the article, and as such constitutes an important element of the text.

Given the nature of the article, reporting on research findings, it is hardly surprising that the information is presented in a relatively impersonal form of language, with frequent use of the Passive voice and forms of indirect speech, whether explicit or implicit. The article attempts to convey a positive interpretation of the findings of the report, as far as employer–employee relations are concerned, but attitudes towards the Training and Enterprise Councils are shown to be less positive.

Sentence Structure
The desire to report all major findings has resulted in a presentation of a sequence of items of information, rather like a list, and the article might have benefited from a different layout which could have conformed to the norm for lists of points, rather than grouping these in paragraphs. There is however some attempt to generate an element of coherence throught the use of anaphoric reference, using a key term from one point to introduce or feature as the main term of reference in the following point. The general pattern of sentence structure would seem to be one of co-ordination or contrast, linked by: *and, or, while, but,* or by the use of punctuation, semi-colon or colon.

Syntax
- *reports Clive Woodcock* (1–2): verb in ST becomes noun in TT following text type conventions, *reportage de.*
- *team players* (title): almost a set phrase to describe certain types of people, this noun group, the object of *search for*, consists of two nouns, the first functioning as an adjective to describe the second. The TT retains the form of noun plus adjective, but expands the single-word adjective into a verb group introduced by a present participle functioning as an adjective, in order to bring out the same meaning, *sachant travailler en équipe,* since the TL does not offer the same facility of use of two nouns in this way.
- *employers are still having problems* (3): use of Present Continuous form gives emphasis to on-gong nature of the experience. TT will have to use Present Simple with *toujours,* hence some loss of impact.
- *having problems finding* (3): ST uses gerund following *problems,* but TT will require a different structure, probably preposition *à* plus infinitive.
- *high jobless levels* (4): ST has adjective plus adjective plus plural noun. TT will

338

require a different word order and will probably prefer to use a singular noun, *niveau*, plus adjective *haut*, preposition *de* plus noun, *chômage* — shift from two initial adjectives plus noun to adjective plus noun group.

- *small service firms* (5): the translator needs to be aware of the syntax here, with the adjective *small* being used to describe the compound noun, *service firms*.
- *it is a matter of having* (6): this impersonal construction with gerund in the ST finds its equivalent in the TL *il s'agit de* plus infinitive.
- *this is because* (5): introduction to clause of reason: in the TT the verb *to be* is replaced by a more explicit verb carrying the concept of reason, *ceci s'explique par*.
- *they are very careful about whom they take on* (6): this clause becomes more impersonal in the TT, *un processus de sélection très exigeant*.
- *say the authors* (8): a commonplace verb used to report direct or indirect speech. The TT prefers to substitute a demonstrative noun phrase, *voici l'avis*.
- *common in* … (11): similar expansion to give more precise reference in the TT, this becomes *ce qui est fréquent*.
- *where employees have contacts* (10): adverb of place is expanded in TT to become more explicit, *dans un secteur où*.
- *conflict-free* (13): SL construction of adjective *free* used as a suffix to create an antonym to the noun with which it is used. TL has a similar procedure but uses instead preposition plus noun, *sans conflits*.
- *while* (24): can be an indicator of time or contrast. Here it denotes contrast, hence the TT use of *tandis que*.
- *recently expanding* (25): the ST uses an adverb to modify a gerundive (present participle which is used as an adjective); the TT substitutes a noun phrase qualified by an adverb, *en voie d'expansion récente* (created by analogy with *en voie de développement*).
- *the increasing importance… means that if trades unions are to reverse… they need to* (32–34): this sentence has been reformulated, involving shifts in immediate syntactic relationships but without any significant alteration to or loss of the overall meaning.
- *they need to recruit* (34): following the reformulation of the entire sentence, this is replaced by a singular verb plus noun phrase, *exige une politique de recrutement*.
- *to reverse* (33): this synthetic verb is replaced in the TT by an analytical verb group, *effecteur un renversement*.
- *were against* (38): this analytical use of verb to be plus preposition is replaced in the TT by a synthetic verb, *s'opposer à*.
- *are generally seen as* (41): Passive voice in SL replace in TL by third personal singular construction with *on* and a more specific verb, rather than *seen — on a tendance à considérer*.
- *keen to tailor pay* (44): expansion by insertion in TL to bring out meaning: SL adjective plus infinitive is replaced in TT by expanded construction — *partisans enthousiastes du principe de l'adaptation du salaire*.

Lexis
Analysis of meaning required:
- *choosy* (title): the translator needs to analyse the component meanings of this word and select the one most appropriate to the context: these include *fussy*, *difficult, demanding, hard to please*. TT uses *exigeants*.
- *the service sector* (1): icon for icon: the most appropriate TL form would seem

to be, *le secteur tertiaire*, not a literal translation of transparent form, *secteur des services*.

- *the right kinds of staff* (3): an example of polysemy: the ST term *right* can have many meanings, including *correct, appropriate, acceptable, meeting certain criteria, suitable*. The translator needs to identify the meaning intended in the SL before selecting the appropriate TL equivalent. In this context, given the reference to the *processus exigeant de sélection*, the TT uses, *aux aptitudes voulues*.
- *skills* (7): TT uses *aptitudes* (more general term of reference) rather than *compétences* which would seem to have a more specific reference, usually used in conjunction with an adjective defining the area of skill, e.g. *compétence linguistiques*.
- *'fit in'* (7): a more idiomatic use of a phrasal verb in the ST, the register being indicated by the use of inverted commas which also maybe seen to imply that this is a quote from the report. The TT has used a 'buzz' word, *intégrer* and reproduced the use of inverted commas.
- *having the right skills* (6): TT prefers a more specific verb, *posséder*. But when this verb appears at the beginning of paragraph 2, the TT opts for a different verb which more aptly describes the action involved, *se doter de*.
- *common in services* (11): possible polysemy, as *common* can mean: *not unusual, ordinary, shared by two or more, frequent...* The possible transparent equivalent of *common* is rejected in the TT in favour of *fréquent*, an adjective denoting frequency of action, the underlying meaning of *common* in this context.
- *the right social and personal skills* (11): the TT rephrases this, making personal skills an aspect of social skills rather than giving the two equal weight, perhaps in a desire to be more explicit or accurate — *des compétences sociales en relations personnelles*. In this way the TL avoids the need to look for an appropriate alternative to *voulues*, as used in paragraph 1.
- *sweat shops* (19): SL specific term has to be explained in TL by introduction of the noun phrase, *du genre* and the use of inverted commas to show an intended neologism of use, implying a loan construction.
- *fringe benefits* (41): index for index: a fixed term, expression in the SL, translated by *compléments de salaire*, hence giving a rather clumsy element of repetition in the TL.
- *poorer* (41): the meaning needs to be assessed and analysed in context; here the reference is not focusing primarily on financial levels alone but on general standards, being weaker or better, hence the TT use of *moins favourables*.

Collocations:
- *to have problems* (3): *éprouver des problèmes*.
- *marked feature* (28): *caractéristique frappant*,
- *carry out training* (48): TT omits verb, inserts noun, *l'existence d'une formation*.

Intensifiers:
- *a high proportion* (25): *une proportion importante*: intensifier of size or degree.
- *a substantial number* (27): *un nombre signicatif*, to avoid repetition of *important*.
- *big variations* (43): *des variations*: another intensifier of size is required here, again to avoid repetition of *important*: think of different synonyms in SL in order to search for appropriate TL equivalent. TT uses *sensible*, by analogy with *différence sensible*, having looked for synonyms for *important*, *significant*
- *big increases in training* (50): *un accroisssement considérable*.

Cultural References

- *Kingston University Small Business Research Centre* (8): in the body of the text where it first appears the individual units of this name have been translated where possible to explain the function of the centre and its relevance to the report. The name appears in its SL form in the reference given at the end of the article, to enable those who wish to write for further details.
- *the Training and Enterprise Councils* (46): there may not need to be a footnote to explain the function of these, as their names, when translated, are fairly transparent and permit identification of the intended meaning and fucntion.

Stylistic Devices

Not many instances of these as the article is intended to have a factual and objective tone.

Anaphoric reference through the repetition of a key word or concept, or a substitute pronoun, from one sentence to another, one point to another: *jobs* (26, 27, 28, 29); *unions* (33, 35, 37, 38); *benefits* (41, 44); *training* (46, 47, 48, 50).

- use of plural nouns without a definite article to show generalisation of findings of report: *employers* (3, 12, 17, 22, 37, 41, 46); *employees* (10, 13, 17, 19–20, 22, 35, 36, 38, 40, 45, 49).

Ellipsis:

- *essential to* (15): this is expanded in TL by insertion of *ce qui est*.

Accumulation: of points from the report in the form of brief sentences containing one unit of information (22–31, 32–40).

Reported speech: introduced in the SL mainly by verbs such as *say* (8, 32); *point out* (16); *felt* (13); *suggested* (35); *they reported* (47), but mainly understood by virtue of both the preceding verbs of saying and the general purpose of the article, to report on findings by quoting the results and points made by the authors.

Punctuation

- *'fit in'* (7): use of inverted commas to imply quotation from report.
- use of dash for ellipsis, omission of verb: — *essential to the successful running* (15).

Marks & Spencer

This advertisement appeared in the EC *European Graduates' Career Guide*, simultaneously in the two languages and presumably in other EC languages as well. Despite its billing as an major international retailer, it is to be supposed that the source text is English, given the origin of the company. The aim is to present the company, explain where graduates fit into the company's career structure, and describe in more detail the particular posts to be filled, concluding with details of qualifications required and an address for further details. This text thus corresponds to the norms and conventions of a job advertisement; although somewhat more extensive than some found in the national press, it compares well with other international anglophone models. It bases its approach on what the company offers the employee rather than the European model which prioritises what the company requires of potential employees, reflecting perhaps a less formal approach to the management of human resources.

The text has a clearly developed and visible structure, enhanced by use of space and typographics. Some rhetorical devices used in advertising may be present, but the aim is clarity rather than dramatic impact, and memorability in a serious tone, not by sensation or contradiction of conventions. Linguistic economy will be an important consideration.

Sentence Structure
The first section is concerned with presenting the company's profile and consists of lists of information, grouped where possible in threes for memorability.

Sometimes sentences are linked together in the TL to facilitate coherency of syntax:
- *Stores were opened... The company aims* (33): becomes, *après avoir ouvert... , la société projette...*

but in general sentence structure is simple, with one point per sentence.

Syntax
- *a major international retailer selling...* (2): this gerund becomes a Present Simple finite verb in the TL.
- *a range... is sold* (6): this passive verb becomes an active one, *commercialise*, with a new subject inserted, *la société*, but in the following sentence we find *quality clothing is sold*, for which the TL retains the passive, *articles... sont vendus*, having first ensured that the correct agent is understood by the insertion of *la société*.
- *is committed to providing* (10): this passive verb form and dependent gerund following SL requirements is replaced by a noun plus verb *to be: la politique... est de* plus infinitive.
- *quality and value* (11): two separate concepts are linked into a single compound noun, *un rapport qualité-prix*.
- *through Brooks Brothers* (8): insertion of a prepositional phrase for greater explicitness, *sous l'enseigne de*.

342

– *stores were opened in Spain* (33): becomes an adverbial clause of time, *après avoir ouvert*.

Lexis
– *trade mark* (3): *nom de marque*: an indexical relationship between SL and TL terms.
– *retailer* (2): *détaillant*.
– *clothing* (2): *articles de confection* — also an indexical interlingual link.
– *foods* (3): *produits alimentaires*.
– *consumer goods* (7) *articles de consommation courante*.
– *customers* (10): *clientèle*.
– *turnover* (14): *chiffre d'affaires*.
– *pre-tax profits* (15): TL seems more general — *bénéfice fiscal* — but does this really mean the same thing? One would expect such a large international chain to have taken steps to ensure the accuracy of all TL terminology but...
– *AAA credit rating* (19): *degré de solvabilité AAA*. According to Quid (1992: 1302a) AAA is 'la note la plus élevée pour les obligations et pour des établissements financiers'.
– *community activities* (20): this could refer to activities of help within a given socio-cultural group or community, but is more likely to refer to the EC. The TL choice is equally open to interpretation.
– *selling space* (34, 45): *surface de vente*.
– *square feet* (26–27): is defined in the TL more clearly as *surface d'exploitation*.
– *opportunities* (37, 39): the TL has resisted the temptation to use *opportunité*, which is becoming increasingly common in the spoken language but is still a faux ami in formal written language, thus using *débouchés* instead.
– *cost effectiveness* (49): *rentabilité*.
– *benefits package* (63): *avantages sociaux*.
Collocations:
– *maximise sales* (43): *accroître les ventes*.
– *controlling costs* (46): *contrôler les couts* (here the TL is using *contrôler* in an almost neologistic sense of the SL meaning, not the original TL meaning.
– *high standards of service* (45): *service d'une qualité irréprochable*.
– *manage computer systems* (58): *gérer les systèmes informatiques*.
– *a valuable resource* (49): *une ressource precieuse*.
– *personal skills* (60): it is not clear whether the TL choice, *les qualités de l'individu* do in fact refer to the same concept as the SL.
– *of the highest calibre* (37): does *des plus compétents* really convey the SL sense of excellence of personal qualities?

Stylistic Devices
Repetition of:
– the company name, for reinforcement and promotion (2, 10, 75).
– the key concept of a section in the sub-heading (1, 13, 23, 30, 38, 42, 48, 55, 65).
– the use of key words relating to success in the retail trade in both the presentation of the company and the different job descriptions (10–11, 45–46, 51–53, 56–59).
Alliteration:
– *plus précieuse... personnel... application... politique...* (54–55, 55, 56): this gives

a kind of coherence to the key words in the TL but may have occurred simply as a result of choice of lexis rather than as a deliberate ploy.

Cultural References
- lists of countries where the company operates (2–9), also languages (73–74) which may have TL specific forms.
- units of measurement and finances are expressed in SL sociocultural units in section 3 (13–20, 25–28)and these units are retained in the case of pounds sterling, but changed to follow TL usage in the cases of references to square feet, which become square metres.
- *high street, edge of town* and *neighbourhood food stores* (27–28): of especial interest is the term, *high street*, which is the central focus of most UK towns and is often named as such, translated in the TT as a more general, non culture-specific concept, *en centre-ville*.
- *'St Michael'* (3): the company trade name is retained in the TL.
- *Kings Super Markets* (9): a company name, hence not translated.
- *on the Continent, Europe* (31, 34, 73, 77): a very SL cultural habit of making a difference between mainland Europe and the UK; translated as *Europe Continentale* (unusual use of capital letter here for the adjective, perhaps due to interference from the SL form).

Punctuation
- *'St Michael'* (3): the company trade name is retained in inverted commas in the TL to indicate its function.
- numerals are written as numbers in both languages (13–35).